Moving through Grief, Reconnecting with Nature

Moving through Grief, Reconnecting with Nature

Jay Dufrechou

mhp

muswell hill press

London • New York

First published by Muswell Hill Press, London, 2015

www.muswellhillpress.co.uk.

British Library CIP Data available
ISBN: 978-1-908995-10-0
Printed in Great Britain

To Max, Audrey, and Tess

Contents

Acknowledgements

This book was a long time coming. I first wrote about grief in response to nature in a seminar taught by Rosemarie Anderson at the Institute of Transpersonal Psychology (ITP) in the mid 1990s. Without Rosemarie's mentoring and support over the years, the seed that grew into this book would never have germinated. More generally, I am indebted to the faculty at ITP, including Robert Frager, Arthur Hastings, James Fadiman, Hillevi Ruumet, Kathleen Wall, and many others, for creating a transpersonal doctoral program that could function as a container for spiritual emergence as well as training for scholarship and service. I was particularly fortunate in the friendship of the late William Braud, a gifted scholar, researcher, and teacher, whose generosity of spirit and time helped guide a generation of ITP students both professionally and personally.

In more recent years, the personal and professional journey woven into this book was supported by the offerings and international community arising through The Grof Transpersonal Training Program, emerging from the work of Stanislav and Christina Grof and continued by Tav and Cary Sparks. My particular gratitude extends to my friends Carolyn Green and Jane Cooper for facilitating my return to Holotropic Breathwork in the mid 2000s, which helped me find the stamina and confidence to write this book in the midst of many other commitments. Through the international Holotropic Breathwork community, I met Tim Read, M.D., who, along with his colleague Mark Chaloner, founded Muswell Hill Press to support the work of new writers in the transpersonal field. Without Tim's belief in this project, it would not have been finished. My deep appreciation extends to Keiron Le Grice for his expertise in shaping and editing the final version of this book, and more importantly for his friendship as a fellow traveler on the psychospiritual path.

In my personal life, the love and generosity of Margaret Dufrechou made possible the writing of this book and the actualization of my calling into the psychospiritual journey. Thanks to our children Max, Audrey, and Tess for being who you are and indulging your appearance now and then in these pages, and to my parents, Raymond Edward Dufrechou and the late Audrey Ladner Dufrechou, for believing in education of any kind and releasing their children into the life journey. So many others over the years have supported and encouraged my becoming the person who would write this book. To name but a few, since I was a teenager I thought if I ever wrote a book I would thank my middle school English teacher Irma Goldstein, whose encouragement of my writing set the stage for a lifelong love of pouring myself into words. Synchronistically, just as I was finishing this book, Irma contacted me out of the blue after being out of touch for nearly forty years. My draw to writing was fostered in the undergraduate Creative Writing Program at Stanford University under the guidance of John L'Heureux and Nancy Packer, though for most of my life I followed the wise advice of John L'Heureux to just take an aspirin and lie down when that urge to write hit; it was safer than actually picking up the pen.

Special thanks to my friends Joan Dionne and Paul Durante and their children Amelia and Alex for hosting me for several weeks during the latter stages of writing and editing this work. Without those nightly Scrabble games, it would have been much more difficult to get up early every morning and turn the computer back on. Fittingly enough, this book was finished in New Jersey, across the Hudson River from New York City, with the loving support of my father and my sister, Michelle Kaiser, who also made valuable contributions to the book itself. I hesitate in attempting to thank the many people whose friendship over the years has sustained and enlivened me in the life journey as it is impossible to name you all, but I want to send my appreciation to Frederick King, Larry Kornman, Kim Sutton Allouche, Whitfield Neill, all of my classmates at the Metairie Park Country Day School, Steve Sulmeyer, Steve and Carolyn Spitz, Charles and Margaret Charnas, Kristina Warcholski, Richard Cutler, Lisa Francis Holcombe, Katharine Donnelley, Maija Schellhardt, Patrick McCue, Amelia Pillsbury, Margaret Churchill, Diane Grieg, Shawn Katz, Valentina Meic, Hasan Arslan, Clara Wilson, Jackie Poole, Mike and Dorothy McCarter, all of my friends and colleagues in the Montana Workers' Compensation system, the Funk family, Theresa Wold, Orlinda Worthington, Joe Maphies, Sally Mueller, Trish Sternberg, Gwen Pincomb, Molly Holz, Tom Palmer, Marina Smirnova, Amber Balk, Holly Harmon, Debbie Dunning, Marianne Murray, Paul Griffin, Ryan Westrum, and all of my friends in India and in Holotropic Breathwork workshops worldwide.

Finally, my gratitude extends to the many people who wrote to me with their stories of grief, weeping, or deep emotions in response to nature. These people include Gayle Abbott, Guy Albert, Ana Ines de Avruj, Ingrid Ammondson, Marilyn Armstrong, Amber Balk, Valerie Becker, John Bullaro, Adam Butler, Ruth Davis, T. Ryan Davis, Christine Dudoit, Gerry Eitner, Elaine Gallovic, Lisa Graiff, Joanna Graves, Susan Gray, Linda Carroll Hassler, James R. Hipkins, Laura Huber, Louis Jeremias, Joybeth, Peter Kessler, Sue Kronenberger, Rosie Kuhn, Michael Leas, Jenny P. Lee,

Jaene Leonard, Ralph Litwin, Julie Longhill, Marie McLean, Louis A. Nielsen, Nancy Russel, Roseann Seryak, Laurel Smith, Emily Squires, Janet Taylor, Terry Taylor, Ray Voet, Diane Waddell and Rhea White. Your generosity in sharing your stories has allowed this book to reach out to others who may be ready to remember our place in the natural world.

JPD
Ridgewood, New Jersey
April 2015

CHAPTER 1

Coming Home

"Weep at least once to see God," said Sri Ramakrishna, a nineteenth-century Indian mystic.[1]

Rain

One morning in the winter of 1998, when we were still living in California, I woke up just before five and heard rain. At that time, I was getting up before everyone else in our family to have time for meditation and exercise. On this particular morning, I lay in bed for several minutes, enjoying the warmth beneath the covers, the nearness of my wife, and the sound of the water falling against the house. I could hear the rustling of wind in the trees outside our bedroom. When the wind died down, I heard the quieter sound of rain hitting leaves in the trees and bouncing off the glass panes of the window. I drifted in and out of sleep. Eventually, I brought my consciousness to the surface and ventured out of the warmth of the bed.

Making my way to my office, a converted garage, I sat on my meditation cushion and directed attention to my breath. As often happened when I began to meditate, my attention went to the familiar chatter in my head. What did I need to do today? Did I have any appointments? I had to remember to bring envelopes and that research book to class. We better go over Max's vocabulary words with him one more time before carpool came. What would I make for dinner tonight? We could have ravioli, which was in the freezer, or I could stop by the grocery store. We needed milk anyway, and I could also pick up some other things. What else did we need?

When I noticed this chatter, I tried to return attention to my breath. On this particular morning, something interesting happened because of the rain. When I returned attention to my breath, I noticed that I actually heard the rain. Simultaneously, I realized that when the mental chatter had been running, I had not been hearing the rain. As I stayed with my breath, and continued hearing the rain, I began to notice details about the rain that had previously escaped me. The rain on the roof sounded different from the rain falling against the bedroom window and trees outside. This sound was louder, for one thing, and it seemed closer, more physical, as if each drop individually, and thousands of drops collectively, were making an impression on my nervous system. I could feel within my body the cacophony of raindrops hitting wood shingles above me. At that point, as I began to notice this, I started to weep.

I believe the main part of the weeping came from some part of me remembering how it felt to live with my senses open to the immediate, physical presence of nature. I was obviously still having thoughts, but the thinking part of me was less present. I seemed to exist more as the sensations arising inside me, directly linked to the rain and the outside world. The distance between me and the outside world seemed very thin, if it existed at all. My body seemed to recall how it felt to live in synchrony with nature. This felt like a homecoming, like walking into a familiar place where you are known and loved. I felt strangely whole.

While this experience felt good, my immediate reaction was to weep. This was grief. It was poignant, even slightly painful, but it was not unwelcome. The weeping felt like an easing open, as though something inside my body was finally allowed release, as if a blockage had begun to dissolve. Without much thought, I understood this implicitly as some kind of breakthrough for me, but the understanding was more intuitive and emotional than cognitive. It would take me years to feel any sense of completion in unpacking the multiple levels of what I was feeling. Now I understand the tears were multi-layered and multi-determined. I was crying with joy at a deeply felt sense of connection with nature, but there was also a very strong presence of sadness. As is the case with grief, there was longing for something missing, but understanding what was missing would require unweaving much of my life, perhaps even unweaving all of our collective history. Eventually, there arose an emotionally driven question of *how did this happen, how did we lose our connection with nature?* This book is an attempt to answer that question, but obliquely, emotionally more than historically, by feeling into contemporary experiences of grief and weeping in response to nature, by following the path of grief.

Back then, as I was crying in response to the rain, I could only stay with the physical experience for so long. Soon enough, my attention was no longer on the rain, nor even on my breath. I began to think about what was happening, to reflect on it. I started wondering what parts of this experience I should try to remember, for I knew the specifics of experiences like this often disappeared from memory, like dreams. My mind automatically started phrasing language as a means to hold onto what had been happening, making mental notes. Soon enough, even this cognitive-linguistic endeavor was interrupted by the more typical chatter that came with my attempts to meditate. When I noticed the chatter, I realized the weeping had disappeared and I had stopped even hearing the rain. I tried to return attention to my breath. Soon enough, I was in my breath, then in my body, and then I was again hearing the sound of drops on the roof. I felt as though I had eased my consciousness out of my head and back into my body. I had not exactly gone after the rain; there was not quite that element of seeking. It was more an easing out of buzz through attention to my breathing, an easing out of my thinking, and then it was there, the intimate sound of the rain against the roof, scores of raindrops in my body.

Reconnection with the rain brought a resumption of the weeping, as with the flick of a switch. Once again, I was feeling in my body the rapid, continuous, individual and collective drops of rain on wood shingles, almost sensing the bounce of each drop. It was impossible to notice each of the thousands of raindrops through focused attention but if my attention was diffuse, they were all there, simultaneously individual and collective. I began to play gently with my attention. I found that I could allow myself to move between two very different states. If I followed my breath and relaxed into the rain, my senses came alive and I felt part of something larger than myself. With less of my attention ricocheting around in my head, my sense of self expanded into the environment, into the rain. It felt as though this happened through my body, as if my consciousness were dispersed throughout my body. The world suddenly felt more complete, more immediate, and more real. I could not have articulated this immediately, but the sense of belonging in the natural world was very much present. It was not merely connection with the rain; it was more like the rain and I were part of the same seamless whole.

And yet I was also a distinct observer, just one who was completely open. I could pull out of the experience by moving attention back into what felt like my head, somewhere behind my eyes. I recognized this head-space as more familiar in many ways, more where I lived most of my life. Although I did not realize this at the time, I think it was more comfortable, safer, to be in my head. Eventually, I realized the way in which this head space was refuge from feeling, even an avoidance of the intensity of the world around me. But there were many layers that would need unpacking before I could understand these mechanisms.

Though it would be several years before I could articulate what I am about to say, something happened to my sense of time and history in these few moments. My experience with the rain was highly personal, intimate, and time-space specific—it involved my unique life in the moment: Jay at age 39, almost 40, living in San Jose, California, three children under 12, on hiatus from work as a lawyer to study transpersonal psychology, a thinly disguised search for what I do not mind calling God. I had been having spiritual experiences of various kinds for a few years, some of which I will share later in this book. But this experience with the rain brought me into connection with the heritage of our species, as well as our connection to all life on the planet. I knew immediately, and deeply, that I was just one of the billions and billions of creatures before me who had been with rain on the earth. This was, oddly enough, neither a particularly humbling nor an empowering experience. Mostly, it was a relief.

Following the Grief

Soon enough, the beeper on my watch signaled the end of the meditation and I got up to begin my day. I wish I could say that everything changed immediately, but the intensity of the experience quickly faded as all the other concerns of my life moved back to center stage. What remained was an underlying longing, and grief that came to the surface now and then, often in response to contact with nature. My experience of the rain did not cause this undercurrent of longing, but was an illuminating moment in a trajectory that had been building for some time and would continue for many years. Gradually, my sense of reality and my sense of self were shifting more into nature and easing out of the human-made world. As this happened, a sense of longing intertwined with grief became a vehicle for my unfolding experience.

Back then, I was still very much engaged with my urban-suburban life in Silicon Valley of the late 90s. While California offers an abundance of nature and natural wonders, the lifestyle in populated areas, as in many populated areas around the country, even the world, can feel dominated by crowds, traffic, and techno-civilized buzz. Feeling more and more drawn to nature, I became increasingly aware of the ways that civilization grated on me. There were cars, strip malls, chain stores, endless construction, television, and all the Silicon Valley talk about stock-options, early retirement, and new granite countertops in renovated kitchens. The culture around me assumed life could not be otherwise than this. Then there was me: in the midst of an experientially-based doctoral program in transpersonal psychology, while simultaneously dad and usual grocery-shopper, carpool runner, and meal-cooker. I felt both in the mainstream world through time and place and outside the mainstream world by what was going on inside me. In the course of all this, there were moments of excruciating intimacy with nature, usually unexpected, almost always heart-breaking in some way.

I remember one time rushing from Palo Alto to San Jose to pick up my older kids from school. I was on Interstate 280, probably one of the most beautiful highways in the world, a straight line through hills, passing large bodies of blue water cradled in the voluptuous earth. But then you suddenly see a blaze of brake lights and come to a stop in the middle of six lanes of traffic. Stop and go, with your foot back and forth between the brakes and the gas pedal, the radio telling you about the traffic you're in. One afternoon, it was raining and there must have been an accident. We were moving forward just a few feet at a time, then a complete stop, leaving me increasingly stressed I would be late to pick up the kids. I looked out my window and noticed rain collecting on the driver's side mirror, running down to the bottom of the plastic housing, and then falling out of my sight to the pavement. There was no flood of tears this time, but my chest was burning. My heart felt like it was breaking open.

Around this time, we added a collie puppy to our family. I started taking long walks with Geordie at night in the dark. We lived in an old San Jose neighborhood quickly changing with the money coming into the area. Modest homes from the depression and post-war years were coming down, replaced with square heavy blocks of bricks built practically to the edge of the neighborhood's old, compact lots. These new structures seemed closed, impenetrable. The original, much smaller homes felt more accessible. Set back from the street, typically with large front windows, they had an open feeling. Glancing in from the outside, I would often see the comforting glow of television changing colors against painted plaster walls. In the dark from a distance, the glow of television is not unlike the glow of a campfire. With my new canine friend, I would think about the billions and billions of dogs whose lots had been thrown in with humans over the last several thousand years. Instead of the well-kept houses I was passing, I would imagine living in earth-constructed dwellings, sitting around a campfire, the dogs keeping watch over the human group. I was starting to identify with the outside world, winding back through time.

As our California-born children grew older, we began taking trips out into nature. Not wilderness trips by any means, just day hikes and car camping with friends and neighbors a few hours from home. My favorite was Pfeiffer State Park in Big Sur, across Highway 1 from the Pacific Ocean. The land was mostly flat, with groves of Redwoods, but backed up into mountains. A stream ran down through boulders, with just enough water to float inner tubes and rafts as it flattened out in the park. We would start with a hike up the mountain to a natural pool, deep enough for dives and swimming. Then we would climb back down and float back to the campsite. The kids called this "going with the flow." Fun as this was, the experience was only slightly wilder than Disneyland. The first night I spent in Pfeiffer State Park, I sat around our campsite at dusk in my folding camp chair, counting the number of cars and trucks within my line of sight. There were twenty-six.

As we lay in the tent, the three kids sleeping heavily all around us, I was not so much hearing wind in the trees as the intermittent slamming of car doors, dogs barking, and parents shushing their children to obey the ten o'clock park curfew. There was nothing wrong with that, but there was little chance a deer would walk by, no beaver dams to cross, no need to watch out for bears. As with most of my life at that time, there was little opportunity for stillness, no place without humans.

Around this time, I watched the movie *Out of Africa* one afternoon when I was home sick from work. The trajectory into nature has never kept me from a good movie. Alone in our darkened basement, in the glow of our thirty-five inch Mitsubishi television, I was transfixed by panoramic scenes of the continent on which our species had its origin. I have always been fascinated by our evolution, finding that long journey into our current form as Homo sapiens more sacred than any scriptures. Even the title *Out of Africa* moves me, with its focus on leaving and origins. While some of us stayed in Africa, others walked out in successive waves, eventually leading to human domination of the planet. This began around 100 to 120 thousand years ago, not very long ago in the scheme of things.[2]

Out of Africa is based on an autobiographical book by Karen Blixen, writing under the name of Isak Dineson. Meryl Streep plays Karen, a Danish woman. Escaping a bad love affair and a life she does not want, she marries her lover's brother and follows him to Kenya. Karen buys a coffee plantation, which she owns and runs from 1914 to 1931. The marriage does not work and she reluctantly takes up with Denys Finch-Hatton, an English adventurer played by Robert Redford. The narrative is framed as Karen's reflection, beginning after she has lost the farm and returned to Denmark. She is writing at a desk. Through the nearby window, we see an overcast, cold-looking city. In Streep's sonorous voice, accent perfect, we hear: "I had a farm in Africa . . . at the foot of the Ngong hills." My heart was burning from the very beginning, already in the realm of loss and longing. That Karen *had* a farm in Africa meant she no longer has a farm in Africa, as we could see from her civilized surroundings and the gray outside the window.

In the opening moments of the film, Karen recalls flying over the highlands of Kenya with Denys in an open cockpit plane he has just purchased. As the scenery unfolds, she is saying, "he gave me an incredible gift—a glimpse of the world through God's eyes and I thought yes, I see, this is the way it was intended." Later, in the chronological flow of the story, we rejoin their flight. Denys has arrived unexpectedly for a visit, landing in grasslands near the farm. They take off almost immediately, with Karen sitting in the open cockpit in the front of the plane. As they fly over grasslands, alongside mountains, over valleys like craters, I feel my own grief returning, coming up in my chest, moving toward my eyes.

Tears flowing, I watched African rivers winding through dense green treetops, waterfalls dropping thousands of feet from cliffs. Herds of hoofed animals stampede through straw-colored grass. A lake is covered with birds. As the plane passes overhead, thousands of cranes take flight, a single slow-motion wave of white wings leaving the water, pressing upward through the air. White transforms into pink as a flock of flamingoes skims the surface of the lake. By this point, watching the film, I was back to the heavy weeping from my rain experience. I was crying in response to the beauty of the landscape, but more deeply I was weeping for myself, for a deeply-buried, body-level loss. My body seemed to remember this was "the way it was intended." The whole film was about loss, including Karen's personal losses—of her husband, of Denys, of the plantation—but the deepest loss was intimacy with the heartbeat of the wild.

Something in me was starting to realize how deeply I wanted closer contact with nature. Having learned to put up tents and cook on Coleman stoves, our family began venturing around the American west during successive summer vacations. In our white Ford Windstar Mini-Van, we drove around Arizona, New Mexico, down into Mexico's Baja Peninsula. But it was Montana during the summer of 1998 that changed our lives. In Big Sky Country, "the last best place," we saw the National Parks, rode horses, camped, panned for gold, rafted, and just looked at all the mountains. Summer was hot in Montana, but the specter of winter was always present, intriguing to me. The hiking guide in Glacier Park told us the glaciers had been melting for many years, suggestive of global warming. On the other hand, the electrical cords extending from just about every vehicle engine told me this was a place where it got cold enough in winter that you had to plug in your car.

There was one night by the campfire on a river west of Glacier National Park, when a cowboy singer entertained our group under the stars. With one of the children sleeping heavily on me, another on my wife, we looked at each other, eyes brimming over. The summer evening was chilly, the air was clean, and the stars were dense enough almost to make me nauseous. The day before, sitting on the back of a horse, I developed an intention to make this way of being more consistently my life. Intention turned to scheme one night in Kalispell, in a Montana-style pizza restaurant (horns and pseudo cattle skulls everywhere, muted colors of the West). We had come into town after our camping trip had been cut short by a minor fishing accident. Just after our son Max started casting a fly, another child ran in front of him. He jerked back his rod suddenly to avoid hitting her. The torque of the fly line came back at him strong enough to imbed two prongs of a three-prong hook deep into the flesh of his neck. In the emergency room, digging into poor Max's neck, the doctor told me he and his family had just moved to Montana from California. This guy could do it—why not me? I started scheming with my wife over pizza. To my surprise, even with her practical side, she did not shoot me down. It must have been that singing under the stars.

When we arrived back in San Jose, as I was unloading the mini-van, some neighbors came up to welcome us home. I was talking about moving to Montana. One neighbor-lady told me point blank, "You can't just go on vacation some place and then move there." Well, actually, you can, with some luck and hard work. As sometimes happens in life, various threads came together to make a move not as insensible as our neighbor seemed to think. We needed a new school for our older children; the youngest was about to enter kindergarten, so could start fresh in a new town. My wife was ready for a new form of work. I was completing the residential phase of my doctoral program in transpersonal psychology and needed to return to gainful employment. The only remaining school work was writing a dissertation. I had entered the Institute of Transpersonal Psychology more to hold and frame the experiences I was having than to gain a doctoral degree. But I found the process of research and writing another way to continue the unfolding of what had come into my life.

For a dissertation research topic, I focused on the experience of grief in response to nature. In transpersonal psychology, researching a particular type of meaningful experience is fair game. Considered the "fourth force" in psychology—after the psychoanalytic, behavioristic, and humanistic movements—transpersonal psychology includes the study of the human urge to connect with something larger than ourselves, something *trans* (or beyond) the individual sense of self. Seeking as much to understand and convey the experience as analyze it, I gathered brief narratives written by people who resonated with the question, "Have you ever felt really connected with nature and found yourself weeping, or feeling grief, loss or other deep emotions welling up in your body?" [3] Many of the stories I received in response to this inquiry appear in this book. When the book shifts into the writings of others, the typeface will shift into italics.

The following chapters follow a trajectory based mostly on my desire to invite readers into the experience of grief in response to nature. Actually, grief in response to nature is better considered a range of experiences, in many ways unique to each individual, but with a number of common threads. While there is plenty of analysis in the coming pages, my purpose is less to explain and more to consider where these experiences come from and where they lead. In developing these trajectories, reflections from my own life and narratives from others are blended together with what I have gathered from psychology, sociology, anthropology, ecology, and a range of other disciplines. Taken as a whole, the book contains my understanding of the possibilities of an embodied psychospiritual path of personal growth involving incorporation of nature into the sense of self.

Before you consider where you are going, you need to know where you are. We begin with feeling into where we as a human collective have come cognitively and emotionally over the last several thousand years. This is not intended as an historical argument but as a means of noticing the strands of civilization that seem to structure our ways of being. The second chapter considers our move out of nature into agriculture and out of agriculture into industrialization. Chapter 3 describes what I call our third removal from nature, into what I describe as postmodern times, when we are surrounded by images generated by media and culture, with increasingly few of us having much actual experience of nature. Chapter 4 moves into the longing for wholeness in nature some of us experience when waking up to our lives in these times. This is the pull of grief into the natural world—sometimes felt as a spiritual calling. In this chapter we read the story of my friend Grace, who for a time felt she could only find God by the sea.

In Chapter 5, I frame internal experiences of deep connection with nature through the work of psychologist Stanislav Grof, who along with his late wife Christina developed an experiential modality for inviting transformational nonordinary states of consciousness called Holotropic Breathwork. Some of my experiences in breathwork illustrate the ways in which an internal sense of nature may transform our experience of separation from the natural world into a renewed sense of wholeness and connection. Chapter 6 looks into the psychology of grief and weeping, seeking to understand the mechanisms of our psyche involved in these experiences. Chapter 7 continues an attempt to understand weeping—and the longing often behind weeping—through the experience of sacred or joyful tears.

In Chapter 8, we read stories from people who have found psychological healing through immersion in nature, particularly in times of crisis or loss. These experiences are placed within the context of psychological theories and therapeutic practices focusing on including nature as part of an "ecological self." Continuing with stories shared by others, Chapter 9 looks into—and out from—experiences of grieving *for* or *about* nature in the context of our developing environmental crisis. Given our escalating use of natural resources, global warming, pollution, and intrusion of humans into environmental niches long belonging to other species, many people now feel grief in response to the destruction of nature. I call these experiences ecological grief. While experienced as grief about harm to nature, those of us grieving for nature may also be grieving for ourselves at some level, suggesting the ways our personal psyches are intertwined with the natural world.

This takes us into Chapter 10, titled "Psychological Immersion in Nature." We begin with the observation of psychologist Carl Jung that humans were once psychologically entwined with nature, but through civilization have lost this connection, with our innate orientation toward the natural world having sunken into the unconscious. We imagine the ways some of us may be projecting our own psychologies into nature or blending our personal or collective psychosocial issues with elements of nature. This includes mixing our fears, aggressions and the darker elements of our psyches with nature. Among other things, we consider the "bears" part of the angst felt by Dorothy and company en route to Oz, as they came into the territory of "lions, and tigers, and bears." Chapter 10 concludes with considering the contemporary possibility of experiencing our psychologies deeply blended with nature, but with consciousness, from the perspective of people with an independent and individual sense of self. We may find ourselves dispersed out into nature in ways that make all of life feel sacred.

This takes us to Chapter 11, where we awaken into the experience of sensing God in nature, though the term *God* is used more to describe an experience than an entity or concept. Always part of our spiritual history, these experiences continue into our times, typically appearing spontaneously. Almost always, people cry during these experiences. In the final chapter, I imagine into the future from a more global perspective, understanding that from now on, it seems, we are once again one people in an instantaneously connected global community, like it or not. Remembering our place in the natural world may be the one thing that unites us into a safer and sustainable future. On the other hand, if we do not find a way to make it, with a few million years the life force behind nature might just well produce some other creatures better able to appreciate this beautiful blue-green planet.

Feeling the Earth

Like many people, I am aware of the precarious environmental situation we humans have created over the last several decades. I did not set out to write an environmental polemic, but grief in response to nature exists in this context. We are living in what scientists call the Sixth Extinction

Event, characterized by the loss of 17,000 to 100,000 species per year, described as a silent extermination.[4] The grief experienced by me and others in response to nature is not separable from the awareness that our species has become a scourge on the planet, and I say that with compassion for all of us. Prior extinction events have resulted from meteors, weather changes, or geological shifts. This one is manmade.

Horrible as this destruction feels for many of us, to me, at this point, it feels like a stage in our development, practically inevitable. We have developed ourselves into a situation where our conduct has dire consequences for nature. This is happening at the same time we have developed technologies that could kill huge swaths of humans as well as the natural world. I am not expecting extinction of humanity, but if it is to occur, I suspect the more likely causes would be nuclear happenings or bio-hazardous plagues than tidal waves or depletion of resources. What is interesting to me is that getting our act together with respect to nature might be excellent practice for getting our act together with respect to each other. In the end, to me, it is the same issue. We all come from the same place and that is nature. Opening to ourselves as nature, finding the sacred in nature, just might lead to transformation that will make it difficult for us to objectify and kill each other. Life might become sacred, human and otherwise.

The important question involves what we do next. Laws and treaties protecting nature seem part of the future, but if we are to save ourselves, and the planet, inner transformation will be required. The laws and treaties will not be passed unless enough of us come from a place of understanding what we are about to lose. Opening to the specifics of nature—and grieving through the process that arises—might just point toward a future. This is why I have labored long amidst an already complicated life to tell this story. I will not say something irritating like I have written this book for nature, but I will say it feels like this story is coming from the depths of our collective, from the goddesses and gods of the planet, who want to help us save ourselves. Or maybe not save ourselves exactly. Maybe it is more about coming home.

My daughter Audrey was born July 20, 1989, twenty years to the day after Neil Armstrong took that "one small step for man, one giant leap for mankind." From one perspective, journeying to the moon seems like one more technological accomplishment among many in the last amazing few centuries. But consider that for millions of years our ancestors gazed up at the moon—a distant, different, shifting body in the sky, so close and yet so far. And then suddenly we could look back at ourselves from our moon.

Even before Neil Armstrong took that first step, preliminary journeys were sending back photographs of the earth floating in space. On Christmas

Day 1968, the following words of American poet Archibald MacLeish appeared on the front page of the *New York Times*: "To see the earth as it truly is, small and blue and beautiful in that eternal silence where it floats, is to see ourselves as riders on the earth together, brothers on that bright loveliness in the eternal cold—brothers who know now they are truly brothers."[5]

While circling the moon, Apollo 8 astronaut Frank Borman said: "The view of the Earth from the Moon fascinated me—a small disk, 240,000 miles away. It was hard to think that little thing held so many problems, so many frustrations. Raging nationalistic interests, famines, wars, pestilence don't show from that distance."[6]

More from Borman: "When you're finally up at the moon looking back on earth, all those differences and nationalistic traits are pretty well going to blend, and you're going to get a concept that maybe this really is one world and why the hell can't we learn to live together like decent people."[7]

From Roger B. Chaffee, another astronaut: "The world itself looks cleaner and so much more beautiful. Maybe we can make it that way—the way God intended it to be—by giving everybody that new perspective from out in space."[8]

The first Arab astronaut, Sultan bin Salman Al-Saud, said about his time in space: "The first day or so we all pointed to our countries. The third or fourth day we were pointing to our continents. By the fifth day, we were aware of only one Earth."[9]

After his journey to the moon on Apollo 14, astronaut Edgar Mitchell founded the Institute of Noetic Sciences (IONS), an organization supporting the transformation of individual and collective consciousness through research and education. Interestingly enough, I found most of the people who contributed stories to this book by contacting local IONS groups around the world. Looking back at the Earth, Mitchell said:

> You develop an instant global consciousness, a people orientation, an intense dissatisfaction with the state of the world, and a compulsion to do something about it. From out there on the moon, international politics look so petty. You want to grab a politician by the scruff of the neck and drag him a quarter of a million miles out and say, 'Look at that, you son of a bitch.'[10]

From one final lunar astronaut, Alan Shepard: "If somebody'd said before the flight, 'Are you going to get carried away looking at the earth from the moon?' I would have said, 'No, no way.' But yet when I first looked back at the earth, standing on the moon, I cried."

CHAPTER 2

Recalling Our Loss

From Rumi, the beginning of his poem *The Question*:

One dervish to another, "What was your vision of God's presence?"

"I haven't seen anything. But for the sake of conversation, I'll tell you a story." [11]

The Gaze of a Deer

Dana had two children under the age of ten, a million-dollar home in Connecticut, a husband who just made partner in a Wall Street law firm. Many would think this family was living the American Dream. There was success through hard work, focus on the children, intelligence and generosity. Operating this one household fueled a small corner of the suburban economy: there was a housekeeper five days a week, in-home help with the kids in the morning, a second round of child care in the evening, gardeners, catered dinners. With a master's degree in social work, Dana developed programs for local non-profits and mentored high-school girls in foster care. She was also learning to teach yoga, reading about shamanism, and studying a healing practice known as Polarity Therapy, a method for reaching the subtle energy systems of the body. Friends from her Polarity group were taking her to lectures at the Open Center in Soho, introducing her to various spiritual practices and forms of bodywork.

If there were a fissure in this family, it was the growing distance between Dana and her husband. Rob woke up before five every morning and made his way into Manhattan on the train. A star athlete in high school, he approached work with a fierce determination and intention to win. He rose quickly in the law firm and was increasingly involved with national power brokers, taking advantage of the pro-business climate in Washington. Rob's legal acumen helped devise the bundling of financial instruments that eventually brought major institutions to collapse in 2008.

As often happens, as his career took off, Rob's outlook shifted over time, little by little, to accommodate the needs and assumptions of the system which provided his paycheck and self-esteem. It was not something he talked about with Dana, but she noticed his increasing alignment with power and decreasing patience with the messiness and confusion of life below the upper echelons. Rob did not openly criticize her new spiritual interests, but Dana felt the edge that arose if she mentioned these activities in front of his colleagues.

The events of September 11, 2001—the Twin Towers coming down virtually around Rob—impacted their lives in ways that were deeply personal. On that bright late-summer morning in lower Manhattan, Rob was evacuated from the Wall Street skyscraper where he worked. He learned what was happening by emailing friends on his Blackberry as the crowds walked uptown. The sense of life-threatening danger and confusion never left him completely. With two close friends and many acquaintances dead in the collapse of the Towers, disbelief mixed with outrage and shock. Within a few months, he was seeking transfer to a new branch of the firm opening in Florida. Dana resisted, not wanting to uproot the children, nor wanting to leave behind her new friends and spiritual interests. There was an unspoken stalemate. Inside, she was going numb, yet to most of the world, she was increasingly hardened, even brittle.

One summer weekend, not long before the kids returned to school, Dana took Rob to a retreat center in upstate New York. She writes: *I felt at home immediately. White, clapboard cottages blended into forested hills in a way that felt natural, almost wild. This was very different from the more expensive, elite, manicured spas we had visited previously. After walking the grounds to get our bearings, I went off alone to a shiatsu bodywork session. I had worked with shiatsu practitioners before, but this man was different. He was quiet, calm, and very intuitive. As he moved my body into various stretches, I felt supported in a way that was emotionally intimate, but entirely safe.*

With this sense of physical and emotional safety, I began to realize how guarded I had become, how little I let close to me. I started to remember an old part of me that was more open, trusting, and spiritual. As I relaxed the weight of my limbs into his steady hands, he kept reminding me to breathe. I looked up at the ceiling. There was a large skylight. I could see blue sky and I noticed the depth of the color. I felt a fluid peace, as if blockages were draining from my body as this man massaged my arms, legs, and head. When the session ended, I was sad to lose the connection to this stranger, but even sadder to lose connection to that old part of myself he had been able to reach.

As I walked back to our cottage, I passed a grassy clearing sloping upward to the forest. I sensed something moving and turned to find a young deer no more than fifteen yards away. She stood quietly watching me. When I was a child, I would sometimes try to make eye contact with animals, often the squirrels that lived in the tree outside my bedroom window. If the animal held my gaze for a few seconds before scurrying away, I felt as though I had overcome some barrier, as though my loving interest had momentarily hushed the instinctual fear of the animal. Although I knew very little about Christianity as a child, I was drawn to St. Francis of Assisi, imagining him immersed in the animal world. I longed for that kind of connection with our many pets, with the birds that sang outside my window, with any animal that wandered into our yard.

And now there I stood, gazing into the face of a young doe, many years and defensive walls separating me from the barefoot child I had been, running free in the grass. In that moment, I was back to that simple place of hoping this beautiful wild creature would hold my gaze. As she continued to look at me, with apparent interest, and no detectable fear, I began to sob. In the minute I spent in tears, I realized how far I had come from myself, from the person I was supposed to be. I knew the life I was leading was some kind of mirage, grounded in imagery and disconnection. On the city side of a vast river, I sensed the other side and I felt tricked into believing the life we were leading was reality. I felt sadness and remorse for what felt like thousands of small decisions accumulating into where I now stood. I realized I wanted something else.

Eventually, the deer ambled back into the woods, not bothered in the least. As my crying eased, I tried to take in the beauty and peace of the clearing, but I could only go so far. I didn't know how to be still enough. A man and woman came down the path, talking quietly, respectfully. I saw them hold hands and my heart broke a little. I wandered back to our room. Something had changed in me, though it was difficult to put into words. Now I can explain it like this: for a few moments, I remembered the possibility of connection and, at the same time, I realized the depth of my disconnection. For most of that day, my body felt lighter, as though a release of some kind had occurred. As much as I wanted to hold onto this experience, after we left the spa, I returned to my usual self, focused on the next thing to do, and moved forward at the speed that was our life.

Separation from Nature

Like Dana, most of us in the industrialized countries have come a great distance from nature. Some of us have grown distant from nature in our own lifetimes. Others, particularly many younger people, have never known nature intimately. This is increasingly true in the industrialized countries with our ever-expanding, increasingly technological economies. Even in developing countries, the relationship to nature is changing. The designation "developing" suggests that soon enough these countries will join the worldwide industrial-technological marketplace. When I travel, I see signs on airport ramps proclaiming the good news that soon there will be no more developing markets, just a global economy. I believe the posters. Unlike some of my environmentally-protective peers, I have no interest in fighting against globalization or pretending we will roll back development any time soon. Mostly, I am interested in noticing the impact of loss of nature, feeling what we feel, and then seeing what happens.

Issues of development are complex, but I am reasonably certain that if I were living in a developing economy, I would want the conveniences and improvements in daily life so readily seen on television and now the Internet. On the other hand, when considering we are reaching the last days of human communities interacting with nature in ways similar to the hundreds of thousands of years of our heritage, it is difficult not to feel the loss. With globalization, even nature-based subsistence economies are being pulled into the world marketplace, with lands, waters, minerals, and energy supplies increasingly owned by large international interests. There are few places left on earth where people live more in synchrony with nature than as participants in an economic system treating nature as resource. This is happening after thousands of generations in which nature was simply the world around us.

For all of us, collectively, the trajectory of our species over thousands of years has involved gradual separation from nature. As Dana said about her personal life, there were many small steps, but in our collective history there were some large ones. In this chapter and the next, we shall feel into those large steps as a means of noticing how we have constructed our internal worlds as reflection of changes in our external relationship to nature. For now, the rough outline. Ten or twelve thousand years ago, we began to dominate nature through agriculture and domestication of wild animals. In geographically separate parts of the world, around roughly the same time, various groups of humans turned wild grains into tended fields for harvests. Previously free animals were domesticated and tended by humans, kept in pens or under our control through dominance, ready meat for slaughter. Wiley monkeys that we are, we directed most of our attention to herd animals, learning to stand in for the herd leader and have them follow us. The very evolution of several lineages of animals came under our control for our benefit. We created domesticated cattle, goats, sheep, chickens, pigs, horses, oxen, dogs, cats, and various other animals for service or food.

Civilization emerged, for better and worse. For thousands of years, the civilizations arising around the globe were mostly separate, though more interchange has happened all along than most of us realize. Gradually, worlds came together through trade and exploration. Various cultures in various parts of the world dominated smaller or larger areas for various periods of time. Western Europe rose from relative wildness into seafaring peoples capable of global colonialism and imperialism. Business was good for some of us. Others were killed or enslaved either literally or effectively. Then, just over two-hundred years ago, industrialization brought the machine age. What had been feudal and then mercantile economies morphed into capitalism, with some experiments in socialism along the way. Capitalism seems to be enduring, though socialist ways and means influence distribution of some resources in some places.

A few decades ago, we moved into electronics and cyberspace. With this last step, millions of people have ceased to know nature as much more than an idea. This is not conscious for most of us. Even if we have some understanding of this latest psychological trajectory out of nature, most of us have not accessed either our individual or our collective emotional response. This book is about noticing and processing those responses. Lest this quick history seem too negative, along with these trajectories have come, for the most part, an increase in health, life span, and living conditions. Many of us enjoy the possibility of individual autonomy and self-determination in ways literally unimaginable for most of our ancestors. The pursuit of education is possible for billions of people. My great-great-grandfather handing down my last name could not even write that name, signing birth certificates with an "x." These few generations later I am able to write this book and can look up anything at any time on the Internet.

Jean Marie Dufrechou likely had no longing for nature as much as desire to make a living in the swampy land of Louisiana at the seaport of New Orleans. I imagine he would have readily exchanged mosquitoes and southern heat for some air conditioning and television, at least during the summers. When I go to Louisiana in the summer I tell myself I am going to do without air conditioning, but five minutes in a hot automobile and I am setting the temperature at 65 with the blowers aimed right at me. I am grateful for the times in which I live. Perhaps this is mostly because I love to imagine. The media revolution, particularly television and the Internet, have given billions of us access to the world around us, providing an endless source of ideas, places, cultures, narratives, extending our imaginations in ways our ancestors would never have believed possible. Knowledge is power, said the philosopher Francis Bacon in 1597, echoed by many people after him.[12] No matter what you think about consolidation and abuse of power in our times, the Internet and global media are a game changer, a good thing as far as I can tell.

More of us have the capacity to learn, communicate, and create in ways never before experienced in the history of our species. While I level a fair amount of criticism at my home country, I am an enormous fan of the American dream. I enjoy sharing a first name with Jay Gatsby, the tragic hero of F. Scott Fitzgerald's classic American novel, *The Great Gatsby.* Things did not end well for that Jay, but he was able to reinvent himself. In our times, we can not only invent ourselves in the American dream, now increasingly a world dream, but we can publish that self, even evolve it on a daily basis, on Facebook, Twitter, LinkedIn, and scores of other electronic means of spreading our word. But Jay Gatsby's problem was an American problem and is now a world problem: confusing image with reality, falling into illusion.

Our image-based electronic world is a double-edged sword. This is the subject of Chapter 3. For now, I will note that nature has become, for many of us, something on television. This is not entirely bad. When I exercise on the gym treadmill, I look for something I can stand to watch on the thirty channels pumped into the screen facing me. At any given moment, half of those channels are showing commercials, another large segment with sports commentary, news, or reality television. I often find respite in images of some gorgeous part of the world that can take me away, a travel or adventure program. But images of nature are not nature. Actual time in the natural world has decreased for so many people in the last hundred years. Even when we are in nature, I suspect many of us are not able to take in where we are.

Much has changed even in my lifetime. Many of the elders among us, even those in middle age, recall fields at the outskirts of town. Even more importantly, they recall having time to meander and simply *be* within nature. But those folks are becoming increasingly rare. In some places (like Montana), we can still reach the outskirts of town within a few minutes, with actual wilderness not much further away, though the definition of wilderness starts to get complicated when bears and wolves are not all that far from Starbucks and Wal-Mart. In the two places I have lived near Helena, deer are plentiful, herds of elk sometimes graze the hills, coyotes call and make an appearance some times of year, along with a rare bear and even more rare mountain lion. Grizzlies and wolves are within an hour, better than at my doorstep from my perspective. Hikes that feel wild enough are just outside of town. Many of us in Montana are fortunate enough to have hiking trails just steps from our front door.

But mainstream life in the United States and similar countries takes place in cities and suburbs, with some effort necessary to reach nature. Many of us know only downtowns, interstates, neighborhoods, shopping malls, big-box stores, and the next town starting where ours ends. Parks and spaces of green may provide pockets of nature, but the wild is not often part of daily life. In California, walks in the mountains or on the coast are accessible, yet we typically find scores of other people with us. On a recent visit to California, a friend invited me to hike in the Rancho San Antonio Open Space preserve in the mountains between Santa Clara Valley and the ocean. It was a weekend. When I arrived in my rental car, I spent twenty minutes trolling around the dozen or so parking lots. Every space was filled. Cars were idling, waiting for someone to leave. When hikers returned, drivers slowly cruised behind them, hoping to get their spot. Just like the mall at Christmas. I gave up and left.

Even in a place like Montana, where I have been fortunate to know nature intimately enough, the natural world is not interwoven into life as it was for my ancestors. Like almost everyone else, I am part of the national economy, earning money by providing services in the context of a complicated insurance system. During all my time in Montana, I drove to work and sat in front of a computer like many people. Daily life still kept nature separate from me, unless I made an effort to connect. Just a generation or so before us, even in developed countries like the United States, time in nature was a given in many people's lives. When older generations moved into cities, something from the wilds remained in their hearts and souls. There may have been loss registering as grief, but there was memory based on experience, an etching of the natural world on the soul.

Peter's Lot

Before her passing in 2007, Rhea White wrote to me about her memories of nature from her childhood. A career librarian and researcher, Rhea lived most of her life in New York City, where she was long-time editor of the *American Journal of Psychical Research*. One of her many contributions to the field of consciousness studies was the concept of *exceptional human experiences*, often abbreviated as EHEs. Rhea coined the broad term to encompass psychic, mystical, healing, death-related, and peak experiences, as well as any experience of consciousness considered anomalous in the scientific, materialist model.[13] She encouraged incorporation of these experiences into our realities as a way for transformation of self and culture. Rhea was interested in my experiences in nature as exceptional human experiences. She was among the people encouraging me to write openly about these experiences.

Rhea took time to describe for me how meaningful nature had been in her youth. She wrote: *I grew up on sixteen acres of pasture land, and woods behind our house. My cousins next door and I did seventy percent of our playing in those fields and woods. I knew every inch. In eighth and ninth grades, I walked our pasture and along the edge of the woods, about three miles, every single day of the year. I knew every shrub, every cocoon, every bird's nest. In tenth grade, I started to become friends with a group of girls and boys and began more of a social life. I also became very interested in golf and began playing in local tournaments. This became my consuming interest. But I remember being very sad, and writing in my diary about it. Although I loved golf and the competition, and the good friends I was making at school, I hardly had any time for my beloved fields. I had left a very precious highly prized friend. I felt very badly and cried about it.*

Though I left the fields behind, I still went back during times of high excitement or defeat, to my favorite rock, on a gentle rise just before the woods. There I could cry or exult (over golf or school) or just sit still and let the beauty of the fields sink in. I wrote essays and poems about the fields in school, and they were tinged with sadness because I had to leave them behind. Even when I went there, it was not the same. The easy intimacy was gone. I couldn't stay for hours. I was there for a brief bit and then had to get back to rehearse for the school play or to do homework or play a round of golf with my father. It never came again as it had been.

Rhea encouraged the writing of EHE biographies, where we feel free to describe experiences that may seem strange to the mainstream world. In one of her own EHE biographies, Rhea wrote about her childhood connection with nature, particularly a part of the woods she called Peter's Lot. *I awoke this morning with a bright memory in my mind. I was able, without thinking, to place it in time. It was a beautiful day in 1949—my senior year in high school. For all intents, I had already "left" the fields, because I could not remain with them and also enter the world of people, where I wanted to go. My aim of becoming a top-notch golfer was deeply entrenched in me by that point. And I was on the brink of graduation from high school and starting college in the fall.*

After school on that beautiful day, I went up to the fields. I crossed over the fence at the top of the slight rise in the middle of our side, into Peter's Lot. I was more aware of my sense of connection with the wildlife, insects, amphibians, reptiles, small mammals, fish and, on that afternoon, the explosion of blossoms everywhere I looked, as if I were up in an apple blossom cloud somewhere, caught up in heaven. I was the blossoms and

*they were me. The new greenery was sprouting everywhere, matching the
new life awakening in me and reaching into the world.*

*The perfume of the blossoms up close to the trees was almost choking
as I walked the familiar paths fashioned by the cows, whose munching and
comings and goings had created country lanes with grass as short as if it
had been mown. At a little distance, I noticed that many flowering shrubs
and trees had grown since I first had come there when I was ten or eleven.
It seemed to me the entire three or four acres were nothing but blossoms. I
could not remember a time when they were so billowy. The breeze was just
a bare zephyr carrying their scent, the sky such a light blue, only a small
part revealing dark blue depths. The air temperature was that of a kiss, and
the birdsong was so varied, issuing forth from countless shrubs and tall
tufts of weeds and grass.*

*For a moment time stopped. While I knew this was farewell, this
beloved piece of Earth was affirming everything I was. I knew it had never
been like this before and never would be again—at least for me. I loved it
so and ached with the thought of parting at the same time that I was eager
to go. I felt very close to God, and to the life that burgeoned here so
bounteously for this final occasion. Mostly, I was thankful. So thankful for
all that Peter's Lot had given me. It was so special, every bit of its wondrous
and varied places: trees, shrubs, rocks, berries, pond, stream, woods. It
brought together the best of what I knew.*

Nature Deficit Disorder

Even though she rarely returned to those particular fields, Rhea lived her
life with Peter's Lot still in her heart. For many children born in the last
few decades, nature has never been part of their experience. In *Last Child
in the Woods*, Richard Louv brought attention to the concept of *nature
deficit disorder* in children.[14] Like many of us, Louv views this absence
as dangerous not only for individual children, but for the health of our
culture. "How the young respond to nature, and how they raise their own
children," he writes, "will shape the configurations and conditions of our
cities, homes—our daily lives."[15] If future generations have no internal
sense of nature, Louv fears we will lose our way.

Sounding much like Rhea White, Louv recalls the natural world of his
youth, which stayed with him. "I knew my woods and my fields; I knew
every bend in the creek and dip in the beaten dirt paths. I wandered those
woods even in my dreams."[16] Louv believes this provides a necessary
grounding in our humanity. He writes: "Immersion in the natural
environment cuts to the chase, exposes the young directly and immediately

to the very elements from which humans evolved: earth, water, air, and other living kin, large and small."[17] But most children from industrialized cultures in the last few decades do not have these memories. Children without exposure to nature, Louv argues, risk numerous problems, including attention deficit disorder, obesity, and myriad physical and emotional difficulties prevalent among contemporary children and adolescents.

In the last few decades, we have raised the first generation to come of age immersed in electronics and technology. If you grow up in this environment, Louv writes, "nature is more abstraction than reality. Increasingly, nature is something to watch, to consume, to wear—to ignore."[18] He laments a television commercial depicting "a four-wheel-drive SUV racing along a breathtakingly beautiful mountain stream—while in the backseat two children watch a movie on a flip-down video screen, oblivious to the landscape and water beyond the windows."[19] I remember seeing this remarkable commercial myself. I think it should be stored in the Smithsonian as an important record of life in our times. From an advertising perspective, the positive adult emotional connection with nature—or at least the positive adult emotional connection with the idea of vacationing in nature—is used to create a positive feeling for the SUV. Then the commercial draws on another completely different adult need. This is to have the children keep quiet in the back seat so you can enjoy your vacation. So many children are addicted to constant stimulation, usually from electronics; the commercial suggests there can no longer be the perfect road trip without television to hold their attention.

I direct no judgment toward those imaginary parents. I have been there myself. After a year of hard work in a stressful office environment, who wants to manage bickering from the back seat while driving along a mountain road? When we were cruising around the American West in our mini-van, there were many times when I would have gladly turned on a television. But what does this say about where we have come? The children in the back seat are happy enough in their electronic world. What about the adults? What is their experience? They look like they are having a great time, but are they in nature—or are they experiencing a head space of vacationing in scenery? Is this anything like what Rhea White and Richard Louv experienced in their youth?

In Chapter 3, we shall return to the subject of what happens to nature in our consciousness in our times, particularly with mass media. For now, I will confess that at some point, several years after I moved to Montana, I realized the American West was merged in my psyche with cars and car commercials. One day I walked out of my house and saw my aging red Volkswagen Jetta framed by the mountains. I caught myself having a moment of pure bliss, a sense of "having it all," and my love for the car and the mountains were just one and the same. As I thought about it, I started to wonder whether the *real* reason I had moved to Montana was car commercials. All those years watching successful, good-looking, happy people speeding through those open roads, or hugging curves around those sensuous mountains, maybe nature was just an image and I was no less lost than Jay Gatsby.

Welcome to America, and increasingly, the world. The loss of nature from mainstream culture is not just loss of proximity to the natural world, but banishment of nature-as-real from our construction of reality. In a sense, nature has birthed us and held us as we evolved into creatures capable of consuming our parent, both physically and mentally. Sounds like a Greek myth, or a tragedy. In Chapter 3, we return to this part of our story, loss of reality into mental constructs in what I will call postmodern times. In the remainder of this chapter, we will consider how this happens in a psychological, or psychospiritual, sense. We then consider the psychological impact of two of those "large steps" that took us out of nature—agriculture and the industrial revolution—as ways to feel into the cultural imprinting separating us from an experience of nature. Before turning to these particular constructs, we look to the basic idea—well known in many spiritual and psychological systems—that we humans absorb and live through the constructs of reality implicit in our cultures.

Consensus Reality

Like it or not, what we experience as reality is largely a construct of consciousness. This is how our body-minds work. For centuries philosophers have been debating whether we can know any reality out there other than as constructed by our minds, but that particular argument as a matter of "either/or" is not interesting to me. I hold that debate similarly as the nature versus nurture question. On nature-versus-nurture, obviously each of us has certain instinctual and genetic orientations (and astrological imprinting, if you lean in that direction) with which we are born. Then what comes to each of us in the world, as experience, through our parents initially, then our families, school, communities and cultures, layers over our initial orientations and we exist at any given moment as a combination of nature and nurture. Sometimes the layering is smooth, sometimes problematic, for each of us personally. It is the same with construction of reality: we are each individuals, with particular orientation as embodied beings, and then with the layering from experience in the world we construct a reality that becomes habitual, the sea in which we swim.

While constructing our experience is done by each of us individually, what we construct is shaped and reinforced by what we internalize from culture. Mostly this happens unconsciously. To some extent, this is basic behaviorist psychology. Just like the rats renowned for running through the mazes built by psychology doctoral students (though not in a transpersonal program), we often react and create cognitive interpretations based on our conditioning. Our emotions are also influenced by conditioning. This is how we evolved, particularly before we developed the more recent brain structures allowing complex reflection and mental imaging. Conditioning equates to survival in most of our animal incarnations through evolution; it is learning and adapting to environment.

At the most immediate level, how we experience nature is no different. What we internalize about nature from both culture and personal experience builds a mental construct of nature, interwoven with various emotional aspects that may or may not be directly related to nature. This influences how we experience nature. In our times, most of us have developed psychological constructs creating distance between our experience of ourselves and our experience of nature. This happens mostly unconsciously, habitually, so that we may not realize we operate with a nature-excluding perspective. That we are separate from nature—that we are not nature— just seems to be reality. This is ironic, from my perspective, because existing in the natural world led to our development of habits of conditioning and construction of reality and then we evolved to a point where we began to exclude that natural world from our unconscious sense of what is real. But this is a habit of civilization.

Charles Tart, one of the pioneers of transpersonal psychology, developed the concept of "consensus trance" to describe our acceptance as real and inevitable the beliefs and implicit assumptions of our culture. In *Waking Up: Overcoming the Obstacles to Human Potential*, Tart observes, "From a culture's point of view, it is far better if your everyday mind, the habitual, automated way you think and feel, is shaped to reflect the culture's consensus beliefs and values."[20] We are born "a mass of potentials, possibilities waiting to be developed," but we all tend to become "normal" members of our culture through absorption, imitation, and shaping of our ways of viewing the world.[21] Long before the emergence of transpersonal psychology, spiritual teachers understood the first step in "waking up" involves recognizing the existence of the consensus trance. This is difficult, Tart notes, because cultures "almost never encourage their members to question them."[22] Rather, one of the "interlocking set of beliefs" of consensus trance is the "belief that we don't have a 'belief system.'"[23]

In contemporary mostly-capitalist culture, economics is the glue for the fabric of consensus trance. Like Dana's husband, and like the rest of us, albeit with infinite variations, those participating in the economic and social power structures usually come to believe in the inevitability of the system in ways intermixed with their own interests, self-esteem, desire to provide for their loved ones, and needs for power and social acceptance. Some of us in these systems know better at various levels, but feel we have no choice if we want to survive, much less have the comfortable, safe, and vibrant lives we want for ourselves and our families. Those further down the economic chain are usually trying to make ends meet within the realm of the possible in their experience, meeting what psychologist Abraham Maslow called physiological, safety, and love/belonging needs. Obviously, there are variables and sub-cultures within cultures, sub-trances within consensus trance, involving gender, race, class, and myriad other circumstances. But most of us, most of the time, go right along, immersed in consensus trance, worrying about the next thing.

In *Waking Up,* Tart describes techniques for easing out of consensus trance. He draws upon spiritual teachings, particularly those of G. I. Gurdjieff, a Russian mystic whose influence remains behind the scenes in much contemporary psychospiritual work.[24] Gurdjieff taught a spiritual practice known as the Fourth Way, involving techniques for working on one's own psychology. Like most genuine spiritual teachers, Gurdjieff understood the way toward enlightenment requires dismantling the unconscious elements of thinking and feeling, which includes becoming conscious of consensus trance. The two most important Fourth Way practices are "self-remembering" and "self-observation." The first builds a muscle; the second uses the muscle to break through our personalities and the assumptions and habits instilled by family and culture.

Self-remembering, as Tart explains, "is the term for gathering our dissociated faculties into a more unified whole."[25] Consciousness becomes less rigid and habitual and more inclusive of different ways of experiencing and knowing. "It is remembering our body and our instincts and our feelings as well as our intellectual knowledge, and so promotes the development and integrated functioning of our three brains [body/instincts, feelings, and intellect]."[26] Very importantly, this helps recover the dynamism of our individual bodies. As Tart writes, "consensus trance involves a loss of much of our essential vitality. It is (all too much) a state of partly suspended animation and inability to function, a daze, a stupor."[27] He considers consensus trance "a state of profound abstraction, a great retreat from immediate sensory/instinctual reality to abstractions about reality."[28]

"Self-observation" involves "understanding how your psychological machinery functions."[29] This does not happen all at once, but is a lifelong practice. Some spiritual systems call this "witness consciousness" or "mindfulness." The Mindfulness Based Stress Reduction Program developed by physician Jon Kabat-Zinn, now taught around the world, incorporates similar practices, helpful for physical as well as psychological health. Many forms of psychotherapy encourage insight into what lies behind our behaviors and mental and emotional states, helping us make particular changes, but more generally teaching us the one essential skill for psychological healing and growth: self-observation. As Tart explains, self-observation "is simply a matter of paying attention to *everything*," with everything understood as "a mixture of perceptions of external events and your internal reactions to them."[30]

Self-remembering and self-observation move us toward experiencing ourselves as individual beings. When we are less gripped by consensus trance, our attention moves naturally toward our own thoughts, emotions, and bodily responses. We begin to discern the difference between cognition, feelings, and body awareness. We continue to live within our culture and surroundings, yet we are increasingly able to understand our reactions as manifestations we can observe and work with, not merely the inevitable result of what is happening around or even inside us. This is similar to the practice of "going vertical " (taking your attention down inside yourself) taught by Tav Sparks in the Grof Transpersonal Training community.[31] Rather than attribute our internal states and external circumstances to the "horizontal" world around us, we direct attention into our own minds, emotions, bodies, and through them into our personal histories and conditioning, with an intention to release that which no longer serves us.

We do not abandon the external world, but enter into a different relationship with the life events and circumstances coming our way. As we shift within ourselves, we tend to experiment with new interests, behaviors, and people, noticing what happens inside ourselves in relationship with our new connections and activities in the world. Some people find the world then seems to bring them into contact with people, experiences, and events that carry forward the internal transformations taking place within them. These happenings may feel extraordinarily coincidental and meaningful, known as a synchronicity in the work of Carl Jung and several others.[32] Life begins to feel like a "journey" or unfolding, with internal "work" seeming to encourage happenings in the external world, which then fuel further personal development. Some people now call this following your "process."

The practice and general outcome of Tart's self-remembering and self-observation are similar to embodiment as described by some contemporary teachers. With embodiment, we move toward primacy of body experience, preferring sensation and emotion, de-emphasizing intellect, at least initially. Psychologist Eugene Gendlin pioneered exploration of the "felt experience" of the body in psychological healing. Some of his research indicated accessing internal body experience during psychotherapy was more predictive of psychological healing than any particular style or theory of therapy.[33] Gendlin described the "felt-sense" as follows:

> At any moment we can individually and privately direct our attention inward, and when we do that, there it is. Of course, we have this or that specific idea, wish, emotion, perception, word, or thought, but we always have concrete feeling, an inward sensing whose nature is broader. It is a concrete mass in the sense that it is "there" for us. It is not at all vague in its being there. It may be vague only in that we may not know what it is.[34]

Perhaps paradoxically, as our attention turns inward, we release more and more conditioning, developing a spaciousness and presence allowing us better to perceive the "reality" of "external reality." We experience others more as they really are and less as we expect or need them to be. We may connect more genuinely and compassionately. Perhaps we begin to see parts of the essence of other people hidden even to them. We start to feel we are "seeing through" the elements of consensus trance. Sometimes we may develop an attitude toward the lack of authenticity in external culture. We may assert independence that is not particularly great for existing relationships and positions in the world. We may feel ourselves a bit of a rebel, an "outlaw" from consensus trance. One of my teachers at ITP, Hillevi Ruumet, borrowed the term "outlaw" from mythologist Joseph Campbell to describe this orientation.[35] Given my draw to the American west, considering myself something of an outlaw appeals to my sense of abandoning the cultural herd, perhaps becoming a bit shadowy, adventuring out into the wilds of the prairies and mountains, into individuality. In my case, that individuality is connected with nature.

I believe this happens with most people, a draw to nature in this process. With self-remembering, an orientation into nature simply seems to emerge. Less embedded in consensus trance, we notice the natural world and find solace and normalcy. We may begin to feel more embedded in the natural world than in culture. Experiencing oneself embedded within nature in turn assists further release of consensus trance and conditioning. As conditioning is released, we feel more alive, perhaps longing for more immersion in nature. Conditioning tends to involve repression of various instinctual urges; some of these repressions are released and new longings emerge. As this happens, we may experience grief and weeping, as well as joy and happiness. We return to these subjects in Chapters 6 and 7. For now, we continue examining the psychological structuring existing in consensus trance. Like many people, the more I felt drawn into nature, the more I needed to understand what had happened in our civilized trance creating the distance most of us feel from the natural world. I wanted to understand why so many of us in contemporary culture find ourselves, like Dana, "on the city side of a vast river... tricked into believing the life we were leading was reality."

Control over Nature

One of the oddities of global history is the seemingly coincidental development of agriculture around roughly the same time period, ten or twelve thousand years ago, in different parts of the world. For millions of years, our ancestors hunted and gathered; in the form of Homo sapiens for the last one hundred and fifty thousand years or so, and before that as the more distant ancestors we describe as different species. Then suddenly agriculture appears in different parts of Asia and the Americas. Some historians have suggested reasons for this relatively contemporaneous development, such as climate change, but no single causal factor provides a completely acceptable reason for the timing. Some peoples, of course, continued hunting and gathering in flourishing tribal societies for thousands of years, but the trajectory toward removal from nature had begun. Plant agriculture and the domestication of animals was indisputably the watershed moment in our long-term history. Bigger even than the Internet.

The big change involved controlling nature rather than participating in the natural world as one of many species. Agriculture began a trajectory of control we are still playing out. Rather than moving around with hunting and gathering, we stayed put, stockpiling grains and keeping watch over animals, developing villages, then towns, cities, and civilizations. All these things needed controlling in new and different ways. The surpluses of food generated by agriculture and keeping animals began the economic reality of wealth, leading to structures of power and hierarchy we have taken for granted in most places for several thousand years. Within early civilizations, some specializations in social function began, leading eventually to castes and classes. Many people were controlled down through the generations; this is still playing itself out.

No longer hunting, men in particular played out our instinctual power and dominance needs in more focused and institutionalized ways. Surely there had always been struggles for power within hunting and gathering groups, as there are struggles for dominance in any herd of animals. With civilization, those instincts tended to act on each other, down through families, within communities, leading to consensus realities in culture based on implicit levels of control. Some writers have seen this as a fall from grace, a departure from earlier non-patriarchal societies not based on control. From having considered some of those arguments, and from exposure to biological anthropology, I do not believe there was any Garden of Eden in our past, no idyllic time when humans got along without effort and everyone was happy and safe. Nature was often violent, which is part of why we tamed her, and we were once nature. As for violence against each other, primatology and anthropology suggest even our ape-like male ancestors sometimes attacked and killed each other. [36]

All pack and herd animals, which we are, establish hierarchies based on dominance and control. But with agriculture, this extended to nature. This is not just a matter of human history, but planetary history. Our control over nature has become the dominant biological and environmental force on the planet. As noted by paleontologist-biologist Niles Eldredge, "Agriculture represents the single most profound ecological change in the entire 3.5 billion-year history of life." [37] With agriculture and animal domestication, Eldredge continued, "humans did not have to interact with other species for survival, and so could manipulate other species for their own use; humans did not have to adhere to the ecosystem's carrying capacity, and so could overpopulate." After this turning point: "Humans do not live with nature but outside it."[38]

Over time, nature became a force we manipulated. Sure, vagaries of climate, disease, and other variables often left us at the whim of nature. Some of us railed against her and some of us worshipped her, at least until our attention was directed skyward with the origin of religions mirroring our new social systems more than nature. We take this so much for granted it is difficult to see it, much less imagine how things could be otherwise. In other words, the trajectory into control-based cultures is part of consensus trance. Almost everywhere in the world, our economies, social systems, religions, world views, even relations between the genders and family systems, are products of cultures that assume the right to dominate nature. If anything, we are flummoxed, even irritated, that we still cannot control earthquakes, hurricanes, tornadoes, and floods.

Lamenting our loss of nature is not new. The desire to return to nature arises throughout our history, often in times of change. In the first century A.D., from the heart of Rome, Pliny the Elder wrote about returning to naturalistic ways. Nature romanticism famously arose in the arts of Europe and North America in the nineteenth century, just as nature was becoming more and more subjugated through the industrial revolution. The transcendentalist movement in New England of the 1800s celebrated nature in prose held as part of the foundation of the United States. Sometimes when I have described my interest in what has happened to nature and humanity, someone says, "Oh, like you mean Thoreau and

who's that other guy, Emerson?" Then they may tell me, "I had to read
Walden in high school. It was really hard to get through, but I know what
you're talking about."

"Exactly," I respond. "Thank God for Cliff Notes."
While I was not around during those earlier times of nature-lament, I
cannot help thinking something is different now. Perhaps there is nothing
new under the sun, or maybe we have come to a different place, a new
spot. An increasing number of people seem to be questioning our position
as dominators of nature. Some people are angry, others despondent. Paul
Shepard, one of my favorite environmental philosophers, understood our
situation, and felt both anger and despair. Like Rhea White and Richard
Louv, Shepard grew up with nature inside him. Born in 1925, Shepard
came of age during World War II, just before the massive urbanization
and suburbanization of North America. With his father a horticulturist and
director of the Missouri State Experimental Farm, Shepard knew both
agriculture and nature. His partner in his later years, Florence Shepard,
wrote that he grew up "atop a hill that overlooked woods and farms and
the town of Mountain Grove... surrounded by a rich natural environment...
wander[ing] freely as a child through the countryside."[39]

Shepard considered his writings a "lament for the land and its fate, a
painful sense of the vanishing wild and, what had seemed to me as a boy, its
perfection."[40] Moving past simple longing for his sense of nature in youth,
Shepard awakened to a deeper, instinctual memory of living within nature,
recalling the time before our ancestors subjugated the natural world with
agriculture and herding. He described an internal state, "more provocation
than uneasiness, [that] was generated by the study of biological evolution
and a growing sense of my own distant ancestry, no less emotionally felt
than the lost landscapes of my childhood, and yet intellectually satisfying in
a way that no other religious ideas are."[41] From this perspective, Shepard
imagined what it was like to live as hunter-gatherers, slowly evolving into
Homo sapiens during the Pleistocene, 1.8 million to 10,000 years before the
Common Era. Particularly in the northern latitudes, the Pleistocene was
characterized by repeated cycles of glaciations and the flourishing of wild
animals. We lived among them, preyed on them, and prayed to them.

In his last book, *Coming Home to the Pleistocene,* Shepard suggested
the way back to our humanity is less through criticism of our present and
more about "remembering beyond history," back to when we were
embedded in nature. "To have lived through a large part of the twentieth
century, with its catastrophes of violence and greed," Shepard wrote, "is to
have realized ruefully that during the three million years of the Pleistocene—
the era of our becoming—humankind was few in number, sensitive to the
seasons and other life, humble in attitude toward the earth, and comfortable

as one species among many."[42] During this era, Shepard believed, "group size was ideal for human relationships and human freedom, health was good despite (or perhaps because of!) high infant mortality rates, diet was in accord with our omnivorous physiology and sapient flexibility, and our ecology was stable and nonpolluting."[43]

Of course, no compassionate person regrets the advances in civilization which have decreased mortality rates, particularly among infants and children. But we can notice the elements of deep humanity lost in our moving away from life in small hunter-gather groups. We can take into our consciousness, both mentally and emotionally, our millions of years as part of nature, noticing our sudden (in the scheme of evolutionary time) jump from participation to domination. When we hunted and gathered we did the same things other species have always done—the same things we ourselves did all the way back through our evolutionary lineage when we *were* other species. We ate the plants that nourished us and hunted animals for meat, not so different from a cougar hunting a deer, though by the time we became hominids, we had some evolutionary assets better than the cougar and some not as great. When we gathered plants, we foraged like the herbivores and omnivores, looking for what was good to eat, remembering the best places to find the best things, moving when necessary.

When agriculture began, our ancestors were likely just looking for assurance there would be a next meal, and a next year's meal, but what happened changed everything on the planet, eventually permanently. Shepard brings attention to the fundamental shifts in our experience of ourselves and the world around us. "When people began cultivating plants, moving from a world of perennials to annuals, they created a new mode of perceiving reality, an altered sense of time." [44] With agriculture came a need to focus on hardy plants that would produce food on an annual cycle and the necessity of intervening in natural cycles in order to eat. Food came from tended fields or penned or tamed animals. Sustenance depended on disturbance of nature and enforcement of uniformity rather than appreciation of what nature provided and gratitude for our skill and good fortune in finding it.

No longer was there an implicit sense of nature as bountiful, mysterious, endless provider. When we hunted and gathered, we knew nature was sometimes harsh, but we also knew she regenerated new life without human impetus. In such surroundings, time stretched out into the future—while our bodies might succumb within nature, we were part of an endless time. As controllers of plants and animals, and participants in cultures developing from these practices, human perspective on the future, according to Shepard, was no longer open-ended, no longer hopeful, no longer worshipful. We began guarding against the tendency of nature to interfere in our plans for a good harvest. Our short-term focus switched to *this year,* to success or defeat within seasonal parameters. With our long term survival dependent on control over nature, the future became dependent on the present, but the present involved the need to dominate our surroundings.

Simple existence within what was happening began to be lost. From the perspective of some contemporary (and some ancient) spiritualities, this was a shift of enormous consequence for human well-being. Perhaps paradoxically, if you have a sense of endless time, you also have a sense of the present moment, for you can be present to what is occurring without imagining you need to control a future result. So many spiritual seekers now work diligently to recover a sense of the present moment not controlled by habitual ruminations about the future or the past. It may be fantasy to believe our hunting and gathering ancestors lived in the present, but then again, it makes sense, particularly because this seems to be part of what nature brings back to us. Nature seems to offer and perhaps require a certain diffuse alertness. When we lived in the wilds, if we were not alert to the present, we tended to be eaten.

Morris Berman, a cultural historian and social critic, describes a form of consciousness he believes was the experience of our distant hunting and gathering ancestors. As Berman concedes, such explorations are "necessarily speculative," since "quite obviously, [we] have no way of interviewing Paleolithic peoples or of conducting evolutionary brain experiments."[45] Berman named this form of consciousness "the experience of paradox." Berman believes it was consistent between our animal and early Homo sapiens ancestors, and still resides within us as "a very old genetic memory, in that it seems to be continuous with the kind of alertness that animals often display."[46]

Berman describes this way of experiencing the world as an "experience of 'space'"[47] The nomenclature of "paradox" comes from a natural holding of "contradictory propositions, or emotions, simultaneously; sustaining the tension of conflict so that a deeper reality can emerge."[48] There is no "insistence or hope that the world be this way or that" but a simple acceptance of "the world as it presents itself, and in that sense, it would seem to require a very high level of trust."[49] In contrasting the experience of paradox with the form of consciousness he believes we later developed, termed "the sacral authority complex" or SAC, Berman writes:

> Trust in the world is now much less, and fear of death has assumed a prominent place. The human being has not so much a world as a world *view*; and the perception tends to be vertical in nature. In other words, whereas with paradox the "sacred," such as it is, simply is the world, in the case of the SAC sacrality has been projected upward, into the realm of the gods.[50]

What Berman describes as paradoxical consciousness strikes me as very similar to what therapists and personal growth facilitators encourage as an ability to hold the "both/and" as opposed to an "either/or" way of relating to the world. Years before I read Berman, I described an approach to life recognizing that "many things are true at once" without contradicting each other, much the same as Berman's experience of paradox. Interestingly enough, much of the pre-agriculture ways of experiencing the world described by both Berman and Shepard feel extremely similar to forms of consciousness emerging from psychospiritual practices and taught and encouraged in contemporary spiritual growth movements. This is particularly interesting with respect to Berman, who is openly caustic in his writing about Jungian and transpersonal psychology. For instance, he refers to "Jungian/gaian foolishness," with "gaian" referring to the practice among some spiritual seekers to consider the earth a living, and feminine, being, Gaia having been one of the primordial Greek Goddesses who personified the Earth. Berman similarly hopes his readers find "this transpersonal tyranny as scary as I do," and views the observation of transpersonal writer Rick Tarnas that Western culture is re-orienting toward feminine values as "Come to Mommy, she will make you whole again."[51]

Nonetheless, anyone reading Shepard, and Berman in particular, will wonder at the similarities between their suggestion of pre-agricultural ways of being and the forms of awareness that emerge through spiritual practice. Mind you, I am not talking about beliefs, catch phrases, enculturation, or personality-based performance that emerges from listening to teachings or adopting tenets of faith. Nor am I talking about such things as striving to be good or compassionate. I am talking about orientations toward the world, forms of consciousness, which in my experience tend to emerge from spiritual practices such as meditation, yoga, and Holotropic Breathwork.

These contemporary orientations toward experience include an attention to, and acceptance of, what is emerging in the present, without attachment to controlling an outcome. Many in the transpersonal and personal growth movements report an emerging desire for surrendering to "the mystery." This means not pretending to understand how and why everything that happens seems to be happening, much less to control it. This does not involve relinquishing the sense of personal self, freedom or free will, but rather involves opening to the possibility that we do not always control our own fates, even if we shape them through our choices, attitudes, beliefs, hopes, and dreams. From such spiritual practices tend to emerge an intention for *not knowing*. Room is left for chance and the unexpected, for miracles of surprise. Way before I read Berman, I thought this was not unlike walking in the wilderness—who knows what is around the bend. It may be beautiful, it may be dangerous, but it will be a part of nature, situating our lives as part of what is, part of a whole.

Berman's suggestion the experience of paradox is consistent with how animals experience the world makes particular sense to me. I suspect this is partially why so many of us are drawn to animals, particularly those in the wild. In Shepard's view, our domestication of animals was more tragic in consequence than our dominion over plants. Shepard considers animals—the "Others" as he calls them—to have made us human.[52] He argues our cognitive processes and psychological tendencies arose through relationship with animals, during all those eons of the Pleistocene when we both ate and were eaten by animals.

In those formative years, we survived by knowing and imitating the ways of the "Others." We wore their skins, drew pictures of them, and communed with their "spirits" to understand the world around us. In Chapter 10, we will consider the draw to "shamanism" experienced by thousands of contemporary people as a desire for psychological immersion in nature. In neo-shamanic practices, we seek an internal sense of these very animals Shepard believes helped to shape our souls. I suspect we may be attempting to remember some of our own ancestral forms of consciousness.

Through wild animals, we were in touch with nature and her potential for offering us a glimpse into ourselves. Wild animals had their own lives, even if we learned to outsmart them by understanding them. Outsmarting wild animals in the hunt is different from penning them up or breeding the wild out of them. In Chapter 10, we shall consider more deeply the current fascination of many people with wild animals, particularly wolves and bears in the American West. As I will suggest, the very conflict between our need for the wild and our need for control—as well as our contemporary loss of reality about nature—seems to play itself out in personal and cultural attitudes toward these animals. As we became civilized, the wild that fed our psyches through our animal acquaintances moved into the recesses of our unconscious. Before we entered civilization, Shepard writes, "animals were seen as belonging to their own nation and to be the bearers of messages and gifts of meat from a sacred domain."[53] But "[i]n the village they became possessions."[54] As much as I respect animals, wild and otherwise, I suspect the real issue involves our loss of this sacred domain—and our loss of a certain way of being in the world.

Sometimes when I read Shepard or Berman, I sense an implicit anger or blame toward those of our ancestors who took the road of agriculture and domestication, as though a better path may have been taken. I sense something similar from a good many others now lamenting the impact of the civilization we have created—as if many of us suffering these times would be here if humans had stayed hunters and gatherers. I hold our history differently. While I want to feel my emotions around our loss of embeddedness in nature, I greatly admire our civilizing ancestors, particularly at the stage of agriculture and domestication. I would love to meet those geniuses who realized seeds could be gathered and planted, animals controlled and then interbred with the least violent and most controllable in the herd. If I had been the guy who realized I could drive wild aurochs into pens and have ready meat, I would still be proud of myself. If I had realized how to breed out the troublesome characteristics, to make my job as auroch-keeper safer and easier, you can bet I would still be patting myself on the back.

My interest lies in understanding what we have done to nature in our consciousness and what we have lost within ourselves. If we feel into our unconscious presumption of entitlement to dominate nature, we may open into the possibility of remembering another way of being. This is far different from feeling guilty for our heritage—and not everything can be blamed on agriculture and herding. The behavior of our chimpanzee cousins, the species with whom we share the most recent common ancestor, indicates our ape ancestors dominated each other within their communities and very likely killed each other across communities.[55] But of course they were still living within nature, still feeling the natural world around them, not going to work in an expensive car, wearing an expensive suit, and sitting in traffic, any Hollywood movies depicting our ape cousins in these ways notwithstanding.

Almost all animals struggle in various ways against nature, seeking survival in competition with other life forms and the forces of the natural world. The instinct to control nature for our survival may simply be part of our life force, part of our animal instinct. Evolutionary biologists even talk of the "arms race" that began billions of years ago as some species developed protection against others (such as hard shells) leading evolution to produce other species with means to break those shells and devour the once-protected. Then even harder shells were developed, followed by more effective predatory means. Like it or not, competition and conflict seem inherent in life on the planet. Yet the form of control arising with agriculture and domestication of animals does seem qualitatively different. As Shepard notes, we had been animals competing with other animals for an evolutionary niche. Then we became presumptive masters of the universe, presumptuous in our expectation of entitlement to control.

As agriculture and animal domestication removed us physically from nature, this shift in consciousness brought into our psychology a human-dominated "world view" in which nature was conceptually as well as physically separated from us. Berman suggests this shift in consciousness—even the very creation of a world view—broke our psychological link with our animal ancestors. We exchanged presence for certainty. What Berman describes as "certainty" in post-agricultural consciousness feels much the same as what Shepard describes as control. We control in order to have certainty; we have certainty only if we are in control—or if we are able to imagine someone is in control, be it general, king, priest, or God. This is obviously a personal psychological issue for each of us as well as a structural component of the consensus trance we inherit in post-agricultural times.

Needing certainty or control is also a spiritual issue. I suspect the patriarchal God we created in later stages of civilization reflects this need for complete control, manifesting a longing for a unitive protective force. Consistent with the views of many anthropologists, Shepard argued the agricultural shift led to invention of a God in our own civilization-based human image—quite a reversal in our history. This may be the ultimate hubris of human civilization: the vision of the creative energy of the universe in human form. Sadly, this brought the sacred down to our level of imperfection, masked by an inflated view of ourselves. As Shepard asks:

> Is it any wonder that we came to think of the natural world as inferior, as created by a human-like deity, as an enemy to our civilized interests? What could religion do in such circumstances but invent an anthropomorphized God the creator, place evil in the wilderness, reserve the soul as a human possession, and locate heaven somewhere else?[56]

By no means would I advocate for a reversal of what we have created through civilization, even if that were remotely possible. I, for one, am not ready to give up access to emergency rooms and antibiotics, nor to relinquish the innumerable other trappings of contemporary life that sustain our health, safety and happiness. Very practically, I am grateful to have minimized the chances that I will have to watch my children taken away by eagles or cougars, though of course even contemporary parents live with fear of the hazards to our children in present life, including the possible explosion of that suitcase nuclear bomb haunting my own personal imagination. I am also content with my experience of individuality which seems to have arisen through the separations we created by moving out of nature. We likely needed civilization and the growth of rational processes in order to experience ourselves as unique individuals, at this point able to crave a return to nature. I do not want to relinquish my sense of individual consciousness, even if that were possible.

Yet for our individual and collective salvation, we might rediscover what Shepard called the "generic human." He writes: "The generic human in us knows how to dance the animal, knows the strength of clan membership and the profound claims and liberation of daily rites of thanksgiving. Hidden from history, this secret person is undamaged in each of us and may be called forth by the most ordinary acts of life." [57] Those of us with the inclination to awaken our generic human need to find our own individual way back. Even while writing all these words on my computer, one thing I know is that this has to be more about living a life—or even better dancing a life—than figuring anything out with my head.

World as Machine

If agriculture took us out of the wilds, starting our battle for control of nature, industrialization brought the assumption we have won the war. There may be some cleaning up to do—we may still need to tighten all the screws on nature, nail her down completely—but for the most part we believe we have prevailed. We have entered a whole new territory of hubris with respect to our attitude toward nature. Our sciences are smarter than nature; we know how to crack her secrets and use them for our will and whims. Even the human DNA code is pretty well cracked; it is just a matter of time until "they" (the scientists) have it all figured out. It is all written down out there somewhere; and now it is on computers. When we cannot figure something out, our computers can pick up the slack.

True enough: the sciences developed in the last few hundred years have yielded stunning levels of understanding about our world, our biology, and the universe. Rationality and the scientific method work wonders for weeding out falsities and biases and giving rise to understandings as beautiful as they are useful. Yet lurking within the industrial age is the idea that nature is something to be subdued in an intellectual sense, just as we subdued her physically. It is not simply that we are smug for being smart, for we are smart. Rational science is amazing. The issue in this section is to feel into the attitude that has developed within consensus trance about nature. Now we are into mind control with nature. We know how to extract nature's secrets, tease them out of her, use them to control her at the chemical, biological and even atomic level. Agriculture reminds me of a form of physical control, like imprisoning someone. How we conceive of nature in the age of science feels like we are into her nervous system, controlling her from the inside out. If you control someone's mind, I suspect you lose even more respect for them than if you happen to become able to lock them up.

I call this our second removal from nature. We are no longer just con-trolling animals and plants. As a culture, as we entered the industrial age, a part of us started to look down on nature as beneath us, dirty, messy, not organized and rational like a good machine. Now machines, they work in an orderly fashion. You put gasoline in a car and maybe sometimes take it to the mechanic, who now even plugs the machine into a machine for some computer diagnostics, but cars like the other machines work according to schematics. It all makes sense; someone understands it, even if you do not. Not like horses, which are ornery, have a will of their own, and crap all over the place, something you have to clean up. Some of us, I think, being good industrialists and rational thinkers, are even irritated about the continuing chaos of nature, somewhat like a wife out of control.

Industrialization seems merged in our psyches, in collective trance, with the scientific paradigm and methods that brought about industrialization. I am using the term industrialization broadly to include the process beginning a very few hundred years ago, through which increasingly sophisticated use of scientific principles gave rise to machinery, factories and vehicles, which in turn completely altered social structures and the ways most of us live. This began most forcefully in England, and also in Germany, then spread around Europe, North America, and other parts of the world. From industrialization emerged the United States as a dominant world power, where it remains, though now challenged by the financial (and perhaps soon military) prowess of countries outperforming the United States economically. All of this performance—this relatively new form of economic competition—is based on the assumption of world as machine.

As we moved into the machine age, economies were no longer primarily based on agrarian interchanges, which were still within the milieu of nature, but shifted toward another form of exchange. We moved into capitalist economies, with ownership of means of production, laboring jobs, businesses, and professions. People moved to cities. Farmland was aggregated, evolving eventually, at least in the United States, into corporate agribusiness. Individuals, families, and communities no longer produced their own food, clothing, tools, and goods, nor even exchanged those things with people they actually saw. Rather, everything became a commodity of value, offered in a context of alienation. In the economic sense, alienation is not a psychological state but a separation between the physical transformation of natural resources into something with specific particular value and the user of that thing of value. That said, psychological alienation quickly became part of the picture, as we all became, to one extent or another, cogs in an economic machine.

The social transformations accompanying this shift were revolutionary and complex, giving rise to well-known and varied economic, sociological, and political theories. Adam Smith imagined the invisible hand productively directing capitalist markets. As with all rational thought and emerging science, there was something clean and inevitable about the invisible hand, at least in capitalist imagination. A good strong hand, working hard, can caress you for good behavior or give you a smack if you need it. In reaction, feeling the alienation and the growing social injustice, feeling into the smack more than the caress, Karl Marx thought the workers would unite, take over, and soon enough manage an economy without dictatorship. We all know how that turned out. The tensions of the industrial age still remain in our world, with some developing countries only now beginning to feel them. On the other hand, some of the nineteenth and twentieth century tensions have eased in many places, through democracy and increasing individual freedoms—and through diversion of our energies into ever new and amazing opiates of the masses, also known as consumer products, now in electronic guise.

For present purposes, we can simply notice in a very broad sense the structures of the cultural trance that have roots in industrialization and the scientific paradigm. Like many before me, I am equating industrialization with the development of a mechanical view of the universe. Not just a mechanical view of the universe, but a paradigm in which human understandings implicitly rise above nature. Through detailed knowledge of the workings of the component parts (e.g., physics, biology, chemistry, even psychology), we imagine ourselves capable of redesigning nature as a machine to be used for our purposes.

Control was not enough; we became creators. Most of us do not consciously think about this, but the assumption that we are creators of the universe through science and rationality is implicit in consensus trance. As Nietzsche said in the dawning days of the industrial age, God is dead.[58] As my father would say: dead and rotten. Millions of us in industrial-technological times never even knew God, like he was a grandfather who passed away before we were born. We may hear about him, but we have no visceral sense of him. He means nothing to us personally. I am not saying there are not people out there finding meaningful, deep, and personal relationship with their experience of God. I am saying that consensus trance in mainstream educated culture has assumed we are smarter than what that consensus trance imagines as a fairy tale God. Of course, within certain sub-cultures, there is a continuing resentful and sometimes violent reaction to the death of God and this view of him as a fairy tale. This goes hand in hand with a hatred of the rationalism that killed him, taking the form of fundamentalist religions, but that is a story for another day.

In place of God, we have machines, and now machines are computers. Some of them are starting to think. My son Max talks about the coming "technological singularity," when artificial intelligence will surpass human intellectual capacity, raising the science fiction-y possibility computers will take control, as foreshadowed by many movies.[59] Let us hope they are not as jealously murderous as Hal in *2001: A Space Odyssey*, or, perhaps even worse, the "love 'em and leave 'em" type like Samantha in *Her*. Max suggests humanity should begin a new calendar in the year of the technological singularity, predicted by some to occur as soon as 2030, by others more like 2045.[60] He makes this suggestion in part because he chafes at a calendar beginning with the presumptive year Jesus was born, which brings us back to God being dead and the future being handed over to the rational intelligence of machines. How fascinating that the slightly apocalyptic flavor of the imagined technological singularity involves our fear of losing control to the machines we created in our own rational image.

In this second removal from nature, we began to assume we are smarter than nature because we can discover the universal principles which nature herself must obey. Subjugation became not just physical in the sense of controlling crops and animals, but had moved to a mental realm. The issue was manipulation of the foundational laws of the universe, previously the working of the gods. With the machine age, we ascended Mount Olympus, where causal agents play. Those who follow science no longer needed a god in man's image, so the great demise of the religions based on agriculture came upon us. We were smart enough not to need gods. Through this process comes a shift in consensus consciousness in which "science" becomes more "real" than nature herself. The sun still rises and the seasons come; but more real is astronomy and laws of rotation and gravity.

Most of us in the industrialized societies attribute a god-like power to science as a cohesive knowing-force. Most of this is not conscious. And yet, sadly, even while we imagine science as omnipotent, almost all of us are removed personally from access to the omniscience, as we do not really understand the principles or particulars involved. Somebody else does; "they" do. Almost all of us talk about a collective "they" with respect to science and scientists: "they" just discovered this; "they" are about done working on that. We wonder what "they" are going to discover next. We assume our future is in the hands of science, though with the coming technological singularity the future may be in the hands of machines. We are conditioned to believe ways of knowing and learning not adhering to objectivist machine-like scientific principles are not legitimate and thus not "real." This means what can be "legitimately known" and hence considered "real" becomes constricted to what can be researched and described by scientific method. Once again, God is out the window, replaced by the "they" of science; or God is moved to an emotional-fairy-tale realm held separately from scientific reality.

The scientific method, for better or worse, cannot directly access consciousness or experience as lived. For most of the twentieth century, this meant the study of consciousness and human experience was not considered real in a scientific sense. Striving to be a "real" science, psychology as an academic discipline developed as the study of observable and measurable behavior, relegating human experience into some place that was not-quite-trustworthy, not-quite-real. This is no longer the case in all academic psychology departments, many of which now recognize the value of qualitative research, seeking to understand and document human experience. The exclusion of consciousness from psychology is certainly not the case in the discipline of transpersonal psychology. My friends Rosemarie Anderson and William Braud authored two research methodology books now widely used in transpersonal and humanistic research describing alternative, but nonetheless empirical, ways of discovering and knowing.[61]

At the same time academic psychology was excluding consciousness from scientific reality, the disciplines of biology, neurology, and medicine were describing consciousness as an epiphenomenon of the brain. An epiphenomenon is a secondary effect, or by-product of a primary phenomenon.[62] Brain functioning was the primary phenomenon, the material event, the actual reality. What we experienced as consciousness—our very lives—became simply a by-product, even an accident in the view of some people, of mechanical brain functioning. This meant science had removed primacy from our very consciousness, making our reality suspect, casting doubt on the meaningfulness of our experience. Along with God, our sense of self as a valuable reality went out the window. This left us with the divide between science and religion that many people now living cannot bridge, so either operate as atheists or agnostics, or pretend the God of agricultural religions and the "they" of science do not need reconciling, repressing the schism that eats at the psyche from creating such false divisions.

I consider the assumption that consciousness is not primary as the biggest "elephant in the room" in science. In fact, there is no proof consciousness arises only from the brain and some proof that it exists separate from brain functioning.[63] This issue is part of the larger question of whether the material world manifests from another realm, a realm in which consciousness participates separate from our physical manifestation. As described in numerous books over the last few decades, such as Fritjof Capra's *The Tao of Physics: An Exploration of the Parallels between Modern Physics and Eastern Mysticism,*[64] twentieth-century physics reached understandings, through the scientific method, of the interconnection of material entities outside the means of communication considered possible in the mechanistic paradigm.

For over a hundred years, physicists have noted the interplay of consciousness and matter. I personally have come to understand symbolic meaning as a basic organizing principle of the cosmos. In *The Archetypal Cosmos: Rediscovering the Gods in Myth, Science and Astrology*,[65] Keiron Le Grice draws upon current understandings from physics and depth psychology to describe a universe in which matter and consciousness arise from a more fundamental underlying "archetypal" reality, which is the source of meaning. Insofar as we may have access to meanings arising from an archetypal reality, many of those meanings appear to us through images and symbols involving nature. Whether nature is a manifestation of processes in an archetypal cosmos or somehow helps to create those meaningful imprinting processes, many people experience the natural world as reflecting the deepest parts of ourselves.

As discussed more directly in Chapter 10, our return to involvement in nature can take the form of a psychological immersion in nature, through which aspects of our consciousness or even deeper unconscious recesses of our psyche interplay with nature on imaginal or symbolic levels. Through such connections, we re-enter mystery, a realm where the universe is not a knowable, reducible machine. In an archetypal cosmos, rationalism associated with "world as machine" is not the singular entry point into knowledge, but may even interfere with our understanding of realities about ourselves and the world around us. The mechanistic-rationalist paradigm may be something we need to move beyond without abandoning it, as described in depth in the works of developmental theorist Ken Wilber, who formerly identified himself with transpersonal psychology, but now uses the designation integral.[66] Rationalist ways are an important part of us, a necessary stage in maturation of our species, but there are stages beyond that may be necessary if we really want to know the universe.

With respect to releasing the hold of the mechanistic paradigm, we can begin to notice whether the assumptions of world as machine are part of our consciousness. The negative impact of the mechanistic paradigm on our consciousness—and ultimately our morale—has been observed by numerous writers. My friend Whit Neill, a frequent visitor to Montana for fly fishing, gave me books by Lewis Mumford, an American sociologist, well known for his work on urban planning and the study of technology. With his life spanning almost all of the twentieth century, Mumford observed the urban-suburbanization of the country, along with its move toward worship of technology. His two-volume work, *The Myth of the*

Machine, was written in the 1960s, just before we moved fully into the electronic age.

The Myth of the Machine illustrates the angst of becoming conscious of ourselves as nothing more than cogs in an industrial machine. Mumford described the 1900s as producing "a radical transformation in the entire human environment, largely as a result of the impact of the mathematical and physical sciences upon technology."[67] He distinguished between the polytechnics of earlier societies, in which different modes of technology offered a complex interwoven framework for social infrastructures, and the monotechnics of the machine age, characterized by single forms of technology sweeping wide swaths across social structures. An important example involves the automobile. As Mumford notes, in most of North America, cars have caused the structuring of the urban and suburban environments. Until very recently, in almost all parts of the country, this led to virtual exclusion of other modes of transportation, such as walking, bicycling, and public transport. Cities and suburbs shaped themselves to the automobile, as did the human animal. This left most of us without much effective choice in how our physical selves met the outer world, and hence subject to alienation.

Not long ago, it occurred to me that the cars and trucks in which I drive feel more real to me than my body as my agent of motion. I realized I do not like it. As the result of frequent walking in the mountains of Montana, I began to recover a sense of my own body as that which carries me from place to place. I began to recover a better sense of the space around my body. I realized the way in which I had unconsciously understood the body of the car—and its place and possibilities in space—as the real way that I moved from place to place. Those walks in the mountains brought me into contact with nature, contributing to a sense of nature as that which surrounded my body as I moved. Even when I am in cities, I prefer walking from place to place, continuing my sense of bodily agency moving in the real world, noticing the cars, buses, buildings, and roads as things we humans have constructed out of materials from nature. For the most part, I prefer older cities, with urban layouts arising prior to the world-shaping force of the automobile, though of course even older cities, at least in North America, accommodate this Trojan horse of modernity.

I believe my experience would have made sense to Mumford. He was concerned with "alterations in the human personality" with our new technological lifestyle.[68] In his view, we were "passing from the primeval state of man, marked by his invention of tools and weapons for the purpose of achieving mastery over the forces of nature, to a radically different condition, in which [man] will have not only conquered nature, but detached himself as far as possible from the organic habitat."[69] This created what he called megatechnics, through which "the dominant minority will create a uniform, all-enveloping, super-planetary structure, designed for automatic operation."[70] Rather than acting individually and autonomously, "man will become a passive, purposeless, machine-conditioned animal whose proper functions, as technicians now interpret man's role, will either be fed into the machine or strictly limited and controlled for the benefit of de-personalized, collective organizations."[71] Surely Mumford could not have been talking about us.

Mumford understood the machine-age to have produced, in our consciousness, a "mechanized world picture" in a "de-natured environment."[72] The systematic scientific descriptions "of space, time, motion, mass, gravitation eventually brought about a major shift in technology: from the workshop to the laboratory, from the tool-using craftsman and artist, himself a prime mover as well as a designer, to the complex power-driven automatic machine under centralized direction and remote control."[73] Mumford believed "it was this world picture, not individual mechanical inventions alone," that contributed to the "final apotheosis" of our shift toward experiencing ourselves as a part of a "megamachine."[74] Mumford did not talk in terms of consensus trance, but his "world picture" is another way of suggesting our semi-conscious assumption of our new role as humans.

As parts of a megamachine, we are further removed from our embodied, natured humanity. Our (mostly unconscious) locus of agency has shifted *away* from ourselves as individual, autonomous beings *to* whatever is the source of the mechanization. Mumford wrote about the assumption of "remote control" of the machine. This is the "they" of science that I notice in common parlance. It is important to note the assumption that the machine is singular, one mechanism pulling us all into it. Stanislav Grof has described the underlying paradigm of scientific assumption as "monistic materialism"—the assumption of a singular mate-rial world reality describable by one set of laws. Nothing exists outside the material world and that world is described by universally-operating scien-tific principles. For most of us in the industrialized world, I believe the assumption of monistic materialism blends together with the myth of the machine so that we envision the universe as one complicated machine, controlled remotely. Those of us believing in God may imagine God as controlling the machine, but even this assumption may leave God as the Wizard of Oz operator of an impersonal infrastructure, not so much inti-mate knower of our animal souls.

If we are cogs in a remotely controlled machine, where is our value, except as commodity? In that respect, perhaps we become one with nature, all of us commodity. When the world has become a machine, nature is merely the source for operational parts. Trees exist to become timber, mountains are there for mining, animals and plants have their functions as part of a mechanized economy. Nowhere is this more tragic than in terms of the human body. Particularly within the United States, our national economy and individual lives are sometimes dragged down by medicine as business, with our bodies a commodity on which profit is made. This is possible because consensus trance holds our bodies as machinery. A few years ago, I heard a story on National Public Radio about the awarding of the 2013 Nobel Prize in Medicine to researchers who described important aspects of cell physiology, known as vesicle transport and fusion. Radio journalist Steve Inskeep remarked this discovery "will help to figure out what to do when the machinery goes awry." The written version of the story on the NPR website described the cellular process as "cargo delivery." This is just an example of "body as machine" in consensus trance.

I mean no disrespect to all those dedicated, intelligent, hard-working people in the medical system, nor a lack of appreciation for the scientists who have made discoveries, invented machines, and found chemicals that keep or restore our health, minimizing our suffering and loss. Like most people, I cherish the benefits of modern science, including allopathic medicine. When something is wrong with me or my loved ones, I want you guys thinking rationally, figuring out what is wrong with my machine. But many of us are sitting on some feelings about what we have lost by envisioning ourselves as part of technology, including our bodies. This book is about the grief many of us feel for our loss of nature, ultimately a loss of ourselves. Before we reach grief, many of us find anger. Technology sometimes becomes a scapegoat for this anger, an easy modern culprit.

In various settings over the years, I have noticed the way some of us need to defend technology by arguing that technology is nature. The argument usually goes: "If people are part of nature, anything we make is nature, so technology is nature." Drawing on the work of James Lovelock, Bill McKibbin noted this argument in *The End of Nature,* where he wrote: "One can, of course, argue that the current ecological crisis is 'natural,' because man is part of nature."[75] McKibbin acknowledged the suggestion "that 'our species with its technology is simply an inevitable part of the natural scene,' nothing more than mechanically advanced beavers. In this view, to say that we 'ended' nature, or even damaged nature, makes no sense, since we *are* nature, and nothing we can do is 'unnatural.'"[76]

Granted, when I am walking through cities, I understand everything around me as constructed from nature, the ultimate source of our materiality, including the substance of our bodies. But the suggestion "technology is nature" seems to ring hollow, to bypass the point. McKibbin puts it this way, "one can argue this forever and still not really feel it. It is a debater's point, a semantic argument."[77] Of course we are nature, and the constituent parts of our machines come from nature. But most of us are no longer surrounded by wild animals, plants, and geological forms not shaped by human agenda. We engage with human-made contraptions, live within structures with technological parts, and conceptualize the world as machine. The answer, as far as I am concerned, is not rejecting the astoundingly successful world rationality has built around us, but feeling our loss around other ways of being, and remembering, and then remembering some more, while seeing nature in the midst of all these human-made things.

Hawks in the City

Having begun this chapter with Dana's story, we return to her in its closing. She wrote about her childhood draw to St. Francis of Assisi, "imagining him immersed in an animal world." Dana longed for that kind of connection "with the birds that sang outside my window, with any animal that wandered into our yard." Before founding the Franciscan Order within the Catholic Church, St. Francis was an itinerant preacher, during an era of rampant corruption among clergy, including the Pope. In response to a religious structure seeming more about material indulgence than spirit, St. Francis began walking through the Italian countryside, preaching wherever he found himself. According to legend, sometimes this meant preaching to the birds, squirrels and deer. That his communion with nature became part of the Catholic tradition is unusual in a religion rarely inclusive of the natural world. The song of St. Francis to brother sun, sister moon, mother earth, and brother fire is one of the few nature hymns found in the hymnal books in many Christian churches.

Some historians consider St. Francis to have saved the Church through his opening to nature. This began with rejection of the ways of his particular culture, radical action in his time. As the story goes, his father, a wealthy cloth merchant, called upon a local bishop to talk his son into abandoning his spiritual pursuits for work in the family business. In a dramatic confrontation in the cathedral of his town, Francis broke ties with his father, literally removing his clothes and handing them back to his earthly parent. The story of St. Francis offers a symbolic model for the spiritual return into nature. Discarding the clothes given by our culture, we walk naked into the woods. No wonder Dana recalled his relationship with nature when writing to me.

What happened to her? Here is a story close enough to the truth. With care and compassion for all involved, she ended her marriage to Rob, finding her own niche in the world. She now lives in Chelsea, in New York City, working in non-profit and teaching yoga part-time. Her children are grown, happy enough, pursuing their own lives. She still enjoys her spiritual friends, and travels when she can—often to foreign lands where nature still openly thrives. She recently made her third trip to the Amazon of Peru, where she works with an indigenous healer. The power and essence of animals and plants is now part of her daily experience, part of her internal experience of herself and her world. Rob eventually remarried, happily. He, Dana, and the kids still form a tribe.

Dana happens to thrive on the energy of New York City, though it helps to get away from concrete and crowds when she can. But no matter where she is, Dana sees nature all around her. She sits on benches watching pigeons, notices hawks living at the upper reaches of tall buildings, and is constantly amused by the procession of dogs being walked on the city streets. She loves the urban hawks in particular, watching them soar in the spaces between buildings, wondering whether they find any difference between mountains and skyscrapers. Those hawks invite us to consider whether it is possible to exist as creatures within civilization while recovering our instincts of the wild. Fundamentally, this involves our outlook, how we hold nature, and perhaps whether we can move into and through our grief for what we have lost. Before turning fully to grief, we look in the next chapter into whether nature has ceased being real in the consensus trance, for we cannot grieve that which does not exist.

CHAPTER 3

Nothing is Real, Not Even Nature

A lawyer friend of mine named David Sandler told me about an extraordinary recommendation made to a group of trial lawyers at a seminar he attended. A master trial lawyer was describing contemporary best practices for winning jury verdicts. Jury trials are often won or lost based on how much the jury believes your experts as compared to experts testifying for the other side. The recommendation from the master trial lawyer was to present your most important expert testimony to the jury through video, not with real-life testimony. In the past, video testimony was considered second-best, a last-ditch effort if your witness could not come to trial. But now, those of us "in the know" are learning video testimony is more persuasive than live testimony. Jurors trust what they see and hear on video more than what comes from a person sitting before them. Image holds more truth than reality.

Enter the postmodern realm. While the term *postmodern* may be familiar to many, particularly those involved in academics in the last few decades, it is a strange term when you first hear it. I used to throw it around now and then in front of my kids, amusing myself by telling them something they did or said was very postmodern. As they would ask before they went to college and learned some sociology, "How can something be *post*modern? You don't get past modern by definition." Well, you do when modernity starts to reference a specific historical time period with certain characteristics so that trends or characteristics "post" that time period can be described and discussed as *post*modern. First used in particular disciplines, such as art history and literary criticism, the term postmodern initially described a style that came "post," that is "after," a style previously considered modern. For instance, during the late 1800s, Impressionist art was considered "modern" because the style was avant garde, then when some paintings moved into a different style, that style was called "postmodern" because it abandoned characteristics that had been described as modern. Over time, usage of the term postmodern broadened. By the latter part of the twentieth century, "postmodern" described a range of writers considering the lack of mooring in concrete reality that seems to arise within a mass media culture. In a sense, these writers wondered whether we have moved "post" reality.

Interestingly enough, as we will come to see, even the phrase *postmodern* is postmodern in the sense that the word *modern* has been defined to mean something other than its straightforward meaning, removing the word from its usual mooring in common lay speech. To grasp "postmodern," you do something characteristic of "postmodernity." You base your orientation on an interpretive idea in a shifting sea of concepts, interpretations and images. In the postmodern context, "modern" does not mean contemporary or "now" but points toward a particular period in the past, so in some sense, one of the words for "now" no longer means "now" but rather means "then," leaving me with a vague sense that "now" has lost its mooring. I am in some kind of head space rather than in the actual orientation of historical time and place. There is meaning but the meaning is referential more than concrete.

Why talk about postmodernism in connection with nature? The postmodern viewpoint provides a lens into what I call our third removal from nature, the time in our history when nothing is real, not even nature. For many people in our times, nature is no longer grounded in actual experience of the natural world, but has become an image bouncing around like all other images in a culture dominated by media. In the last chapter, I used the example of the interweaving of automobiles with the panoramic vistas and mountaintops in the American west. Those scenes generate feelings and reference points within us, but those feelings and reference points are intended to point me toward purchasing a car and participating in the car based lifestyle. Nature becomes a sign pointing in that direction more than an experience in space and time. Then, even when I am in nature, the question arises as to what I am actually experiencing. When I walked out of my house and felt the bliss of seeing my red Jetta against mountains, the question arose as to where I really was. Was I in the mountains or was I in the head space of a commercial?

There is nothing particularly evil in this and it is a matter of degree. Many of us still do have some experiences in nature and even the television images probably pull at some of our actual memories. But for understanding our present level of removal from nature, it is useful to consider nature as image separated from both the natural world and from our direct sensory and emotional responses in the natural world. In later chapters, we will consider how many of us in our times have lost an ability to consider nature as real, sometimes leading us into dangerous situations, such as when we are tourists in Yellowstone or Glacier National Parks and fail to take in the "danger of death" signs at the base of trails with respect to the danger of grizzly bears, getting close to said bears in order to take pictures with the unconscious assumption that these bears are not actually real but are there to provide us with an image we can capture and share. In this chapter, we look into some ways to understand our predicament in our third removal from nature, beginning with some of the perspectives of postmodernism.

Postmodernity

As we moved into the middle and latter parts of the twentieth century, a general "postmodern theory" arose through writings of intellectuals and academics, mostly European, predominantly French. Michel Foucault wrote about the relationship between knowledge and power in a twentieth century context, while conducting an "archeology" into the social construction of madness, sexuality, medicine, and other social institutions and ideas. Jacques Derrida wrote volumes in the philosophical and historical traditions "deconstructing" the assumptions of Western civilization. Broadly speaking, on a social level, this is analogous to investigation into consensus trance that happens in spiritual work, such as that described by Charles Tart.

Attention to the underlying structures and assumptions of societies became a hallmark of postmodernism. Along with "poststructuralism," postmodernism became a description for the commonalities of writers such as Foucault and Derrida, including their questioning whether there is any underlying structure to social institutions and cultures other than as created through forces mostly unseen by most people. Postmodern writers often linked these unseen forces to the implicit or explicit desires to maintain power by certain groups and institutions. As a broad categorization for a mid-to-late twentieth century trend within the humanities, postmodernism began to characterize the understanding that "reality" is constructed through social discourse, particularly power discourse. This coincided with an interest in the constructed "signs" within linguistic and social systems that simply refer to each other, maintaining the systems but lacking reality outside the system.

In the latter half of the twentieth century, according to some postmodern thinkers, we began moving into a period characterized by "meta-narratives," broad and increasingly homogenous constructions of reality by forces of media, industry, culture, and globalization. Meta-narratives emerge from the presentation of would-be experiences such as those depicted in media. Most postmodern theorists would argue meta-narratives are not disinterested but arise from a series of attempts to cause us to do something, as in, to buy products. I would put it this way: meta-narratives come together into a consensus trance involving the implicit assumption that consumer culture is inevitable, just the way it is. Among other things, this diverts attention from whether there are other ways of being that might provide additional meaning in our lives, if we even knew how to notice the issue.

From these perspectives emerge a picture of what I am calling postmodern times. Others have designated our era the information age, the post-industrial age, the electronic age, or the age of image. To me, the idea of image is central, both in the literal sense that so many of us spend time absorbed in electronic images and in the psychological (or psychospiritual) sense that our attention is drawn into mental images of things and processes more than direct sensory and emotional experience. For those of us desiring a reconnection with nature, it is not necessary to judge these developments but it may be useful to understand how they influence us through consensus reality. In our first removal from nature, with agriculture, we ceased participating in the natural world in the same way as other species, moving into control of nature. In our second removal from nature, with industrialization and the explosion of rational science, nature became a commodity, a source for resources. In our third removal of nature, as we have entered what I call postmodern times, we have moved out of the real world itself, entering a head-space of image and lives in an electronic realm. Interestingly enough, the "post" prefix has been used to create the words "post-nature" and "post-natural," predicting an era when nature, even human biology, is decreasingly relevant when compared to technology and the realms of artificial intelligence.[78]

My favorite postmodern writer is Jean Baudrillard, originator of the concept of *hyperreality*. Baudrillard described a mental realm in which simulations interact with simulations and consciousness is unable to distinguish reality from a simulation of reality. *The Matrix* film trilogy by Lana and Larry Wachowski draws on the ideas of Baudrillard in creating a science fiction world where artificial intelligence has taken control, using humans for a source of biological energy. To keep us alive and unconscious, we are incubated in womblike structures, stacked in an endless space of black tubes and conduits. Our consciousness lives within a complicated computer-generated world of images, where our simulated bodies interact with other simulated bodies. The Matrix police hunt down and eliminate anyone who might start to realize this world is simulation and not reality. Since we are bred from the beginning as participants in the simulation, we do not know there is an actual reality unless we manage to "wake up."

The filmmakers pay homage to Baudrillard by having a copy of his book *Simulacra and Simulation* as the place where hero Neo stores his contraband items.[79] Neo, in the form of Keanu Reeves, is "the one" who might lead humanity back into the real world. The most important contraband item is the famous red pill. If you swallow the red pill, you are suddenly jolted back into real time and space, where you are hooked up to all those tubes, and await physical rescue by a band of renegade "awakened" humans. If you take the blue pill, you remain in the world of illusion. For me, "waking up" from the Matrix is the same *Waking Up* recommended by Charles Tart and countless spiritual teachers before him. This may be why the film pulls at so many of us—okay, the spiritual underpinning along with all that action and those good-looking people. The metaphor of needing to battle the agents of unreality in order to wake up is real: this is the work of psychospiritual practice.

In *Symbolic Exchange and Death*, Baudrillard claimed Western culture has followed a precession of simulacra, which are representations, insubstantial images of things. Like many others, Baudrillard observed that we live within consumer culture in the privileged countries, with much of the rest of the world wanting to follow along. Baudrillard contends most of the items offered for purchase in consumer culture have no specific utility, possessing value related only to image. Primary meaning is detached from utility, resonating only with constructed image. "Gone are the referentials of production, signification, affect, substance, history, and the whole equation of 'real' contents that gave the sign weight by anchoring it with a kind of burden of utility."[80] Value, in Baudrillard's view, has become entirely relative and generalized: "from now on signs will exchange among themselves exclusively, without interacting with the real (and this becomes the condition for their smooth operation)."[81]

In hyperreality, without realizing what has happened, we are lost in a sea of images and associations pretending to have some value or utility in our lives, but ungrounded in actual needs. I suspect even the experience of "needs" no longer has concrete meaning in the postmodern world. For many of us privileged types, most of our actual material needs are met but we may have little idea what we need emotionally and spiritually. "In truth," Baudrillard wrote, "there is nothing left to ground ourselves on."[82] While our distant ancestors were grounded in the natural world, we are surrounded by consumer items. In the postmodern world described by Baudrillard, more and more of the real things around us exist in our mental reality as signs, fused with complex reverberations from ideologies and slogans we have ingested, enmeshed with our various actual instinctual human urges, twisted together in ways that Baudrillard calls, in some instances, obscene.

As much as I enjoy the postmodern critique, and find it useful in talking about what has happened to nature in our minds, at some point I wake up myself and realize we are not as mindless as all that, most of us perfectly able to discern our needs and sort through the consumerist melee making up our surroundings. Postmodern description of the lack of actual utility in consumer items loses energy for me when I consider how much I love so many of the gadgets that have come into existence in my lifetime, particularly in the last twenty years. In fairness to Baudrillard and other postmodern critics, most of them were writing before some of these gadgets got really good, such as cell phones, computers with Internet, and then cell phones with text messaging, Internet, email, *and* cameras—not to mention technology and infrastructure allowing me to download movies and television shows without commercials, not to mention pay-at-the-pump gasoline and pre-washed salad in those little plastic bags. Once again, I am not so much complaining about the miracles of modern technology— which increase our health as well as ease and enjoyment of life. I am noticing one of the ways to consider what has happened to nature in our awareness.

In the remainder of this chapter, we look into some other aspects of life and reality-generation in postmodern times. We consider other frameworks for understanding the relationship between our habits of cognition as compared to experiencing our sensations and emotions. We will consider what this means for our relationship with nature, not so much to criticize our contemporary culture as to develop ways for noticing what happens in our experience. The hyperreality of postmodern times may actually offer us more opportunity for psychospiritual growth than initially appears. Some of my favorite teachers of spiritual practice have suggested that image (also known as illusion) is always what holds us back from a sense of the sacred. The fall into hyperreality may be the rock bottom before waking up. Somebody give me the red pill. On the other hand, maybe not. I have some good friends who assure me they would take the blue pill and remain in illusion with no questions asked. The trouble with waking up is that it is often painful, which will eventually bring us back to grief.

Monoculture

Like most people in the United States, Canada, and an increasing number of other countries, I have spent my share of time sitting in traffic at stoplights on urban-suburban corners, surrounded by likes of Home Depot, Lowe's, Starbucks, and Wal-Mart, maybe an Applebee's, Olive Garden or similar national chain restaurant, not far away from a few banks with drive-through windows. If you change a detail or two, I could be just about anywhere in North America, probably some parts of Europe or Australia, maybe even a few parts of Asia or Africa. I recently drove from Montana to San Diego, then up to Vancouver, British Columbia, and then across country to New Jersey. It was comforting to find Starbucks at many exits for morning coffee and croissant, not to mention Subway for lunch. Staples or Office Depot were reliably in strip malls when I needed to print from the Internet or a USB stick. The same self-service, self-pay, copiers/print-ers are being installed at Staples across the country, in similar alcoves of the stores. As I traveled across the continent, I would be standing in what felt like the exact same "place" but in different states or different coasts. Sometimes I would have to stop, focus and think to remember where I was.

At this point, where is "here"? The scenery changes, and sometimes the accents, and certainly the weather might be different in some places at some times of year if you are not inside air conditioning or heat. But our sense of where we are may not be the same as it was even a few decades ago. Airports provide another good example. If I am walking through an airport in various parts of the United States or even many other countries, I am seeing identical or similar stores with identical or similar items for purchase. Where am I really? Am I *in* any particular city or am I *in* Starbucks? Perhaps the nuances in the experience of the particular international chain shops and restaurants are just as distinct as the nuances in the different forests, prairies, or deserts in various parts of the world. Hard to tell, but I doubt it.

This is monoculture, the tendency for everything and everywhere to become the same. Political theorist Benjamin Barber calls this new planetary sameness "McWorld."[83] Originally a play on the ubiquity and uniformity of McDonald's fast food, "Mc" was at one point defined in the Oxford English Dictionary as a prefix used "to form nouns with the sense of 'something that is of mass appeal, a standardized or bland variety.'"[84] McDonalds apparently argued successfully for removal of the "Mc" definition, but we get the point. Barber suggests a McWorld trajectory he summarizes as follows:

> a future in shimmering pastels, a busy portrait of onrushing economic, technological, and ecological forces that demand integration and uniformity and that mesmerize peoples everywhere with fast music, fast computers, and fast food—MTV, Macintosh, and McDonald's—pressing nations into one homogenous global theme park, one McWorld tied together by communications, information, entertainment, and commerce.[85]

Part of me thinks, "wow, sounds great, I love theme parks," particularly Disneyland. Yet outside the *Happiest Place on Earth,* homogeneity often involves lack of imagination and a learned inability to feel the distinctness of surroundings. It becomes hard to imagine any reality other than the singularity of consumer culture, with the world around us increasingly structured physically and psychically with ubiquitous corporate sameness. With respect to nature, the trajectory toward McWorld makes it easier for us to assume unconsciously there is one reality out there *and that reality is not nature.* Nature becomes something that is separated from the *actual* reality described by McWorld, as if all nature were kept in a zoo. Even putting nature on a pedestal in the decades-old environmental tradition can involve an implicit assumption that nature is separate from us. McWorld allows, and certainly knows how to sell, an "experience of nature"—but this is very different from nature as just simply what is.

I realize all of us experience locality in our communities and the natural world in particular places. I am glad to have spent much of my life in two places lying on the extreme ends of nature and weather: Louisiana and Montana. Taking a walk on a shell path next to a swampy bayou in August is quite distinct from walking up an icy path from my barn to the house in twenty-below-zero Montana. While the airports in those two disparate places may have the same airport quality, I know how hot and humid it will be from May to September when I exit the airport in my home town of New Orleans and how the bitter cold may hit me on the other side of the airport doors during October through March in Montana.

But even in these places, there is pull into McWorld. The French Quarter in New Orleans provides an example. Decades ago Disneyland created a New Orleans Square to simulate an experience of the French Quarter. Then, over time, parts of the actual French Quarter in New Orleans have started to look less like the messy place I knew in my youth and more like New Orleans Square in Disneyland. As many locals lament, parts of the French Quarter have conformed to tourist expectations and marketing in the vacation-consumer-meta-narrative. We miss some of the strange peculiarities of the seventeenth through nineteenth century melting pot culture. This leads to wondering about the experience of tourism more generally: sometimes it feels as though the actual experience is "tourism" and not visiting any particular place. Ode to the French Quarter—may you never lose that smell of beer spilled on sidewalk in steamy heat, air conditioning flowing out of the open bar doors. Otherwise, how would I know I was home?

Monoculture is not just about urban and suburban sameness, but suggests a pulling toward uniformity of experience. My favorite example involves "the holidays." Honoring diversity, many of us (Fox News notwithstanding) strive for diversity within the winter holiday season. We envision not only Christmas, but also Hanukkah, Kwanza, and any other holiday we can find to include within our inclusiveness. This feels great (to some of us at least) and vastly surpasses exclusionary alternatives. And yet, in America at least, I wonder whether our desire for honoring diversity masks the underlying sameness of what is *really* happening for most of us. What is really happening—it seems to me—derives to large extent from McWorld and monoculture.

Consistent with life in a consumer culture, what happens around the winter holidays is an economic experience—a singular shopping extravaganza. I mean no offense to the many religious or spiritual people who experience meaning within their traditions during December, but the main event, the postmodern reason for the season, is consumption. The holidays are the apotheosis of consumer culture. We could call it McChristmas or, as my son Max would prefer, Santa Claus Day. Adding Hanukkah and Kwanza to the meta-narrative seems mostly to make some of us feel better and draw more people into the shopping spree. Hanukkah is by no means a major Jewish holiday and yet most of the United States pretends we have Christmas and Hanukkah as equivalents, now throwing in some other holidays: monoculture pulling everything together.

In the United States, Thanksgiving has essentially been pulled into the holiday of consumer consumption. Stuffing ourselves and enjoying company aside, Thanksgiving is now "the day before Black Friday," so named for the day retail stores traditionally "go into the black" of profit. For me, "Black Friday" appropriately conjures up something else in the holiday of consumer culture, a macabre image, vaguely witchy, a Freudian slip of the cultural tongue involving unconscious knowledge of the endless pit of consumption. The media dare us into consumerist frenzy with images of people lined up for hours to rush into stores to grab bargains before somebody else gets them. Now *that* is a religious ritual. I suspect the phrase Black Friday might even conjure up vague ancestral memories of mayhem in other religious rituals in our more distant past. In the last few years, "Black Friday" has started to happen in the United Kingdom, odd since there is no Thanksgiving, but understandable since the British isles are increasingly part of McWorld.

To illustrate loss of nature into monoculture, imagine living in a culture creating itself more in synchrony with the natural world in holidays and festivals. When we were part of nature, we gathered our food and made our homes based on what was available around us. Celebrations took place within nature. Way back in our earlier days as Homo sapiens, we likely met up with other clans or tribes at places for ritual celebrations. We borrowed from nature to create our rituals. The rituals honored nature and the goddesses and gods who once arose from nature. It is interesting to me that in ancient times people understood that different places had different gods. This was not like a present-day knowledge that other people *believe* in different religious figures but an acceptance that in different places there *were* different actual gods with reality of their own. Sometimes people moved to a place and worshipped a different god if they came to experience this god as more beneficial.

These other gods in different places lived in the places where people worshipped them. When you went to a different place, you might gain a sense of the gods and rituals of that different place. If so, you were not in McWorld, not in just another Starbucks in another airport. You were in a geographical place with a character and a specificity that was tied to an experience of the sacred. At least in my imagination, this had everything to do with nature in the particular place. But we live in different times. In many ways, McWorld feels inevitable to me. As the Borg Queen said in *Star Trek*, resistance is futile. Yet we can re-invent ourselves, we can remember, within the global culture emerging. We can bring nature back to life in place to place, season to season, celebration to celebration, moment to moment.

Swiss psychiatrist Carl Gustav Jung wrote: "Matter in the wrong place is dirt. People got dirty through too much civilization. Whenever we touch nature, we get clean."[86] Part of me admires the cleanliness of McWorld. No trash on the ground in Disneyland. Another part of me recognizes what Jung means by dirty—not healthy, not robust, not living on the planet. Perhaps McWorld reflects back into itself just a bit too much, endless images in a mirror maze. McWorld may not provide the guidance back into ourselves offered by nature. It may not be as clean as it looks. There is something seductive and yet ironic about the shimmering image of McWorld. As in *The Matrix,* it is comfortable, safe, what we know. But at some level, we know it is not real.

Television as Reality Generator

Not long a friend of mine in Minneapolis left a relationship and moved into his own apartment. He bought new furniture and had it delivered. He did not buy, and does not own, a television. He is just not that into it. When the two delivery men walked into the apartment with the first piece of furniture, a couch, they turned to my friend and did *not* ask, "Where do you want us to put the sofa?"

Rather, one of them asked, "Where's the TV gonna go?"

Implicit in this question was of course the very reasonable assumption that there would be a television and the equally reasonable assumption that from the placement of the television would flow the structuring of the rest of the room, including most importantly for present purposes where to put the couch. And so it goes with the structuring of just about everything, not just my friend's new living room. It all flows from the television. It seems the world of the delivery men was turned upside down by my friend's confession: "I don't have a television." Leading to their disbelieving response: "Man, what you talking about, no TV? What the hell you do all night?"

Even before encountering the postmodern theorists, I came to my own shorthand description of the reality many of us have started to inhabit. My rant was that we are now living in our television sets. I did not just mean we were watching too much television, but that television had become our unconscious source of what we experience as real—as now corroborated by those jurors believing video testimony over a person before them. I joked for years that television was the originator of what was *really* happening. Nothing happening outside the television had much juice by comparison. Those people who are actually *on* television: now they are really real. The growth of "reality television" in the last few decades adds an interesting twist. "Real" people entering a television world and acting unreal, catapulted into hyperreality through their willingness to make their lives into image.

With these ideas wandering around in my head, I came across *Four Arguments for the Elimination of Television*[87] by Jerry Mander, a former advertising executive. Mander explores our transformation into a culture of television after World War II, when the small screen came into almost all homes in the United States, then spread around the world. No one, least of all me, would realistically imagine the elimination of television from the world, though some of us may unplug from the tube in our individual lives, at least for a time. Mander's four arguments are useful for considering the place of television in our removal from the world, including nature. Number one: "In one generation, out of hundreds of thousands in human evolution, America has become the first culture to have substituted secondary, mediated versions of experience for direct experience of the world."[88] Mander describes "a strange change in the way people received information, and even more in the way they were experiencing and understanding the world."[89] Like other postmodern theorists, Mander worries this leaves us "adrift in mental space."

Argument number two: the "reality" given to us by television is not without agenda. Mander observes it is "no accident that television has been dominated by a handful of corporate powers. Neither is it accidental that television has been used to re-create human beings into a new form that matches the artificial, commercial environment."[90] He considers it "inevitable" that the joining of technical and economic factors makes television a vehicle for creating consumers—not just consumers of particular products advertised in particular commercials, but "lifers" in a culture of consumption. The implicit primary product we unconsciously "buy" is the culture of consumption itself. Several years ago, I took my older children to a conversation with *X-Files* creator Chris Carter at Montana State University in Bozeman. Pressed by some member of the audience about why he had not fought the Fox Network for more creative control, Carter asked us to remember television shows exist to hold our interest between commercials.

Mander's third argument for the elimination of television highlights the impact of the light-flickering medium on our neuropsychology. He believes this visual stimulus over time may create illness and "certainly produces confusion and submission to external imagery."[91] I imagine most of us humans were always confused and submissive, but it is hard not to notice the fugue emerging from too much of those flickering electronic images. According to a 2012 Neilson Report, "the average American over the age of 2 spends more than 34 hours a week watching live television . . . plus another three to six hours watching taped programs."[92] An eMarketer study the following year suggested television watching per day for the average American had been increasing through 2012, but went down by a few minutes in 2013. As it turns out, electronic screen time was not decreasing, but rather shifting to Internet viewing, including watching program on computers through downloading and streaming services.[93]

While these new proclivities mean more choice and fewer commercials, our flickering image time is not waning. As most parents calling children for dinner have known for decades, humans enter a trance based on reception of information without our interaction. This produces relaxation for many of us, but a relaxation without thinking. In that fugue state, we are more inclined to accept what is presented without thinking, so to speak, outside the box. As argued by social critic Noam Chomsky, the *range* of possible views presented on television is relatively narrow, and always within the scope of the dominant political-economic powers.[94] In a submissive state, the possibilities for living outside the accepted range of "reality" may become difficult to imagine, much less to enact.

Mander's final argument focuses on the inherent biases in the medium, such as toward simplified linear messages. Complexity and nuance are lost through reduction of stories to the infamous sound byte, resulting in "information loss." We lose not just information about the incidents reported, but information about everything else happening in the world. As Mander notes, national television operates as a kind of telescope in the sky, flying around, constantly looking. When it zooms down to a single spot, this becomes what is happening at the moment. At that moment, Mander writes, the "telescope did not select views of the ocean as the tide comes in, or people sitting on front porches, or young people knocking on doors to tell a neighbor about a zoning hearing."[95] All those events are "lost information."

I was recently in Kalispell, Montana, watching my morning news program while I dressed for work in the area. The national news kept breaking through with the latest developments in a search for a child missing on a river in Sacramento, California. We saw the helicopters arrive, we had updates on the search, we knew who was holding out hope and who seemed to think the child would not be found alive. While my heart went out to the people involved, I wondered why I was watching this story in Kalispell, Montana. Well, I knew why I was watching this breaking event: someone had selected this "edge-of-your-seat" story with ratings in mind— and ratings lead to money. In terms of location in place, most television unmoors us from our actual geography. If the "main event" is taking place somewhere else, then the reality of life is shifted someplace else, if not *into the television set,* then at least away from *here* into *there* as represented by national media.

When nature is reported on the news, this is often because nature is a problem: too much snow, a flood, a fire, something lamentably out of our control, an agent we need to be aware of and sometimes work against. Weather reporting is a staple on local news programs. Often the weatherman or woman provides some heart on the program, sometimes comic relief. For years, there have been cable weather channels. Nothing against the weather on television, but I think this contributes to an objectification of nature. The weather is going to be bad or it is going to be good: it is not just what is around us.

In the last few decades, numerous television shows have arisen depicting the dangers in nature, often dangerous animals or treacherous areas of the world. This seems to have particular appeal for certain types of people. I have a friend in Montana who is addicted to shows about sharks. "What is it about sharks?" I asked him.

"I don't know," he responded. "I'm just so scared of them. They just keep moving and they can tear you apart." Good television. Inflammatory depictions of nature on television may keep the natural world in our consciousness as a chaotic opponent, something out there that can get us, something we can battle against. This continues the struggle we began with nature long ago. With respect to my friend, I do not object to him having a place to project out his fears. Better than if that angst was going onto his wife or kids.

Billions of people have seen and learned about the wonders of nature through television. And yet, how real is nature on TV? Televised nature remains an electronic image we take in visually, sometimes with sound, but without the more subtle arousal of all our other senses. No temperature, no humidity, no smells, no feel of wind or water on the skins. Thirty below zero in the Antarctic, Alaska, or Montana may *look* cold but vision and even sound do not convey the searing bite. A huge wave swelling up behind a surfer may look overpowering, but watching the wave and surfer is nothing like feeling the power yourself, the temperature of the water, the salt, the wave throwing you around in its turmoil.

With televised nature, at best, there is a hint of presence within the natural world. No discomfort, no danger, only a surrogate thrill, a second-hand sense of majesty. The television camera directs us to images, but we do not wander on a trail in dense foliage making noise in case there is wildlife ahead. Television needs to hold our limited postmodern attention, so cannot provide a sense of endless time, or waiting, or seeking for ourselves in the natural world. I suspect many people react to televised nature as just something else on one of the channels, boring to some, captivating for others. If nature exists for postmodern people as something else shown on television, I worry the natural world becomes an implicit commodity to keep us watching between commercials, different only in form than *X-Files*, perhaps just as scary if we are dealing with sharks.

Increasingly over the last few decades, I have become somewhat obsessed with what feels like doublespeak involving nature in some commercials. Apparently originating in George Orwell's dystopian classic *1984*, the term doublespeak suggests using communication to divert attention from actual reality. A classic example is "support the war for peace" (which strangely enough was the headline on a billboard in Helena, Montana, in the early days of the Iraq War, with no irony intended). It is one thing to draw on positive feelings for nature in creating pleasant associations for such things as an SUV you can drive through the mountains. It is another to use nature in commercials to create positive associations for companies that, while providing materials we use, are part of the machine destroying the natural world.

For instance, a company has questionable environmental ethics so we are given a commercial with images of nature and a voiceover telling us the company is building up the environment. Or we have computerized video images pretending a car is constructed from wood around a stream. Is it moral to cause me to associate construction of this car, and all cars, positively with nature, even while I know vehicle emissions and our need for oil and gasoline are destroying the planet? Logos for oil companies superimposed over scenes of nature and I am left with a good vibe about that company as sincerely dedicated to protecting the natural world? Even if I credit people in those companies as having actual good will toward the environment, it feels like the image of nature is being used to cover up what is actually happening in the world: doublespeak.

Having grown up on television and commercials, I should be used to these things. My concern for nature in postmodernity runs more deeply. Once we are trained toward unconscious holding of nature as image, it becomes possible to project all kinds of associations into nature. As discussed more fully in Chapter 10, many of us project into nature in ways that run deeply into our personal and collective psychologies, including playing out the cultural issues of our times. I wonder whether this is easier in a postmodern world where nature has become an image on television. For instance, in my travels in various personal growth communities, I have met a great many people who seem to idolize nature as a purely benevolent sustainer. They may talk about the mystery of nature and the need for the wild but this has sometimes felt to me like an idea not moored in the fullness of reality in nature.

I will imagine an example not based in any one life but drawn from people I have known. I imagine a friend from my youth whose family was part of the Catholic tradition in New Orleans. Sadly, his mother passed away relatively young, before my friend was fully grown, and his father was somewhat tyrannical. It is no stretch to wonder if my friend blames his father for his mother's early death and blames the Catholic God for not saving her. My friend became enamored of the Goddess in nature, reading each of the numerous books published in the last several years about feminine nature deities. He finds comfort and meaning, a beautiful thing, and yet his ruminations about how we fail to see the good in Nature seem fueled with anger, emotional pain, and enormous lingering grief, now enmeshed and perhaps repressed through use of the image of a beneficent nature Goddess.

My friend is not imagining the type of goddess who contains the fullness of nature, the dark as well as the light. He is not imagining a Nature Goddess who ruthlessly and capriciously claimed his mother. He is not communing with Kali, for instance, the Hindu goddess of destruction, a feminine force of violent regeneration, which is part of nature. I cannot help but imagine that if he actually knew the natural world, he would not be describing a Nature-Mother who seems just an earthier, more sensual, version of the all-good Virgin Mary. I do not discount the right of my friend to invent the Goddess he needs, and yet my sense is that his wounds remain unprocessed, sapping him of life.

Let me contrast this imagined friend to my other friend who watches all those shark shows on the tube—seeing a nature that is relentlessly evil. Seeing whatever we want in nature, constricting her, seems all the easier when she is just something else we can watch between commercials. Nature as image may rob us of the fullness of nature as inclusive of all that we are—and all that nature is. If we re-imagine or re-invent nature deities, please God let them contain all the realities of the natural world. Otherwise, we might be using nature-as-image as a commodity in the same way other images are used as commodity in postmodern times.

Loss of the Body—Abstraction

Having considered the three levels of removal from nature, we turn to consideration of a longer evolutionary trend separating humans from our natural surroundings. This involves development of the brain that makes us Homo sapiens, conquerors of the known world. Through our millions of years of brain evolution, we have become creatures capable of abstraction, experts at leaving our senses and emotions for the mental realm of thinking, planning, and rumination. As we evolved from monkeys to apes to humans, we developed the means to conceptualize, to hold representations in our minds, to live in those representations more than in the actual world around us. Even if our ancestors continued to live immersed in nature for thousands of years, the evolution of our capacity for abstraction began our journey out of nature. This was simultaneously a journey out of our own bodies.

As we begin talking about brain structures, I will note that I am not suggesting our consciousness is only a product of the material structures of our brains, though those material structures influence our experience. As noted previously, I have come to believe some essence of consciousness exists separately from what is "produced" as experience by our nervous systems. The metaphor of a television set has often been used to describe how the brain influences consciousness.[96] The signal producing the television image—whether from broadcast television, cable, or Internet—comes from someplace other than the television set, yet the material structure of the television influences and produces what is "seen" as the image. I believe the brain, and entire body, operate similarly. Although some essential aspect of consciousness exists separate from the material world, we usually work within the image produced by brain.

Examining the human brain is like looking at an archeological site under excavation, noticing the functional layers built on top of earlier structures through evolution. Our brain stem structures correspond to the brains of our distant reptilian cousins. Mid-brain structures, including those mediating emotional responses, resemble those in our closer mammalian relatives. The cortex (outer brain) is well developed in most mammal species; it facilitates more complicated behaviors and adaptation to environment. Although our human brains are more complex than those of our evolutionary predecessors, the brain structures developed by our more distant evolutionary ancestors (reptiles, then mammals, then primates) remain within us, perhaps corresponding to some of our continued "primitive" behaviors.

One of the primary ways human brains differ from the brains of other mammals involves the complexity and size of our prefrontal cortex. This part of the brain is important in all primates, but expanded in humans. If we compare the areas of our brain cortex to those of other primates, we notice that humans have relatively small cortical segments responsible for primary processing of vision, motor actions, and smell, but relatively large sections responsible for auditory processing, necessary for language. It was different for one of our closest hominid cousins, the Neanderthals. After their ancestors walked out of Africa, this species evolved for thousands of years in Europe, until our closer-genetic ancestors, after another walk out of Africa, met up with them again, likely contributing to their extinction.

Neanderthals had larger cortical space devoted to visual processing. They likely saw well for hunting through many ice ages, perhaps with more depth and nuance than we see, but ultimately lost in competition for big game. Vision was no match for the talents of language and planning of our *Homo sapiens* ancestors, called Cro-Magnons in Europe. Even though we are mostly descendants of this later evolved species, most of us have some Neanderthal genes from relatively late interbreeding between Homo sapiens and Neanderthals, likely occurring in the Near East. My personal Neanderthal gene percentage, according to genetic testing, is 2.7%. I proudly wear a t-shirt so proclaiming.

As you would imagine, the prefrontal cortex has been associated with activities leading to our domination of the planet. This part of the brain facilitates thoughts and actions as related to internal goals, including conformance of thoughts and actions to socially acceptable modes of behavior and belief. Some neuroscientists suggest human cognitive control results from signals emerging from our prefrontal cortex which guide the flow of activity along neural pathways in other parts of the brain.[97] The prefrontal cortex has been described as important in "top-down control of behavior."[98] This area of our brain is part of what makes us Homo sapiens and not the same as our earlier ancestors or cousins. Among other things, this part of our brain allows me to formulate these thoughts and put them on the page. The prefrontal cortex might be understood as the enforcer of the status quo, the maintainer of the consensus trance we learn to inhabit. Without it, there would be no status quo in the sense of civilization.

Another main difference between the human brain and those of our nearest relatives is the adaptation of our brain to language. The last few decades have seen the popularization of discoveries regarding the differentiation in function between the right and left brain hemispheres in humans. In most right-handed people, the left brain hemisphere is dominant;

it is responsible for controlling the right side of our bodies and, more generally, for linguistic, linear, and analytic processing. Left-handed people have the reverse situation, though some evidence suggests their hemispheric differentiation is less marked than in right-handed people. For simplicity, and with apologies to the lefties, I will follow the lead of many others in discussing "right" and "left" brain functioning, though literally these references apply only to right-handed people. In this manner of reference, the "left" brain is important in marking time, abstraction, conceptualization, causality, and creating dichotomies. The "right brain" is considered the hemisphere of creativity, artistic activities, and easing out of "unoriginal" or black-white thinking.

If the left brain tends to divide, the right brain understands more holistically. Leonard Schlain, author of *The Alphabet versus the Goddess*,[99] describes the right brain as nonverbal. He believes this hemisphere has more in common with the experience of non-human animals. The right brain understands cries, gestures, and authentic states existing behind linguistic or social presentation. Schlain characterizes the right brain as expressing more *being* than the left, including feeling states not readily describable in words. He argues the right brain perceives "concretely," closer to a "direct appreciation of reality."[100] Some brain imaging suggests we draw on the right brain when dreaming more than the left. Consistent with this notion, the right brain works with metaphors and understands holistic connections.

Schlain's primary thesis in *The Alphabet versus the Goddess* is that literacy in human history brought patriarchy: the dominance of men and certain forms of masculine functioning over more holistic and inclusive feminine ways of being. I am inclined to believe male dominance has roots deeper in our genetic heritage, but that is not important for considering Schlain's argument. Language certainly contributed to the general dominance of "left brain" functioning. As early human social groups became civilizations, those civilizations were structured through language and those parts of our brain allowing us to think linguistically, to separate and divide, to analyze, and to plan. In contemporary times, some people may consider a way of being characterized predominantly by these activities as masculine in a pejorative sense, in contrast to a more accepting, feeling-oriented, and holistic "feminine" attitude. In this way of thinking, a pre-left-brain way of being may be considered more in keeping with harmonious living within nature, in contrast to dominance and control of nature.

Linguistic ability obviously gave our ancestors advantage in the competitive natural world. Those of our ancestors with brain structures facilitating language were more successful, had more descendants who survived, and contributed these linguistically-useful brain capabilities to the gene pool of the species. Once hominid culture began to work in tandem with biological evolution, the linguistic structuring of social groups, along with our increasing success in planning and other mental activities, contributed to an ongoing evolution of our biological species, and then to successful social evolution within our species. Our success, and our building of civilization, derived from our great capacity for experiencing ourselves (thinking) linguistically and from our talent for holding concepts of both the past and the future through conceptualization or linguistic maneuvering.

Our biological and social evolution over thousands of years gave us a life of the mind with a tendency to preoccupy with language and representations, removing us from a sense of simple presence within a natural environment. We spend a great deal of time within the internalized representations of the world we are able to hold in awareness, in other words, within the image we construct of reality. When compared to other animals, even primates, human brains devote more space to *secondary* processing of sensory information than to primary processing of direct experience of the outside word. Secondary processing means cogitation regarding what actions to take, or how to conceptualize, in response to particular sensory input. This involves comparing sensory input to what has been learned and internalized as a representation of reality, shaped by the consensus consciousness of the particular culture. This brings us back to the prefrontal cortex and its talent for "cognitive control."

Lest I sound antagonistic toward the prefrontal cortex, let me add this part of our brain likely permits us to rise above actions flowing solely from instincts and emotions. Those instincts and emotions still work their way into our thoughts, behaviors, and conceptions of the world, but do so unconsciously. Self-remembering and self-observation lauded by spiritual and psychological teachers is possible through our higher brain functions, allowing us to develop means to reflect on our images, then allowing a more free flow into awareness of those emotions and instincts, but held by a meta-observer part of consciousness we have developed. It is a gift to be able to create a mental abstraction of our abstractions, learning how to ease out of them. But many of us do not open up this emotional flow, staying in a world of abstraction, concept, and control, not particularly conscious that this mental realm is not as rational as we imagine.

Much of the remainder of this book involves the ways in which nature seems to facilitate a return to ways of being other than the head space of "top down" cognitive control. For now, I will share the story of the several summers I walked through the mountains to work. We lived down a dirt road ten minutes from downtown Helena, where I had my office. If you walked over a steep hill just in front of our house, rocky old roads from the days of mining and ranching took you to public trails maintained for hiking and biking. Once I left my house, I would see no human structures other than a few old wood fences until I reached the subdivision just a few minutes from my office. These walks were intended as my time before I started working, but given my personality and habits of mind, the cogitation started as soon as I left the house.

As I walked, I would notice when I started shutting out the sensory and emotional world by planning what I would do next in the legal work. I would joke with myself—"oh there I am in the prefrontal cortex"—and remember to linger a bit in the breeze and the smell of the pines. Interestingly enough, solutions to whatever problems were running through my mind often then arose seemingly out of nowhere. Perhaps I had eased out of the left brain and allowed the right brain to produce its wisdom. As I noticed this shift, I sometimes said to myself, "thank you right brain." More commonly, I would feel gratitude for the mountains, trees, grass, wildflowers, and dirt around me, as well as thanks to all those volunteers and professionals maintaining the trails.

For me personally, it helps to move my attention to other areas of my body in order to ease myself out of the cogitation I sometimes call mental looping. I allow the emergence of a form of being that moves (temporarily) away from language. Perhaps aided by many years of activities such as meditation, working with dreams, and Holotropic Breathwork, I can ease myself out of "language" space into a mode of consciousness that seems to exist somewhere less inside my linguistic head. This seems easier as I become older. While it is frustrating to find that particular words and names sometimes seem difficult to access, this shift seems to create more space between my consciousness and the constant running of language. Now it seems more a choice to engage in a language-based way of being. It seems more possible to release language and conceptualization into what feels more like simple being. There is no better place for this release than in nature. Indeed, the natural world seems to pull us back into this place.

Phenomenology

During the last century, several European philosophers known as phe-nomenologists articulated distinctions that I find useful in understanding our tendency to leave being for abstraction. The phenomenologists have always struck me as strange because they wrote about experience not dom-inated by abstraction and conceptualization, yet they wrote some of the most difficult prose you can read, full of abstraction and conceptualization.

Oh well, they were philosophers. Here we go with some concepts that I believe will help frame an understanding of opening to nature.

Edmund Husserl, a German philosopher, invented the term *Lebenswelt* (*life-world* in English) to describe experience based primarily on input from the sensations and emotions of the body, prior to shaping by thoughts and conceptualizations.[101] Husserl was reacting against the objectification of experience prevalent in Western thought. He argued that conceptualization separates understanding from "lived experience." The concept of lived experience has become commonly used in the qualitative research branch of psychology, with many researchers seeking to describe aspects of "lived experience." Myself, I have often wondered what would be the opposite of "lived" experience, but I will not go there. The popularity of the phrase derives from the frustration many people interested in psychology have felt when they realized that much of psychology felt more about abstracting and categorizing life than understanding it. Thus there arose a new tradition of investigating "lived experience," grounded philosophically in phenomenology.

Martin Heidegger, another German philosopher, described our underlying beingness, which he called *Dasein* (there-being in English).[102] Heidegger described *Dasein* as a "thrown projection" because it is situated within understandings inherited from culture, but projects itself into the future. Heidegger believed individuals could never entirely free themselves from their situation in historical-cultural context (which he called their facticity). Nevertheless, he encouraged recovery of the beingness that exists for each of us beneath the dominant conceptual categories of our culture. Dasein can be understood as a "clearing" in being. I think of it as "being there" with grounding in the past and orientation toward what happens next, but presence in oneself.

Maurice Merleau-Ponty, a French phenomenologist, described the body as the source of unmediated experience, called preconceptual experience. This is experience before it has been slotted into our habitual filtering and automatic interpretation of what comes our way. Even while embedded in the *Lebenswelt* and thrown forward as D*asein*, the body for Merleau-Ponty exists "on the side of the subject: it is our *point of view on the world*, the place where the spirit takes on a certain physical and historical situation."[103] For Merleau-Ponty, the individual body remains a touchstone for our unique beingness, which is individual and subjective.

David Levin, a more recent American philosopher, similarly described our bodies as offering a realm of senses and emotions lost to most people by forces of socialization.[104] In Levin's view, Western culture indoctrinates the sense of separation from our bodies and our environment. Quoting Lame Deer, a sage of the Lakota Tribe, Levin wrote that people "seem to have forgotten 'the secret language of their bodies, their senses, their dreams.'"[105] Levin considered this loss related to the domination of binary, mutually exclusive oppositions, polarizations of experience which he believed deeply pathologize the nature and character of our experience. Examples include: "inner/outer, public/private, personal/non-personal, self/world, subject/object, me/you, mind/body, matter/spirit, animal/human beings, nature/culture, human world/thing world, living/dead."[106]

Levin considered this related "to the domination of a paradigm of knowledge, truth and reality which has favored the advancement of science and technology at the expense of lived experience."[107] He was essentially describing, in philosophical language, what has been written in other contexts by other writers I have gathered into this and the prior chapter. Bringing nature into the picture, Levin recognized the possibility of recovering experience of the natural world through experience of the body. He described an "elemental body-self" with the capacity for integration into "the elements" through a "bodily belonging to the earth."[108] Buried within us, "we have some understanding—a certain bodily felt sense—of our elemental nature, our elemental composition."[109] I hear Levin talking about the same thing as Paul Shepard when the latter wrote about our ancestral memory, remembering how to dance as the generic human.

In *The Spell of the Sensuous*, eco-philosopher David Abram draws on the phenomenologists in articulating the possibility of a tandem recovery of our senses along with recovery of an intimate experience of nature.[110] Abram particularly resonates with the work of Merleau-Ponty. Drawing on Merleau-Ponty's interest in perception, Abram described perception as participation in the world because "it always involves, at its most intimate level, the experience of active interplay, or coupling, between the perceiving body and that which it perceives."[111] Nowhere is this intimacy more intense than in nature. As Abram explains, if we consciously experience the active interplay of our sensations with the natural world, "we gradually discover our sensory perceptions to be simply our part of a vast, interpenetrating webwork of perceptions and sensations borne by countless other bodies."[112] In other words, if we follow our sensations into experience of our bodies in the present moment, in relationship to nature, we recover not only ourselves, but also nature. Abram wrote: "the recuperation of the incarnate, sensorial dimension of experience brings with it a recuperation of the living landscape in which we are corporeally embedded."[113]

Abram wrote about *Becoming Animal* in a more recent book.[114] To become animal is "to discern and perhaps to practice a curious kind of thought, a way of careful reflection that no longer tears us out of the world of direct experience in order to represent it, but that binds us ever more deeply into the thick of that world."[115] Abram is interested in a form "of thinking enacted as much by the body as by the mind, informed by the humid air and the soil and the quality of our breathing, by the intensity of our contact with the other bodies that surround."[116] To do this requires, "Owning up to being an animal, a creature of the earth. Turning our animal senses to the sensible terrain blending our skin with the rain-rippled surface of rivers, mingling our ears with the thunder and the thrumming of frogs, and our eyes with the molten sky." [117] In this chapter, I am content to let David Abram have the last word. If we think with the body and not the mind, as he puts it, we will find ourselves, "Becoming earth. Becoming animal. Becoming, in this manner, fully human."[118]

CHAPTER 4

Longing for Wholeness

Grace worked for over twenty years as a computer scientist and director of research and development in technological fields, first on the East Coast, then in Silicon Valley, the heart of the new California Gold Rush. In the mid-90s, she became ill, but her physicians had difficulty discovering the source of her symptoms. She quit her fast-paced lifestyle and began to study transpersonal psychology. *During July of 1997, my partner and I were invited to house-sit for friends. Their small cottage was one block from the Pacific Ocean. Though I had lived several years in California, I had never been to the northern coast. Exiting Highway 280 by the Hecheche Reservoir, we began the ascent up the green hills of Highway 92.*

I was in awe of the simple beauty a mere hour from my suburban home. It was a sunny afternoon, with light playing through the branches of the eucalyptus and cedar trees growing along the mountainside. I felt I could breathe for the first time in memory. As my lungs expanded, my body felt less cumbersome, as if I were filled with light and air rather than some dense, impermeable material. I felt my throat tighten with inexpressible emotion and a sweet longing for something un-nameable. I chose to call it "wanting to move to the coastside."

During our stay on the coast, the weather was exquisite. At night, we were rocked into peaceful sleep by the rhythmic sounds of the ocean and a nearby fog horn. Mornings were crystal clear. Before John left for work, we would walk along the beach. There were few people, only the overwhelming majesty of the ocean. We saw lone fishing boats on the bay, and gulls and pipers about their daily work. When John drove away, for the first time in my life, I was alone in a place where I wanted to be, with the wherewithal to appreciate the experience. In a cottage filled with the love of our friends, I felt at home, surrounded by cypress trees, open park land, and, of course, the ocean. I felt a stunning sense of peace. Years of striving seemed to leave my body as the tension in my muscles and heart lessened, eased open by the air that became my breath, drawn in from the sea.

One morning, as I walked along the shore, the only other person on the beach caught my attention and pointed toward the ocean. Looking out, I saw a whale, moving gracefully through the waves. I had previously paid money to ride in a boat, crowded with people, to look for whales, and not spied a one. At the end of this day, I prepared a simple meal and left a note for John, asking him to turn on the pot and bring his lounge chair to the beach for the sunset. This simple pleasure touched me at a deep level: a ready meal for my loved one, a coming together at the end of the day, a sunset within a few steps of a modest home. I felt full and satisfied, much more satisfied than through prior costly and glamorous experiences in my life.

Several weeks later, back in the hectic pace of Silicon Valley, I sat in the office of my spiritual director. I looked out the window at the sun on the leaves of the trees. Through the branches I could see the incessant Santa Clara Valley traffic whizzing by. I cried as I told my spiritual director of my deep longing for contact with God. I said I could only find God by the ocean.

As I described my deep grief, he reminded me that God is everywhere, not just by the ocean. While I understood him intellectually, my body did not believe him for a moment. I left his office in one of my states of self-pity, mixed up with anger. God was one way to describe what I was seeking, but it was both simpler and more complicated than looking for God. I was seeking myself, but a different kind of self, one that opened into nature, one that merged with the wind, stars and waves.

Over the Christmas holidays a year later, John and I stayed once again at the cottage by the sea. We were alone, with no family. The weather was very clear and cold, with almost an East-Coast-crispness in the air. One night we walked along the path by the ocean, holding hands through our gloves, our ears muffed from the wind. My heart was full, expanding in my chest with the millions of stars, the moon, and the goodness of God.

At the same time, I was experiencing a bittersweet longing. As my heart grew with the greatness of Nature, the size of my longing increased. I felt a great sense of hopelessness that I would never have this connection with nature as a permanent part of my life. For as long as I could remember, I had desired to live by the ocean, but I always lacked the necessary fortuity and finances. As we strolled along the path on this dark night, I looked up into the Milky Way, which I had rarely seen in the midst of city lights. It seemed so far away.

Walking back to the cottage, I counted the houses along this small patch of beach: there were fifteen. Imagining their cost, I felt myself grow tighter and smaller. The beauty of the night and the companionship of my loved one were entwined with tendrils of longing and hopelessness.

I began to feel that my life had little meaning. Unsure of my health, I wondered if I would leave this world without ever feeling fully alive. The husband of a friend, a man who had symptoms similar to mine, passed away with the doctors never finding the cause of his body's failing. Not having raised a traditional family, I wondered if I would leave any mark on the world. I wondered if I would be remembered. My longing for nature was as much about desire to be known by nature as to know nature myself.

I told my spiritual director that I felt a concurrent desire to be held and to hold, to feel connected with a part of life, to move with the rhythm of life. I feel this as an ache, sometimes an expansion that moves with my breath. I feel it in my arms as they yearn to reach out. I feel it in my hands as they wish to grasp, to stroke, to touch, to entwine. I feel it on my skin, as I want to feel the drops of meaning, connection, and emotion like cool drops of rain on a hot summer night, changing my temperature, penetrating into my soul. But most of all, I feel this in my chest, as my heart desires to beat with the rhythms of all that surrounds me. As I fall into this desire, I feel my heart opening, like the time-elapsed photograph of a blossoming flower, yielding petal by petal, layer by layer.

One afternoon in May of 1999, I ran into Grace at school. ITP was then on San Antonio Road, the border between Palo Alto and Mountain View, a main street heading toward the open wetlands of San Francisco Bay. Years later, Google would claim a large piece of that territory, Facebook a smaller share. Back then, I often ran the path along the muddy shore with my friend Rich, another lawyer escaping for a time into transpersonal psychology. When I saw Grace after a mid-afternoon class, I told her my family was moving to Montana. She said, "Come sit with me in my gas guzzler." Grace drove an old SUV, ready for the wilds or the pavement of Silicon Valley. I was generally irritated by the scores of expensive sports utility vehicles prowling the urban suburbs, facing nothing more challenging than puddles in the rainy season. But it was different with Grace. I thought I understood her motivation, her need to be prepared for rough terrain. It was a kind of hope.

On this late afternoon in May, the glorious California sunshine was all around us. We sat in the parked car, with the incessant Santa Clara Valley traffic moving by us, not yet clogged, but getting there. "Montana!" she exclaimed, and we sat in silence. I had already been explaining myself to all kinds of people for weeks. Most could not understand why we would leave a good life. Jay going to school in psychology was crazy enough; moving to Montana was even worse. I relished the likelihood Grace would understand without all the words. She and I were in different programs at the school, but our paths had crossed several times. We recognized ourselves as kindred spirits. Both entering midlife, not unusual for this particular educational path, we had burned through ourselves in the mainstream high-pressured working world in ways different than many of our student peers. Like Grace, I had left a well-paid job because there was something inside me I needed to save, something that needed to grow.

In the mid-1990s, ITP was still a strange little school in a hippy-dippy branch of psychology. It seemed the right path, but I was following the flow rather than any concrete plan. Many people from my ordinary world considered me self-indulgent, irresponsible, or worse. They wanted to send sympathy cards to my wife. Grace and I had only spoken a handful of times, but she knew the way the soul shriveled if you found yourself out of synch with the world around you. She knew the risks you take, and the pain you cause other people, when the need for change becomes unbearably immediate. I had been in school for four years, with only dissertation-writing remaining. That had not been enough; now I needed to move to Montana. There were many explanations for the move, including my wife's readiness for a new adventure and our joint hope for better circumstances for our children. But my motivation was also deeply personal, that need to save myself, to find a new way of being.

The summer before, on our vacation to Montana, the idea to move first appeared when I was on horseback, trotting down a dirt road just west of Glacier Park, near Kalispell. In what Montana folks would find an extraordinarily California-like move, my wife had responded to an Internet advertisement for a wagon-ride camping experience, three days, two nights, fully catered. A retired fish-and-game warden, along with several of his extended family members (that part was very Montana), took us into the woods with their horses, wagon, and camping gear. Years later, I would recognize the difference between riding down some dirt roads and camping near a stream and actually heading into wilderness.

As we trekked into the surrogate wilds, I was riding a big dun Belgian Warmblood, up ahead of everyone else. As a child in New Orleans, I had ridden ponies around a ring on Sunday afternoons in City Park often enough. Since then, I had been on horseback no more than half a dozen times, mostly just sitting on a trained trail horse, whose job was to follow the tail of the nag in front of it. This was not much different, but I was more or less on my own. Now and then I learned forward to pet the horse on the neck, and smelled that horse smell, and could hear my family and the other family behind me. I felt a strangely familiar and intimate connection to this big animal who was allowing me to sit on his back. He trotted if I pressed my legs against him, and then slowed down like a long exhalation of breath. I was just another human on his back, but I felt connected to him. I felt longing for something inside myself that remembered how to connect with an animal. This was a year or two after my rain experience. I was feeling exhilaration more than grief, and yet grief was not far below the surface, rising in the form of longing.

The next morning, in our camp, I woke up early and left the tent to find an appropriate bush for morning relief. I stopped still, heart pounding in a new way, when I saw a black bear about fifteen yards away from me. Later, I learned the guide had left out boxes of apples and oranges, sloppy for a ranger. Apparently bears do not care for oranges but the apples were gone. I saw the bear before he saw me. There was not much context in my life for this particular experience. Was I afraid (yep), was I thrilled (yep), did I have any idea what to do (nope)? I found my way back into the tent and unzipped a window flap to look back at the bear. My hands were shaking. I was unable even to wake up my family. I watched the bear lumber back into the woods. I think I was sorry to see him go, but the feelings were mixed.

In the SUV with Grace almost a year later, I told her about my grief around nature. I was en route to using these experiences as the basis for my dissertation. She described her desire to live by the sea, a story she would later tell in writing. Then she said, "Tell me about where you're going. I drove through Montana years ago. The parks are beautiful." I described a home we bought in the mountains outside Helena. Our lot was five acres, but we bought another twenty across the road. There was a barn and much of the land was fenced for horses. We were on a dirt road, with a septic tank, and a well for water. I had no idea how common this was in Montana or in other semi-rural places. Later another friend told me, "Yeah, I remember when you thought you were going into the wilds because you had a well and a septic tank." She lives "off grid" in New Mexico—much higher status among us greedy-for-nature types.

In defense of my sense we were abandoning civilization, much of suburban rural Montana retains some real elements of wilderness. When we first moved into our house, the former owner told us he had recently seen a mountain lion walk along our back fence. When a new neighbor came over to introduce himself, he commented, "Don't let your kids play in them woods up over there. There's a bear in there. When I get some time, I'm gonna go in there and shoot him out." Another neighbor cautioned against letting our younger daughter walk alone on the dirt road near her house. "All those pine trees are just where the mountain lions like to sit up in." Even then, I was not sure how much of this was true and how much was the Montana way to welcome Californians. We discovered soon enough the verb form for what Californians do when they move to Montana: *Californicate* the place. Nearly fifteen years later, I am yet to see a mountain lion, though my neighbor saw one recently run across the road near our houses. Bears are more inclined to make their presence known, carrying out your garbage if you don't close it up, lumbering across a road unexpectedly when you're on your way home from work.

After a few years in our first Montana house, I started to feel I was living in dense civilization, even if there were animals around. I could see three houses from my front yard and hear traffic on the road to the lake. I was already spoiled. And yet, when I needed complete isolation, if I sat on the wooden fence and looked in a certain direction, the other houses disappeared. I was looking towards the Big Belt Mountains, the Missouri River down amidst the folds of distant canyons. I loved how the mountains changed colors all the time: green, blue, purple, sometimes white with snow. Their layers and curves pulled at my heart. In the early years, every time I walked out the front door it was like falling in love.

In the evening, you sometimes heard coyotes in the distance. A neighbor claimed she could hear mountain lions late at night; they sound like a woman screaming. One summer, bright orange-red spots of fire appeared on the green and brown of the mountains across the river. Hawks were often gliding in circular motion in the sky. Ravens swooped down to take the smaller creatures. Deer were everywhere, though I had to tell hunters driving up the road there are not any elk. "Well, there used to be 'em up here," one of them told me, accusation mixed with defensiveness, a reference to the general Californication of the place.

I didn't know all this yet when I sat with Grace in her gas guzzler, but I knew what my heart wanted.

"It's cold up there," she said.

"I know," I responded. "But that feels right to me." Though I grew up in the South, and spent twenty-something years in California, winter has always felt normal to me, as if my body and soul remember the cold and the darkness. When it gets seriously frigid, twenty or thirty below zero, I feel like I am riding the freezing temperatures like an ocean wave or a rough horse. Though many Montana people do not believe in global warming (thank you once again, Fox News), they are fond of saying it is not as cold as it used to be. Sometimes it feels like they want to blame this on Californication. Many winters, you can count the days of sub-zero on your hands, but you hear about weeks and weeks at a time in years past. The natives say snow used pile up like walls on the side of the road, but not anymore.

In the SUV with Grace, she asked me, "What are you looking for?"

"I think you know."

"I'd like to hear it in your words."

The traffic on San Antonio Road was slowing down, congealing, starting to creep. It was reaching the point where you didn't get through the traffic light the first, or even the second, time. "Well, sometimes I think I am running away."

"From what?"

"From a life that's hard for me to keep up with. Everybody else seems to do it, but I don't know. . ."

"You're not going *to* something?"

I stayed quiet. I could feel it in my chest, right in the center, spreading out, that burning, almost a stabbing. I just pointed to the indentation beneath my sternum. I was choked up. It was hard to speak. Grace nodded. Tears rolled down both our faces. I grabbed her hand, squeezed it, and left. The last time I saw her she was turning to look into the lane of slow-moving traffic, hoping for someone to let her in.

Two years later, Grace wrote: *On January 1, 2000, we move into a home by the sea, purchased through a set of fortuitous circumstances and the courage to undertake a massive fixer-upper project. Our house is one of the fifteen homes I counted on that Christmas vacation two years earlier. The day we move into our new home is sunny and clear, with the smell of the sea filling my lungs, opening me to possibilities. After we walk in the front door, we run around the house and open all the windows—and breathe. I feel the expansion that comes to me by the ocean, as if I could fill the whole room, as if my body becomes warm liquid that flows out over the park land and into the sea.*

Over time, I realize I had become smaller than God had intended, living in congested cities and cramped spaces that had come to reflect my inner life. Now I watch the pelicans dive for fish and feel their lack of worry, my lungs expanding with the sea air. One morning as I run along the beach, I send greetings to the sea otter swimming along the shore. He looks at me with curiosity (perhaps wondering about a creature so clumsy and slow), and keeps pace with me for awhile, then moves swiftly ahead. I weep as I see one of his sisters dying on the beach, evidently shot by a fisherman— or when I see a crow tearing at the flesh of a dead gull. I am often reminded of the fragility of life. I carry with me an appreciation of what I have been given, both desired and undesired.

Living by the sea, with few neighbors and little of civilization's machinery, my experience is filled with gratitude and wonder, no matter what is occurring at the moment. While I know God is everywhere, for my particular life circumstances, it was necessary for me to live in a place where I could be surrounded by Nature. As the rhythms of the ocean have become mine, I have felt myself heal in an internal sense, even while my illness continues. This is akin to finding one's center, that still place we may discover during meditation, the safe place to which we can always return.

For me, this sense of myself in nature is my safe harbor—not safe in a material world sense, for this house is anything but safe, and nature is anything but safe. I mean a safe place of the spirit, fostered by immersion in nature.

Moving into Nature

We can't all move to the beach, not even the mountains. Many environmentalists go crazy about people who want to live "in nature" because if hordes of people move into nature, it is no longer nature. Much of the coastline in the United States is already precarious with development. Building in the woods and mountains of the American West puts life and property in danger when the natural world brings wildfires, not to mention enormous public cost for firefighting. We are losing forests and flora of all kinds by the minute to development. Development is the driving force of the loss of species in the sixth extinction event. Nevertheless, the longing many of us feel for nature is taking thousands of people out of cities and suburbs. Moving into nature is possible for more and more people with telecommuting jobs. Given contemporary technologies, many forms of entertainment come to us via satellite and almost anything can be purchased on line.

In *Building within Nature,* Andy and Sally Wasowski describe the recent reversal of the flow between urban and rural settings in the United States. [119] For well over a century, "there was a major exodus out of rural America, where opportunities ranged from few to nonexistent. People moved into urban areas for jobs, educational opportunities, and 'the good life.'"[120] In recent years, "urban and suburban crime, congestion, pollution, and a skyrocketing cost of living are causing a large number of people to reevaluate their definition of the good life and to begin packing."[121] Unfortunately, without great care, nature is destroyed in the process. The Wasowskis write:

> Every year, many thousands of acres of natural land—woodlands, deserts, meadowlands, savannas, coastal scrub—are turned into home sites by disenchanted city dwellers and by developers eager to tap into this ready market of expatriates. Ironically, by the time the moving vans pull up to many of these newly completed homes, the beauty and character of the land—the very things that attracted the buyers in the first place—have been harmed or destroyed. Bulldozers have scraped the land clean of all vegetation, in many cases leveling lots so that all traces of the original topographical features— arroyos, slopes, rock outcroppings, etc.—have been eradicated.

Development of nature leads to thousands of displaced species of plants and animals. Many individual animals are pushed into places they cannot survive, with the natural ecosystems thrown into disequilibrium. Most environmentalists would prefer we humans move into denser concentration in existing cities or plan dense new communities, leaving nature alone in the areas she remains vibrant. Others, like the Wasowskis, find ways of making homes within nature that minimize impact on the natural world. A growing number of architectural firms and urban planning consultants have an ecological focus, while studies in sustainable planning are taking root in universities and colleges. The term *permaculture* was created by Australians Bill Mollison and David Holmgren to describe a permanent, naturally-sustaining culture.[122] Builders practicing permaculture take time to observe the flows and interrelationship of species, land, and weather in a particular place, then design human systems (buildings, industry, or agriculture) to fit within the rhythms of nature.

Meanwhile, organizations have arisen to support people in placing natural lands out of the reaches of development. In Lewis and Clark County, Montana, the Prickly Pear Land Trust provides information, educational programs, and legal options (such as conservation easements) to assist landowners in committing particular tracts to nature down through future generations.[123] In rural places, not everyone is willing to make personal sacrifices so those living elsewhere can believe nature still exists, *somewhere*. I have Montana friends whose families are fourth or fifth generation—nothing compared to Native Americans but long term for European settlers in one of the last lands to be populated by immigrants. These families face difficult decisions when one generation ages and ranching or farming is no longer in the blood. When your family has owned large tracts of land for years, and you can help your children and grandchildren financially—or even create an enjoyable life in retirement for yourself—it is not the obvious choice to say no to developers. Certainly choices to sell to development in such circumstances are not subject to questioning by well-off urban nature lovers.

I did not cut down trees or build roads to construct a home, but I was more than happy to buy an existing residence close to nature. I am honestly not sure if I feel guilty, indulgent, or just grateful for a chance to live close to animals and open lands. I consider my time living close to nature as a form of recovery. Chellis Glendinning wrote a book called *My Name is Chellis and I'm in Recovery from Western Civilization,* playing off the opening statement people make in meetings in the Alcoholics Anonymous community.[124] She provides my excuse and I am sticking to it. Glendinning describes our civilized life as an addictive process in need of conscious recovery. A large part of the recovery is recognizing who we are and what we have lost. Another part is admitting our suffering.

Glendinning writes: "You and I are not people who live in communion with the Earth and yet we are people who evolved over the course of millions of years—through savannah, jungle and woodland—to live in communion with it."[125] Rather than living within nature, she continues, we find ourselves "dislocated from our roots by the psychological, philosophical, and technological constructions of our civilization and this alienation leads us to our suffering: massive suffering for each and every one of us, and mass suffering throughout our society."[126]

Glendinning understands our suffering for loss of nature as both individual and collective. Individually, we suffer "in our personal lives, in our relationships with ourselves and each other, by the numbing and abuse of dysfunctional behaviors."[127] Collectively, "we express our suffering in our relationship with the Earth by the numbing and abuse we enact through ecological destruction."[128] Glendinning calls our process techno-addiction, the tendency within technological societies to live in a state of "out-of-control, often aimless, compulsion to fill the lost sense of belonging, integrity, and communion" with any number of available stimulants, not just alcohol, food, or narcotics, but cultural addictive behaviors such as consumption and control. She concludes: "It is well past time for us to come home, to return to the matrix from which we came, to recover what we have lost, to remember again the wisdom and balance of the natural world."[129]

I will admit that Glenndinning is talking about a psychological process of recovery—and we are back to the reality that not everyone can move into nature. But nature sure helped me. After I moved to Montana, Grace emailed me that she still needed the ocean, at least until she managed to "permanently internalize what I absorb from nature." My friend and former ITP teacher Hillevi Ruumet moved to California after many years in Hawaii. She said she was able to leave the islands when she felt the islands inside her. In defense of people like Grace and me, maybe our own recovery in nature serves the planet in some sense; at least that sounds like a good story.

How one returns home, in actual life, is complicated enough, and varies person to person. For most of us, it is a combination of going within and reaching outward to nature—releasing the internalized grip of civilization; allowing nature to enter into the body, mind, and soul. As Grace wrote, when she felt the rhythms of the ocean become hers, she felt herself heal in an internal sense. She described this as "akin to finding one's center, that still place we may discover during meditation, the safe place to which we can always return." I felt something similar, but I would describe my personal feeling as a sense of internal spaciousness akin to the expanses in Montana, the reaches of the mountains up into the sky, the absence of people and presence of animals and trees.

When I imagine what has transformed inside of me, I think of a range of mountains in south-central Montana known as the Crazies. I know a few people who might consider this a form of self-diagnosis, but I am not alone in loving those mountains. They rise high up from the plains as if out of nowhere, isolated, sharp, and jagged, snow capped for much of the year. Most of this side of Montana is mountainous, with the Bridger Range not far southwest, and the Gallatin, Absaroka, and Beartooth Mountains straddling the border to Wyoming and hugging the northern rim of Yellowstone Park. But the Crazies, considered an "island range," stand alone. They are self-contained and form a kind of circle, plains on all sides of them.

I have never hiked inside the Crazy Mountains, but for over a decade I have driven back and forth between Helena and Billings for work several times a year, passing just south on Interstate 90. I force myself to keep my eyes on the road but I want to keep looking at them. In the way they seem extreme, they are almost a caricature of mountains, not quite a joke, but at least a quip. You are not quite sure what they are doing there, how they got there, what is their meaning, what is their intention. I have thought to myself that must be why they are called the Crazies, as they seem to make no sense, though the real story of their name is more poignant. In *Crazy Mountains: Learning from Wilderness to Weigh Technology*, eco-philosopher David Strong gives two theories for the origin of the "white man's name":

> The most common is that a woman left a wagon train near the town of Big Timber, got lost, went insane, and lived in the foothills of the mountains. However, I find it hard to believe that these mountains, these first definitive mountains of the Rockies, did not have a settled white name long before the wagon trains. The story that makes the most sense to me is the following: When the first white people came to the region, they asked the natives what they called these mountains. Not understanding each other's language, they had to communicate in sign language. The natives tried to tell them that they were a place of visions. The whites interpreted the signs to mean that these mountains were a place where people went crazy.[130]

Strong uses the Crazies, and their precarious ecological situation (roads being built, lack of designation as protected), to illustrate what is happening specifically and concretely in one wild place in danger of taming. Like David Abram, Strong combines philosophy with concrete and descriptive writing. About the Crazy Mountains, he writes:

The vast expanses of central Montana have an edge and a suddenness. Along the Yellowstone River, sandstone rimrocks line the horizon. Beyond these rims, the flats, benches and swells of the high plains, arid and mostly treeless, yet gold in autumn with prairie grasses, define a precise division between a yellow earth and a youthful sky. As a boy I was told that "Montana" meant land of the shining mountains. Mountains, especially the Crazy Mountains, seem to explode here into the blue as a child might draw them.[131]

As tends to happen when people pay attention to the concrete, Strong is realistic more than theoretical. While urging a deep ecological perspective, he wants to talk about what would happen if a deep ecological perspective were to become a mainstream reality. "Most of us," he writes, "sense the need to dwell again," but, he asks, how is that really to happen?[132] He continues:

Yet consider how much remains in the dark. How does tomorrow, even, call to be shaped differently? How should we be different in our work and our leisure, with others, with friends, with family? What would the reform of technology mean for agriculture, towns, and cities? What would it mean for businesses? For travel? For Third World countries? For symphonies, theaters, restaurants, and television? For the homeless and for children?[133]

As Strong explains, "we need to realize first that expecting a program is itself a sign of the unreformed, universal and a priori approach of technology."[134] This is because "much that matters most cannot be laid out in advance or be articulated in isolation from the context of each of our individual lives, communities and regions."[135] He writes:

The reform of technology will not be masterminded; rather it will be the result of communities of people who are able to speak and convey to each other what things matter in the way they matter. It will be the result of people working together and taking a few deliberate steps at a time, as possibilities open up. The true frontier for us is not literal wilderness any longer, nor is it a frontier we can conquer without irony and contradiction. Accepting and insisting on a particularist approach to a wilder future is the first of many steps toward reforming technology, toward learning to build again.[136]

I read Strong with great relief, the same kind of relief I feel when looking into the Crazy Mountains from my safe, warm car on the interstate. I am relieved the mountains are out there, still looking pretty wild, and a good place into which I can project my soul and dreams of wildness. I am relieved I am not lost up in the mountains in the cold, trying to stay warm, build shelter, fend off wild animals, and worry whether my children will die from exposure to the elements. I am relieved Strong is realistic about where we are and that he directs the first order of business as insistence on "conveying to each other what things matter in the way they matter." I would add that for some of us, an even earlier, or at least contemporaneous, order of business is to move deeply inside ourselves and find what does matter to us from the inside out. Strange how concretely I feel those Crazy Mountains right in my chest.

Nature in Approaching the Self

Anyone familiar with the analytical psychology of Carl Jung might have noticed that my draw to the Crazy Mountains could be using that rugged isolated range as a symbol of what Jung calls the Self. I did not realize this for many years, but it would help explain why these mountains feel so mysteriously numinous to me—and evidently have felt mysteriously numinous for many people before me, native and immigrant alike. Jung is considered the grandfather of transpersonal psychology in that he ventured deeply into the human psyche and realized we are connected, through the deepest reaches of our unconscious, with all else that is. Nineteen years younger than Sigmund Freud, Jung was for a time Freud's heir apparent in the German-speaking world of early twentieth century psychoanalysis, until their famous break, caused by Jung's refusal to accept Freud's insistence the single driving force in human neuroses is the infantile sexuality dilemma.

Initially devastating for Jung, the dissolution of his personal and professional relationship with Freud led to development of his own understandings, which for many of us opened the door within psychology for connection with what feels like our ancient spiritual heritage as humans. Jung reached his understandings from working with patients, but more importantly from tumultuous investigation of his own psyche, through dreams, drawings, and imagination. Jung is well known for his contribution of the concept of a collective unconscious, a realm within the psyche shared by all humans, appearing to us through symbols in dreams and waking manifestations of individual and collective psychology. He described archetypes existing within the collective unconscious, patterning symbols deeply connected to our shared origins, often appearing in similar myths and practices from a wide range of cultures.

The Self is an archetype of the collective unconscious central to an understanding of the human life journey, particularly if that journey is made conscious and includes a pull to the sacred. Analogized to the nucleus of an atom, the Self is the center of the entirety of the psyche, including both conscious and unconscious aspects, around which other elements of the psyche constellate. Jung described the Self as a God-image, noting an encounter with the Self could feel like religious experience. As with all archetypes, the Self in Jungian understanding is not an entity but a description of a psychological constellation or emergent process. Jungian scholar Anthony Stevens described the Self as "the organizing genius behind the total personality," with "a *teleological* function, in that it has the innate characteristic of seeking its own fulfillment in life."[137]

The goal of the Self is the experience of wholeness. How wholeness manifests for each of us individually depends on who we are uniquely as humans—or more accurately, who we are meant to become, what we are meant to include as our particular means to wholeness. The Self invites a process of psychological transformation known in Jungian psychology as individuation. Jung explained individuation as a "destination, a possible goal," a matter of "becoming an 'individual,' and, in so far as 'individuality' embraces our innermost, last, and incomparable uniqueness, it also implies becoming one's own self."[138]

Through individuation, we begin a process of experiencing ourselves (our conscious ego) in a way more authentic to our actual individuality in relation to pull from the deepest part of ourselves. This involves separating out from those assumptions and behaviors we absorbed from family and culture that are not truly authentic to us personally. Jung described as the persona that aspect of our psyche that formulates a surface personality, perhaps understandable as an individual manifestation of cultural trance. In *Relations Between the Ego and the Unconscious,* Jung described the persona as representing "a more or less arbitrary and fortuitous segment of the collective psyche . . . . only a mask of the collective psyche, a mask that *feigns individuality,* making others and oneself believe that one is individual, whereas one is simply acting a role through which the collective psyche speaks."[139]

Jung concluded ego consciousness may move toward the Self or experience its reflective numinosity, but believed the Self—not unlike God as described in many traditions—remains ultimately unknowable in any direct sense. He wrote "that man is also what neither he himself nor other people know of him—an unknown something which can yet be proved to exist...an ineffable totality, which can only be formulated symbolically."[140] As Stevens articulated, because the Self "carries us...into the ineffable mysteries of the world," we generally encounter the Self and its invitations toward wholeness through projection "onto figures or institutions perceived as possessing pre-eminent power and prestige—either onto human figures like presidents, kings or queens or, more readily, onto suprapersonal entities such as the State, God, the sun, Nature or the universe."[141]

The Crazy Mountains surely pulled at the part of my psyche seeking a symbol of wholeness, including my need for separation, perhaps a time of isolation, some courage in the form of ruggedness, and a goal of containment of what is uniquely mine. It is interesting that symbolism of the Self often involves a circle and the Crazies are essentially an island of mountains. What all nature means to me can never be fully known but will always exist as a pull, an invitation into a process of becoming. It would be inaccurate to equate the Self directly with nature in Jung's understanding, yet nature, as we shall experience throughout this book, seems particularly suited for mediating a mystical connection between a smaller sense of identity and a larger experience of all that is. Theories and concepts can never completely capture our draw to the numinous, or our draw to what feels like the deepest reaches of ourselves, but the Jungian conception of Self helps me understand why I feel the Crazy Mountains so deeply—and why, like Grace, I felt I had to move into nature.

For Jung, movement toward wholeness involves immersion within the primordial instincts of the human, yet with sufficient awareness to distinguish oneself from these instincts. Jung understood the instinctual depths of the psyche as "the place of primordial unconsciousness and at the same time the place of healing and redemption, because it contains the jewel of wholeness."[142] This is "the cave where the dragon of chaos lives and it is also the indestructible city, the magic circle or *temenos*, the sacred precinct where all the split-off parts of the personality are united."[143] For people like Grace and me, nature may call to us from this place inside us, which is also a place outside us—nature—holding our projections of wholeness and our instinctual memories of the origins of the human animal.

Jung lived before Western consciousness moved through technology into postmodernity, but he understood our twentieth-century psychological trajectory out of nature. On occasion he discussed the American example of conquering nature only to lose the instinctual that is part of our collective heritage. Meredith Sabini, a depth psychologist focusing on dream work, gathered writings of Jung into a collection called, *The Earth has a Soul: C. G. Jung on Nature, Technology and Modern Life.*[144] As recalled by Sabini, as far back as 1925, "Jung gave an interview to the *New York Times* in which he commented on how much had been sacrificed to achieve the domination of our wilderness; how Americans tend to think in great abstractions and emphasize control over emotions and instincts."[145] Several decades later, in 1957, Jung again discussed the American loss of nature when interviewed by University of Houston Professor Richard Evans. Sabini notes: "Jung stated frankly that America was so uprooted and divorced from Nature that the 'real, natural man' was in open rebellion against the utterly inhuman form of life. . . . Jung told Evans that something must be done 'to compensate the earth.'"[146]

Sabini invites an imagination of Jung as a tribal healer, a twentieth-century psychiatrist wanting humanity to remember the "archaic, natural, primordial, or original."[147] She describes Jung's recollection of one of his dreams, suggesting symbolically his hope for our reconnection with our past. In the dream, Jung was with a primitive tribal chief sharing knowledge that "at last the great event has occurred; the primitive boar, a gigantic mythological beast, has finally been hunted down and killed. It has been skinned, its head cut off, the body divided lengthwise like a slaughtered pig, the two halves only just hanging together at the neck." Along with the chieftain, Jung struggled to bring the meat to the tribe. There were obstacles. The boar meat fell into a rushing river and was swept into the sea. After retrieving the meat, Jung and the chieftain reached the tribe. Sabini quotes Jung's description: "The camp or settlement is laid out in a rectangle, either in the middle of a primeval forest or in an island in the sea. A great ritual feast is going to be celebrated."[148]

I imagine myself there for the feast. I can almost smell the boar roasting in an open fire, hear the fat popping, taste the wild in the juicy, scorched meat. The night is all around me, but I am with my tribe, my people, having come home. We give thanks to the boar and celebrate all he means that can never be expressed. We start to dance and there is singing. It feels like even the trees in the night are echoing the song. That image, a manifestation of Jung's access to the collective unconscious, perhaps a reflection of our collective Self, pulls at me from the same place that pulled me into Montana.

In Montana

Montana gradually opened something inside me. Little by little, all that space, land, and sky seeped into me. The rivers, lakes, mountains and trees became familiar, as though I could count on them. It stopped being a surprise to live amongst elk, deer, rabbits, coyotes, hawks, eagles and ravens, though the more elusive big cats, bears, and wolves remained mysterious and numinous. When we moved to Montana, much was different in our lives, and yet of course we were still living in the United States, still dropping off kids at school, working in an office, watching *Star Trek* on Sunday nights while eating spaghetti. The time I first really knew things had changed came one Saturday afternoon during our first fall in Montana. Our daughter Audrey, starting fifth grade, had invited a new friend over for the weekend. I was in our bedroom upstairs with the windows open. I heard some very quiet talking coming from the big deck downstairs. It was the hushed tone that caught my attention.

I stepped out onto the small deck off our bedroom and looked down. The two girls were sitting in chairs by the railing, watching a storm drop rain on the Elkhorn Mountains across the valley, probably five miles away. One of my favorite things about the American West is how you can see rain storms in the distance—discrete, slanting, shimmering lines reaching from the clouds to the ground. I watched the girls as they watched the show across the valley. They were talking so quietly I could hardly hear them. Even their laughter was quiet. On the balcony I could feel shifts in the wind. Sometimes the smell of fresh rain became so strong I could taste it. If I hadn't known before, I knew in that moment that coming to Montana was the right thing for my family. That afternoon there had been no arguments over television, no whining about boredom, no pleading to be driven across town in dense traffic to some other end of the endless suburbs. Just two girls watching one of the best shows on Earth, the space and the rain instilling a hush no suburban parent ever could.

After the brief Montana fall comes winter, generally arriving right around Halloween. This was not my first experience of winter in a northern latitude, but entering the first one in Montana felt serious, like a commitment. Having animals to feed in the winter was more a blessing than a curse, as it forced me outside twice a day in all temperatures. Sometimes the air was so cold it was painful to breathe. I quickly learned the compensation for the most bitter cold was often a sharp, clear sky, sometimes little ice crystals floating around in the air. While below zero Fahrenheit gets your attention, for me, the salient feature of winter in northern latitudes is not cold, but darkness. The summer is bright and expansive, with light and possibilities everywhere. Then winter returns, sending you inside—both inside dwellings and inside yourself. Summer expands, winter constricts. Winter constricts, and then summer expands. And yet a taste of winter can hit you any time of year, reminding you who is boss. Montana people are fond of saying it can snow in any month. Everyone has their story of the snowed-out August barbecue. One of the most treacherous crosses I ever made over McDonald Pass—the route over the continental divide on the way to Missoula—was in June.

Winter can send you a message in any month, but Father Cold pretty well owns Montana from early November through late March, though in most years temperatures move above freezing now and then, long enough to melt snow and let it all start again. The sense of coming winter starts in September, even late August, around the first days of school. The air in the mornings and nights feels different than the weeks before, a bit of warmth is missing. Around the end of the month, I would begin the ritual of moving summer things into the barn. Sometimes the smell of snow was in the air. I would hang tarps on the open side of the hay shed, mend a few fences, and make sure the stock tank heater coil still worked. One Saturday afternoon, I was using a sledge hammer to restore fence posts moved for the hay delivery when I looked around and noticed this was my life. Light snow was blowing in the mountains on both sides of us. The horses were standing around nonplussed but knowing something was about to change. I was not fighting the elements in the ice age, or even battling Montana nature in past decades, but something inside me was deeply satisfied to be moving around in the first cold of the season, getting ready.

That first spring, we added goats, chickens, and horses to what a friend from the east coast had named "the ranchette." Admittedly, hanging out with domesticated animals is not exactly living in the tundra hunting wooly mammoths, but it was a step back a few generations. Domesticated animals still have much to teach us as household intimates. When our daughter Tess turned six—her first birthday in Montana—she wanted a baby goat. We complied, which was not difficult since there was a goat farm on the way into town. As my wife said, there are few things in life as good as watching your six-year-old run around the yard with a baby goat following her.

Oliver was a Nubian, his ancestry in the Middle East. He was black with white markings, including white floppy ears. He grew into a large goat, but only lived several years. We buried him in the back pasture when there was deep snow on the ground. We maneuvered his heavy body onto a sled and Tess helped pull. For a grave, we used a hole from a failed attempt to transplant a tree the summer before. No way could we have dug in the frozen ground. Years later, Tess was out in the pasture and realized an animal had scavenged Oliver's bones. She found the sun-bleached, gnawed white remnants scattered around in the dry weedy grass. That experience led to one of the most moving art projects of her youth.

When Oliver was still a baby, our older daughter wanted to be part of the goat experience, so we soon had a female Alpine. She looked like the goats you imagine on the mountains in Switzerland. Light brown, with pointed ears and a beard, Chloe was feisty and loved to get on top of things, such as motor vehicles, or inside them. As one of our friends said, you shouldn't have goats if you mind them eating your upholstery. Goats are demandingly inquisitive and love affection, at least until they get tired of it. Our son called the goats "livestock dogs."

My wife became interested in the possibility of goat milk and another generation of little goats. Oliver had already been neutered, so she took Chloe back to the goat farm for breeding. Our two girls went along for the ride. The goat farm owner, a no-nonsense Montana woman, brought out a ram. He was a Nubian, looking something like Oliver. The decidedly unneutered ram quickly jumped Chloe, performing his role once, and then again, in the time it took my wife to write a check for twenty-five dollars. The knowing goat farm lady looked at our two young daughters, nodded toward the breeding activity, and said, "See girls, remember this, that's all it takes—it can happen in a few seconds."

Two kids were born in the spring, an interesting cross between Alpine and Nubian. My wife woke up in the middle of the night and knew to walk out to the barn just as Chloe was about to deliver. We watched Choo-Choo and Peter (alternatively named Chaw) slide out onto the straw on the barn floor. Though Oliver was only their father in spirit, the kids looked like both mom and dad. Milking did not go well. Chloe never forgave us for trying. Even worse, Chloe refused to let one of the kids suckle. On the positive side, with bottle feeding by daughter Tess, Peter grew up more oriented to us than his brother.

Chloe, on the other hand, became an eternal head-butter. For years, we walked with the goats in the mountains. At the second place we lived, they roamed freely most of the year, except during the warmer months when they ate the neighbor's flowers or followed hikers down the dirt road. Domesticated goats will pretty much follow you anywhere, though it helps to have a big stick to pound on the ground. It sounds to them like the hooves of the herd running off, so they instinctively follow. As with horses, humans become the herd leader with goats, though you cannot ask them for much other than to come after you. And, yes, they do eat anything vaguely digestible. My son actually had to use the excuse, "Our goat ate my homework." Fortunately, in Montana, a kid with that excuse has a chance of being believed.

Compared to the thousands of years some of our ancestors kept goats for life-sustaining meat and milk, our suburban-rural experience seems just play. And yet we had the chance to remember something. A few years ago, a friend of mine from California posted on the Internet a picture of his young son at a petting farm in Sacramento. My friend had written a caption below the picture, "John pets a sheep." A few moments after seeing the picture, I emailed him, "Actually, John is petting a goat." The goat in the picture was not one of those breeds that look like they might be either a sheep or a goat. I am talking about an obvious goat. "How can you not know a goat?" I emailed my friend.

"Who knows the difference between a sheep and a goat—what's it matter?" he joked.

My friend is no dummy, having a few advanced degrees, a responsible job, and impressive, up-to-the-minute knowledge of the standing of numerous sports teams, not to mention the intricacies of national politics. "How can you expect this civilization to survive," I inquired, "when people don't know the difference between a sheep and a goat?"

And of course, the chickens. As silly as it is, knowing chickens over the years has put so much in context for me. Well over a hundred chickens lived and died on our little ranchette. I am not proud of this record, but I was not about to lock up chickens—the point was for them to free range, to live. Apparently chickens can live up to twenty years, but none in our brood made it longer than a season or two. As one of my new age friends remarked, it may not be the karma of chickens to have any single long life on the planet.

Though I was not able to protect them from the reality of free-range chicken karma, I have enjoyed many chicken friends. Some I could even tell apart from the others. Poor Jakimo, I will never forget her, particularly because she was the namesake of our middle daughter's strange self-designated nickname. A show bird, Jakimo was gorgeous, a sculpted array of white and gray feathers, somehow bred to look manicured. A fluffy white plume stuck up from her little head, very dignified, a Park Avenue hat from the fifties. Flustered when she suddenly saw me walk into the barn one morning, she broke her own little neck flying into a wall, a fatal mistake.

Other chickens drowned in the stock tank. Most were taken by other animals, sometimes our own dogs. One year, an unknown creature took nearly twenty. It happened so fast over a few days, during the middle of a week when I was busy at work, I could not figure out how to stop the slaughter. Life is cheap in nature, I suppose. Another time, as we were getting in the car for me to drive the children to school, a fox ran into the yard and started chasing the free ranging chickens. I tried to shoo the frantic birds into the barn, but they just ran around in chaos, too flustered even to take refuge on a fence rail. Deciding I had little choice but to leave them to their fate, I got back in the car. As we drove out of the yard, my daughter Audrey leaned out the window and shouted, "Good luck, chickens."

Having chickens free ranging around the yard felt healing in my heart. I loved their ways, scratching around for bugs, cackling at each other, running away from me, but coming back as a collective wave if I am about to throw some grain. My wife was convinced they kept down the number of grasshoppers, a good thing in summer. I enjoyed their chicken habit of roosting on the rafters in the barn, all in a row. I amused myself greatly by learning how to "discipline" the roosters who would run at me in attack mode. Silly on their part, as they did not know who they were dealing with. This is the trick. You imitate the behavior roosters use to establish dominance with each other, which is pinning the challenging rooster down by the neck. Roosters use their beaks for the pinning, but a human pinch with the first two fingers works very well. Of course, you have to grab them first and before that you have to catch them because as soon as a charging rooster sees your big human form running back at them, they do an about-face and run the other way. One morning I went through this routine while wearing a suit for work. Just as I stood back up, having dominated some poor misguided rooster, I realized a new neighbor lady was watching me from the road, her mouth slightly open. I had lived here long enough to give others moving in from out-of-state my own welcome to Montana.

I cherished eating eggs laid by our own birds. The yolks are bright orange, not yellow, and stand up firm in the pan. The taste is not all that different from store-bought eggs, just more fresh. Most of the satisfaction is from involvement in the process that brought eggs to the table. Raising chickens from chicks, feeding them grain, watching them roam the yard doing what chickens do, establishing their "pecking order," starting to lay eggs when they were ready. I loved finding eggs around the barn and then coming to know where particular hens would lay. One of my favorite "contrast to California" stories involves my daughter's friend from San Jose who visited our second summer. Our twelve-year-old visitor would not eat a fresh egg I had fried for her—because the yolk was bright orange and not the bland yellow color she was used to seeing. The orange yolk was "gross," she said. "It's not normal."

"Well, actually . . . ," I started to say, and then thought better of it. After all, not my kid.

There is a remarkable scene in the movie *Babel*, in which suburban American children find themselves at festivities preceding a wedding in Mexico. With their southern California parents traveling on another continent, the children accompany their Mexican nanny across the border. They arrive in a place with chickens milling around the yard and start running around, chasing the birds, having fun. The next moment, a young Mexican man grabs one of the chickens and kills it, by holding its head and flicking his wrist. (I am told my great-grandmother was particularly good at this wrist-flick manner of getting Sunday dinner, particularly with a chicken that had been irritating her.) While these fictional southern California children presumably had eaten their share of Chicken McNuggets, their look of shocked amazement captures the divide between contemporary mainstream experience in the United States and our heritage. Chickens are in cartoons and barnyards, but they are not really what we eat, are they? Those must be different chickens.

I will confess to slaughtering a few chickens myself. This is how it happened. Our first spring in Montana, we took the whole family to the ranch store. Chicks of all varieties are for sale. You walk down a row and look them over while the hatchlings sit hunched into their little feathers amidst sawdust in big aluminum water tanks, under heat lamps. Fourteen-year-old Max was as much into this chicken adventure as his sisters. But he made a slight mistake, which I did not catch until several weeks later. Max thought a sign reading "Roasters" meant "Roosters." This was well before the children and my wife developed their intense, experience-based fear of roosters. A few years later, when visiting a faux-Colonial historical re-enactment village on the east coast, all three children were staying well clear of the roosters milling around a woman dressed in seventeenth century garb and pretending to churn butter. She saw them keeping their distance and said to me, "Oh, they haven't been around chickens?"

"No," I responded. "Actually, they *have*. But your roosters seem pretty nice." Those particular chickens may have been selected for their tourist-friendly behavior, but my children, a few years of rooster charges behind them, were not taking any chances.

"Aren't all roosters nice?" she remarked.

"Not really," I informed her. So much for faux-Colonial authenticity, or perhaps those Mayflower types brought over nice birds.

In that first ranch store outing, Max was still thinking we could use a little "cock-a-doodle-doo" in the morning when he handed me a little cardboard box containing several chicks he thought would grow up to be roosters. By the way, some of them call out "cock-a-doodle-doo" all day, which I found quite funny, as it seemed like they had just woken up, having slept in late. When I gave over my credit card at the ranch store check out, I did not question who in particular I was purchasing, but I did remember Max being excited about picking out roosters. Raising the chickens was my gig, so I had them in the tack room of the barn, in circular tubs previously used only for holding beer and soft drinks at California parties. I did notice the little canary-colored birds Max picked out were growing rather quickly, but I did not think much of it.

A few weeks later, the mom of Audrey's new friend came to pick up her daughter one Sunday afternoon. We went out and walked around the barn. "Those are roasters," said Theresa, who was raised on a farm in South Dakota. "In a few weeks they'll be too fat to stand up. You need to eat them." Sure enough, those little canary-colored chicks were now huge yellow chickens, growing fatter by the day because they were bred to become quickly enormous for slaughter. Oh, I realized, *roasters,* not *roosters.* In fact, none of them were roosters; they were all roaster hens. "Isn't it ironic," sang Alanis Morissette.

A week later, Theresa came back out to teach us (or rather me) how to kill and dress chickens. I bought a new hatchet, mercilessly sharp. Theresa told us to boil some water in a large pot. I found a piece of cut log that was too big for the wood stove, but just right for an executioner's block. There was a nice flat surface just at knee height. I caught a roaster; poor thing didn't have much chance to flee given her fat genes. Theresa took her, held her head against the wood, and voila, guillotine by hand. Yes, the bird flapped around headless. Then we dipped the body in scalding water, which makes it easier to rub off the feathers. With wet feathers on my jeans and all over the yard, we took the headless chicken inside, opened her up with a knife, and took out the guts. What amazed me most about the whole thing was how fast this bird went from live animal waddling slowly around my yard to exactly what you get at Safeway. Who knew?

We served the chicken that evening. Our youngest daughter, then around seven years old, sat there silently. "You're not going to eat?" I asked.

"I'm not going to eat a bird what I knew," she replied. Tess has now been a vegetarian for a decade and a half.

While playing farmer is slightly embarrassing, slaughtering chickens removed one small disconnect in my life. When I buy the chicken under saran wrap at the grocery store, I know I am eating an animal that lived. If I am mindful, I even envision the bird that once was. I am at peace with my carnivore side, earned through a few million years of evolution, but I know the animals I eat were really not all that different from me. I don't hunt, but I wish I knew how. People have offered to take me hunting, but there are already enough things I am learning how to do in my middle age. When he was in high school, my son learned to shoot, with the stated goal of finding his own food, but he later reverted to city life. He now lives in the heart of Hollywood, working in advertising, creating some great commercials.

Thousands of Montana people hunt to fill their refrigerators with meat for the winter—and as part of their heritage. Most of them have grown up hunting, but for people like me, hunting would be another way to remove a piece of the disconnection. If I ever learn to shoot and bring home my own meat, I am just crazy enough to want to skin the beasts myself, tan the hides, and wear the skins outside in the depths of winter sitting around a campfire. Maybe I will also find myself a cave and go in there with a lighted torch and some charcoal—and draw myself some animal portraits on the limestone. Am I playing—or remembering?

Our ancestors looked in the eyes of scores of animals as they died. Sometimes, it was our ancestors who died, gored, stomped, thrown or bitten by animals that fought back for their lives or outsmarted us. As our successful hunter ancestors sat around the campfire, the meat in their mouths still had some essence of the living creature who roamed the earth that very day or the day before. This is a different experience from buying food as part of the economic chain of things in contemporary life—and yet we can remember, each in our own way, our own version of Jung's dream of the tribal feast, whether lived, dreamed, or imagined. Come to think of it, neither hunting nor a ranchette is necessary to remember. Nor is eating meat, and maybe someday I will join the ranks of the compassionate world-conscious vegetarians—or, wait a minute, maybe not. To remember you just need a little imagination, a bit less illusion we have always lived the way we live now, a feeling back into yourself.

The Meaning of Raven

Living closer to nature breathes life back into culture. I began to realize that some symbols and images well-known in civilization have lost their moorings after a few generations of cities and suburbs. In middle school, like most American kids, I read Edgar Allen Poe's *The Raven*. Growing up in the city of New Orleans, I am not sure I had ever seen a raven. If I had, I would not have distinguished it from any other bird, maybe just noting it was black, maybe assuming it was a crow. Reading the poem in school, I could tell from context a raven was a black bird, but I had no associations from life to the bird. The only associations I had to ravens as a symbol were from within the poem or from other literary or civilized references, an example of postmodern self-reference within culture. The teacher explained, of course, that the raven was a symbol for death, but I heard this in an intellectual sense. There was nothing emotional about it, nothing visceral.

Fast forward thirty-five years or so and I am walking in our woods in Montana. I round a bend, and suddenly come upon a deer carcass, bloody, sinewy, bone showing. Three or four raven are pulling blood red meat from the body, lifting their necks, and swallowing it down. That is the part to remember: *lifting their necks and swallowing it down*. The smell and visceral feel of death hit my body with shock, revulsion, almost nausea. Ah, I thought, even with my disgust, *thank you, God*. This is raven, *this* is what was knocking on that chamber door, once upon a midnight dreary. *That* changes everything, I thought. Even though it was daylight and just a ten minute walk from my house, I cleared out quickly, as a dead animal with meat still on its bones can mean the return of a bear or a mountain lion.

This experience had some energy for me; I formed a relationship with ravens. One spring, stupidly, I thought to let half-grown chicks out in the yard on a bright sunny day, to give them some space from the tub they had nearly outgrown. I created a small enclosure around a tree by unrolling chicken wire, extremely amused to be using chicken wire for its named function, restoring another disconnect. Unfortunately, I did not have sense enough to put chicken wire over the top of my make-shift pen. In my defense, I was not used to death descending from the sky almost instantaneously. After all, there have been a few thousand generations between me and when the children of our ancestors were routinely snatched up by raptors and eagles. On my happy-go-lucky sunny Saturday in Montana, I went inside for not more than twenty minutes. When I came back out, I saw a raven flying away with the last of the half-grown chicks in its talons. I felt a mixture of guilt and anger, mostly guilt for my carelessness in allowing the death of those six little chickens. Now I am more likely to think, well, the raven also needed to eat and this is what happens in nature.

Around the same time, I experienced a series of synchronicities involving "raven." At a Holotropic Breathwork workshop, I met a woman who goes by the name Raven. A man who needed to give me his address lived on Raven Road. A woman told me a dream featuring a raven. My seventh-grade daughter had to learn a poem. Sure enough, it was *The Raven*, a selection from school having nothing to do with me. I heard her practicing for several days, repetitions of that midnight dreary weak and weary right back in my life.

I sat listening as she recited. The beauty of the rhyming was still there. The haunting image of Lenore remained. But now raven was no longer just an intellectual concept, not just a learned connection of image to idea. That sudden knocking of the raven was mortality, a symbol maybe, but based in experienced reality, grounded in life and death. With the tapping on the chamber door was the nonchalance, the enjoyment, of the raven picking muscle from the dead deer as meat, jutting back its beak, letting the meat slide down its throat. With the tapping was the experience of walking out my own door and watching a chick I had held in my hands an hour earlier, and carefully placed in the grass under the tree, being carried away by a black form. Lenore was there, then she was gone; and death was not a literary specter, but a real part of life.

After living in Montana for several years, I was at a seminar on shamanism in California. We had just watched several videos about indigenous shamans. People were discussing the aspect of shamanism involving dismemberment, wondering why a shaman in one of the videos had drawn images of animals in apparent reference to the experience of dismemberment. I was hearing an attempt to link the symbolism of particular animals as learned in a Western thought-based manner to dismemberment, discussing meaning in what felt to me a linear, analytical way. I heard it as a tedious thought-process moving from learned symbolism *about* particular animals to speculation on a thinking level about what the shaman had been *thinking*.

Eventually, I raised my hand and said something like, "I'm not sure I get it either, but my sense is that in the wilds, you walk around a corner and see a carcass torn to pieces and lying there, dismembered." I paused, trying to figure out how to explain what I meant. Not easy, since even I was not sure. "It's not a head experience," I tried. "It's not something for discussion or making mental connections or leaps. It's a visceral experience of the body. Maybe these are animals the shaman has seen dismembered, and he remembers it in his body, and he takes that energy into his journey, the experiential energy, his memory." I think my comment may have shut down the line of conversation but I am not sure anyone knew what I was saying other than the workshop leader. In retrospect, if I could have pulled it off, a more helpful comment may have been that we might try dancing the question rather than analyzing it from our heads.

Riding It Out

My deepest recovery in Montana came through my relationship with horses. You can ride anywhere, but horses more easily become part of life in a place like Montana. A friend named Anne O'Leary, who lived in our house before us, heard about an old ranch horse one of her new neighbors was about to sell to a slaughter house. For a hundred dollars and some old hay, she talked the neighbor into letting us take "Little Joe." He was probably over twenty years old and had an injured hip. There was a Montana story to explain the hip. A few years before, the rancher's soon-to-be ex-wife took a bit of revenge by stampeding his horses out of the corral so they would spread around the ranch. Little Joe, who was short for a horse, around 14 hands, and hence the name, struck his hip against a fence post as the stampede ran out of the corral. Our vet said the hip was just a "mechanical problem" and was a good thing as he would not be able to buck us off. He was still fine to ride and as it turned out, would still gallop when he felt like it, but had long since lost any inclination to cause trouble for green horns. Joe, as I called him, seemed palpably grateful for an easy life, a stall to stand in at night, hay thrown to him twice a day. We should all be so lucky in our later years.

In the spring, a 16-year-old quarter-horse joined Joe in our ranchette stable. Brown, though dappled with gray in the winter, "Poco" had a rough trot, but he was patient with learners. In the early years of learning to ride, that rough trot gave me some pretty firm calluses in the place earlier generations described as "where the sun don't shine." That same spring, I brought home a yearling black and white paint filly. Oddly, I am unable to name her. On her registration with the American Paint Horse Association, her name is Midnight Satin Jewel, but none of those words fit. I have rejected each and every name suggested to me by family and friends over the years. I think this is because no name can sufficiently carry what she has meant to me. It reminds me of knowing someone intimately enough that use of their given name feels awkward, as if the name should not be spoken because you sense something more intimate than a name.

There is an old saying, made famous by President Ronald Reagan, that "there's nothing better for the inside of a man than the outside of a horse."[149] This has been my experience with each of the several horses who have lived with us for a time in Montana. Leaning against their bodies, interacting with their ways, recognizing their questioning of my ways, so many unknown memories seem to arise, so many unknown questions answered. All the small connections are heightened in the rugged rhythms when galloping across an open field. There is a way to melt into the motion, while remaining alert and connected. My horse and I never quite got there, but good riders hardly use their hands on the bridle and bit. Requests to the horse for direction and gait are conveyed by the slightest shifts in position of the legs and seat. "Just turn your head and look where you want to go," a trainer once told me. "Your body will follow and she'll know what you mean."

Gayle Abbott, who grew up with horses in Texas, described a similar relationship with horses when writing about her emotional response to nature. *I feel most comfortable and relaxed on horseback. When I ride I am very tuned in to the rhythm of the horse's gait, and in giving in to the rhythm, it's almost as if the rider and horse become one. When I ride in Texas, the land is flat and I can see for miles. I am usually not concerned with where I am going, only that I am relaxed and content. I am very appreciative of the colors of the earth when I am riding, how the blue sky meets the red clay of the ground, and how the various shades of green on the small, sparsely spread trees add interest to the landscape. I am also appreciative and respectful of the horse's power—especially since I have been thrown a few times. If I have stress, it melts away. If I have things on my mind or decisions to make, riding seems to bring clarity. My heart and body feel lighter; there is a feeling of freedom. I often end up singing when I ride—my voice seems to merge with the landscape and the rhythm of the horse.*

Much of this book was written on Saturday and Sunday mornings across several years. Except in the depths of winter, a writing session was often followed by horse time. When I started writing this section, the sliding glass door next to me was open; outside was the first summery day of the year. That was my day to remember the smell of pine trees in warm weather. To me, this is the smell of the Rocky Mountains. It pulls me into them. This smell does the same thing to my body as when I see a hawk circling in the brilliant blue air of a warm spring day. Even after living in the mountains for several years, the smell still holds that bittersweet longing for nature, mixed with pleasure, and now the longing involves first-hand knowledge of the brevity of summers in this country.

For several years we had a hammock stretched between two pine trees in an area to the side of the house. That particular ground was rippled with abruptly sharp clefts formed by hundreds of years of quick snow melts, rushing gutters of water sculpting the earth. As summer arrived, I would lie in the hammock, called out by this smell of summer. In the shade of the trees, I would feel pockets of coolness now and then wafting by me, dislodged from between tree branches, pushed loose by a breeze, not yet mixed in with the warmed-up air of the day. The hammock was in an area where the horses could come, so they sometimes sidled up to investigate the guy who throws hay and rides us lying prone at the level of their chests. As much as I trusted them, I would have to relax myself out of fear. I did not believe they would hurt me; it was just my instinct to be wary of animals larger than me who would bolt suddenly into action if something happened to spook them.

On many glorious afternoons, I went out to the barn, saddled up my black and white paint mare, a ritual. First I put goop in her ears to keep out the flies. This helped soften up her ears, which were sensitive. The touchiest moment in getting ready to ride was when I pulled the bridle over her head. If the leather touched her ears the wrong way, she jerked her head away and we might start an argument. I tore a rotator cuff one year by not flowing with her fast enough when she pulled her head away. I could not sleep on that shoulder for over a year but the pain took me back to the moment and I did not mind.

In the early years, if she jerked her head away more than a couple of times, I would get out the whip and make her run in the round pen in the hope she would lose some willfulness. If we went that route, she would eventually get tired, forgot why she was upset, seem to relax, and we would try the bridle again. The problem was that sometimes she remembered both her ears and the argument when I eased up the bridle. So I would still have problem number one and had added problem number two.

After seeing that movie a number of times, I realized it might work better to flow my energy with hers in putting on the bridle. I had to start before the problem point. It was not all that different from riding her. Come to think of it, it was not that different from riding my own tension in thirty below zero weather. You relax and ease yourself into what is presenting itself. With her on one of those warm spring days, I would breathe in the mountains along with her smell, feel how it centers all my energy in my gut, and then start slowly with the bridle moving up her head, noticing my own breath, all the while attempting to blend my energy with hers. Over the years, we learned how to manage this together; or maybe her ears just got less sensitive. Once the bridle was on, I would bend down to pick out her hooves before riding. Then I would have one last swig from a bottle of once-cold Corona, now warm and a little bit brackish, and count myself lucky to be alive in this place at this moment.

The moment I haul myself up into the saddle is always one of complete attention. Since I trained her myself, there is always the memory of those first times I got up on her and had no idea what would happen. This was always in the round pen, so she could not run far, but she could buck and kick and get rid of me if she wanted that. I started the process slowly, building up over a series of weeks. We got saddling down without much hoopla. I had her run for several weeks in the round pen so she would grow accustomed to the saddle on her back, with the stirrups hitting her belly. But I knew a human on her back was a different story. More weight, different weight, weight shifting all the time, me behind her instead of where she could see me. I had tried laying blankets across the saddle to add some weight, something I had read in a book. But both of us knew that was stupid and nothing like what would happen when I got up there.

I tried to ease into it, several times of pushing my chest against the saddle, easing up in stages. Then I had to get a foot in a stirrup and pull myself up so she would feel that kind of weight, only going just so far one time, then a little further the next time. Eventually, with her standing right next to a round pen panel, I swung my leg over and sat down on her gently. She waited a few seconds and bolted like a racehorse. It is actually pretty funny that she waited until the moment I sat down to bolt. I guess maybe suddenly it became real to her. I managed to grab hold of the top metal tube of the round pen panel and held on while she ran out from under me. Fortunately my feet came right out of the stirrups. My body slammed into the panel and I slid down the rest of the way, having survived well enough. Then I tried again.

It was a slow matter of building trust, an easing between her body and mine. It was nothing you could think about; it was something you had to feel, as it gradually arose. Though she is a registered Paint, her mother was a pitch black Thoroughbred, the stock of race horses. Perhaps from her Thoroughbred genes, she has power—what they called horsepower. Over the years we grew accustomed to each other. We walked, and trotted, and moved with a smooth enough lope. Sometimes, particularly if we were heading up a long upwards slope, I signaled with my legs and posture that she could let loose and run as fast as she wanted. The power would kick in gradually at first, and then suddenly with full force we pounded the earth as I realized why they call it breakneck speed. That could very well happen if I fell off in an unlucky way. Yet even while she runs, I can feel her continued attention to the two-legged animal on her back. She knows I am there. She is showing me the depths of her strength, which feels effortless from my perspective on her back, though beyond any force a human can generate.

I have fallen off, but always in minor jumps she tends to make to the side in a sudden moment of fright. I have never fallen in a full run, knock on wood. Fortunately, the most I have broken are fingers. Though minor, it is dramatic enough to fall off in a field and stand up to see one of your digits at ninety degrees to the others. I ratcheted it back straight. It is still kind of crooked but I like that; it reminds me of riding.

For the first many years in Montana, I was still longing for nature. With less desperation, assuredly, but the steady pull remained. And then gradually it was enough and the mountains and rivers and lakes and animals began to feel a part of me. I never became a mountain man by any means, but reality had shifted into the natural world. One of the gifts of my time in Montana was frequently traveling the state—mostly the western, mountainous part—over the course of fifteen years for work. I came to feel the place inside me, as a whole and as distinct parts. In the early years, we took many trips to Glacier and Yellowstone Parks, including glorious hikes. A handful of Montana camping experiences taught us our lives at home were close enough to camping, including a fire pit in the front yard. So we put away the tent and released the need to worry about bears and food, and, well, just bears. Some day, I keep telling myself, my life will include more extended adventures down rivers and into the wilderness.

As "enough nature" has come into my external life, the pull of the grief has started to shift. It is starting to feel more historical, social and global. It feels like a longing to understand something else, to remember something else. Maybe this involves the loss of tribal community—to feel the loss of connection and the possibilities for remembering connection through the human community as people who belong to nature. Even if shifting, nature remains part of the longing. It remains internal, instinctual. I want to experience all of the intricacies of our ancestry on the planet through my body, inside my body. I would like to ride our collective ancestral memories of life within nature just as I have ridden the paint at full gallop, trusting in what happens.

CHAPTER 5

Holotropic Experience

Writing from the perspective of a mental health professional, Chellis Glendinning recognized the place of grief in recovery from Western civilization. She shared the story of loss and longing told by Carole Roberts, a 45-year-old educator who spent time in Costa Rica, then returned to San Francisco. At some point, living in the jungle, Roberts realized something inside her had changed. She described the experience:

> One morning, sitting on the porch and listening to the chattering of birds and animals, I found myself speaking with a parrot in calls back and forth. It was so natural, at first I didn't know I was doing it. It was as if I was becoming dispersed into the environment, like a hallucinogenic drug experience in which there is a reduction of ego so you can feel a direct experience of other. [150]

When Roberts returned to urban life, rushing to a meeting on a college campus, there came a moment of realization: "everything here was laid out—manicured lawn, little hedges on one side, flowers in boxes—and I burst into tears! I had this sudden, overwhelming flash of loss and longing. Here the presence of life was reduced and controlled in a way that felt unacceptable. I felt, and still feel, deprived."[151]

Grofian Psychology

When Carole Roberts felt her consciousness dispersed into nature—"like a hallucinogenic drug experience"—she was in the territory Stanislav Grof has been exploring for decades. Born in 1931 in Prague, Grof was a child when Hitler's Germany occupied Czechoslovakia. When his country came under Soviet influence after World War II, he was in his teens. Grof trained as a medical doctor within an official atmosphere of Marxist orthodoxy, in which spirituality was viewed as outdated superstition, the opiate of the masses. During his residency in psychiatry, Grof heard about experimental sessions with a chemical recently synthesized in a Swiss laboratory. Albert Hofmann had been working on the properties of ergot, a fungal substance that grows parasitically on rye, once used by midwives to instigate uterine contractions. Hofmann synthesized lysergic acid diethylamide, more commonly known as LSD. While he was working in the laboratory, LSD accidentally entered his bloodstream, evidently through his skin. The rest is history.

In *LSD, My Problem Child: Reflections on Sacred Drugs, Mysticism and Science* Hoffman describes what happened at work on April 16, 1943. After handling LSD, he began to experience "a remarkable restlessness, combined with a slight dizziness." [152] He went home, where he "sank into a not unpleasant intoxicated-like condition, characterized by an extremely stimulated imagination," including "an uninterrupted stream of fantastic pictures, extraordinary shapes with intense, kaleidoscopic play of colors." [153] Three days later, intrigued by this initial experience, Hofmann intentionally ingested LSD, this time leading to frightening perceptions and the sense he might be going insane. As the session continued, the frightening feelings subsided and Hofmann realized LSD opened a door to the deepest realms of the psyche, perhaps even to realities beyond the individual psyche. Subsequent experiments indicated LSD had similar effects as other psychoactive substances, such as mescaline, long used by indigenous peoples in sacred ceremonies.

For as long as he could remember, Hofmann had been interested in extraordinary inner experiences. A childhood encounter with nature stayed with him, perhaps guiding him toward research with substances producing mystical states. As Hofmann recalled, when he was walking on a mountain above Baden, Switzerland, "through the freshly greened woods filled with birdsong and lit up by the morning sun, all at once everything appeared in an uncommonly clear light." [154] He wondered if he had simply failed to notice this before. "Was I suddenly discovering the spring forest as it actually looked? It shone with the most beautiful radiance, speaking to the heart, as though it wanted to encompass me in its majesty." [155] Over the course of his youth, Hofmann experienced several more instances of "indescribable sensations of joy, oneness, and blissful security" in his rambles through nature. [156]

As a research chemist, Hofmann recognized the potential of LSD to evoke visionary states similar to his spontaneous experiences in nature. Even after psychedelics fell into disrepute in the 1960s, Hofmann continued to believe in the healing potential of nonordinary states of consciousness, including heightened emotional connection with nature. Like many others, he felt humanity was facing a deep spiritual crisis. He hoped experiences of nonordinary states of consciousness might point the way "toward a new consciousness of an all-encompassing reality, which embraces the experiencing ego, a reality in which people feel their oneness with animate nature and all creation."[157] After decades of prohibition on LSD research, the healing potential of LSD is again finding documentation through projects such as those sponsored by the Multidisciplinary Association for Psychedelic Studies (MAPS). This includes studies into the value of psychedelics in "treatment of anxiety associated with life-threatening illness, as well as for spiritual uses, creativity, and personal growth."[158]

As a young psychiatrist in Prague, Grof quickly understood the value of LSD in psychotherapy. In addition to working with hundreds of patients using LSD under controlled circumstances, he experimented with the drug himself. It became clear to him these nonordinary states of consciousness opened an inner wisdom, capable of illuminating psychological issues for those who could process them, as well as offering what he later called transpersonal experiences. Integration of the experiences and the psychological insights gained from the experiences was particularly important, which is partially why LSD was problematic as a party drug. With integration and professional support, life-changing psychological shifts could be made.

Grof described his own first experience with LSD in *When the Impossible Happens: Adventures in Non-Ordinary Realities*.[159] Initially, he experienced a rapturous display of "colorful abstract and geometrical visions," which he understood years later as "similar to graphic representations of nonlinear equations that can be produced by modern computers."[160] Then came encounter with his unconscious. Grof described "an intoxicating fugue of emotions, visions, and illuminating insights into my life and existence in general that became available to me on this level of my psyche."[161] Later, when a research assistant introduced a strobe light into his session, Grof "was hit by a vision of light of incredible radiance and supernatural beauty."[162] He felt his consciousness catapulted out of his body, with "no more boundaries or differences between me and the universe."[163]

From this experience, Grof immediately understood consciousness as more primary than matter. Eventually, from his study of various cultures and meeting numerous indigenous healers, Grof realized humanity had always been entering nonordinary states of consciousness for healing and vision, including access to those realms of consciousness beyond the personal sense of self. Various plants found in nature had been used to assist these journeys, as well as techniques such as drumming and forms of breathing. Eastern and indigenous cultures hold many experiential practices for encouraging experiences of the sacred. Western civilization, Grof came to understand, is the aberration in missing this part of human heritage.

The framework for understanding human potential for psychospiritual development, including the potential efficacy of nonordinary states of consciousness, is known as the *holotropic* paradigm within Grofian psychology. Grof coined the word holotropic to suggest an innate human orientation toward psychospiritual growth. Derived from the Greek words *holos* (meaning whole) and *trepein* (meaning moving towards), holotropic means "moving toward wholeness." This usage is similar to the description of plants turning or growing towards the sun captured by the word *heliotropic* as used in plant biology, with *helios* meaning sun in Greek. I like imagining humans naturally moving toward wholeness in the same fashion as some plants growing toward the sun.

Like the Jungian process of individuation, the Grofian holotropic journey is a lifelong process, captured by the "moving toward" aspect of "holotropic." Wholeness is understood as something you can move toward but never fully reach, as there is always something else that arises for inclusion within wholeness. In contrast to the analytical psychology emerging from Jung's work, the holotropic journey envisioned in Grofian psychology tends to focus more on embodied processing through nonordinary states of consciousness and opening to the experience of transpersonal realms. I do not believe Jung would have disagreed with the understandings Grof has articulated—at least not most of them—but Grof has articulated a paradigm based in experiential practices opening a wider range of avenues for the psyche to manifest than are typically included in Jungian work. Grof noted Jungian analysis focuses on more subtle techniques than the many "new powerful experiential approaches" with strong psychosomatic components emerging in the 1960s and beyond. The Grofian model arose from, and provides theoretical context for, psychological work emphasizing "deep, direct experience that has both psychological and actual physical dimensions."[164]

If Jung is considered the grandfather of transpersonal psychology, Grof is one of the founding mothers and fathers. The word *transpersonal* was used only sporadically in some contexts by early American psychologist William James and Jung. Grof proposed the term as the descriptor for the new vision of psychology shared by several theorists and practitioners coming together in northern California in the late 1960s. This group included Abraham Maslow, James Fadiman, Anthony Sutich, Miles Vich, Sonya Margulies, and several others. Together, they realized the spiritual dimension of the human psyche was missing from psychology.[165] As Grof explains:

> The renaissance of interest in Eastern spiritual philosophies, various mystical traditions, meditation, ancient and aboriginal wisdom, as well as the

widespread psychedelic experimentation during the stormy 1960s made it absolutely clear that a comprehensive and cross-culturally valid psychology had to include observations from such areas as mystical states, cosmic consciousness, psychedelic experiences, trance phenomenon, creativity, and religious, artistic, and scientific inspiration.[166]

This was the framework to which I gravitated after various experiences began to emerge in my early and middle thirties. The experiences bringing me to transpersonal studies could be called spiritual emergency, a phrase used by Stan and Christina Grof to describe "crises of the evolution of consciousness . . . comparable to the states described by the various mystical traditions of the world."[167] As Stan Grof explains, "this term is a play on words reflecting the similarity between the word 'emergency' (a suddenly appearing acute crisis) and 'emergence' (surfacing or rising). It thus suggests both a problem and opportunity to rise to a higher level of psychological functioning and spiritual awareness."[168] From a mainstream perspective, spiritual emergency may be understood as "a form of identity crisis where an individual experiences drastic changes to their meaning system (i.e., their unique purposes, goals, values, attitude and beliefs, identity, and focus) typically because of a spontaneous spiritual experience."[169]

My experience of the rain shared in the opening of this book was a particularly poignant entry point for me into emerging grief in response to nature. But that experience was only one among many experiences pulling me into a different way of understanding myself and the universe in which I am situated. Some of my early experiences were not unlike those described by Hofmann and Grof as offered through LSD, but came to me spontaneously or as the result of "energy work" offered by various people coming into my life. By "energy work," I mean intentional practices based on experiencing universal or life energies associated with psychological or spiritual development. That work has not been a large part of my personal growth, but was important in the early years. Once I was on the path offered by these experiences, the holotropic model became the central framework through which I understood what was happening in my life. As noted previously, an experiential practice developed by Stan and Christina Grof, called Holotropic Breathwork, has become an important part of my work both personally and professionally.

After describing Holotropic Breathwork, including my initial experience in breathwork, the remainder of this chapter turns to some of the most important understandings within Grofian psychology. This includes the "cartography of the psyche" articulated by Grof, including what are known as the Birth Perinatal Matrices (BPMs) and Grof's description of systems of condensed experiences, abbreviated as COEXs, a way of understanding the interrelationship of manifestations in experiential processing as well as life unfolding. Reference to these understandings helps me explore some of the ways deep internal connection with nature arises through psychosomatic work involving nonordinary states of consciousness. The Grofian framework is particularly relevant to moving into and through grief in response to nature because the recovery of nature through grief is ultimately a matter of deeply personal inner experience arising through the body.

In my own life, an enormous amount of grief involving the loss of nature came into my awareness and was processed through my body and emotions in the course of Holotropic Breathwork over the last two decades, most importantly during the last eight years. Through these experiences, I came to understand that humans, and all the other life forms on the planet, are intertwined in a way that feels sacred. All of the natural world is not just out there, but is inside us. My experience has been that loss of this internal feeling of nature represents an unprocessed wound (understandable as a COEX) impacting many of us individually as well as our emerging global culture as a whole. When the loss of this internal sense of the sacred in nature is remembered, grief tends to emerge for many people, similar to the experience of Carol Roberts bursting into tears when she remembered the ease that had led her spontaneously to call back and forth with a tropical bird, an experience she contrasted to her experience of the manicured nature of city life.

Holotropic Breathwork

After his initial work with nonordinary states of consciousness in Czechoslovakia, Grof embarked on a long career he describes as the "systematic exploration of the therapeutic, transformative, and evolutionary potential of these states."[170] Moving to the United States in 1967, he continued psychedelic research as Assistant Professor of Psychiatry at Johns Hopkins University School of Medicine in Baltimore, then as Chief of Psychiatric Research at the Maryland Psychiatric Research Center. In 1973, after LSD research was halted by the United States government, Grof was invited to the Esalen Institute in Big Sur, California, where he was Scholar-in-Residence until 1987. There, he and Christina developed Holotropic Breathwork as a natural means for inducing nonordinary states.

The Grof Transpersonal Training (GTT) program describes Holotropic Breathwork as "a powerful approach to self-exploration and healing that integrates insights from modern consciousness research, anthropology, various depth psychologies, transpersonal psychology, Eastern spiritual practices, and mystical traditions of the world." [171] As described by GTT, Holotropic Breathwork "combines accelerated breathing with evocative music in a special set and setting. With the eyes closed and lying on a mat, each person uses their own breath and the music in the room to enter a non-ordinary state of consciousness."[172] This activates an "inner healing process of the individual's psyche," bringing a particular set of internal and/or embodied experiences.[173]

Holotropic Breathwork is typically experienced in sessions lasting two to three hours. Trained facilitators and a "sitter" or "breathing partner" provide support and assistance when requested. An important principle within Holotropic Breathwork is recognition that only the breather is an expert on the experience he or she is having. Facilitators trained in Holotropic Breathwork or those who have studied Grofian psychology will likely have seen or heard of similar experiences previously, but there is a fundamental practice of "not knowing" that protects the freedom of breathers to have their processes emerge as they emerge without interpretation or shaping by anyone else.

In this way, Holotropic Breathwork differs from other modalities—for instance the shiatsu bodywork described by Dana in Chapter 2—in which a facilitator, healer, body worker, therapist, or shamanic practitioner has training or forms an idea about what might assist the individual and takes action on that basis. Other than as requested by the breather, or in order to keep the breather safely on the mat, the holotropic paradigm respects the autonomy and wisdom of the individual's "inner healer." The boundary on non-interference is held even if a sitter or facilitator experiences a strong intuition of an appropriate action or has been trained in another system to provide certain interventions in certain observed or intuited circumstances. Experiencing the urge to intervene or "help" when you are a sitter or facilitator is common. Resisting these urges to become part of someone else's process without invitation or necessity becomes a psychological and spiritual growth process of its own.

Integration of experiences is considered essential, with group settings provided for sharing experiences without interpretation or analysis from others. Breathers are encouraged to document and bring forth their experiences into material form through writing or creation of mandalas (art work within a circle) with art materials or magazine cutouts. Many, but not all, people report a sense of deep and lasting transformation from experiences in breathwork. Fashion designer Eileen Fisher recently described breathwork in an interview for an article in the New Yorker magazine: "You lie on the floor breathing in a specific way, a kind of heavy breathing that gets you into a sort of dream state. You go through all this stuff and let it go. It's like thirty years of therapy in an hour."[174] After experiencing Holotropic Breathwork, Father Amirtharaj Arockiyam, a Salacian priest teaching at the Don Bosco Theological Centre in Panpakkam, India, remarked: "This is a deeply spiritual practice, leading us beyond the level of dogmas and doctrines of organized religions; as such it could transform the world."

While no two Holotropic Breathwork experiences are completely identical, individuals breathing over numerous sessions often experience recurring themes and successive opening or release of internal energies associated with various parts of the physical body. Over the years, my experiences in Holotropic Breathwork have tended to focus for periods of months or years on particular areas of my body and the felt-sense of energies clearing in or through those areas. Sometimes involvement of a part of my body or sensations or movements in a part of the body is fleeting and does not return; other times an opening in a part of the body remains a theme for months or even years.

Though not the case for everyone, these areas of my body have generally corresponded to the chakras of the energetic body noted in Eastern practices and spiritual understandings. Images, memories, and emotions have typically arisen that make sense to me in association with the qualities and experiences of those particular chakras as I have come to understand them through other teachings. Developments in my life, both as lived externally and psychologically, have seemed to parallel these physical sensations of opening, which seem to spiral through and among various energetic centers. This is consistent with the understanding of patterns of psychospiritual growth and processing described by Hillevi Ruumet in *Pathways of the Soul: Exploring the Human Journey*.[175]

The holotropic paradigm discourages an overlay of the chakra or any system over experiences in Holotropic breathwork, consistent with the fundamental principle that only breathers interpret and find meaning in their own experiences. None of my descriptions of my own experiences in breathwork, or my understanding or interpretation of them, should be considered prescriptive or even typical, as a main principle of holotropic work, as noted, involves the freedom of every person to bring forth their own experiences. Indeed, for many of us, Holotropic Breathwork functions in part to release the hold other people's experiences and understandings have on us. Nevertheless, Grofian psychology includes, as set forth later in this chapter, a "cartography of the psyche" indicating the types of experiences many people tend to have in nonordinary states of consciousness. This map of nonordinary experiential states grew from Grof's observations of commonalities in experiences across thousands of experiential sessions, not from any particular preformed theoretical system.

In any work with nonordinary states of consciousness, experiences differ between people and between the sessions of any one person. Some experiences are more visual, others more physical or emotional. Some experiences feel more important or life-changing than others. Some experiences feel like "breakthroughs," while others feel challenging, like facing demons or reliving difficult experiences. There can be periods of "feeling stuck" and learning to recognize and work through such feeling states can be life-changing. From a Jungian perspective, breathwork provides an opportunity for emergence of shadow material, both from the individual biographical life and from our collective histories. In contrast to Jungian modalities, such as dream work or active imagination, nonordinary states of consciousness emerging through Holotropic Breathwork facilitate experience of psychospiritual material through the body, emotions, and visual experiences, so the shadow has more modalities for expression. Repressed experiences often seem to emerge through these non-linguistic and non-rational channels.

Marina Smirnova conducted research into "dreadful manifestations of the sacred" within Holotropic Breathwork. Analogous to experiences of a collective or transpersonal shadow, these experiences illuminate the dark side of reaching into the transpersonal realm or collective unconscious. Smirnova defined dreadful manifestations of the sacred as "fierce, tempestuous, shuddering, seemingly sacrilegious, or otherwise unfathomable, yet profoundly enrapturing, complex and wholesome, life- and death-giving expressions of the sacred that evoke a feeling of dread and awe."[176] Drawing on the work of Rudolf Otto, Smirnova explains:

> While dread as a feeling "may indeed be so overwhelmingly great that it seems to penetrate to the very marrow, making the man's hair bristle and his limbs quake," a combination of dread and awe, in Otto's terms, is "blending of appalling frightfulness and most exalted holiness."[177]

From discussions with nine people reporting such experiences, Smirnova developed an understanding of "atonement" with dreadful manifestations of the sacred through nonordinary state experience. The "dreadful" aspects of the sacred, for these people, contained "fragmented and alienated experiential realities imbued with pain, judgment, stigma, or taboo."[178] These experiences were understood as "a potential catalyst of the embodied experience of the Self/God-image, which is summarized as one's deepest identity rooted in the sacred and a healing agent that bestows relational symbiosis and conscious wholeness."[179] Through accommodation of these experiences into their sense of themselves—a process which happened through experiences of the body, emotions, and visions—these breathers reported a "sense of psychospiritual healing, transformation, and conscious wholeness."[180]

Many people report a "working through" or integration of difficult or traumatic life experiences during sessions of Holotropic Breathwork. Insights or understanding of life events or relationships are common. Often these understandings involve deep compassion in the sense of feeling into the emotional or bodily experience involved. Sometimes what feels like biographical material is "worked through" symbolically through images or somatic or emotional experience having no direct analytical correlation to the biographical incident, yet the breather feels an existing, and sometimes long-standing, biographical issue has been raised and resolved, at least to some extent. Grof observes the residual effects of difficult, even traumatic, experiences tend to dissipate, perhaps even disappear, if the energy produced by embodied consciousness matches the intensity of an original incompletely processed experience.

In *Waking the Tiger: Healing Trauma*, Peter Levine describes trauma as becoming stuck in the immobility response, which he considers the only alternative mammals and reptiles have to fight or flight. [181] In the wilds, if an animal is unable to fight or flee, it freezes, which may preserve its life if the attacker believes it has become non-threatening or has already died. If the animal survives, it eventually completes the process started by the nervous system by then fighting or fleeing. In our human case, Levine believes we find ourselves in situations where fighting or fleeing is either impossible or judged improper by our civilized brain, but we never become able to complete the process. Levine believes traumatic symptoms are not all caused by recollection of the triggering event, but "stem from the frozen residue of energy that has not been resolved and discharged; this residue remains trapped in the nervous system where it can wreak havoc on our bodies and spirits." [182] In his view, the persistent and disabling symptoms of post-traumatic stress disorder (PTSD) "develop when we cannot complete the process of moving in, through and out of the 'immobility' or 'freezing' state." [183]

For many people, nonordinary states of consciousness, introduced by Holotropic Breathwork or other modalities, offer a clearing of that which is holding us back from "unfreezing" with respect to traumatic experiences. This clearing also permits emergence into embodied consciousness of joyful and loving experiences or any other experience existing in the near or far reaches of our psyches. That which invites us toward wholeness offers into awareness—whether through images, emotions, or somatic experience—that which allows us to process and move through frozen experiences and also move into the next experiences that may assist us in our holotropic growth. Quite often I have experienced a feeling state or way of "being" during Holotropic Breathwork that was not previously in my repertoire—such as, for instance, complete equanimity or self-confidence—that I am able to remember in an embodied sense and then draw on during unfolding life.

Trauma is rampant in our techno-industrial world, not just from the suffering experienced by individuals in response to actions from family members or strangers, but from the underlying social experience, including violence within nations and wars between them. Trauma may arise even from the difficulties in finding employment, affording healthcare, or understanding how to create a meaningful life. There is much in our culture that leads to frozen rage or fear for many of us. There is also much in our culture that seems to circumscribe our easy experience of joy, connection, and the sacred. Deep embodied connection with nature is one of the experiences many of us now have difficulty accessing. As we shall discuss in more depth later in this book, despair and anger at the destruction of nature by humanity seems to lurk beneath the surface for many of us. I believe most of us are frozen to this trauma.

At the risk of oversimplifying the enormous range of experiences offered through nonordinary states of consciousness, I will say that there are two frames with which I look at my experiences. One frame notices the way in which experiences open and transform the frame of reference I bring to life and being. This involves how I hold and understand the world and what is possible for me and others in the world. The second frame notices the elements of nonordinary state experiences that seem to involve a more particular processing of particular wounds, needs, or desires that seem to be lodged in my body-mind-spirit.

In the sixties and seventies, people talked about an experience that would "blow your mind"—after which nothing was the same because your sense of self and the universe had changed. Once the mind is "blown," then it becomes easier to move away from the existing narratives, conceptualizations and categorizations—including the elements of consensus trance or persona—that have been holding us back from processing our way through that which is frozen or not yet experienced. In the next section, I describe an initial experience in breathwork that set the stage for many subsequent experiences, helping create the framework that would eventually hold a deep experiential understanding that I am nature and nature is me.

Rocket Man

In the autumn of 1995, on the carpeted floor of a living room in Palo Alto, still not knowing what to expect even after an explanation about the breathwork process, I lay there next to a friend, my eyes closed behind an eye mask. Loud, driving music began pounding from huge speakers behind me. As instructed, I started to breathe deeply, in a circular fashion, no space between breaths. Within minutes, my body went rigid and I felt stuck, unable to move. Then images presented themselves like images in a dream but with emotions more intact, more like memory. I seemed to be experiencing rapidly successive births and deaths. The deaths were more specific than the births, though they flashed by rapidly. The births were more about going rigid in my body, feeling trapped, unable to move. After I was "born," there would be a relaxation of my body, more images, and then more rigidity, like thousands of minute spasms I could not feel, holding me tight, freezing me, all accompanied by relentless images.

The birth and death cycle felt endless, with many of the deaths violent, but interspersed at least once or twice with what felt like hovering near what felt like God. That was an experience of complete understanding and seeming access to infinite knowledge—and yet within an experiential place where knowledge did not matter; it simply was. I did not want to leave that place, and I seemed to remember and long for it "between lifetimes," and yet I was repeatedly sent back into embodied form, into embodied experience, into rigidity. Moments after a new rigidity gripped my body there were flashes of what felt like recollection of death experiences. There seemed countless ways to die violently, through accidents, as food for predators, through being murdered. I was shocked at the number of sudden, surprising deaths. You think you have just taken a bad tumble and then, surprise, you are dead. There was one death in which I was struck on the back of the head with a stone—a recollection which has stayed with me in an embodied way, such that sometimes I want to turn around and make sure no one is coming up on me.

There were few ends of life that seemed peaceful, maybe because a soul tends to forget peaceful deaths. I remember only one extended death scene, exquisitely and preciously peaceful, seeming to culminate a lifetime lasting into old age. I was lying on a bed in a large room, surrounded by a dozen or so family members and friends who loved me. Their love was palpable, as was their grief that I was dying. The love and the grief were the same thing. There was a sense of a life well-lived, manifested in the love of the people around me. I think of that experience very often, probably every day for nearly twenty years. It pulls me forward in this lifetime, in a way that could be described as teleological. If I get to that moment again, then whatever all this has been in this lifetime, it was worthwhile. Lest anyone mistake me, this does not mean I try to be good, perhaps to the contrary. It means I try to fulfill being me.[184]

There was something about this initial breathwork which taught me that grief was an entry point, a companion. The transpersonal element of grief in this first breathwork experience focused on my loss of the sense of hovering near God in between lifetimes. It hurt to be sent back into a rigid body; it was a shock, experientially violent. There was grief from being pulled away from God, yet there was the sense that God had done the pulling—not God as a person but as a force, perhaps better described as karma, inevitability, continuation of an inevitable process. As I remember the experience all these years later, I notice a strong element of confusion, even dissociation. Why was this happening? What had I done? I had no sense of any particular sins or wrongdoing. I seemed to be just living a succession of ordinary lives. The consequence was some brief moment of peace, then being once again stuck in a rigid body, wriggling down the carpet on the floor of a living room in Palo Alto, perhaps an echo of struggling to be born. Then my body went lax, some images of death, and it all happened again.

From the beginning, nature was part of my experience in Holotropic Breathwork because so much of my experience involved images of living (and dying) in times when we were immersed in nature. Nature was not something separate from us, but was the context in which we existed. Initially, I was more taken with the aspects of experience seeming to bring me into contact with energies or realms other than the earthly plane, as exemplified by the experience of "hovering between lifetimes" described above. This was also my initial orientation to other "spiritual emergency" experiences, a fascination with experiences that seemed to suggest we have access to realms or means of communication outside the scope recognized by materialist science. It was not exactly that I believed in the literal factual reality of any particular experience, as part of what happens with these experiences, at least for me, involves reaching a place where you are not concerned with the literal reality of images, but understand their emergence from a fundamental realm of connected consciousness that feels experientially more real than the physical world.

Working with the buzz of these experiences was difficult but eventually I got used to it, more or less. Without a doubt, I have never been the same. It is not easy getting used to being a rocket man—and the journey can be solitary, lonely. Elton John sings about another kind of *Rocket Man* but the idea feels the same: "And I think it's gonna be a long long time, Till touchdown brings me round again to find, I'm not the man they think I am at home, Oh no, no, no, I'm a rocket man, Rocket man burning out his fuse up here alone."[185] Fortunately, eventually you find even Rocket man can come back to earth. This is when nature really seems to help.

Nature through the Inside

Over time, the accessibility of what felt like transpersonal realms became an experiential given for me, and my orientation moved into experience of the sacred within nature. I began to research experiences of grief, weeping and other deep emotions in response to nature. We moved to Montana. The reality of living an American life continued, including in 2006 a demanding transition in my work life as my wife and I began a law firm. Wanting a way to process the stress, I thought of Holotropic Breathwork. There was a group in Seattle offering breathwork, but I thought of Calgary, Canada, a seven-hour drive north of Helena, a short hike in the Montana scheme of things. When I made my Internet search, Carolyn Green and Jane Cooper—both trained through the Grof Transpersonal Training Program—were about to offer their first workshop in Calgary. I registered.

As similar as Canada is to the United States, I liked the idea of a journey to a different country for breathwork. Later I realized the journey reminded me of ancient times when humans would travel long distances for spiritual gatherings often involving nonordinary states of consciousness. Albeit on twenty-first century North American highways in my Subaru, I was following an archetypal pattern instigating an inner journey with an outer one. I drove up to Calgary on a Friday, the first of many such drives over the next several years. You travel mostly through prairie, with the mountains of Glacier National Park, and its Canadian sister, Waterton Lakes National park, rising on the horizon to your left. Then you reach the border and some excitement about how you are going to explain why you are going to Canada. "I'm going for a Holotropic Breathwork experience" leads to a blank stare mixed with suspicion. You certainly do not want to start talking about a nonordinary state of consciousness "like with LSD." I have arrived at "breathwork, think of it like a cross between meditation and yoga." I leave the "on steroids" unstated.

At some point I realized there was something practically nonordinary about leaving Montana. Having come to this nearly empty northern border state from California, I realized I had been thinking I had gone so far north there was no one left. I assumed more or less unconsciously I had reached the edge of the earth: seemingly endless open space; fewer than a million people in the fourth largest state geographically; one area code for the whole state (so if you see t-shirts or bumper stickers reading *406*, you will know you have encountered someone from Montana—*406* is something like a secret handshake). Then I drove into Calgary and thought I was back in San Jose, California.

Calgary is a large city thriving on commerce from Alberta's rich oil and gas fields, with relentless strip malls, subdivisions, and a glimmering new downtown. I put myself up in a business-class motel, had dinner in the bar, and noticed these people seemed to be experiencing themselves as living in a different country. I made conversation with people who had never been to Montana but had lived in Quebec, Ontario, or British Columbia. These were years when United States politics were hurting my soul, so it was a relief to feel myself somewhere else. In later visits, I stayed closer to downtown and walked around 17th Avenue, feeling a bit like I was in Europe.

On that first trip, on a Saturday morning, after getting just a bit lost, I found the straw bale building where Jane and Carolyn were offering breathwork. I was in a subdivision just off the Trans-Canada Highway heading out of town toward Banff, not far past the ski jumps left over from the 1988 Winter Olympics. Carolyn and Jane were welcoming. I started to relax. After several years in Montana, my outward grief in response to nature had significantly waned, but there was a deeper part, transpersonal and collective as well as personal, I was about to discover.

I am not sure what I expected in that first Canadian breathwork—maybe release of some anxiety and anger involving stress. Then I started to breathe and immediately tapped into a well of grief that took years to cry out. This grief was different in that it started from images and experiences inside me, but involved the same longing for wholeness within nature. I was back to that deep grief for what had been lost, described in my response to the rain, but experienced even more intensely given the enhanced state of consciousness with the breathwork. Also heightened and extended were the awe and gratitude for an internal connection with nature, a life-changing sense of the sacred all around me in the natural world—all of it making me weep through many sessions.

One of my first experiences in Calgary breathwork involved the motion in my body when on the back of my galloping horse. I found myself moving my hips, and my whole body, with the simulated motion of a hard ride. After a bit of this, I wept. Maybe I was processing emotionally what I had come to experience on the back of a horse. Maybe my body, mind, emotions, and soul were coming together in experience of the gallop. Later I came to the metaphor of riding our ancestral history, taking it back into my body and emotions. Many of my experiences in breathwork in the next few years felt as though I was remembering how it was to live enmeshed with nature, as nature. I had come a long way with my animal friends on the ranchette and my love affair with the mountains, snow, and wild animals that ventured around us. But this now in breathwork was internal, outside present time, yet eternal in the way that the cycles of nature feel eternal. While outside of present time, all these experiences of grief in recollection of intimate connection with nature were occurring within a context of my contemporary knowledge of the precarious state of the environment and the world.

Renewed involvement with Holotropic Breathwork rekindled my interest in Grofian psychology. The "cartography of the human psyche" developed by Grof formed the background for understanding experiences in breathwork. This map of the potential reaches of consciousness describes the terrain people typically encounter as their inner healer moves them— usually gradually, over a period of years—toward an experiential wholeness. Knowing the terrain can be useful in the way that any map makes it easier to understand where we are and where we might be going. The Grofian cartography of the human psyche includes not only our biographical memories since childhood, but also perinatal (in utero) memories, as well as access to transpersonal domains. During experiential work, there is not necessarily any delineation between such experiences, but it can be helpful later to place them in context.

One of the criticisms directed toward Grofian psychology and the experiential modality of Holotropic Breathwork is that the Grofian system of understanding conditions people to have certain experiences. That is a fair criticism from the perspective of seeking proof of the reality of these experiences as something other than simply experiences that are emerging. Seeking that kind of proof has never been of much interest to me, though I am deeply interested in the healing potential of holotropic work. It has never felt to me that understanding the cartography of the psyche developed by Grof has done anything more than deepen my understanding of the healing potential of experiences arising through me, in the same way that coming to understand dream symbolism deepens the healing potential of working with dreams. Because biographical experiences are self-explanatory (memories, catharsis from processing life trauma, developing compassion for ourselves and people in our life), we turn to the initially strange terrain of perinatal experiences. We will return to transpersonal experiences in the discussion of COEXs and the sharing of some of my experiences as illustration of emergence of an internal experience of the natural world.

Perinatal Experiences

Experiences that seem to reflect the process or stages of birth may appear in nonordinary states of consciousness in a variety of ways, including literally as memories; through the emergence of emotional reactions repressed during birth; as embodied processes (for instance, re-enacted birth through body sensations or urges toward movement that may be carried out with assistance from facilitators); or symbolically through images or narratives metaphorically suggesting aspects of the birth process and associated meanings. Repressed energy related to the trauma of birth may be released through any of the means through which process emerges in nonordinary states: emotions, physical sensations, symbolic or literal images, movements or postures.

"Going into a birth process" during breathwork happens to me often enough, not because I am thinking about or imagining it, but because I follow what seems to be emerging in my body. One of the typical ways I enter into the process is through experiencing a need for pressure on my head. I will start pressing on my head and then often my sitter or a facilitator will offer to put pressure and I will accept. Often enough, this then turns into a situation where on the mat my body feels as though it is being born and wants pressure in certain places and movement, then a sense of release. None of this is an idea or an intention. It is more like an emerging urge to feel pressure and containment, and then slow release of that pressure and containment as part of moving along the floor or through a cave of pillows or bodies constructed to assist me in the process.

Following this process frequently leads to understandings, memories, and catharses relating to whatever issues seem to be up for resolution or understanding. Usually these are not necessarily directly or solely related to birth or birth trauma. For instance, I remember more than one "birth experience" involving my realizing, and feeling, that my children are growing up and need less involvement from me in their lives. This "realization" is not just an idea but includes a range of emotions including grief and joy, and reflects back into experiences in my own family of origin. After one such process in Calgary, I ended up sitting up on a cushion cradling a pillow remembering viscerally what it was like to hold my children as infants. That feeling compared to their "being" as teenagers was held together emotionally. Obviously, I was weeping. I believe very deeply that having this experience allowed me to begin letting them develop their own lives with less interference from me than might otherwise have occurred.

This is the way in which I understand, from a breather's perspective, Grof's observation that perinatal experiences are a doorway to healing and the transpersonal. Transpersonal experiences or understandings in particular tend to open up through "birth experiences." In my example of experience arising involving my children, images and emotions followed one another involving a feeling of my own birth, a feeling of the birth of my children, a sense of all children being born, and all mothers giving birth, such that the biographical, perinatal, and transpersonal are intertwined. Deep compassion and connection with all of us develops. One realizes, and feels, that all of us animals start out helpless through a messy process of birth. Not just humans, all animals, all nature. Envisioning our younger goats sliding out from their mother Chloe is an image that comes to me often enough in these experiences.

Appearance of the perinatal in nonordinary experiences (initiated by psychedelics or Holotropic Breathwork) was not something anyone thought up or taught, but simply something that appeared repeatedly in the experiences of people in these states. Grof noticed and sought to understand. While no systematic documentation exists to my knowledge, there are anecdotal reports from people who have re-experienced some aspect of uterine or birth trauma during breathwork or psychedelics, and later confirmed with their parents the historical accuracy of the details they experienced. The possibility of remembering birth is not generally accepted by the mainstream medical field. But well before I studied transpersonal psychology or experienced breathwork, my son Max, when he was approximately two and one-half years old, said something to me demonstrating he remembered his birth.

When Max was born, my wife's later stages of labor were halted by the hospital staff because she was suddenly ready to deliver—much quicker than they anticipated—and no obstetrician on call could be found in the hospital. For what seemed like close to an hour, she was instructed by the nurses not to push, though contractions were hard and Max was in the birth canal. Unfortunately, at the time, I did not have the wherewithal to challenge the instructions for my wife not to push. When he was born, Max had a large bruise on one side of his forehead. He was rushed to a neonatal unit and then eventually returned to us. Two and a half years later, my wife was nearing the time for the birth of our second child. Little Max was standing in the kitchen and I thought to prepare him for what was about to happen. I said something like, "Max, soon Mommy will go the hospital for the baby to be born."

Max said, "That *hurts.*"

Assuming he was talking about his mom and the labor, I said, "Mommy will be fine; it will be okay."

Putting his hand to his forehead, to the spot where he was bruised during birth, he said, "No, not *mom,* it hurts the baby." I am certain no one had ever talked to Max about his birth. There would be no reason for anyone to tell him he was born with a bruise on that part of his head. More importantly, his matter-of-fact demeanor left me no doubt he was remembering his birth. Within a few years, he would neither remember making this comment nor anything about being born.

I do not have conscious perinatal memories or memories of my biographical birth other than what seems to arise in nonordinary states as a "process" mirroring birth. But I believe there are aspects of my birth that linger with me. I have noticed that when I reach a certain point in breathwork—particularly during what feels like an embodied process to recover, release, or open energy in my body—my energy (focused will power is another word for how this feels) rises to meet the challenge and then I will suddenly collapse and stop. I have come to associate this, in part, with the pain-killing gas given to my mother during my birth. Like many women delivering babies during the 1950s and 1960s, my mother had a gas, almost certainly nitrous oxide, available to her in order to ease the pain of giving birth. My mother recalled something attached to her wrist from which she could take a whiff and knock herself out. She apparently did this frequently, presumably knocking me out as well, given transfer to me through her bloodstream and the umbilical cord.

As I imagine into this experience from my perspective as an infant being born, it feels as though I am marshaling energy to meet the challenge of staying present to the contractions pushing me out of the birth canal, but then suddenly lose the ability to be present to what is emerging. In my case, this feels less like memory and more like imagination put together from information and the physical sensation of going slack at challenging moments in embodied process. In analogy, or in reenactment, during breathwork, as I am trying to stay present to the energy rising within me, I feel myself wanting to stay with the rising energy, but then I suddenly "lose it" into a collapse of my body and an experience of mental-emotional dissociation from the felt-sense of what is arising.

Putting this into the context of Levine's model of stored trauma from a frozen response, if I was unable as an infant being born to stay present and responsive to the pressure of the contractions on me, there may be something unfinished about an ability to stay present and responsive to difficult pressure in life. Levine's model involves times when we have spontaneously frozen rather than moved into a fight or flight response; my example from birth involves losing consciousness as the result of an anesthetic, perhaps dulling me from being able to fully experience an imprinting of "fight." In terms of how the experience presents itself to me, there was something unfinished in my meeting the birth process; the movement toward wholeness offered to me in breathwork brought me to the place where I could try to stay present to something emerging within me; the resolution would involve finding a way to remain present (and willful) through what feels like an internalized collapse under pressure. This is a work in progress.

Some have wondered whether the drug and alcohol tendencies of my generation are linked to the provision of medications to delivering mothers during labor. In a series of studies, Swedish researchers concluded that children born to mothers using pain-relieving drugs in labor, when compared to children not so exposed, were significantly more likely to have challenges with drug addiction.[186] One study, focusing on use of nitrous oxide during labor, indicated that children born in this process were 5.5 times more likely to become amphetamine addicts than brothers or sisters born to the same parents without use of laughing gas.[187] Although I find such studies generally helpful in understanding my experience, I am not arguing for the literal truth of a correlation between experience and behavior in adults born in the midst of nitrous oxide and what was likely experienced as an infant in the birth process. Rather, the nitrous oxide narrative serves as an illustration of how perinatal memories, particularly as stored in the body, may appear in breathwork, reverberate with life issues, and offer resolution of unfinished experience.

When first encountered, the emphasis on perinatal experience in Grofian psychology may seem excessive. This may be one area in which Jung would have disagreed with Grof. As Jung observed in his 1957 interview with Richard Evans, birth is "an event that happens to everybody that exists."[188] Given the universality of birth, Jung refused to consider "birth trauma" as having a profound effect on individual human psychology as had been postulated by psychologist Otto Rank, another one-time member of the Freud contingent. Jung took this position because he thought there was no way to develop a base of knowledge about the psychology of people who had *not* experienced birth, since everyone has been born. Jung said to Evans in the interview:

> Don't you see, this is an event that happens to everybody that exists—that each man once has been born. Everybody who is born has undergone that trauma, so the word has lost its meaning. It is a general fact, and you cannot say "it is a trauma"; it is just a fact, because you cannot observe a psychology that hasn't been born—only then you could say what the birth trauma is. Until then, you cannot even speak of such a thing; it is just a lack of epistemology.[189]

Yet it does not follow that each birth is the same, so it is possible to develop objective knowledge about the relationship between different experiences during birth and different psychological experiences throughout the lifetime. As Grof has pointed out, it is strange that mainstream psychology accepts that particular experiences during infancy have a deep impact on individual psychology yet excludes the possibility that particular experiences during birth or in utero impact individual psychology. There is also the interesting question of whether our human births, which are collectively difficult since we developed large brains in relation to women's pelvic bones, impact our collective psychologies and ways of being. It is possible that the common experience of struggle and trauma during birth impacts us collectively—that we are as a species continuing to struggle in reflection of the struggle we have to be born. The more experience I have in Holotropic Breathwork, the more profound becomes my understanding of the psychological and spiritual impact of the usually unconscious influences of perinatal experience, so we turn to articulation of the stages of birth recognized in Grofian psychology.

The Birth Perinatal Matrices

Within the perinatal realm are four stages of the birth process identified by Grof, called the Birth Perinatal Matrices (BPMs). These involve:

BPM I—a sense of oceanic oneness we tend to experience in the womb prior to the onset of contractions, absent various toxic possibilities;

BPM II—the experience of no-exit angst and depression when contractions have begun, but the mother's cervix has not yet dilated;

BPM III—the life-or-death struggle we tend to experience when moving through the birth canal; and

BPM VI—the sense of arrival, accomplishment, success, and liberation we may experience upon birth, full of exhilarating possibilities.[190]

Impossible to describe fully with simple phrases, the attributes and associations of the BPMs are complex and subtle, reaching into all life experiences. Similar to the way any one experience of grief may feel layered with many experiences of grief, any particular experience within nonordinary consciousness—or, for that matter, within life—may feel associated to other experiences, with a BPM serving as an experiential or imaginal container for the association among experiences. Periods of life may seem to make sense in the context of a particular Birth Perinatal Matrix. For instance, we may endure a period of months or years when life circumstances seem to hold us in a pressured grip without movement, corresponding to BPM II; and then we may suddenly experience release from a stagnant period, corresponding to BPM IV.

The BPMs may also describe the energetic nature of some embodied processes enacted by people in breathwork. A breather may, for instance, experience a dullness of emotion, even a sense of inability to have emotion, and yet feel a constricting sense of judgment, punishment, failure or rejection. As with some people who begin to feel suicidal in life, there may seem "no way out" of the situation, as though no future with any sense of vibrancy is possible. Images or memories of experiences in nature may accompany the experience, such as being swallowed by a snake and stuck inside or trapped in a bleak winter or oppressive heat with no escape. The room in which one is breathing may start to feel excessively hot or cold with no possibility of finding a comfortable temperature.

Intellectual understanding is rarely enough to move fully into and through such experiences. But going with such experiences as an embodied process if they arise during a nonordinary state may prove useful in breaking free of patterns that may exist in life as well as on the breathwork mat. In further working with the experiences, for instances in artwork or movement practice, an association of the experience with the constriction of BPM II, when uterine contractions exist but there seems no way to move, may arise. How we experience ourselves in nature may then also change, opening a form of dialogue between inner and outer, including nature. There may be memories of times in nature (or at the same period of life actual experiences) involving a sense of alienation or hopelessness, such as looking into a dark night sky or the endless ocean. All of this may resonate with BPM II. If there is an unrelenting or non-moving sense of grief in response to nature, this might resonate with this second perinatal matrix.

Returning to the struggle of birth experience, understood as reflected in BPM III, there have been numerous times in breathwork when I have experienced such a struggle. Sometimes this appears as a reenactment of birth and sometimes as a desire to enact aggression within constriction or have aggression enacted on me within constriction. I have had numerous images or internal experiences during breathwork that have involved "scenes" of violence or struggle within nature, typically leading to an acceptance that this is part of nature. This is hard to convey in words, but understanding and accepting this and feeling experientially the struggle of being born come to be felt as the same thing. As Grof has described in several books, each of the BPM processes may manifest through myriad ways, with each BPM describing a range of experiences enacted in nonordinary states and in life, culture, and nature. The innumerable "internal nature" experiences I have had reflective of BPMs have worked to imprint nature more deeply within me.

During a breathwork process, none of this feels planned, intended, or thought through. Where intention emerges for me involves putting my attention and will into merging with the emotional, physical, kinesthetic, proprioceptive, or imaginal process that is arising for me. This is very similar to placing my attention on my breath during meditation, and allowing my attention to follow whatever emerges during meditation. This is not the same as becoming lost in head-based thoughts as in listening to chatter, but involves noticing and merging with what seems to arise from other parts of my being. In meditation, I notice and allow what arises to move through in an easy flow. In Holotropic Breathwork, I move my attention (or emotions, or movement, or sensations) fully into a process that has been activated and heightened by the nonordinary state of consciousness generated by breathwork. Then I follow where it leads in my body, emotions, and mind.

In the example of enacted birth, typically Holotropic Breathwork facilitators—on my signal, verbal request, or through the need to keep me in the space of my mat—would provide resistance to my body, with use of pillows and/or their own bodies simulating the experience of resistance or pressure from being surrounded by the birth canal. This heightens and increases the intensity of the experience for me, both in terms of movement and more importantly in terms of the emotions and felt internal sense. Often this moves into a sense of struggle, enacted to some extent externally, but felt intensely in my body and emotions. Associating these experiences to BPM III assists a general sense that I am moving through something, that a new experience of myself is being born. Coming to know this experience as a pattern—valiant struggle in order to be born into a new sense of self—allows me to envision this experience as part of a human archetype, perhaps the archetype sometimes called the heroic journey. This is by no means to reduce the complexity of a heroic journey to the reenactment of a birth process, but rather to suggest that an understanding of Birth Perinatal Matrices may expand into a felt-sense of relationship to life process, even history.

After laying a bit more groundwork in Grofian psychology, we shall notice more generally the ways a practice such as Holotropic Breathwork may become the vehicle for emergence of an internal experience of immersion in nature—of being nature. At this point an example of a BPM IV experience will illustrate what I mean. In breathwork, sometimes after a reenacted birth process or sometimes spontaneously, I will experience a great emotional catharsis, what feels like an acceptance that I am "okay" just as I am, that everything is in place, a deep appreciation for all that is unfolding. The "struggle" has been resolved into "being." Quite often, but not always, this is accompanied by a particular internal image, vivid as a dream, but with more emotional resonance, of standing at the edge of a primitive village, looking out over a jungle, watching the sun rise.

The rising of the sun takes a few moments and provides warmth as well as a growing glow all around me, through me. I know that my village is behind me, that I am awake early before others. I feel the village as a circle of huts around a central campfire. (Note how this resonates with a Jungian conception of Self.) The jungle is vibrant in front of me, dense and mysterious, even dangerous, not in a way to be avoided, but in a way that is realistic. Sometimes there is an elderly dark man who is coming out of the jungle toward me, using a walking stick. He is ancient and wise. He is always awake before me.

I watch the sun rise, experiencing myself as part of nature. I feel the rising sun now as I type these words and my eyes are full of tears. Golden yellow sun rises over deep green of the tree canopy. On the breathwork mat, I weep in gratitude and awe, sometimes held by a sitter or facilitator if they have been part of a birth process, but often alone externally, though accompanied internally by all those in my village and all the animals and jungle in front of me. If not wholeness, this is a reflection of wholeness. BPM IV, the moment of birth and release from struggle, including a sense of liberation and emergence, frames my experience of the rising sun. One of the perks of internal images, deeply felt and permanently held, is the ability to return to them anytime you want. This is how my presence at the sun rise serves me in life when I need it. I can remember the experience and then the sunrise, village, and jungle are experiences inside me, a return to embeddedness in a specific moment of immersion in nature.

Systems of Condensed Experiences (COEXs)

Grof describes *systems of condensed experience* or *COEX systems* as "consisting of many layers of unconscious material that share similar emotions or physical sensations."[191] This concept is similar to, but not identical with, the concept of complexes articulated by Jung. Jungian analyst Barbara Miller succinctly defined a complex as "a structure of the psyche that gathers together similar feeling-toned elements."[192] Like all Jungian concepts, a complex is more a process than a static entity, even when the process becomes entrenched. Miller explained: "Each complex is united by the same emotion and each complex is united and organised by a mutual core of meaning. That is, the complex organises experience, perception, and affect around a constant central theme."[193]

In *Beyond the Brain: Birth, Death and Transcendence in Psychotherapy,* Grof discussed similarities and differences between Jungian complexes and his COEX model.[194] On the biographical level, the concepts are quite similar. Consistent with the general differences in Jungian and Grofian psychology, the COEX model emphasizes a more expansive understanding of manifestations of the psyche, including perinatal experience, a full range of possibilities of psychosomatic processing, and a broader inclusivity of transpersonal elements. With respect to the perinatal dimension, Jungian psychology, as Grof recognized, understands the death-rebirth process as an important archetypal theme. This process is more central in the psychology developed by Grof. From years of observing people in nonordinary states of consciousness, Grof came to understand "perinatal phenomena with their emphasis on birth and death [as] a critical interface between the individual and the transpersonal realms."[195]

Grof describes the layers of the psyche weaving together into a COEX:

> More superficial layers contain memories of emotional or physical traumas from infancy, childhood, and later life. On a deeper level, each COEX system is typically connected to a certain aspect of the memory of birth, a specific BPM; the choice of this matrix [by the inner healer] depends on the nature of the emotional and physical feelings involved . . . . The deepest roots of COEX systems underlying emotional and psychosomatic disorders reach into the transpersonal domain of the psyche. They have the form of ancestral, racial, collective and phylogenetic memories, experiences that seem to come from other lifetimes (*past life memories*), and various archetypal motifs.[196]

About the transpersonal domain of the human psyche, where we find the deepest roots of COEX systems, Grof wrote:

> Transpersonal experiences have many strange characteristics that shatter the most fundamental assumptions of materialistic science and the mechanistic world view. Although these experiences occur in the presence of deep individual self-exploration, it is not possible to interpret them simply as intrapsychic phenomena in the conventional sense. On the one hand, they form an experiential continuum with biographical and perinatal experiences. On the other hand, they frequently appear to be tapping directly, without the mediation of sensory organs, sources of information that are clearly outside of the conventionally defined range of the individual.[197]

As Grof wrote, with respect to movement toward the transpersonal, "Experiences of death and rebirth are instrumental in the individual's philosophical dissociation from an exclusive identification with the ego-body unit and with the biological organization."[198] In this regard, it is interesting to note that my own initial experience in breathwork, as described earlier in this chapter, involved the sensation of repeated births and deaths. This experience included images and emotions in my awareness (feeling somewhere between a dream and a recollection), but impacted me on a life-changing level through its physicality, including rigidity and movement in my body. There was a link between death and birth that was palpably physical, unforgettable due to its emergence through my body. This has everything to do with my emerging experience of nature because, in the animal world, the most impressive physical enactments are birth and death. These processes *are* nature: birth and death are what make us inextricable from nature. Birth and death are the life force coming and going through what we call nature. Recognizing this at an experiential, physical level is part of a return to nature.

I understand the experience of loss of nature, including grief in response to nature, as part of a COEX bringing together many elements. For me personally, there are many biographical elements involving nature and grief itself. I touch upon some of the biographical elements later in this chapter, in the next chapter, and throughout this book. This COEX seems to be collective as well as personal. As a species, we have lost nature and there seems to be something felt by many of us calling for a return. I have noted several times the deepest element of grief for me involves loss of an experience of the sacred in nature, such that this COEX, as experienced by myself and I think by many others as well, involves not just loss of nature, but loss of the sacred, and a cultural "forgetting" of how to experience the sacred in nature, including a forgetting (or repression) of our heritage in using nonordinary states of consciousness to contact the sacred, which throughout our heritage has involved nature and her elements. Understanding of this process through the COEX model, which includes a gathering together of many types of experiences, including physical experience, seems particularly appropriate with respect to healing our loss of nature, because it is through the body that we realize our bodies are simultaneously nature and consciousness, as are all the myriad other bodies we find within the natural world, present, past, and future.

Jungian psychology, in the view of Grof, developed quite thoroughly "the dynamics of the archetypes and of the collective unconscious, mythopoetic properties of the psyche, certain types of psychic phenomenon, and synchronistic links between psychological processes and phenomenal reality."[199] Grofian psychology includes heightened "recognition of transpersonal experiences that mediate connection with various aspects of the material world."[200] This includes "authentic identification with other people, animals, plants, or inorganic processes, and experiences of historical, phylogenetic, geophysical, or astronomical events that can mediate access to new information about various aspects of 'objective reality.'"[201] In the next sections of this chapter, we shall explore how these particular types of experiences may provide an existential awareness of oneself as nature. In other words, the identifications referenced by Grof which often accompany nonordinary state experience leave one with experiential knowledge that we *are* nature.

Remembering Ourselves in Nature

Many of my Holotropic Breathwork experiences have felt like embodied memories of moments in a lifetime experienced within nature—deeply embedded in nature physically, psychologically, emotionally, and spiritually. These experiences have included a sense of "being" an animal or, more commonly for me, a sense of being a person living a particular moment in a way of life embedded in nature. As these experiences occurred, they felt real, that is, they felt as though they were actually occurring or had actually occurred, somewhere between internally lived experiences and recollections. Many such experiences have felt more real in some fundamental and authentic sense than occurrences in my actual life in the material world. Nonetheless, it seems more useful—and more honest—for me to hold these experiences as potentially real in an objective sense; even though as they are occurring, I experience them as real, and with respect to the way of being in the world they suggest, or cause me to remember, I interpret them as real.

In discussing the transpersonal domain, Grof notes that "many experiences belonging in this category are interpreted by the subjects as regression in historical time and exploration of their biological or spiritual past."[202] Sometimes, he writes, an individual "has a convinced feeling of reliving memories from the lives of his or her ancestors, or even drawing on the racial and collective unconscious."[203] Some subjects report "experiences in which they identify with various animal ancestors in the evolutionary pedigree or have a distinct feeling of reliving episodes from their existence in a previous incarnation."[204] For example, in *Beyond the Brain*, Grof describes the "fascinating category of transpersonal sexual experiences" involving "full identification with various life forms."[205] Through such experiences, it seems possible to recall the specific sexuality of the life force on the planet as manifested in innumerable species. Grof writes:

> Whether these are other mammals, lower vertebrates, or such invertebrates as insects, mollusks, and coelenterates, these episodes entail the corresponding body image, emotional and other experiential responses, and characteristic behavior sequences. All the sensations involved appear to have a very authentic quality; they are always quite specific and unique for the species in question and typically far beyond what the fantasy of an uninformed person could contrive. Like the experiences of the collective and racial unconscious they frequently mediate a great amount of accurate information that far transcends the educational background and training of the individual involved.[206]

Although without the specificity suggested by these particular experiences, I have felt myself "as" various animals numerous times in breathwork, as have many people. Often I am a bird, flying, looking down at the earth. Once I was a bird of prey attacking a smaller bird in flight and then simultaneously I was the bird being attacked. In a longer experience, I was the raven living around our barn at the time. I wrote earlier about my relationship with ravens emerging in Montana. Within the experience of "being" the raven during this particular breathwork session were woven many actual experiences in my Montana life, felt more vividly in the breathwork session than when lived. This included a deeply felt connection I had created with this particular raven.

One winter the grain in our tack room had become sustenance for a growing population of mice. This was when I was still leaving oats and feed in the fifty-pound paper sacks I bought them in, before I learned to use hard plastic trash cans with lockable lids. The rodents slowly made their presence known. When I was in the barn to throw hay to the horses and goats, the mice would appear as dim swift images in my peripheral vision, or as scurrying noises. I could not face mice eradication in the frigid cold. Consequently, when spring came, there were hundreds of them. I bought traps, the re-useable kind you bait with a scoop of peanut butter. Every morning, I would find one or more dead mice; there were more and more every night over a period of several weeks. I felt badly for the mice I was killing, but mice can bring disease, including deadly Hanta Virus in Montana. Twice daily, I would empty the mice traps in a particular area a few steps from the barn. The remains were always gone the next time I came out. Eventually, I realized I was providing a meal ticket to the raven who by then was frequently sitting on the wood rail fence next to the barn.

In this particular breathwork session, first I was this particular raven sitting on the fence and then I was this raven flying. I felt the area around our land in a vertical as well as horizontal space. I flew over pine trees and roads and looked down at the grids of fences. I came to know a place where I could find small bits of food, mice not yet hard from death or cold. I put my fingers into them and carried them to a tree where I sat and ate their insides. (I write "fingers" because in the breathwork experience, the sense of inserting talons into the mice was an extension from my actual human fingers, so the word "fingers" best conveys the experience.) Gradually, as the raven, I owned this place. It felt good. Interestingly enough, in my actual human life, while my name was on the deed to 25 acres, I had no sense of owning the place. Yet through the raven, including his existence in the three dimensional nature of space, I glimpsed possession and belonging.

As would often happen after I had a visceral, meaningful "experience of nature" in breathwork, as the experience dissipated, I would feel grief and loss and would typically weep. Many hours were spent on a breathwork mat in Calgary, weeping, often with Jane or Carolyn holding me. Sometimes when the weeping subsided I would think about things and come to some understandings. After the experience as the raven, I felt I knew something about the essence of what shamanic types would call "raven," referring to the soul or collectivity of the species raven. There was no Disney-movie relationship with the particular raven living near my barn, and yet I felt as though we were familiar. Maybe I used the word "familiar" in the last sentence in the sense that animals would sometimes be considered the "familiar" of a witch. I do not mean this in a negative or necessarily magical sense, but in the sense of knowing an animal whose wildness may take you into powerful mysterious realms, slightly terrifying if you really open to it, sometimes useful for impacting life in the material world.

With this raven, in real life, I was always glad to see him and I continually hoped he would stay on the ranchette. The next winter, I half regretted putting the grain in hard plastic trash cans, as I would not be raising a crop of mice. When I surmised the raven was the likely cause for the disappearance of the bunny born in our haystack, a bunny who had been adorably hopping around the front yard for a few weeks, I did not hold a grudge. The raven was my friend; he needed to eat. Though I did not dwell on it, there was something about his presence that felt protective. Years later, when we moved out of that particular house, the last thing I moved was the round pen for horse training, which by then was in the large front yard. The round pen was constructed with a series of metal panels chained together into a big circular enclosure. Before I took back the U-Haul we rented, I went back out to the house and loaded the panels. This meant I was taking away a circular structure that by then had been in the front yard for a few years. As I finished loading the panels, I heard the caw of the raven, circling around the yard, repeatedly cawing. I looked up and watched him fly around and around. I told him goodbye and cried as I drove away from the house.

Much later, through reading *Gifts of the Crow: How Perception, Emotion, and Thought Allow Smart Birds to Behave Like Humans,* by John Marzluff and Tony Angell, I learned that scores of my fellow humans have formed friendships (and sometimes enmities) with corvids, the bird family including nutcrackers, jays, ravens, magpies, and crows.[207] Marzluff and Angell begin the book with the story of a blue-black crow living on the University of Washington campus, where Marzluff teaches:

> Almost hourly, he delivers food to his mate and three fledglings, while also keeping watch for any threat to the nest. Suddenly he turns his head, caws softly, and glides away, landing on a lamppost directly above a blonde woman. The woman, Lijana Holmes, smiles and calls him "Bela" as she offers him a breakfast of eggs and meat, which she prepares daily. Bela, in turn, presents his special gift—recognizing Lijana and participating in this routine with her. His gift to Lijana is more abstract than what he provides his bird family, but it is powerful nonetheless—it is the ephemeral and profound connection to nature that many people crave.[208]

My relationship with the raven at our ranchette—and with an archetypal or shamanic "raven"—illustrates what was happening between me and nature in these later years in Montana, facilitated by Holotropic Breathwork. While there were some intimate connections with nature in my actual life, there was an even more vivid internal experience, a sense of an archetypal or transpersonal domain in which experiences *as* nature were linked and existed beyond me, connecting me to nature eternally. Layers of grief poured out of me as I became these experiences. This was deep grief, cathartic, heavy, and yet a profound gift. Almost always, the grief included some awareness of loss of nature in an ecological sense, sometimes an awareness of some specific damage being done to the natural world by humanity. This latter emotional experience is described as ecological grief in Chapter 9. These feelings were then layered into my actual experiences of nature. In other words, now when I was actually in nature, there was a depth of recollection that felt sacred, overflowing with meaning beyond words, deepened in part by the holotropic state experiences.

Back in breathwork, this fuller sense of connection with nature held me as I encountered both personal and collective issues involving my present life. In typical holotropic fashion, energy involving a personal issue could emerge initially as within transpersonal imagery or experience from any level of the psyche. For instance, several times in breathwork, I experienced myself as a large carnivorous cat—a lion, a tiger, a panther, a cheetah. Usually, as this happens, I find myself tearing up an animal I have just killed. The meat is red. Tendons are more bothersome than blood. I get easily around the bones. None of it much matters because all of reality is tearing at the meat and feeling myself growling. The growling is similar to purring, on a continuum. The growling at the harsher end is an extension of my teeth—and in life I can feel my teeth as if from the inside, as if I am feeling the essence of what they are, how they have evolved as part of an evolutionary process involving biting, chewing, sometimes killing. My teeth—even as I feel them now—*are* this process.

In a breathwork session as a big cat carnivore, growling emerges as an extension of the clenching of my teeth. This is an internal experience, with images and the sense of myself as the lion; and it is also manifested externally on the mat with grinding of my teeth, *feeling* my teeth, and vocalization of growling. I realize it feels the same as my human anger. Soon anger itself is the same thing as display of teeth and that transforms into a growing sense of my ability to protect myself from experiences in this human life I do not want. Then I can start to feel how the energy of teeth and growling can manifest through me simply as *No thank you, I do not want to do that,* but the transformation can occur if, and only if, I am fully present to the energy of the anger. If I am less conscious of the depth and intensity of the origins within me, anger and aggression may manifest less consciously, seeping out in various ways, or turning inside against me as shame or depression. Holotropic experiences of gnawing at meat helped me understand these parts of myself.

From this and other similar experiences, I now tend to feel anger in my teeth and jaws before it manifests as an idea about something or an exchange in the world, and then it flows throughout my body. I am more conscious that "I am angry" and less focused on a perceived injustice or response, less needy around taking external action without thought. I believe this makes me more effective in understanding appropriate actions, including drawing boundaries I need to draw or in discerning that I want or need something. When I am angry, I also feel connected to the billions of creatures who have lived and died on the planet, navigating our animal system of defending and aggressing, needing to eat, trying not to be eaten. Defending territory; taking territory. Boundaries, needs, defenses: now we are acting them out psychologically.

Consistent with any COEX, some of my experiences during this time included memories and understandings involving the biographical domain, and then these memories were connected to what was unfolding with respect to nature. Grief in itself was part of the unfolding. In one Holotropic Breathwork session I returned to one of the many moments in my childhood when my mother had locked herself in the bathroom, crying. I was aware of her unhappiness as well as her deep, unresolved grief, which I understood as most directly related to the death of her sister and the absence in her life of her mother, who had died many years earlier. During the experience, I was in my own younger state of confusion, shame, and loss, even helplessness with respect to the unresolving nature of my mother's grief and weeping. Then I was sensing her mother—who I never knew—in her own grief, having lost her two sons to early death, including the son for whom I am named.

James Calvin "Jay" Ladner drowned in Lake Pontchartrain at the age of 16. In the midst of sensing the overwhelming grief in my mother's family, I felt myself briefly as him in the water of the lake, and then recalled myself—a biographical memory—as a four-year-old child, unable to breathe, struggling in water off a beach in Florida. A wave had capsized my small raft and I was stuck under it, the salty water was swirling around me, I was not able to find air. In this swirling, from that part of myself that remains an observer in breathwork experiences, I remembered my sister's wondering whether alcohol had played a role in my namesake's death. I experienced the nature of alcoholic longing—and then mostly it was back to water, the sense of the comfort of water and the surrender of drowning in water, despair and helplessness yielding into release. I had a sense of all the gods and goddesses of water who have ruled over human life—and I needed them to support me as I started to cough on the breathwork mat. As I allowed them to support me, I became generally aware of the gift and danger of grief, both ancestral and personal—gift as an entry point to some types of understanding, to the opening of the heart; danger in the possibility of drowning emotionally, even pulling others down with you.

In later reflection, I remembered how my cousin, Carlton Dufrechou, had worked for years as Executive Director of the Lake Pontchartrain Basin Foundation, whose mission has been to act "as the public's independent voice in the effort to restore and preserve the water quality, coast and habitats of the entire Lake Pontchartrain Basin."[209] Lake Pontchartrain is actually an estuary, a mixture of salt water moving up channels from the Gulf of Mexico and fresh water draining in from rivers and rain runoff. I remembered many times as a very young child sitting on the "seawall" at Lake Pontchartrain with my cousin and our fathers. The seawall was a series of concrete steps down into the water edging the lake on our side. When my cousin and I were young, we were not allowed to swim in the lake due to pollution. The signs prohibiting swimming on the south shore went up in 1962 and remained for most of my life. That is how I learned the word "polluted"—from being told I could not swim in the water. I still "hear" the word "polluted" in a New Orleans accent.

Remembering sitting with my cousin on that seawall, unable to go into that water lapping up towards us, makes me realize how COEXs work themselves out differently for different people. Some people spend years cleaning up lakes, other people spend years considering grief in response to nature. My cousin's contribution certainly feels more tangible but who knows. Many people celebrated in recent years as the ban on swimming on the New Orleans side was turned into an advisory to avoid days surrounding large runoff. It is hard to express the meaningfulness for so many people of once again being able to swim in that water. In this way, you can see how our personal histories with parts of nature are interwoven deeply within us, within our families, in our communities, in our heritage, and deeply inside various levels of the psyche. When my cousin helped clean up the Lake he was cleaning up much more than just the water in one of the largest wetland estuaries on the Gulf Coast. If we can bring clean practices to more and more of our dealings with nature, who knows what will be healed.

Dirt, Drums, and a Turtle

Among Stan Grof's many books is *The Ultimate Journey: Consciousness and the Mystery of Death.*[210] The book covers much terrain around the central awareness that death has been a sacred part of life in many human cultures but has been denied and sanitized in most of our lives in our times. I have come to believe it is difficult for most of us even to think about death. I suspect we dissociate. I am not saying I am any different, but I am open to the possibility of a wholeness including an acceptance that life ends.

The reality of death was present in many of my breathwork experiences, accompanying a general sense of the sacred. The incessant frequency of life and death in the natural world is part of the emerging awareness of the sacred. Aside from experiences that feel like recollection of a death, there have been many experiences of living a life with knowledge of the danger of death present within nature. Recently, there was an experience in which I (a female) was digging in the earth while my male mate was doing something in the forest not far away. These seemed to be loin-cloth years. It was warm but not hot. There was a background sense of needing to be on the lookout for danger, experienced more as habit than fear. I had grown up seeing death all around me and my experience was that all of us in nature killed and were killed.

Within the background of this knowledge, I had my hands in the earth. There was simultaneity of the feeling of the earth on my hands and the sexuality between me and my mate. These feelings were the same thing in some way experientially. We were physically bound to each other through sex in the same way that the plants were rooted in the earth. This was not an idea but how it felt to be "me" in the experience. The sense of love bound through sexuality was the same as the sense of dirt—both felt damp, cool, and endless. The sense that any moment might bring a lion out of the woods to eat one or both of us was part of the same whole. I had read for years in certain esoteric teachings that sex and death were linked, and had understood this in an intellectual sense—of course sex leads to birth and of course birth replaces the dead and of course life then ends in death. But this was different, it was not an idea put together by my intellect, but was an experience in my body, linked with the feel of my hands in dirt and danger in the forest.

In another Holotropic Breathwork experience, I was a prisoner in a tribe that was not my own. It was night and very dark. There was a large fire and drumming. There was a blankness to my experience. I was afraid but not the way I have been afraid, say, when watching a slasher movie. No one was paying attention to me. I think I was going to be killed but there seemed an inevitability to whatever was coming that was almost peaceful, just like the inevitability of the moon changing shapes. Whatever was coming—presumably death—seemed the same as the forest-jungle night and the drums, a continuation of the darkness and the rhythm. Lots of life died in the night; I was part of that. When I came out of that experience, I was not crying, but felt somewhere between confusion, awareness, and peace. My sense of allowing myself peacefully to disappear into the night of nature was a gift. Once again, this experience was inseparable from nature and left me with a deep sense of longing for experiencing myself as part of the natural rhythms of nature, extended into drumming, extending into an acceptance of death.

Most of my experiences have not centered on death but almost always have a background including awareness that, as Shakespeare said, "We are such stuff as dreams are made on; and our little life is rounded with a sleep."[211] A few years ago, my family spent the winter holiday on the Big Island of Hawaii. There was one glorious day when we walked along a red dirt path to the green sand beach at the bottom of the island. The heavy, dangerous surf pounded the porous black lava. At the end of the path, we climbed down steep trails to the cove. Green sand, not emerald green, but a duller, sandier green was surrounded on three sides by cliffs. The fourth side opened to the vast Pacific. After some lathering up with sunscreen and a half hour sitting in the sun, I followed my daughters into the surf.

We played in the water for an hour. There was one moment when a large clear-greenish wave rose up before me and I saw a huge sea turtle floating in the middle of the wave, a few feet from me. He was suspended in the motion of the water; his own movement blended into the motion of the high-rising wave. The turtle's head was curved upwards, as though he was looking for something. I barely had time to call "look" to my daughters before the wave passed beyond the turtle and picked me up in turn. I was up and down with the wave and he was back in the ocean out of my sight. This was only a few seconds, but registered deeply within me. I feel it even now, the up and down motion with the wave forever linked with the brief glimpse of a beautiful, ancient creature.

In Holotropic Breathwork in Canada some time later, I was back in the waves at the green sand beach. The turtle appeared in front of me, the experience suspended in time for me to take it all in. I went into deep weeping in response to the beauty of the turtle and the setting. Without words or even specifics, I had an understanding of the significance of the turtle in various cultures. Old, nearly as old as any other animals living on the earth, from a species-culture that retreated from the violence of nature by developing a shell—some of them inhabiting water, some on land, but they were freer in the water. As I write these words, I happen to be wearing the t-shirt I bought in Hawaii with the image of the green sea turtle so that I can sometimes wear him on my back. As I edit this section years later, I happen to be wearing the shirt again. I just had to look down to be sure. This is a complete coincidence, almost stunning, as I have many t-shirts.

The turtle brought other synchronicities. One I recall: not long after my breathwork memory of him, one of my daughter's teachers vacationed in Hawaii and sent her a postcard of a green sea turtle, virtually the same image I saw. The postcard spent years on our refrigerator door. This is how experiences in breathwork sometimes link with experiences in life.

In the breathwork experience, out of my sense of the turtle came images of brown-skinned men (me among them) on a beach in Hawaii near long boats. There was drumming and the flow of red lava in the distance. Steam rose from where lava met the sea—a new land emerging from fire and water. I felt part of the male group. The women were somewhere else and were held as different creatures. Someone was talking but all I wanted was to push the boat into the water and row out onto the waves. My need to get out on the waves made it hard for me to listen to what was being said. The language seemed pompous and of no consequence. The drumming, lava, and call of the waves were joined aspects of reality. Even as I was "there" in Hawaii, I had simultaneous dim recollection of times on the beach in Florida in my teenage years and some counterpoint from cold winters in Montana. Deep longing for the turtle—awareness of the fleeting preciousness of that one moment—was infused with all these other things.

I have had many breathwork experiences involving horses, not just my first experience in Calgary. One time I was a Native American riding hard on the prairie. I came upon a woman I loved who had fallen in the grass. I was not afraid, but my heart hurt as though pierced by a spear. I bent over her. She was alive but unconscious. Resolute that she would survive, I carried her with me on the horse. Another scene in a different breathwork experience: I am standing by a brown horse on a path in front of a wooden house. The feel is medieval European. I know my lord (or king) is coming for me; I will join him and ride into battle. It is for protection of the land. I trust this man completely. I will follow him. The trust of the horse feels much the same. I trust the horse; the horse trusts me. My "place" in the land and the wooden house is mixed in with this trust. It is about belonging and defending that to which one belongs. It is about being part of these trees and fields. The horse is sturdy, reliable, as am I. Coming out of it, I weep.

When integrating this experience, I tried to understand the many soldiers in the United States whose values around our recent wars seem very different than my own. Having lived my particular life in our particular times, I cannot imagine trusting a king, or any government, including ours. But if I recall the sense of embodied alignment with home and country offered by this experience, I can imagine how some of our soldiers and their families may feel a sense of trust in leadership that allows their service and sacrifice. More important for me personally, I am inspired to work for construction of a group that I could trust. I want to find "lords" to whom I could give my allegiance. They would be "green" lords, like the lush green in this scene. In the background of all aspects of this experience was an embodied sense of personal relationship with the land, the natural world, including animals. The connection is not itself sad, though it is sacred. Longing for it brings weeping. Over time, as nature feels more and more secure inside me, the weeping seems mostly in awe and gratitude, less in need.

Grof contends our culture's banishment of nonordinary states of consciousness is the salient distinction between us and our ancestors. "The differences between the understandings of the universe, nature, human beings, and consciousness developed by Western science and that found in the ancient and preindustrial societies," he writes in *Psychology of the Future*, "are usually explained in terms of the superiority of materialistic science over superstition and primitive magical thinking."[212] Grof believes otherwise. He suggests the differences between present and past cultures do not involve the intellectual maturity of the Western materialist paradigm, but arise from our "ignorance and naiveté" regarding holotropic states of consciousness. Like an increasing number of anthropologists, Grof believes older human cultures "possessed deep knowledge of these states, systematically cultivated them, and used them as the major vehicle of their ritual and spiritual life."[213]

I believe this was true. Like me, many people experiencing nonordinary states of consciousness develop a deep bond with our imagined ancestors, in part because we believe our ancestors lived in cultures incorporating a sense of the sacred emerging from nonordinary sate experience. As Grof writes, in such states "the experiences of other realities or of new perspectives on our everyday reality are so convincing and compelling that the individuals who have had them have no other choice than to incorporate them into their worldview."[214] He continues:

> I have not yet met a single European, American, or member of one of the other technological societies, who has had a deep experience of the transcendental realms and continues to subscribe to the worldview of Western materialistic science. This development is quite independent of level of intelligence, type and degree of education, or professional credentials of the individuals involved.[215]

Consistent with the Jungian-Grofian understanding that our deepest wounds have archetypal-transpersonal connections, those of us moving toward wholeness through nature may feel as though we are involved in something bigger than ourselves, something necessary for our species, a coming shift. As we follow our individual longing for nature, transforming our inner and outer worlds, we may sense the possibility of transformational shifts in the collective consciousness or unconscious. In *Dark Night, Early Dawn*, Christopher M. Bache, a Professor of Religious Studies who has been active in the Holotropic Breathwork movement, suggests the "pulse of a larger story" is to be found "within the rhythms of our personal story."[216] When we discover this, Bache believes, "everything pivots."[217] He writes:

> Our lives are no longer "ours" alone but belong in an unsuspected way to the universe from the very start. They reflect not just our personal karmic history but the history and aspirations of humanity itself. The threads that form the unique patterns of our never-to-be-repeated existence have been spun in the cosmic womb, in the collective evolution of a star-cluster, a planet, a people.

In September of 2011, I attended a weekend gathering at the Joshua Tree Retreat Center in southern California, honoring Stan and Christina Grof. Other than celebratory events, the weekend focused on an Open Forum series of communal meetings, collectively envisioning the future of Holotropic Breathwork. At one of the mealtimes, I found myself waiting for a turn at the cafeteria-style drink dispensing machine just behind Stan Grof. I typically hesitate to take the time and energy of people like Grof, particularly at such a gathering, but I found myself smiling and nodding at him. Without hesitation, and with no words, he put down his drink and hugged me. I was just some guy he had seen around from time to time, but the warmth, kindness and good will was palpable.

If a transformation of our collective consciousness is pressing for emergence, it will happen individually, through moments of presence and love, which then gradually become culture—and are learned by others implicitly. As Bache wrote in *Dark Night, Early Dawn*, the ecological crisis may not bring about the literal death of our species, but may bring about an ego-death, and "what will have died" will be "our sense of being disconnected from each other and from everything around us. As the psychological debris of our difficult past is cleared away, we will begin to experience more clearly the web that weaves all life into a single fabric."[218]

Like many who have entered the depths of human consciousness and come back to talk about it, Grof also displays a grounded sense of humor. A few years ago, I was teaching at a seminar of the Institute of Transpersonal Psychology, where Grof happened to give the daylong keynote lecture. In late afternoon, during the question-and-answer sessions, one of the faculty members raised her hand and pondered, "I guess what many of us are wondering is whether there is meaning in life?" Grof smiled, waited a moment, and with the *gravitas* people often associate with him, responded, "If you have to ask that question, you're already in trouble." After people laughed, he addressed the question with compassion for the fear many of us hold in contemporary times that life is meaningless, consciousness just a fleeting accident of a material brain, our love only a survival mechanism. The answer, of course, involved turning within, perhaps aided by nonordinary states of consciousness, finding out for yourself.

Grof understands turning within as the last best hope for our species. "Many of the people with whom we have worked," he writes, "have seen humanity at a crossroad facing either collective annihilation or an evolutionary jump in consciousness of unprecedented proportions."[219] He references the observation of philosopher and author Terrence McKenna: "The history of the silly monkey is over, one way or another."[220] Grof states succinctly what I have come to believe is the crux of our situation:

> It seems that we are collectively involved in a process that parallels the psychological death and rebirth that so many people have experienced internally in holotropic states of consciousness. If we continue to act out the problematic destructive and self-destructive tendencies originating in the depth of the unconscious, we will undoubtedly destroy ourselves and possibly life on this planet. However, if we succeed in internalizing this process on a large enough scale, it might result in evolutionary progress of unprecedented proportions. As utopian as the possibility of such a development might seem, it may be our only hope for the future.[221]

In my experience, redirection of our human tendencies into internal processing almost always leads us into grief, some personal, some collective, but always felt personally. The next chapter delves more directly into grief. Before making that turn, we follow the awakening of Laura Huber, whose personal process may parallel the path emerging for us as one global culture.

A Weeping Mountain

When I spoke to her, Laura described herself as entering midlife. She was the mother of three children, with over twenty-five years in the working world. She was professionally successful, having climbed the workplace ladder to senior corporate management. One of the details I remember most clearly involved her youth in an orphanage, where she "learned to see the dark side of everything." When she contacted me, Laura was in the midst of many exceptional, life-changing experiences in nature. She told me her experiences were still raw and unfolding. Because she felt she could not communicate these experiences effectively in writing, she poured out her story to me in a telephone conversation. I typed into my computer while Laura talked. What follows are her words, written practically verbatim.

People were often telling me I had an energy about me—they felt it when I walked into a room. I wanted to know what they were talking about, but I couldn't narrow it down or focus on it. It occurred to me to learn Zen meditation. I wanted to find out about calmness.

I went to a Zen meditation weekend. They took us through imagery meditation and asked us to imagine someplace we could be. I looked out the window and saw a little running creek. I became that creek. I soaked into the earth, could feel myself soaking into the earth. At first, I was just aware of flowing, as though my blood and the water were the same and were flowing. I was nourishing the earth. My legs tingled. They are tingling again now, from my shins, to the top of my thighs, and up through my hips. I can picture that moment—I'm there in that moment, soaking down into the earth.

I could see the whole world through a telescope. I said to myself, let it go. Then I cried. I was thinking, how blessed am I. For twenty minutes, I cried. But I was happy, awed with the beauty. I was able to see myself as part of a massive system. I thought: if we don't take care of this system, there won't be a system. I felt very fluid, like mercury in a thermometer, very protected and very fluid. I did not want the experience to stop. Ever since that weekend, only a month ago, I have been flooded emotionally. Blessed and honored.

What emotions? Sometimes I am scared that I am seeing things I did not see before. The other day, I was sitting in traffic, at one intersection for half an hour. The snow was piled high. I stared at one drop of water dripping from a mound of snow. I didn't see cold or gray or time. How awesome to see a little drop of water. It returns into the water system and it was so beautiful. I wondered why I was worthy of seeing this. For whatever reason, I was blessed with being able to see this. My blinders were off. I was happy. Bubbles in a champagne bottle.

Twenty-five years ago, I lived in Tennessee. I went back last fall to sky dive. I fell through a cloud, became one with the universe. I felt like a fairy, like I wasn't real. The whole universe was in front of me for the grabbing. I could see a quarry and become a fish in the water. I never saw such blue water in my life. Then, I had tears of joy, tears of ecstasy. Awe. To fall through a cloud. When I cried, I was not hysterical; I had gone into this with fear and respect. Better than a front row seat. Awe. Full of emotions.

I went back to sky dive eight times. Once, Pigeon Forge, just outside the Smokies, very touristy, but you can see the mountains. I left O'Hare at 6:00 p.m. and arrived in pouring rain. I had to drive in the rain. Black. Mist or fog. I had no idea where I was going, but just followed the road. Every once in a while there was a light and a shadow from a tree, a profile. When my mind would turn to fear, to uncertainty, I would see a white fog formation and say, "thank you." Certainty came back. The roads were treacherous. It took over four hours.

The next day, I practiced sky diving inside a tunnel. There were huge jet engines; it sucks you up. It was for training, to build on skills and posture, but it wasn't right. I wasn't outside. I finished quickly and drove into the Smokies. I saw a mountain weeping. A mountain weeping. Crying. Not water, not a waterfall, not a creek, but weeping. Then I was crying to take care of her because "you're all I've got." If you don't, you have nothing. Now these were tears of sadness.

Later in the day, I drove in the mountains along side roads, being adventurous. It was the first time I saw creeks running along both sides of old dirt roads. I saw a mountain covered in a golden veil and slammed on the brakes. I knelt at the presence of the mountain. Humbled. Truly, truly humbled. Awe. Just stared. Then, emotionally, a lot of turmoil again. Unworthy. What have I missed all my life? Angry that I have always been so busy doing instead of enjoying. Sad for all those cars that were rushing by me. I never cried so much in my life.

But there were two kinds of tears. Tears of sadness that others around couldn't see, they kept driving by. Also, tears of ecstasy and awe to be blessed by this beauty. Angry at myself for not having seen it before, thinking I was always so busy doing. I had cheated myself. I mourned for myself throughout the day. I "mourned"—I don't want to use the word grieved. I mourned. I was thankful I did not let the analytical Laura kick in.

I brought a piece of the mountain back and have it on my desk. It layers my life. I'm part of that system. I have value and the mountain showed me I have value. I can stand tall and proud and the mountain showed me what everyone has been saying about my energy—my rawness, my boldness. There you are Laura, standing as tall as that mountain in natural beauty. The mountain gave me that. The mountain gave me that understanding and helped me see through the layers of steps that I have taken to get where I am in my journey. I touched the mountain. It was cold, wet, hard, strong, but so giving.

I walked through the warehouse today at work, wearing flat shoes. Walking up an escalator, I felt the earth going one way and me another. We held each other in balance. I went to my office and journaled it. Oh my gosh. Oh my gosh. You've got it, now run with it and don't look back.

People ask me what has happened. They say, something is different, the tone of your voice, how you carry yourself, how you walk. I used to wear my hair shoulder length. Clairol bottle, hair toward my face, pixie, with big sunglasses. I was always hiding. Now I have my hair pulled back, totally back. I can run my hands through my hair. I am beautiful. I am unique. There is one of me and I am here to make a difference. Now I don't go anywhere without index cards. I want to record what I am smelling, feeling, who was there, what I had on. Then later I go back to the moment and just write.

In my classes, they have wanted me to write about my childhood, about the orphanage. I cannot do it. What I remember is home, all the children with me. Home is the smell of mittens on a radiator and the sizzling sound they make. All those mittens, mittens and mittens. That's what I remember.

At a seminar, someone gave me a little pine cone and said I wish you to grow as strong as a pine tree that can bend through the turmoil. I still have the pine cone. It sings and shares my story.

CHAPTER 6

Grief and Weeping

"Grief is at the basis of life," said Pablo Picasso. "If we demand sincerity of the artist, sincerity is not found outside the realm of grief." [222] This comment, recalled by Picasso's friend Jaime Sabartes, poet, writer and fellow artist, is referenced by art historians with respect to the emergence of Picasso's "blue period." During this period, his paintings were tinged literally with blue, and emotionally with melancholy. This has been understood to suggest the possibility of salvation through grief.

Montana Fires, Louisiana Floods

In August of the year 2000, toward the end of our first full summer in Montana, fire swept through the hills where we lived. On a Sunday afternoon, one of our neighbors threw his barbeque charcoals from Saturday night into some leaves. The weather was drier than dry, what they call fire weather in the American West. A hot wind was blowing. The leaves kindled and the flames were out of control within minutes.

I was napping when another neighbor called to tell me fire was coming over the hill. My wife was out of town for work, the kids were hanging around. I ran outside and saw ominous smoke. I grabbed a hose and started spraying water on the wooden shed where we stored our hay. This was the first building the fire would reach. Within a few minutes a sheriff's deputy was standing next to me and told me, very firmly, "Get your kids and animals and get out *now*."

The fire was already burning in the woods near the dirt road leading out of our neighborhood. Another dirt road ran alongside our house, but there was a wire fence preventing our access. People on our side of the fence did not have the right to use that road. When the deputy started to cut the wire, the property owner from the other side protested. He stood there arguing with the deputy even as heavy smoke and reddish glow was growing over the hill. The deputy cut the fence anyway and we drove out with our dogs. I forgot we even had cats. I let the horses loose as I did not have a trailer and there would not have been time to trailer them anyway.

The neighboring property owner's objection to letting us onto his road was another level of welcome to Montana for me, one I have never forgotten. I would not say his behavior was a Montana norm, but I would say exclusion of "other" happens in Montana as in many other places, perhaps more so, possibly a form of meanness inherited from the harshness in the land and weather. On the other hand, another neighbor eventually caught my horses and trailered them out to rescue stables, another form of Montana neighborliness I have never forgotten.

Later that afternoon, I stood with my kids and several other people on a ridge a few miles from the spreading fire. The flames and our house were hidden behind mountain ridges, but smoke rose steadily. Helicopters with huge dangling buckets were scooping out water from Canyon Ferry Lake and wetting down unseen houses. Other helicopters dropped fire retardants. Now and then you would see a cloud of white-ish smoke billowing up, looking different from the darker gray smoke of the fire itself. A newspaper reporter standing next to me said, "That's a house going up—when you see the white smoke, that's a house." She turned out to be wrong, but I believed her at the time. My fourteen-year old son, having a hard time adjusting to Montana, asked if we could go back to California if the house burned. "Nope," I said. "I'll put up a trailer if I have to, but we're staying." Within a few years, the space and ethos of the place was inside Max as much as the rest of us.

We were evacuated for five days, with sheriff deputies blocking the road back up to our house. Now and then they would let me through, ostensibly to get possessions. On one occasion, my boss, Mike McCarter, Judge of the Workers' Compensation Court, came with me past the road block. We hosed water onto the trees near our house until the well went dry. The fire had passed by our house that first afternoon, but was still burning along the lake. On our property, intense heat still smoldered through underground tree roots. Sometimes a random tree would burst into flames. When the water ran out, we left and hoped for the best.

When it was all over, our wooden fence had burned and our house was smoky, but our home and possessions had been spared. An acquaintance had just moved into a cabin on the lake and salvaged nothing from the ashes of her log home except her favorite ceramic coffee mug. While my cherished view across the river to the mountains was the same, the landscape near our house was permanently altered. The fire had blackened a huge swath of trees and land. The charred landscape was beautiful in its own way, but spoke of the ease of destruction. I took the same walk I always took up the side of a mountain and breathed through some grief and rising tears when I remembered the former green and all the animals. I knew life would rise again, that fire was part of the western eco-system, but I was walking on cinders and stepping over trees that looked like half burned wood in a fireplace.

Many trees were still standing but were blackened. We were told they would eventually fall over, but that might take a few years. That turned out to be correct. At the time, I repaired the fence myself and we lived with the smoke. We used some of the insurance money to pay for Max's orthodontics. With the rest, we hired a contractor to take down some of the trees. He buried them in holes dug with a huge backhoe. Years later, a backhoe would dig a more discrete hole for our horse Joe when he died. Then another one for a rescue horse we had for a time, an excruciatingly thin bay mare, sadly abandoned on a scruffy pasture and never fully recovered.

A few weeks after the fire, my mother suffered a stroke during a medical procedure where my parents lived in Louisiana. I had grown up in New Orleans, in a house with a backyard sloping up into the levee on the 17th Street Canal. That levee broke open in August 2005 just after Hurricane Katrina passed over the city. The neighborhood was flooded up to the second floor of the house, with the water spilling all across the basin that was New Orleans. Nearly two decades before the big flood, my parents had moved across Lake Pontchartrain to what is called the "north shore." Sleepy old towns were becoming bedroom communities for New Orleans commuters. Subdivisions and strip malls were rising up on the edge of southern pines, oaks, cypress, and bayous. You reached the other side of the lake by driving across the twenty-four-mile Causeway, claimed as the longest bridge in the world, but more like an overpass over shallow brackish estuary water. In the old days, if you arrived at night, the darkness was so thick and black it was almost frightening. Then, gradually, as in so many other places, nature gave way to people and concrete, condominiums and houses, fast food, shops and stores.

My parents were among the first wave in the early 1980s. A condominium on a golf course, a nice enough place for their later years, even if an alligator came out of lagoon one day and snatched a neighbor's dog. On another occasion, my father became a hero for killing a snake with his putter after a lady was bitten while walking a shell path beside the greenway. He brought the clubbed-to-death snake to the emergency room in case there was a need for anti-venom. Though opposite in some ways, such as temperatures and humidity, Montana and Louisiana have a fundamental similarity in remaining "places" within their ecosystems much more than many other parts of North America. Nature is still present in her unique form, still responsive to climate and geography.

Just before my mother had the surgery leading to her stroke, she told me she wished she had led a better life. I responded, "I think it was good enough." Both with premonitions, my sister and I were not surprised at the "medical accident." My sister had seen herons flying in a certain way after her pre-surgery call with my mother. Seeing the way the birds moved, she thought she knew.

When I arrived at the Mandeville Hospital, my mother lay in a private room, severely brain damaged, without speech. The stroke was on the left side of her brain, the linguistic-analytic side. She was conscious in a way that seemed to involve her right brain only; perhaps she was in a landscape like a dream. Halfway into another world, she lay there connected to machines through various tubes. She had raised me with the clear instruction to remove any life support machines "when the time came." When I was alone with her, I looked into her eyes and made a motion as if to remove the tubes, asking with my expression. She looked back at me in terror. She managed to shake her head no. Gestures apparently remain accessible to the right side of the brain. As I stood there alone, looking at her, a well-meaning occupational therapist came in, bright and bustling, calling my mother "Miss Audrey" in good old southern style. She managed to sit my mother up on the side of the bed. Talking to Miss Audrey as though she were a child, she put a hairbrush in my mother's hand. With her hand over my mother's, she began brushing Miss Audrey's hair, with my mother's arm limply following along like a doll's. It struck me as macabre, reminding me of a Faulkner story.

When my wife and daughters arrived, I looked at them and broke down sobbing in the hallway of the hospital. I was hugging my older daughter; we were both weeping. I was crying about my mother but the blackened landscape in Montana was still a fresh shock in my body. Within a few moments, a nurse appeared and ushered us into a small room. That level of grief, particularly from a grown man, was evidently not appropriate for public. Fair enough; it was a common hallway and other people had their own problems. A well-meaning social worker appeared within moments. She was kind and showed compassion for our feelings, along with a transparent agenda to shut down grief in the hospital. She could, she made clear, refer us for services.

Many people in our culture are not comfortable with the display of grief, particularly from men. Yet there are cultures where grown men visit holy sites with an expectation and intention of weeping, accepted as beneficial not only for individuals, but for communities. I have been told the Wailing Wall in Jerusalem draws cries of lament that are palpable as prayer, seeming not only personal, but cultural and collective. Perhaps the emotional display is acceptable through a sense of collective link to the sacred. Unlike most places in contemporary life, weeping seems more permissible at sacred sites. James Swan, in *Sacred Places: How the Living Earth Seeks Our Friendship*, writes that "many modern people cry at sacred places because living in the rest of the world requires emotional suppression." [223] As we shall in subsequent chapters, the natural world—like religious sites—seems to allow release of emotions in ways that feel psychologically and spiritually healing. Or maybe we should just consider nature one continuous religious site.

This chapter looks at grief and weeping. We begin with noticing the repression of grief that is rampant in Western, rationalist culture. The relationship between grief and weeping is considered, including the role played by release of repression in the emergence of tears. We consider entering into grief and what might happen if we are unable to process our grief. Then we look at theories about the origin and function of grief, drawing on the object relations school of psychology. This takes us back to my experience in the rain as an example of the core loss some of us may be grieving when we respond to nature with tears.

Repression of Grief

In the broad scheme of things, the same social forces that banished nature from our civilized culture banished the free flow of emotions. I am thinking about preference for rationality, analytical understandings, control, keeping a stiff upper lip, viewing emotions as weakness. This can be seen as repression of the feminine, as many have observed. Certainly there is repression of feeling. Ironically, perhaps emotional control becomes culturally mandated at the same time forces of culture put many of us in alienating, stressful circumstances that generate feelings, which are then repressed by social norms. Grief and weeping still emerge within us, but many people automatically repress both without even knowing what is happening to them. This can manifest in depression, other psychological conditions, and even physical medical problems. On the surface, orderly life seems to proceed. Repression of grief and weeping become a personal and cultural habit.

Free-flowing emotions, including grief and weeping, could just possibly deconstruct much of what holds together national and international power. In an interview with National Public Radio following publication of *Duty: Memoirs of a Secretary at War*, former United States Secretary of Defense Robert Gates openly discussed the emotional reasons contributing to his retirement. Gates had a long career focusing on national defense, including service in the Air Force, CIA, and National Security Council, a tough world of big boys. [224] In the context of the post-9/11 wars, Gates realized protecting individual Americans serving in the military had become his highest priority, more important than the more amorphous goals of national defense or protecting national interests. He understood this shift was "perhaps at the expense of hardheaded objectivity in terms of the use of our military." [225] Breaching a masculine, military code dating back hundreds if not thousands of years, Gates told NPR: "I was becoming emotional when I was around the troops and thinking about the troops. And all of that contributed to my decision on the specific timing that it was time to go."

Sometimes it is necessary to put emotions on hold, for reasons of preservation of self and others. And yet, the hardness of structures—ranging from institutions to our internalized personal psychologies—might soften if we allowed our emotional responses to surface. Given his professional history and national stature, hearing Gates describe his emotional life to Steve Innskeep on National Public Radio seemed significant, perhaps an unstated watershed, though likely unnoticed by most. Gates confessed his increasing determination that service men and women losing their lives would not simply become statistics to him. "And so I started out," he said, "by handwriting parts of the…of the condolence letters." He soon realized this was not enough. He explained: "I started asking that every time one of these packets came to me, that it'd have a picture of the…of the soldier or sailor, airman or Marine who'd been killed, along with the hometown news so that I knew, you know, what their coaches and their parents and their brothers and sisters and teachers were saying about them." On national radio, Gates shared, "in those evening sessions, writing the condolence letters, there probably wasn't a single evening in nearly four and a half years when I didn't…when I didn't weep."

Having grown up in New Orleans, I have wondered over the years if the Latin heritage of the place might have encouraged more feeling in me than in some American men. Like liquor and food, emotions seem to flow in the Big Easy. In my youth, this felt more like messiness and lack of control than a healthy flow of feelings. Though most of my ancestry was French, there was a strong and perhaps dominant line of German. Some of the women on my father's side were fairly stoic, emotions controlled. My mother (entirely French background) was emotional, but her level of emotion, including secluded weeping, was difficult for me. This is not to stereotype nationalities with such a broad stroke, but the lines in my heritage became a theme for me with respect to emotions years later in Jungian therapy, with elements of the different cultures appearing in dreams.

I do not recall ever seeing my father cry. This is in contrast to the experience of my own children, at least in my later years with them, when they sometimes jokingly called me a crybaby. I have sometimes talked about this with other men. A male friend from the Holotropic Breathwork community, after we experienced some emotional sessions together, told me his young daughter once asked him, "Daddy, why are you such a crybaby?" Before I found some emotion, like many contemporary Americans, my feelings were largely repressed, though seeped out through depression and anxiety, sometimes in anger and addictions. I can say with a great deal of seriousness, and some embarrassment, that I did not know what feelings were until my mid-thirties. It took spiritual experience to break me open. Nature not only helped, but became a conduit for emotional release as described throughout this book.

Needless to say, emotional life is complex, including the experiences of grief and tears. We can get lost in emotions and in weeping. If we are stuck in this process, continuous weeping may not seem like movement toward wholeness. I have a therapist friend who tells me she occasionally has clients, usually a woman, whose weeping seems to act as a defense against fully facing the reality of difficult issues in life and relationship. One of those clients would usually start weeping while sitting in my friend's waiting room before therapy. Eventually this particular woman came to understand she used crying to avoid feeling the pain she might feel if she faced reality. This makes me wonder if there are different levels of crying, some allowing us to stay near the surface with our defenses and some taking us more deeply inside ourselves. From a social evolutionary perspective, crying may protect an individual from hurt by appealing to the pity or emotions of someone else. Crying may also elicit assistance from someone in the social group for aid.

In such situations, if independent adjustment is a goal, emotional containment may represent a path of growth. I remember one occasion during a weekend experience of psychodrama, part of the first year of ITP. The facilitator, a gifted teacher named Harris Clemes, worked with a young woman who could not stop crying once she had touched the surface of a deep emotional wound. She seemed stuck, weeping in a way that seemed unresolving. Needless to say, I was reminded of my own sense of helplessness in my youth, when there seemed no resolution to my mother's grief. Harris asked this young woman to walk around the room and look into people's eyes, a means to ground herself. I was learning there is a point of balance, a place of stillness, which allows grief and weeping to flow through us without grabbing hold of our legs and pulling us down into the sea.

There can be repression against opening the flow, perhaps fear the dam will break wide open. Particularly within Anglo-American culture, there may be an implicit belief that structure dissipates with emotion and can be lost. Like thousands of others, I am a fan of Downton Abbey, the acclaimed British television series created by Julian Fellowes. The series follows the lives of an aristocratic family and their servants on a Yorkshire estate in the 1910s and 1920s, with the dissolution of boundaries between social classes a recurring theme. I might argue the show is also about finding authenticity in a rapidly changing world. In a scene that caught my attention, sisters Lady Mary and Lady Edith Crawley are having a conversation with Mary's suitor, Lord Tony Gillingham, at a sumptuous party. Mary and Edith are the daughters of the Earl of Grantham and an American mother, whose heiress money saved the estate a few decades earlier. About an unwelcome guest, Lady Mary says, "Papa is livid, but there's nothing to be done. We can't make a scene."

Though less assured than her sister, Lady Edith is often pointedly accurate. She responds, "I sometimes feel we should make *more* scenes… about the things that really matter to us."

Tony Gillingham says dryly, "It wouldn't be very *English*."

To which Edith replies, "No, but I envy it. All those Latins, screaming and shouting and hurling themselves into graves. I bet they feel much better afterwards."

Lady Mary has the last word. "I wonder," she says. "Once you let it out, it must be hard to put it back in."

During the same time period the Crawleys were finding new ways, psychological talk therapy was emerging, beginning on the continent. The notion of emotional catharsis as healing was first described by Josef Breuer and taken up by Sigmund Freud. Breuer's famous case of Anna O, later described by Freud, presented the possibility of curing symptoms of "hysteria" through re-experiencing the emotions around traumatic incidents. Numerous schools of talk therapy have emerged over the decades, with no agreement that reliving trauma with a goal of catharsis is necessarily helpful. On the other hand, the emergence of grief, when it emerges, is recognized by many as a signal of healing, particularly from trauma. In *The Body Remembers: The Psychophysiology of Trauma and Trauma Treatment*, Babette Rothschild explains:

> Sometimes a client will fear that his grief is a regression into trauma, but it is usually just the opposite, a healing progression. When working with body awareness, most clients will notice that their grief helps them to feel more solid, less fearful, if more sad. Grief usually emerges at various steps along the way in trauma therapy when an aspect of the trauma is resolved and the internal experience changes from present to past: "I *was* really scared," "That *was* really bad," etc. In this context grief is a sign that healing is taking place.[226]

Weeping in particular may signal psychological healing. To get there, we may need to release not only repression against emotions, but repression against weeping. Gestalt psychologists, focusing on the whole or "gestalt" of their clients' experience, have addressed the impact of repression against weeping. Mary Catherine Cosgrove explains that "society has admonished that 'big boys do not cry,'" an admonition including "big girls" in contemporary culture in many countries. Cosgrove believes most of us have internalized "a need to refrain from crying" such that the contemporary "human organism has unwittingly become an expert in not crying."[227] In this cultural context, weeping then involves two aspects of release. First, emotional release from lifting of the repression against weeping, which is more broadly a repression against any form of feeling; and second, lifting of the repression holding in check the particular feelings, for instance, grief around a particular loss or longing.

Psychologist Joseph Weiss long ago noted some people cry only at the "happy ending" of a situation because at that point repression against grief has been lifted. In the next chapter, we shall consider the experience of "joyful" tears, but for now, it is interesting to note the possibility of weeping when a repression has been lifted through a fortuitous result. Weiss wrote:

> Certain individuals cry at the happy ending of a movie rather than, as one would expect, at the sad situation that preceded it. Such people, for instance, are not moved to tears when the lovers separate, but save their tears until the time when they are happily reunited. The grief and impulse to cry are repressed until the situation no longer merits this reaction. Then, at the happy ending, there is no longer any need for the grief to be repressed. When the inhibition is lifted the energy that is used to maintain it is unnecessary, and may be discharged, causing pleasure and allowing for the expression of grief.[228]

Releasing repression is not something most of us can sit down and just decide to do. But there are steps one may consciously take. Wise advise of the common sense variety appears in the Internet article, "How to Cry and Let it All Out."[229] The first recommendation is to forget everything you learned about "not crying" and to recognize the gift of weeping as part of the human experience. Indeed, even Charles Darwin observed that weeping— as opposed to crying out in pain, whimpering, or moaning—is uniquely human, a gift of evolution. Since our ape cousins do not weep, this human adaptation developed in the genus line Homo after our ancestors separated from those whose descendents evolved into contemporary apes.[230] From a hard core evolutionary biological perspective, weeping exists in our species because it serves a purpose. Whether viewed physiologically or psychologically, the purpose is often described as a restoration of equilibrium. I would say the restoration often involves making conscious feelings that have been kept out of embodied awareness, with weeping representing an integration of the feelings into the body-mind.

In learning "How to Cry and Let it All Out," the next recommendation is to consider the reasons each of us has for holding back our tears, whether based on negative beliefs about crying, a need to maintain a particular self-image, or simple physiological difficulty releasing feelings into tears. To find their tears, some people work on giving themselves "permission" to cry. Finding a place with privacy, peace, and solitude can help. As we will see in a subsequent chapter, many people find nature "a good place to cry." Weeping may also flow from journaling about our feelings or artwork, dance, or other movement. And, of course, there are movies, the place where many of us find our feelings and finally cry. I know a number of people who only cry in movies. As described by transpersonal teacher Tav Sparks in *Movie Yoga: How Every Film Can Change Your Life,* deeply feeling into films is itself a spiritual practice.[231]

Entering into Grief

Grief hurts, to state the obvious. Perhaps the most painful experience we humans endure is loss of a loved one to death. Sometimes I have felt embarrassed writing about grief in response to nature when considering the depth of grief we suffer when losing people we love. The painful period following loss of a loved one is commonly called bereavement or mourning. People handle bereavement differently, but despair is not unusual, or a feeling of being stuck. In *Ways of the Heart: Essays toward an Imaginal Psychology,* depth psychologist Robert Romanyshyn described such "shattering personal loss" this way:

> Grief is a cellular matter. When the one who has been your spouse, your lover, your companion, and your friend has died, it is the body in its deepest levels and rhythms which measures the time of grief and mourning. No act of will, no decisions of the mind matter, because grief is the winter of the soul, and like the seasons it can only be endured. And in this time of endurance, there is only a waiting. One lives a kind of cocoon existence: the world fades and the body shrinks into the space of its grieving.[232]

I was recently unexpectedly touched by a clothing exhibit at the Metropolitan Museum of Art in New York City called *Death Becomes Her: A Century of Mourning Attire.* I knew wearing black during bereavement had been customary in earlier times and remembered Scarlett O'Hara in *Gone with the Wind* dancing in full widow dress to the outrage of onlookers. Seeing the actual clothes worn by people, mostly women, hit me viscerally. I had a sense of a time when mourning was externalized. This suggested grief was in some way more shared—or at least not hidden. The exhibit walked you through a range of clothing worn in the United States and England during the nineteenth through early twentieth centuries. I had no idea the appropriate colors of mourning shifted as the time of bereavement passed, transforming from a deep black to a lighter tone, sometimes with thin white stripes in the fabric in the later stages of mourning, sometimes shifting into purple. The interpretive narratives of the exhibit reminded visitors that some people used the custom to exhibit their wealth and some, like Scarlett O'Hara, found the custom stifling and wore mourning clothes without any real feeling. From my perspective, I imagined meaning and comfort in an externalized ritual separating out a time of mourning, including a literal "lightening" over the period of bereavement. In our times, I suspect many people miss a sense of external support for their mourning.

Psychologists recognize a trajectory of bereavement, a gradual accommodation to the reality of loss. Freud described the process of healthy mourning as the gradual withdrawal of libido (life force) from the memory of the loved one and reinvestment of that energy in other people or actions in the world. Some therapists talk about the transformational nature of bereavement, as death of a loved one often requires people to reinvent themselves in new ways. As we shall see in Chapter 8, many people turn to nature during bereavement. Numerous people have told me that when the pain of losing a loved one became overwhelming, the only thing that made sense was being in nature. Perhaps there is implicit knowledge that death is part of nature and new life is always forming in the natural world. On the other hand, I suspect seeking nature during bereavement is simply instinctual, having little involvement with knowledge of any kind. I imagine comfort simply seeps into the soul from the natural world.

The psychological concern with bereavement is becoming stuck in grief, a concern that applies to any form of grief, including the loss of beliefs, abilities, or activities as well as people. In an essay titled "Mourning and Melancholia," Freud described the stuck situation of "failed mourning," where the individual consciously or unconsciously refuses to engage with anything not connected with bereavement.[233] This represents withdrawal from life in general, even from reality. "Failed mourning" is characterized by what Freud called melancholia, an experience we could liken to contemporary "depression," but defined more particularly as grief locked in the unconscious, without awareness of the loss being grieved. As we shall see, this understanding of melancholia has led some in the Freudian tradition to consider what are the sources and objects of grief in the unconscious mind.

The problem with grief involves difficulty with integrating the loss; in other words, not facing it or feeling it fully. Facing grief is a tricky business because entering into it fully may seem overwhelming. We may fear dissolution of all structures holding us together. More simply, opening to grief is extremely painful. I suspect some of us fear reaching feelings even more difficult to handle than sadness, such as anger, blame, or shame. In experiential work such as breathwork, one readily experiences and witnesses the ways grief, anger, shame and blame layer over each other, intertwining and sometimes shifting into each other. Sometimes these feelings are directed internally, sometimes externally. With grief and anger, fully experiencing one often opens the possibility of experiencing the other. To get through grief, we often need to let it roll over into anger. Fully experiencing anger may lead back to grief; and then round and round we go, finding more and more layers, more and more memories, more and more wounds and losses we did not fully feel or even know we suffered.

A few decades ago, Elizabeth Kubler-Ross famously identified five stages in grief.[234] Her well-known book, *On Death and Dying,* focused on facing one's own death, but her model has been widely applied to the general experience of grief. The five stages she named were: (1) denial-dissociation-isolation; (2) anger; (3) bargaining; (4) depression; and (5) acceptance. In 2007, Paul Maciejewski, Baohui Zhang, Susan Block, and Holly Prigerson published the first empirical research investigating whether people actually progressed through the Kubler-Ross stages.[235] They concluded most people experienced some level of acceptance from the beginning, without as much disbelief or denial as suggested by Kubler-Ross. Yearning, an experience not directly named by Kubler-Ross, was identified as the dominant experience within grief. The yearning described by these researchers feels similar to what I have called longing.

If we do not face the grief inside us, we may leave our hearts closed. My personal experience in breathwork has taught me fully experiencing grief is the price of an open heart. If we leave grief unprocessed, it can linger for years, even a lifetime, maybe even across lifetimes if we consider the possibility of reincarnation. New losses may merge into old, never quite resolving. In *The Courage to Grieve: Creative Living, Recovery and Growth through Grief,* psychotherapist Judy Tatelbaum writes:

> Grief is a wound that needs attention in order to heal. To work through and complete grief means to face our feelings openly and honestly, to express and release our feelings fully and to tolerate and accept our feelings for however long it takes for the wound to heal. We fear that once acknowledged grief will bowl us over. The truth is that grief experienced does dissolve. Grief unexpressed is grief that lasts indefinitely.[236]

The Origins of Grief

On our first visit to Helena, Montana, my wife and I shared a curious incident of her crying at a Chinese restaurant. After more than twenty years in the San Francisco Bay area, we were accustomed to the manifestation of cultural diversity in excellent ethnic food. After I accepted a job in Helena, in the midst of scouting out schools and houses, we ventured into a place that looked like a Pagoda. When our food came, Margee took one look at her plate and cried. The restaurant in question is no longer in business, so I am not libeling an ongoing enterprise. Margee's reaction was grief. Immediately present was the impending loss of appetizing Chinese food, but there were so many other imminent losses in the picture, so much transition about to happen. I suspect this is always the case with our grief, even when instigated by something so minor.

Projecting into the situation allows me to illustrate the layers of grief. No doubt about it, Chinese food had been a part of our lives. One of our favorite restaurants when we first moved to California was a hole in the wall in Chinatown. Our Christmas Eve tradition in San Jose had morphed into dinner at a Chinese restaurant near our house. This was just an entry point into all of the parts of her life Margee would be leaving behind in our move to Montana. She was grieving the anticipated loss of California. She was grieving the loss of a degree of sophistication that had not yet appeared in our Montana experience. Once she was into the territory of loss of California, her grief almost certainly contained loss of her friends, her job of fifteen years, our house in San Jose, our neighborhood, probably even the smog and the traffic. Beyond the loss of particulars of our California life could have been an anticipatory grief over loss of the familiar per se, loss of bearings, as well as some fear of the various difficulties in making a new life in a new place. How would the children adjust? Would she make friends? Sometimes grief lies somewhere between fear and hope, perhaps an aspect of that "yearning" identified by researchers.

Then—at least in my imagination—there may have been grief for the loss of her young adult years, spent mostly in California, and perhaps some lingering grief for the loss of her parents, already passed away several years by that time. Her parents had known California, had even lived in Palo Alto for a time in their youth, but would never know anything about her life in this new and different place. Once we are into the realm of lost parents, we are likely into grief for a general sense of unmet needs in adult life, a sense that love as an adult is not typically experienced as unconditional. Not far from the experience of lost parents can be an unconscious sense or dim memory of perinatal states where needs were met in an oceanic sea of non-doing, perhaps even some memory of the soul's existence in spiritual realms where unconditional love was a tangible energy. As with all forms of grief, quite a lot might lurk behind tears over a plate of unappetizing Chinese food, at least in my imagination.

Psychologists known as object-relations theorists have written extensively on the subject of grief. A common thread is the understanding that all grief is superimposed over an original experience of loss. For most object-relations theorists, this original experience of loss is the infant's loss of the mother (or caretaker). This is not necessarily a literal loss, but an experiential loss occurring as an inevitable part of psychologically healthy development. In object-relations theory, there are external objects (people, ideas, or things in the actual world) and internalized objects, which are the representations of these objects created by each of us inside our psyche. Internalized objects are imbued with an emotion-tinged constellation of memories, beliefs, thoughts, and desires. These are considered by object-relations theorists to be superimposed over the experience of the original caretaker. The concept of emotionally tinged internalized objects has functional similarities with Grof's systems of condensed experiences (COEXs) and Jungian complexes. All three concepts are ways to understand psychological processes often playing themselves out below the radar of conscious awareness.

One of the early object-relations theorists, Melanie Klein, traced the experience of grief back to infancy. She noted "the absence of the mother arouses in the child anxiety lest it should be handed over to bad objects, external or internalized, either because of her death or because of her return in the guise of a 'bad' mother." [237] Klein believed psychologically healthy individuals learned in infancy to internalize "objects" capable of self-soothing as a means to adjust to real or imagined losses. The primary internalized object is known as the "good-enough mother." This internalized sense of self-soothing has to be just "good enough" to allow the growing child to navigate the disappointments and losses in the world without developing entrenched defenses that end up causing suffering and being diagnosed as psychological disorders.

Some theorists of psychoanalysis, such as Heinz Kohut, refer to these internalized resources of an individual as the "self." This concept of self is typically designated by a small letter "s" and should not to be confused with the "Self" in Jungian psychology, which is usually designated with a capital S. As noted previously, the Self in Jungian psychology is an archetype of wholeness reverberating with our individuality but contained within the collective unconscious. We will return to the concept of a small letter "s" self as a set of internalized resources in Chapter 8 when we consider the concept of an ecological self inclusive of nature. Successful internalization of self-caretaking allows psychological independence as we mature into children, adolescents, and finally adults. This is because we can support ourselves internally through the inevitable losses we encounter in the world. These "losses" can involve simply not getting everything we want automatically without effort, which is a "loss" of the imagined state of infancy where needs are met magically by the mother.

We are spending time with these concepts as they will help illuminate certain ways of looking at grief and, in particular, at grief in response to nature. From an object relations viewpoint, internalizing a healthy caretaking function involves navigating through the grief that emerges from loss of an internal expectation (sometimes called an infantile fantasy) that our needs will be perfectly met from an omnipotent outside source. Desire for caretaking from an outside source can be experienced as an unconscious expectation of perfect mirroring or an expectation of peace and wholeness without doing anything. Anger (well, actually, rage) may arise within the psyche when we sense we are being asked to release these expectations, particularly if we have not internalized a "good enough" ability to self-care. As noted previously, my experience has been that grief and anger layer over each other, so behind any rage at not finding perfect mirroring or caretaking in the outside world is a deep grief at loss of this experience of "wholeness without doing anything." For most of us, these layers of things are buried within the unconscious.

If this internalization of a self-care function is not successfully navigated for one reason or another (and there are books, articles, and whole schools of psychology focusing on the intricacies and variations of these processes) then people even into adulthood tend to develop certain styles of relating and being in the world that cause them problems or suffering. These styles are called defenses in the object relations system of things. One of the defenses people unconsciously undertake is a repetitious attempt to "fuse" with someone or something else. This is seen as an attempt to replicate an experience of union with a perfect, or even imperfect, mother-image. Sometimes accompanying this desire for fusion is a concomitant reaction against the "engulfment" of fusion.

The object-relations understanding of fusion as unhealthy has led to disagreement with some transpersonal psychologists, who understand humans as having a natural tendency to desire connection, even merger, of the experience of personal self with something "trans" that sense of individual self. From a transpersonal perspective, Ken Wilber has written extensively on what he calls the "pre/trans" fallacy. The "pre" refers to a psychological state without differentiation between oneself and others. The "trans" refers to an ability to connect with others from a healthy sense of separate being. The "fallacy" addressed by Wilber is the idea that any sense of fusion or merger indicates a regressed or undeveloped sense of individual self.[238] The transpersonal perspective is that loss of "self" in an experience of merger with "what is" (or for instance with nature) represents continued development along a psychospiritual continuum, not regression toward an infantile or immature psychology. This is a place where people attached to object relations and people attached to a transpersonal orientation often disagree. At base, this is probably an issue involving whether you believe there is "anything out there" with which to fuse other than an infantile unconscious memory of your own. As I have noted, my experience suggests to me that we are beings of consciousness with the possibility of experiencing connection with other realities.

In real life, in my experience, "pre" and "trans" generally overlap and intermingle as we navigate through life. Sometimes we merge with others and need some unconditional support without the placement of "reality" front and center. This provides us with enough juice to get back up there and face reality. It is completely normal to gravitate to other people who will support us in our endeavors and bolster our self-esteem. Eventually, we all need a healthy dose of reality and some bursting of illusions, but the kindness and unconditional support of people in our lives is a gift. Our deep connection with these people might feel very much like a form of fusion as a deep resonance, even love, develops. That kind of love and support fosters the development of stronger internal resources to help us continue to face the disappointments and harsh realities of life. At a more superficial level, this is how I think connection with nature works. Some of us connect with nature, feel rejuvenated, and then make our way back to "reality."

Returning to grief, the object relations people understand a necessity to grieve the loss of the fantasy of fusion with an omnipotent all-providing, need-meeting mother through gradual recognition of a sense of internal agency able to navigate the world and attempt to meet our needs and desires. There would simultaneously grow an acceptance of imperfection— with grief perhaps necessary in order to fully accept imperfection rather than simply tolerate it. In the object relations dialogues, this is often called adjusting to reality. With grieving the loss of fantasy central to healthy development, we have placed grief right smack in the center of life. An internalized capacity for self-care becomes the ability to face and grieve losses and disappointments without defense, denial, or illusion. Perhaps we have returned to Picasso's statement to Sabartes that grief is at the basis of life. All those paintings in blue felt melancholy, but the melancholy may herald a growth in the ability to feel and the ability to be real.

Now we can return to the question of the origin of grief and why that matters in considering grief in response to nature. I have mainstream psychologist friends who, I am fairly certain, if they had the chutzpa, would tell me that my intense emotional draw to nature and my feelings of grief in response to nature involve a projection of "mother" onto nature. If they know me well enough to know my personal associations of my actual mother with grief, they would think they were really onto something. They might try to put it delicately, but I suspect they believe I am still longing for nurturing by a "good" mother, still looking for fusion with an internalized mother image. They would think I have transferred, or projected, the yearning-laced feeling-tones surrounding good mother onto nature. My interest in pre-agricultural peoples might be seen as a similar fantasy, looking for a time of cohesion in a tribe, a time of fusion. This would be seen as a time that has no reality other than as unconscious memory of a desired fusion with mother—or perhaps as regression to a primitive state experienced in cultures where people do not feel themselves separated from other people or from nature.

In this view, if I feel grief in response to connection with nature, the "real origin" of the grief is an unresolved fantasy of perfect fusion with a good mother. There would be "evidence" for this view in my sharing that after feeling deeply connected with the rain, I felt a sense of belonging I had never felt previously without "doing anything." This would be analogized to the imagined blissful state of the infant whose needs are perfectly met without having to make any effort. My hypothetical friend with object relations orientation might feel this was a relatively harmless projection of "good mother" onto nature that might generally help me cope with stresses in my life. On the other hand, my friend might suggest that I was recreating a sense of fusion with nature in a way that was avoiding reality rather than facing whatever real losses existed in my life that I had not accommodated—or even more problematic, that I was not facing establishing the independence necessary for me to discover and seek that which was realistic for me, which would involve facing the "loss" of imagined wholeness. "Reality" in this view would involve acceptance that life involves limitations and separations rather than belief in a perpetual movement toward a fantasy of "wholeness."

From this perspective, my deeply emotional connection with nature might be seen as feeding a "false self" rather than developing a "real self" aligned with reality. James Masterson, a New York psychiatrist who developed a particular object relations perspective, differentiates between a "real self" and a "false self."[239] He explained: "The real self, from the perspective of object relations theory, is made up of *the sum of the intrapsychic images of the self and of significant others, as well as the feelings associated with those images, along with the capacities for action in the environment guided by those images.*"[240] The real self is "derived mostly from reality and to a lesser extent from fantasy—what one wishes as well as what one is—and its motives are directed toward a mastery of reality tasks as a way of maintaining psychic equilibrium."[241] In contrast, the false self "is derived mostly from infantile fantasies, and its motives are not to deal with reality tasks but to implement defensive fantasies: for example, avoiding self-activation to promote the fantasy of being taken care of which then becomes a way of 'feeling good.'"[242] To mature from a false to a real self involves facing and experiencing the "abandonment depression" that arises through realizing that an imagined fusion with an all-providing mother is not realistic.

Interestingly enough, Masterson considered the life and work of the twentieth century novelist Thomas Wolfe from the perspective I am imagining my object relations friends to have about my connection with nature. First, a glimpse of Wolfe's writing, from a section in his novel, *You Can't Go Home Again:*

> The glitter of sunlight on roughened water, the glory of the stars, the innocence of morning, the smell of the sea in harbors, the feathery blur and smoky buddings of young boughs, and something there that comes and goes and never can be captured, the thorn of spring, the sharp and tongueless cry— these things will always be the same.

> All things belonging to the earth will never change—the leaf, the blade, the flower, the wind that cries and sleeps and wakes again, the trees whose stiff arms clash and tremble in the dark, and the dust of lovers long since buried in the earth—all things proceeding from the earth to seasons, all things that lapse and change and come again upon the earth—these things will always be the same, for they come up from the earth that never changes, they go back into the earth that lasts forever. Only the earth endures, but it endures forever. [243]

From studying Wolfe's semi-autobiographical writing and biographies written about him, Masterson believed Wolfe had a fused relationship with his mother. As the youngest of eight children, with his parents usually at odds, Wolfe spent several school years in travels with his mother rather than centered in any one place where he could develop his own friends and sense of an independent self. Masterson suggested much of Wolfe's life involved a search to recreate, combined with a reaction against, this fused relationship with his mother. Masterson writes:

> It is possible that as the trips with his mother robbed him of his autonomy and individuality, the closeness with her became too great; it reactivated his fear of engulfment to an unbearable degree so that he could not indulge in his reunion fantasies with her in quite the same way. Instead, he projected his need for his mother onto the landscape, so that in his dreams of merging with the land he could feel the ecstasy and wonder that he previously imagined in

a symbiotic fantasy with her. Thus, his lush, grandiose expressions of rapture with the landscape could be partially explained as a substitute for a gratifying symbiotic mother.[244]

I might surprise my object-relations-oriented friends by not disagreeing with them, but taking a perspective based on the COEX system of Grofian psychology. If we remember at some level our perinatal states, then of course at some level our states in infancy impacted us and set templates for our future experience. Most of us would have experienced times of longing for fusion with a mother who provided for all needs without any effort on our parts, as well as some gradual accommodation of an internal capacity to self-soothe through disappointments and losses. That there would be some connection between lingering grief for the times of unmet needs in infancy and grief for other losses would simply involve the connection between feeling-toned experiences recognized by the understanding of Jungian complexes as well as Grofian COEXs. My personal connection to grief during my childhood and adolescence, and in the legacy of my family, would be another natural aspect of the COEX involving grief that played a role in my particular life. Any sense of loss from infancy and childhood would not "explain away" my grief in response to nature but would deepen an understanding of the way all grief and all losses reverberate within each other.

Then we reach the question of whether an emotional attachment to nature fosters a false self based in fantasy or a real self based in adjustment to the harsh reality of disappointment and loss in the actual world. I think this part gets very interesting. As we shall discuss at more length in Chapter 10, "Psychological Immersion in Nature", it is possible to treat nature as a fantasy-land of endless good and meeting of needs as in the imagined Garden of Eden before the Fall. On the other hand, it is possible to recognize within nature the ultimate provider of reality. While we may see beauty and wholeness in nature, any actual contact with the natural world teaches us that loss is the basis of life. Forests burn. People, including uncles you never met but for whom you are named, drown in brackish lakes, even when they are only sixteen years old. Parents, sometimes even children, die before we are ready for them to die. Eventually, each of us returns to nature because our bodies are nature. So with nature it is possible to follow a pull into reality, with an experience of wholeness not felt as a fantasy of fusion with an all-providing good mother, but as acceptance of our place as embodied beings who, for our time on earth, are part of nature.

Where does this leave grief, including grief in response to nature? That is for each of us to understand on our own terms with respect to our own lives. The beautiful thing about recognizing a pull toward nature tinged with grief is that nature might just hold you, connect with you, as you feel into all those places of grief in not only your individual life, but within our collective lives as people who face a number of challenges in this civilized world we have constructed. Importantly, there is also the possibility that our grief in response to nature involves another loss, still unconscious for most of us, called into presence by our renewed intimacy with the natural world.

The Loss of Unmediated Being

Drawing upon object-relations theory, Ina Milloff, a marriage and family counselor in Tucson, Arizona, suggested our experiences of grief are layered upon a different loss than the original experience of perfect caretaking. She believes grief is layered upon an original loss of the experience of unmediated being. In *Loss at the Heart of our Being: Core Issues in Separation-Individuation and the Process of Becoming*, Milloff describes our "core loss" as "loss of access to an immediacy of experience or *being*, free from psychological constructs." [245] She suggests we begin with, but inevitably lose, the experience of a "holding presence which allows us simply to *be*." By this she means:

> *being* that is not based on conditional reactions, on defenses, on early object relations, on losses from the past and failed mourning—but instead is based on one's responses to the present moment, with all the awareness, involvement, and spontaneous experience of affect that is naturally associated with the present moment. The internal holding presence, as I see it, allows for the tolerance and acceptance of increasing levels of reality and that which is increasingly known (on an ego level) can then serve as stepping stones toward more and more access to the unknown/unknowable realm of *being*. [246]

The core loss described by Milloff allows for the possibility of building a life from an original state of presence, rather than requiring us to consider separation as the basis for maturity and self-actualization. This is not to denigrate separation, which I have described in earlier chapters as necessary for individuating away from those aspects of consensus reality that may keep us from becoming our unique selves. Perhaps paradoxically, in our culture, separation from cultural habits is generally necessary in order to remember ways of being connected through presence. This is also not to doubt the necessity of separation from the original caretakers during the course of healthy development. This separation is necessary for us to experience, just as described in the object relations literature, a sense of agency capable of enacting self-actualization in accordance with our unique orientations and desires.

If our original loss involves a state of unmediated being, we can consider ourselves originally oriented toward experiencing our sensations and emotions without the overlay of the conceptualizing and rationalizing habits of civilization. This would orient us within our heritage back through our evolution in the animal kingdom, prior to development of the prefrontal cortex and right/left brain differentiation that leaves us, much of the time, oriented toward past or future rather than a present state of being. I believe loss of a state of unmediated being is the primary loss I was grieving during my experience in the rain. More than that, it felt like I was grieving a loss of a state of unmediated being within an open intimate connection within nature—in my specific case, the rain falling outside.

Interestingly enough, it seems to me that grief, weeping, and intimacy with nature are all experiences of the body, not of the head. Grief itself seems to exist in a place not governed by thinking or conceptualization. In an essay titled "Being Present: Experiential Connections between Zen Buddhist Practices and the Grieving Process," Mark Edwards compared his experience in meditation with his observations from working with clients in a grief support service.[247] Edwards understood the primacy of sensory and emotional experience in both Buddhist practice and grief. "In grief we immediately encounter the loss of someone's or something's physical presence," he writes. "This loss is often felt as a direct bodily fact that is known prior to any rational consideration."[248]

As Edwards explains, Zen practice offers the possibility of "integration of the world of sensations and perceptions into a consciousness that is embodied and present."[249] He continues:

> The somatic aspect of grief, and the bodily focus of Zen practice, seemed to initiate similar body-centered processes. During intensive meditation practice it is not unusual to be aware of powerful emotions experienced in the body. There is one experience, in particular, that has been described as "the body filling with compassion." In this experience there is an embodied understanding and acceptance of loss and of the fragile and transient nature of life. This experience of embodying one's emotional life seemed to have strong parallels with the physical nature of the grief experience.[250]

Like any awareness of suffering, moving fully into grief seems to open us to compassion for ourselves and for what the Buddhists call "all sentient beings," all life on the planet. The transformation offered by grief—into a compassionate presence, an unmediated sense of being—needs to happen in parts of us that do not feel analytical or rational. Many therapists hesitate to intervene in weeping by clients during therapy so as not to risk halting an unfolding process that is not based in analytical thought. Many therapists consider an open presence and calm witnessing at the initial stages of weeping the most healing response by the therapist. Reflection and analysis can come later. As I noted in describing my rain experience, if I allowed myself to move into thinking mode, my weeping and my embodied connection to the rain stopped. If I eased out of thinking, my friend the rain and my weeping returned.

In *Living in the Borderland: The Evolution of Consciousness and the Challenge of Healing Trauma,* Jungian analyst Jerome S. Bernstein tells the story of the "Great Grief" described by a young male client.

> During one analytic session, one man in his 30s talked about his struggles to pull his outer life together—where to live, what kind of work/career he should be pursuing, etc. He stopped talking mid-sentence, and there was a long silence. Then he said:
>
> I carry a Great Grief. I feel it deep inside (points to his heart). It's never not there. I feel its presence. It is never far from me. In Montana I felt connected. (He had just returned from a trip there.) Here I'm disconnected—in my car, living on top of the land. I'm part of the land; that's my home. But I'm a product of my culture and therefore cut off from my home. I felt expanded there; I feel contracted here. When I was at the gathering in Montana (a wilderness experience) I was part of the community. When I was there a voice kept saying, "Teaching kids about nature may be one of the most important things you do."[251]

Bernstein explained his struggle as a therapist to witness the experience shared by this young man without "profaning" the experience with categorical labels. His goal was "to not interpret at all—certainly not in the moment." Rather, Bernstein wanted to stay present to the experience *"between language"* and recognized this involved "the tension of holding one's intellectual and rational breath for far longer than any of us can imagine doing." [252] While releasing "the comfort of rational understanding" takes some practice, the "between language" space allows, as Bernstein described, "some kind of knowing through a holding and a wonderment."[253] This holding and wonderment may be part of an original experience we lose as we mature.

One of the benefits of transpersonal psychology is openness to understandings of human experience that may feel more spiritual than psychological. We are not afraid to talk about the sacred or to consider the reality of non-material realms. In this way, we move into the possibility that our deepest experiential loss is spiritual, not merely of this realm in the sense of originating in one biographical life. I am not the first to wonder whether an original loss of *being* and presence involved our dropping into the earthly plane from an experience of source, where connection was immediate and beingness a given reality. The best way to raise this possibility, which of course can never be proven, is through the experience shared with me by Elaine Gallovic.

Having grown up in the greater Cleveland area, Elaine worked for many years as registered nurse with geriatric patients. When she wrote to me, she was living with her husband on three wooded acres. She wrote: *One summer I was walking frequently in a metro park near my home. I was walking a paved "all purpose" trail. I often noticed a huge old maple tree near the path and would silently greet the grand old beauty with a "Namaste" as I passed it. On each walk, I found myself looking forward to the place on the path where I would see this tree. One time I stopped and noticed how many lower branches the tree had lost. I felt the sadness of the old fallen limbs scattered all around the base of the tree. In my heart, I honored how much this tree had seen, had endured season after season, year after year. A road now runs close to the area where the tree grows and I recognized how the tree now has to deal with pollution from cars driving by. I am sure that when this tree was a sapling, there was no road.*

I observed how many people quickly pass by the tree and most likely never notice its grandeur. I began to think of this maple as "my tree." I felt that the energy of the tree was feminine and was more and more drawn to spend a little time with her. After admiring my tree from the path, one day I felt compelled to go over to the tree and stand with my back against the wide trunk. I stood there for a time, feeling such peace, contentment and stillness. I silently talked to the tree and thanked her for her contributions to life. Suddenly, I did not want to leave, even though I had thoughts of completing my walk. I told the tree I would be back.

As I walked away, I felt overcome with tears and a feeling that I can only describe as pure love. The tears were tears of joy that one only sheds in a divine connection. I touched the spirit of the tree and the spirit of the tree touched me very deeply. In reflecting back now, I can recognize that I was also experiencing sadness and overwhelming grief. I believe the grief was the feeling of loss one has when one becomes separated from the Divine. I believe this experience was of my soul remembering my connection to my source and possibly even remembering the separation I felt at my birth on Earth. I would imagine this separation from our source may be the reason babies cry when born.

So, this was a bittersweet experience—the flow of pure love while connecting to the tree and of the separation from pure love when I chose to step away from the tree. My feeling may also have been related to awareness that I do not feel this level of love with people. One would certainly "long" for this type of love connection with all living things, but mostly, it seems to be a longing of our soul to be one with the One.

CHAPTER 7

Joyful and Sacred Tears

During a visit to the De Young Museum in San Francisco last year, I saw Vermeer's *Girl with a Pearl Earring* on loan from the Netherlands. The subject of considerable hype in recent decades, practically a media commodity, the painting had never particularly interested me, though I liked Vermeer. I had seen images of *the Girl* on book covers and posters—and on banners all over San Francisco the past week. Walking up to the painting was an entirely different experience. The centerpiece of the exhibit, it was hung alone on a free-standing wall in the middle of a darkened alcove. When I walked into the luminescent space around the painting, I was fortunate no one else, other than a security guard, was standing around. I was there only a few seconds when tears started to flow, an involuntary response to what struck me as astounding beauty. It was the kind of emotion for which it is hard to find words. There was something clean and pure about it, almost an impersonal feeling. I kept myself in check as I was in public, though from the look on the face of the security guard, a mixture of familiarity and respect, this was not the first time he had seen this reaction.

If I had allowed myself to move into the associations that were arising, I would likely have reached emotional experiences involving my daughters and wife, and then moved into a sense of all women, to the very experience of love, the sense of youth as a fleeting moment in time, and, likely most of all, the nature of vulnerability, authenticity, and innocence. This did not feel like grief—well, not *exactly* like grief, but there was poignancy and strong emotion. In contrast to other experiences of weeping, this kind of emotional response feels like a free flowing, a polished stream bed rather than full of craggy sharp rocks and boulders. It feels joyful. Not the jump-up-and-down in excitement kind of joyful, but a deep appreciation for a glimpse into something that feels purely good. These tears were seeing into a part of being human full of love and innocence, uncontaminated by the realities of people using each other to gratify needs, untainted by cynicism and harshness, undiluted by holding back of authenticity. As for *the Girl*, she invites us to imagine what is *really* going on behind those beguiling eyes, which has led to a popular novel and film.[254] Perhaps it is actually experience with suffering and the darker sides of human behavior that allows her to show us an openness making us feel we might be seeing into her soul.

The tears flowing down my face in front of *Girl with a Pearl Earring* seemed to appear spontaneously, unexpectedly. These are the kind of tears in which water just seems to well up in our eyes and flow over. Weeping may then start, often slowly and calmly. We may move into personal memories containing joy, longing or grief, but there is something about these tears that seems to involve the more general experience of being human. We may understand that life is just a series of moments in time, disappearing, and know it is possible to see into and through these moments. There may be a poignancy and realization that actually *seeing* through the façade of life is tragically rare. This may feel like grief or contain elements of grief, but there is a more positive tone, as if receiving a gift. There may be something ineffable in the experience, impossible to define in common terms. Many people see no need to imagine beyond an experience of beauty. Certainly there is no need for the kind of analysis that would shut down the experience.

Many people have told me they weep in response to nature simply because nature is beautiful, nothing more explanatory needed than that. Later in the book, we will encounter the stories of people for whom nature arouses a sense of the sacred, bringing tears. The range of tears discussed in this chapter push toward the sacred—even the word *holy* seems to fit. This may involve the sense of purity in these tears. I find it interesting that I want to use the word *unpolluted* about my tears in response to *the Girl,* perhaps because she allowed me to see past various aspects of discord and drama in my life. Then I realize that pollution of the natural world is the problem that has led to the ecological movement and the grief many people experience in response to nature. We will turn to those subjects in later chapters but it is interesting to wonder whether tears in response to nature are longing, at least in part, for an ability to see purity in the natural world.

Part of me simply wants to allow these experiences to be what they are, without dissecting them. Another part is curious about a deeper understanding of this form of tears. What is the relationship to grief? *Is* there a relationship to grief? I am particularly interested in the way this form of tears seems to push toward recognition of a collective experience of being human. This begins to feel even a bit religious. Putting words like *grief* and *joy* aside, I am curious about the experiences that open this kind of flow from some of us. I have used the words *joyful* and *sacred* in describing this range of tears as the title of this chapter, but those are just the best words I could imagine at this time. I am more interested in feeling into this part of the range of human experience producing tears. This feels important to set the stage for understanding many of the stories of deep emotions in response to nature shared later in this book. In this chapter, we consider tears from a psychological perspective, including whether there is a commonality to weeping that feels joyful and weeping that feels like grief. We look into tears of "wonder-joy" and "sacred weeping," with assistance from the writings of two of my ITP teachers. The chapter closes with my consideration of the contexts for me now other than nature that seem to produce tears that feel sacred.

Considering Tears

In the early part of the twentieth century, psychologist Alvin Borgquist distilled three types of crying from responses to questionnaires and observations of people weeping: (1) grief or sadness; (2) "a more or less deliberate, largely vocal, cry, best represented in crying of anger and less perfectly by the crying in fear and pain"; and (3) "the cry in joy, including such forms as cries of gratitude, of tender emotion, of feelings of admiration and for the sublime."[255] Although identifying this third category, Borgquist considered weeping for joy actually to reflect emotions surrounding the period before the joyful event occurred, the time when the outcome of some situation was still unknown. He believed joyful weeping was weeping in relief. Similarly, psychologist Joachim Flescher suggested people cry during a pleasant experience because they are comparing the joyful moment to a previous period of personal deprivation, with repression of emotions around the memory of prior suffering released, allowing tears to flow.[256]

Comparison of something joyful to a background of suffering may be part of the experience, though there is no need to minimize joy in order to emphasize suffering. One could just as easily say we weep during experiences of grief because we are comparing difficult experiences to knowledge of more joyful states. This is where we left off in the prior chapter considering grief. Elaine Gallovic wondered whether her bittersweet tears reflected a memory of divine love and "the loss of not feeling this level of love with people." Just as some psychologists have concluded tears of joy represent lifting of a repression against experiencing the grief of prior periods of suffering, we could wonder whether tears of suffering represent lifting of a repression against remembering the possibility of joyful connection. One thing I have learned on the transpersonal path is that opposites often enough turn out to be two sides of the same thing.

Synchronistically, not five minutes after I typed the heading "Joyful and Sacred Tears" at the head of this chapter, I heard from a friend with whom I had not spoken for over a year. He told me he was happy to report that many of the difficult circumstances in his life had shifted and new possibilities were opening up. "When I cry now," he said, "it's tears of joy, like I'm seeing the beauty in life." After recovering from amazement at what I was hearing out of the blue, I asked him to tell me more about the difference in this experience. He thought for a moment, and then said when he cried in sadness, he was feeling, well, sad, perhaps mixed with some shame, guilt, and misery about why good things in life seemed to elude him but not other people. He found his newer form of joyful tears not as much focused on himself, but recognizing something that deeply touched or moved him, which was increasingly often. "It's like I'm in love with the world," he said.

I considered asking my friend if he thought some part of his recent joyful tears were in relief for changes in his circumstances. I held back, as I did not want to shift the mood or question his joy. If I had asked whether these tears of joy reflected a prior period of deprivation, I imagine he would have responded, "How could they not?" There was no doubt my friend's newer experience involved love and opening to the beauty in life, in contrast to turning inward with sadness and constriction. But I wondered whether his difficult few years, when he knew suffering, and had to keep finding strength within himself to keep going, set the stage for the kind of joyful tears now appearing in his life. Is truly seeing beauty in the world the other side of knowing deprivation, fragility, longing, and yearning? Many people who cry in response to nature mention great gratitude as well as great grief. Perhaps great grief and great gratitude are different yet intertwined experiences within an opening heart.

William Braud, my friend and teacher at the Institute of Transpersonal Psychology, wrote about "Experiencing Tears of Wonder-Joy: Seeing with the Heart's Eye."[257] Braud described tears that were not of "pain or sadness or sorrow" but rather "accompanied by positive affect—by feelings of wonder, joy, gratitude, yearning, poignancy, intensity, love, and compassion."[258] He described the experience:

Tears quickly fill my eyes. My skin erupts in gooseflesh, hairs standing on end. Something literally takes my breath away; I gasp, involuntarily. Chills run up and down my spine. I feel a tingling around my eyes, my head, and the back of my neck. The tone of the experience is positive. Toward the end of the experience, or afterwards, there may be some sadness. In the midst of the experience, I feel love and compassion. My heart goes out to what I am witnessing. I feel gratitude. I feel a yearning, poignancy, an intensity. Around me, and between me and the provoking event, there is what I can only describe as a thickness, as though the air somehow has a greater density. The experience comes upon me—unexpected, spontaneous. I feel "possessed"— my body and feelings captivated and enraptured in the experience.[259]

Braud listed some of his personal triggers of wonder-joy tears:

Finding a small bit of milk, unexpectedly, in the refrigerator, when I "knew" there was none left, and it being just enough to go with cereal—being overjoyed at such a simple surprise and being grateful that I could be moved by something so simple; knowing that my wife would appreciate this and be similarly moved, and that this simplicity is something we share.

…

Attending a performance of a particular entertainer after having wanted to do this for about 35 years, and having missed several opportunities (near misses).

…

Appreciating the meaning of certain buildings at the Acropolis in Greece— how truths and lessons were dramatized, communicated in permanent structures. Connected to this was a feeling of the meaning of the gods, goddesses, and archetypes; an anger and frustration at not having been taught such simple, true things many, many years ago; and a delight that I had at last seen and understood such simple, true things. [260]

Braud was experiencing joy, yet each of these examples reflects something prior, whether real or expected, involving deprivation. Braud included in his list of wonder joy triggers his recollection of an email I sent him years ago about something my daughter said to me out of nowhere: "Reading a message about someone's 4-year-old daughter who asks her father, 'When I'm old and then I die and then I'm a baby again, are you going to be my daddy again?'"[261] Perhaps even this example reflects release of a worry that life and love are finite and disappear at death.

More generally, wonder-joy tears came to Braud through "witnessing anything that is truly honest, open, free from guile or craft"[262] Another trigger for him: "a guided imagery exercise in which I experienced a wonderful ball of light on the banks of a stream near a cliff; it led me to a cathedral, and I was filled with awe, wonder, and a feeling of the numinous."[263] Braud wondered: "Could the experience of wonder-joy tears be the equivalent of the soul's feathering confrontation with forms of beauty that evoke reminiscences of a supermundane realm?"[264] He asked other people if they had similar experiences of wonder-joy tears. They described "feelings of unity, union, oneness, closeness, connection, and immersion….a congruence of themselves and all life….gratitude, blessedness, intensity, yearning, poignancy…feeling cleansed, renewed, a beginning….being at home, of recognition, of safety."[265]

Perhaps wonder-joy tears involve both a witnessing of the good and a knowledge the world is not always this way. Braud described a "sad, bitter aspect" accompanying some tears of wonder-joy. He wondered if this "may have to do with an appreciation of how far the 'usual' has strayed from what could be, how we so often miss the mark. There is a yearning for some goodness or beauty that is intimated, but which is not sufficiently present."[266] It may be knowledge of the fleeting nature of purity that brings the tears.

Bitter elements or not, I am left with an understanding of the ability of the human heart to resonate with all forms of emotion, perhaps the meaning of compassion. I am left with wondering whether suffering and joy are more or less accidental and the movement of consequence is toward openness. Braud observed: "The tears and chills are, to me, my body's way of indicating that the eye of my heart is open and functioning and encountering something of vast importance and meaning…I am having an unplanned, unavoidable encounter with the Real."[267] Even with all the messiness of being human, Braud found it possible to witness "the true, the good, the beautiful, the sacred."[268] In the previous chapter, I wondered whether fully experiencing grief was the price of an open heart. I am back to this place. If avoidance of the pain of grief shuts us down completely, then it may become impossible to see all the beauty and goodness that may bring wonder-joy tears to our lives. If you can hold it all at once, you enter into that realm of paradox where contradictory things may be true at the same time. Holding all these things together moves us toward experience some people describe as sacred.

Sacred Weeping

Rosemarie Anderson, another friend and ITP teacher, was a colleague and intellectual partner of William Braud for many years. Anderson framed an understanding of "transformative and sacred" weeping through review of contemporary and historical experience of mystical tears.[269] She described a "spilling over of tears" as "intense, spontaneous and seemingly involuntarily . . . not caused by obvious immediate stimuli or set of conditions known to the weeper."[270] Anderson articulated nine commonly shared aspects of the experience:

- "relinquishing of superficial concerns and aspects of the self, breaking through the façade"
- "a sense of re-integration of lost aspects of self"
- "being in relationship with the impulse of life throughout the universe or touching reality beyond one's ordinary awareness"

- "holding together the seeming (sometimes bittersweet) polarities of human existence, for example, life and death, joy and despair"
- "apprehension of the tragic dimension of human existence, seen as universal rather than uniquely personal"
- "changes in body awareness, including a felt sense of the integration of body, mind, and spirit"
- "a sense of seeing things in their essence or with more than the physical eyes themselves"
- "a sense of being startled, awakened, and triggered into an expanded awareness of reality" and
- the "inward sense of freedom, or pure consciousness from which all activities begin."[271]

Anderson, who is also an Episcopal priest, drew upon mystical literature within the Christian tradition to deepen understanding of the experience. From Isaac the Syrian, she quoted: "Tears are to the mind the border, as it were, between the bodily and the spiritual state, between the state of being subject to passions and that of purity."[272] When sacred tears come, the tensions and emotions of the body standing between the individual and the sacred dissipate, allowing a sense of freedom and wholeness that may not necessarily be "good" but is experienced as pure. Quoting theologian John Chryssavgis, Anderson described tears "as a divine gift, revealing the intrinsic link and kinship between the intellect and the body."[273] Chryssavgis understood the "gift of tears" as suggesting integration of the individual, through grace, into "the life of God."[274] The life of God, at least for me, is not necessarily adherence to any particular religion so much as feeling oneself in an open flow with the sacred.

The sacred weeping described by Anderson feels along a continuum with the tears of wonder-joy described by Braud. The elements in common include spontaneity, "seeing through" into the essential elements of life, and awareness of a tragic element of "missing the mark" in ordinary life. These tears feel deeply intimate and yet reach beyond the personal into the collective human experience. In Chapter 11, we look into the experience of "sensing God in nature"—with God mostly understood as a sense of the sacred—and will notice many of the same elements of sacred weeping and tears of wonder-joy. For now, we will continue feeling into ways to understand sacred and joyful weeping.

The "missing the mark" element of these tears resonates with the experience of penitence in some religious traditions. Penitence can be defined as showing sorrow or regret for having done something wrong, but sometimes the wrong, even when personal, is just a matter of the inevitable pain we cause others and experience ourselves in living a life. Sometimes penitence is more collective and involves awareness a community has veered away from the sacred. Tears may offer redemption, opening the heart into compassion for self and community. The "awareness of brokenness" element of these tears recognizes there is no solution other than compassion. With sacred tears, much dissolves and one is left with a renewed sense of wholeness of body, mind, and spirit, though nothing in particular may have been solved. The tears themselves may feel like a grace and their own manifestation of forgiveness.

Drawing on the Old and New Testaments of the Christian Bible, Judith Van Heukelem described weeping in penitence and compassion.[275] She considered tears of penitence "the cry of a mature Christian," a witnessing and mourning of the imperfect nature of life on earth. Van Heukelem referenced some of the many instances in the Bible when God responded compassionately to human tears. For instance: "When Hezekiah wept bitterly over his 'mortal illness,' God said, 'I have heard your prayer, I have seen your tears; behold, I will heal you.'" God promised "the people in Jerusalem, through Isaiah, to be gracious at the sound of their cry." David believed God heard his weeping. "In fact, he thought his tears were of such value to God that they might be put in a bottle, and recorded in God's book."[276]

Sacred weeping can be experienced as a form of resurrection, which is reflected in the myths of many peoples. Ad Vingerhoets, author of *Crying: a Natural and Cultural History of Tears,* reports the "oldest written references to tears are the Ras Shamra texts found on Syrian clay tablets, near the city of Ugarit, dating from about 1400 BC."[277] These ancient texts include

> a poem about the death of Ba'al, one of the major gods worshipped in many ancient Middle Eastern cultures, and his sister's response to the news. The story tells that the news caused her to weep, and that her tears brought her satiety and even a kind of intoxication. It is particularly significant, however, that her tears also brought the dead god back to life.[278]

Perhaps that place of returning to life links tears of grief and tears of joy. This can also feel like return from exile. Now and then over the years I have found myself walking into churches as some kind of yearning to return to God. Every time I go down that road, I know full well this postmodern self with all his attitudes and opinions will not likely find solace in any contemporary religion. Still, now and then, a guy has to try. One time in my twenties I tried a Unitarian Church. There was an interesting talk along with the elements of worship. I liked the ecumenical feel. Then I balked when people came up to me to talk after the service. I felt like a vacuum was opening up into which I might be swallowed. This was no reflection on the kindness of those people welcoming a newcomer into their community, but spoke of my need to find God on my own and not be influenced by others until I knew what I needed to know.

Around the same time I was weeping in response to the rain, I tried again. I found a small Episcopal Church near my home in the Willow Glen area of San Jose. On days I did not have morning classes, I would walk there now and then for the noontime service. This took me through neighborhoods during the middle of the day, when part of me felt I should be at work like everybody else and not in a psychology program. I assumed everyone in those neighborhoods was normal, not some oddball like me attending school in midlife. Trying to find my own way in life at my age with my responsibilities left me sometimes hurting other people, which also hurt. I had my opening to "what is" but sometimes I wanted help from somebody else who might have some experience with God. Sometimes there was a longing to return into some existing *normal* structure.

Walking into the small neighborhood sanctuary felt comfortable enough. There were typically only a handful of people, almost all of them elderly women. I would sit alone near the back and often would find myself in tears. I am not entirely sure why I was crying. Sitting in church with elderly women, I may have been crying in memory of my great-aunt in New Orleans, who lived next door to me with three of her siblings when I was growing up. Almost every morning, she went out the back gate onto the levee and walked a few miles to a similar small neighborhood church. That was where I had my First Communion in the Catholic tradition, then complained enough every Saturday morning before Catechism (Catholic religious instruction for youth at that time) that my mother eventually stopped making me go. Still I would now and then wonder what it was like to have faith in a God recognized by other people and worship in mass like other people all over the world.

One day I walked to church and sat at the back as usual. Toward the end of the service, I had my head down weeping, my forehead against the pew. I guess there was some part of me reaching out in some way. The pastor bade goodbye to others at the service. Then he came up to me and started a conversation. He was around my age, late thirties. I told him I was studying transpersonal psychology, a form of spiritual psychology, on a break from working as a lawyer. I said I hoped to find something else to do with my life. Without missing a beat, he told me he was considering resigning from the ministry to attend law school. I have to say I was dumbstruck. I ended the conversation politely enough and walked back home. Later, I thought this pastor could not have said anything more perfect. I have no idea whether he knew what he was doing and it does not matter. Without a doubt, wherever you go, there you are.

Crying in church is nothing new to pastors. "Every once in a while," writes Father Ralph of St. Brigid's Catholic Church in Westbury, New York, "someone confides in me, 'For some unknown reason, I find myself crying when I'm in church.'"[279] Father Ralph says he listens "to what's happening in the person when the tears flow." From this listening, he developed a sermon from the book of Nehemiah. The sermon recalls "a moment in the prayer life of the people of Israel where men, women and children were brought to tears in prayer." This was "when they had come back from being exiled and they found a copy of the scriptures that they thought had long been lost. As Ezra the scribe reads from the scriptures, the people start to weep." According to Father Ralph, "It's not a weeping of sadness. It's not only a weeping of joy, but one of relief, of completeness and wholeness. The people cry because 'everything is all right again.'" As Father Ralph suggests, people cry when they feel they have come home from exile.

No doubt about it, I felt in exile. From what was not so clear. For me, crying in church was a mixture of many things, as weeping almost always is in my case. This was closer to sacred weeping than other forms of tears because I was not completely aware of the cause of these tears. They simply seemed to flow when I sat down alone in a back pew. I was definitely aware of brokenness in myself and the unsolvable nature of being true to oneself while caring deeply for others. Ultimately conflicting needs and wants is not just a personal problem but is the problem of the world, particularly given the limitation of resources and the contemporary state of technology and weaponry. I was grateful for the tears but they were more bittersweet than joyful, even full of a certain strange remorse that I could not turn back from the path I had undertaken for myself. I suppose I wanted forgiveness for not being a more normal husband and father. What came was not forgiveness but development of compassion and strength to continue living a life. Perhaps that is forgiveness. I suppose I was also looking for God through this pastor to see my tears and hold my pain, but if God spoke to me, he was wise enough to signal that I needed to get out of there and figure it out on my own.

Back I went into my transpersonal psychology program where an interesting thing happened that made me accept I would find sacred community in contexts other than church. As will come as no surprise, there were many times within the ITP experience when I was moved to tears. Mind you, ITP was not a school with desks and power points and whiteboards. Almost all classes happened on the floor, with pillows and backjacks. Rarely was there a lecture by any teacher, though we read a great many books and articles and information was exchanged at deeply meaningful levels. When our classes did not involve discussion, we were watching or practicing psychotherapeutic techniques, including various modalities focusing on the body and emotions, meditation, yoga, non-violent communications, movement practices, creative expression, and other possibilities for creating "the space" for whatever to come forward that needed to come forward. My favorite aphorism became a phrase from the Gnostic Gospel of Thomas as translated by biblical scholar Elaine Pagels, attributed to Jesus: "If you produce what is within you, what you produce will save you. If you do not produce what is within you, what you do not produce will destroy you."[280]

Not all the time, but on occasion, I would witness an opening in someone or in our group that would move me to weep. Sometimes the weeping was in compassion for pain or even anger being expressed by someone else. My friend and classmate Rich used to tell me, "Oh, for God's sake, I looked over there at you and your bald head was bent down again bobbing up and down crying." It was nice to have a place where this was accepted. Even my friend's ruthless mocking was an acceptance, important from another guy. Once one of our classmates used this habit of mine to make a point she wanted to make. During a course known as group process, we were discussing issues of race, gender, and sexual orientation at the school, also reflective of society as a whole. It was around the time of the O.J. Simpson criminal trial and public and private emotions, perhaps particularly in California, were running high.

The discussion had been staying at the level of the head, perhaps fueled by the gut, with people talking about slights and omissions, expressing opinions, but with anger, resentment, cynicism, and reactivity just below the surface. Not much was being said that anyone had not heard before, but sides and factions were forming in the group. My friend Anne, a gay woman, wanted to shift things and asked me to sit alone against a wall. She positioned herself nearby along another wall. Then she did something strange enough. She asked other members of our cohort to stand in front of her and yell insults at her about her sexual orientation. When the insults started mild, she asked for more energy, more cruelty. "Insult me like you mean it," she said. "Find some place in you that means it."

Eventually, people got into it and let go. I won't repeat the vocabulary, but you can easily imagine. Some of it was harsh and people had indeed found some shadowy places where they meant it. Soon enough, I was weeping, that bald head down there bobbing up and down. My chest was also heaving as this was the kind of suffering that opened my heart and it was hard to take. There was also something stunningly beautiful about what Anne was doing. It was not for her but for the rest of us. This felt sacred. As I sat there weeping, Anne looked around at everyone else, nodded toward me, and simply said, "See."

All the opinions masking anger or resentment no longer made much sense. Aggression and defensiveness in the group disappeared, at least for the rest of the session, along with dissociation, passive-aggression, boredom, and cynicism. Anne's sense of my crybaby tendencies allowed her to use my weeping as a moral barometer—even more than that, as a waking up. After that one word from her, "See," you could hear a pin drop. Slowly, we settled back into our pillows against the wall and our back-jacks. Real discussion began. Soon enough, the room fell into heart and I was not the only one crying. At some point I thought, okay, I get it, if I'm going to be crying for redemption, for our brokenness, those tears need to flow—at least for me—in a context that engages me with what is happening on the planet. That is how this particular man returns from exile.

In my case, nature has become intertwined with the return. For me the question of returning to nature and returning to each other is the same question. So I continue involvement in transpersonal psychology, have developed work in the law as a mediator, and will take one step after the other as always. What I have realized about my sacred weeping is that it seems most called forth in response to the possibility of humans becoming one with each other and with all life on the planet. Perhaps this is not sacred weeping if I know the stimulus, but the feeling is sacred. This may seem strange, but I am fairly addicted to movies and television programs where aliens invade and this forces people to come together in real communities. That there are a number of these fictional stories emerging in the last few decades is itself something to notice. I hope I do not go outside someday and see that gargantuan menacing alien spaceship hovering in the sky, but the notion of authentic human community is very appealing. Not only that, it makes me weep to consider the possibility.

At a recent transpersonal conference, Rosemarie Anderson gave one of the keynote addresses. Her turn came on the last day. She began by noting the interesting fact that so many of the speakers at the conference—completely independent of each other—had begun their talks by projecting onto the large screen a virtually identical image of earth from outer space, that blue-green globe floating in the black infinite: a circular, nay, even better, a spherical symbol of wholeness. She put the image up herself and then commented that she must have been the seventh or eighth of the speakers to start out with that image behind them. Anderson did not interpret the meaning of this coincidence, which did not so much feel like a coincidence as something emerging. What form it would take none of us know—but it was about the earth as a whole, the human as a collective, part of a larger collective of life on the planet.

I recently cried my way through various parts of the movie *Gravity*, in which the character played by Sandra Bullock, a scientist, not an astronaut, is perilously alone in space after an accident involving meteors, satellites and the space station where she was working. Interestingly enough, Bullock's character volunteered to conduct experiments in space as part of her healing from grief following the death of her young daughter. As my tears came in different parts of the movie, I noticed the different strands in the experience. The aloneness of Bullock's character got me, her finding courage got me, but mostly it was all those scenes of the earth down there below her, sometimes lit up by the sun, sometimes not. But always there was an Earth so close and yet so far.

Bullock's character just wanted to get home. There is a moment in the X-3D version when a tear wells up in Bullock's eye and floats out toward the audience, a three dimensional tear-bubble reflecting Bullock's face. My own tears in those moments were a perfect combination of wonder-joy and grief. So beautiful a planet, yet we have exiled ourselves. Bullock was literally exiled, but we have distanced ourselves psychologically, emotionally, so that most of us do not even realize what has happened.

Can we come home?

CHAPTER 8

Healing Through Nature

Sue Kronenberger came to Montana in the early nineties, leaving urban Ohio to live closer to nature. In Helena, she has worked as a licensed clinical social worker, psychotherapist, and workshop leader. She finds her own emotional healing through walking in the woods. Sue writes: *There is a small trail that cuts along the side of a mountain and leads up into a forest thick with pines and firs. The trail head is about a mile from my home. Regularly I walk there with my yellow lab. I have walked this trail at all times of the day and early evening, and have walked it in every season. Mostly I like to walk there after a new snowfall.*

Windy days there are special. I stop in my tracks and take in the whrr of sound that encircles me. I often contemplate the sound of the wind, rushing past tree trunks, branches and needles. Especially in early morning hours I am likely to see a deer. I like to be still so that the deer and I can watch each other for a long time. I only have to walk a short distance before the trail curves and I can no longer see the city. Before me is an outstretch of seeming wilderness. Mountains, trees and sky are all that I can see.

Several times I have gone there to seek refuge and solace. When I am sad, afraid or at a loss for what to do, plodding my feet on the raw earth helps me hold on to myself or figure out a next step. Throughout several years of a difficult marriage, when I felt so lonely within that relationship, I would find myself on this trail letting the expanse of green trees and blue sky wash through me. I walk for awhile and then the tears come. The woods are a good place to cry. I often let out big heavy sobs and let them keep coming until I feel spent and finished. The crying lasts for several minutes. I am usually unprepared and end up blowing my nose and drying my tears on my mittens or on the sleeve of my sweatshirt.

There is a good sitting place right next to the trail under a particular tree. I have named this tree the Solitude Tree. Sometimes I will sit under the Solitude Tree and have a good cry. I touch the tree and when all the tears feel washed through me, I bow to my surroundings in nature with gratefulness for the plants, animals, and rocks. I want to honor their magnitude, resilience, and beauty.

Within this environment, I can touch my sadness so deeply because I feel unconditionally loved and accepted: I feel that I belong. On this trail, in these woods, in these mountains, I also feel a deep sense of all-knowing. Somehow I realize that I am of this same immense mystery as the trees, the rocks, the grasses, the flying ones and the four-leggeds. It is deeply satisfying. After a good cry in the woods, I may feel restored—ready to move on. Other times I feel exhausted and realize that I need rest. Either way, I feel sustained and held.

Peter Kessler was born in Switzerland before the Second World War. Fluent in four languages, he had a long career in international human resources. In 1980, Peter's wife died of breast cancer. *She was ill for three years, a trying time for both her and me, and certainly for our two girls. She was a very wise woman and died like a saint. During her last few days in this world, she had one visitor after another coming to her bedside. She could hardly speak any more, just whisper words full of wisdom. When I depart from this world myself one day, I hope to leave in the same fashion.*

After she passed, I often went to a forest I loved, one day here, another day to another part. Strolling over the fields or finding the quiet of a deserted forest felt like coming home—to a partly known, and partly unknown, place that was always welcoming. In spring and summer, I could smell the perfume of the woods and hear the birds singing for their place in the universe. I would hug the trees, particularly the large ones, with my arms not even reaching around their trunks. The trees would hear my words and I would feel their bark on my skin. I was at home; they were too. I felt the emotions of grief for my wife, but I could still feel peace. All my senses were re-engaged with the sights, sounds, and smells of nature.

Now I live in another part of Switzerland and am married again. I still find my feelings, sentiments, and sensations in the woods. Just today, I was smelling the moss, touching it lightly, taking in the sun rays as the light shone through the trees, and listening to the birds saying goodbye to winter. I thought to myself, this is great living, this is the way it is meant to be. The sensations of nature are honey for the soul and peace for the busy mind. If I am present when I go into nature; she gives me one of the greatest gifts of this life. I feel empowered; and my hurts seem to wash away into the sensory experience of nature. I know that all life has its season; we are all part of the cycles of nature. I have been working as an outplacement consultant for nearly twenty years now, with executives, managers, directors—people who have lost their jobs, their positions in the world. In these circumstances, sometimes we feel as though we have lost our lives. I encourage them to tap into the resource of Nature—her trees, mountains, and wilderness, with snow, rain, sun, all for healing of wounded souls.

For some people, nature provides solace even without going out into the woods. A few decades ago, Nancy Russell was living the American dream in suburban Pennsylvania. With three children, a career in political consulting, and a wonderful marriage, she was, as she writes, *a soccer mom, normal. Then one evening my husband of twenty-eight years came home from a business trip, collapsed in our family room, and died of a heart attack. He was an airline pilot who seemed in excellent health. In one moment, my whole world changed. I was dealing with my own grief, three children grieving and needing differently, financial concerns and other immediate demands—and it was all mixed in with the loss of my lover and best friend. It seemed surreal. I was no longer a wife; I was a single parent. I was overwhelmed and in physical pain—literal pain with heavy pressure in the area of my own heart. I had never known the term heartache was meant to be so real and so physical.*

As I entered survival mode, I noticed that I could stare at a flower and feel a release. The house was filled with flowers and the doorbell kept ringing, with more flowers arriving. As I think back on this time, it is ever so clear to me that relief came into my body as I stared at a flower. I seemed to merge with the particular flower I looked into. The sharpness in my chest would ease—the pangs would melt away momentarily and I would briefly feel release and relief. Once I realized this new ability, I would intentionally take breaks from what was happening and mentally climb into a flower. I was healing by merging with these beautiful gifts of nature.

As time went on, I found other supports, many in nature. Water, in the bath or at the nearby river, soothed and restored me. Just setting my eyes on water flowing in the river relaxed me. My relationship with flowers continued. There was a yellow lily that became the bridge between my spirit and the solace of nature. My awareness of nature expanded week by week. I became more consciously aware of the possibilities offered by the breeze on a spring day, the crunch of autumn leaves, the silence of a winter evening—and not forgetting the purring of a cat, or the love in the eyes of a dog. All the manifestations of nature balanced and restored me, letting me find the whole being still inside me. To this day, the pieces of my soul that feel battered by the experiences of life, alone and separate, are reclaimed by nature's embrace. I am reminded that we are all connected, that we are all one.

Researching the Healing Potential of Nature

In this chapter, we consider nature as healer. The stories people have shared with me about their emotional healing in nature speak volumes about the solace to be found for many people in the natural world. Interestingly, from the realm of more traditional research comes a growing number of studies documenting the positive impact of nature on physical health, cognitive abilities, and productivity. Conducted through quantitative research methods, these studies provide an "evidence base" that becomes useful in arguing for change within social and business institutions.

Some of the first researchers interested in nature and health looked at whether views of nature indicate better physical health or quicker recovery from illness. Ernest O. Moore compared healthcare records of prison inmates whose cells faced farm fields with those of inmates whose cells faced the internal prison courtyard.[281] He found that prisoners who could see nature used significantly less healthcare services. Conducting similar research in a hospital setting, Roger Ulrich compared the medical records of surgery patients whose windows faced nature to those whose windows faced a brick wall.[282] Patients with a view of nature recovered more quickly, used less pain medication, and received more favorable comments from attending nurses.

According to the American Society of Landscape Architects, gardens are now included in most new hospitals in the United States. In 2012, *Scientific American* published an article titled *How Hospital Gardens Help Patients Heal.*[283] Clare Cooper Marcus, a researcher in landscape architecture at the University of California, Berkeley, was quoted as follows:

> Spending time interacting with nature in a well-designed garden won't cure your cancer or heal a badly burned leg. But there is good evidence it can reduce your levels of pain and stress—and, by doing that, boost your immune system in ways that allow your own body and other treatments to help you heal.

As summarized by Deborah Franklin, author of the article, "Just three to five minutes spent looking at views dominated by trees, flowers or water can begin to reduce anger, anxiety and pain and to induce relaxation."[284] This comes from a range of research into physiological changes in blood pressure, muscle tension, and heart and brain activity when looking at nature. Documenting the positive health impact of exposure to nature is consistent with the biophilia hypothesis of biologist and nature-writer Edward O. Wilson. He believes humans have an instinctive orientation toward nature, including a natural bond with animal and plant life.[285] The landscapes in which humans evolved—layered with trees, flowering plants, and water— seem particularly comforting. We evolved on the African savannah amidst cliffs, hillocks, and ridges, with scattered trees accessible for shelter. There were lakes or rivers to provide natural perimeters, as well as food and water. Thousands of years later, even within the most crowded cities all over the world, humans prefer such territory, often recreated in gardens and parks. Now such landscapes are being built into healing centers.

Our orientation to nature is important in healthy functioning, not just recovery from illness. Several researchers have investigated the impact of nature on our ability to focus and stay productively on task. At the University of Michigan, an Attention Restoration Theory (ART) was developed from studies indicating our abilities to direct attention are improved through exposure to natural environments.[286] Directing attention is important to successful cognitive and emotional functioning. The authors of the theory, Marc G. Berman, John Jonides, and Stephen Kaplan, explained: "Nature, which is filled with intriguing stimuli, modestly grabs attention in a bottom-up fashion, allowing top-down directed-attention abilities a chance to replenish." [287] In contrast, "urban environments are filled with stimulation that captures attention dramatically and additionally requires directed attention (e.g., to avoid being hit by a car), making them less restorative."[288]

Combining environmental and psychological perspectives, Rachel and Stephen Kaplan described nature as a "restorative environment."[289] In *The Experience of Nature: A Psychological Perspective*, the Kaplans referenced growing evidence that people with access to nature in their workplace have comparably less stress and more well-being. Workers who see flowers and trees report higher job satisfaction and have fewer negative things to say about work. Seeing nature from work also correlates with fewer illnesses and headaches. Similar findings exist with respect to life outside the office. Viewing nature from home windows increases satisfaction with one's residence, as well as health and well-being. Jules Perry, another researcher, found that viewing pleasant rural scenes during physical exercise positively impacts blood pressure, self-esteem, and mood.[290]

"Green infrastructure" in urban areas has been shown to positively impact "complete physical, mental and social well-being."[291] Nature "buffers" life stress in children.[292] The Kaplans articulated four elements of the "restorative experience" associated with nature:

- being away from the need for sustained directed attention so common in civilized life;
- sensing connection to something larger in scope than oneself, which they call *extent* (and which can also be described by the word *transpersonal*);
- fascination, defined as interest without directed attention; and
- *action and compatibility*, meaning interaction with an environment that seems to support the individual, like the wind at one's back.

To support research into the benefits of nature experience, Elizabeth Nisbet, John Zelenski, and Steven Murphy developed a Nature Relatedness Scale to quantify "the affective, cognitive, and experiential aspects of an individual's connection to nature."[293] As part of their argument for the reliability and validity of the question and answer assessment, these researchers noted that personality variables, such as "agreeableness and openness," correlated well with scores on the Nature Relatedness Scale. This does not mean individuals might not change and grow over time in both personality characteristics and relatedness to nature, but suggests our psychologies are enmeshed deeply with our orientation to the natural world.

Researcher are beginning to use the Nature Relatedness Scale to establish relationships between various other measures of psychological health. For instance, Patricia Martyn and Eric Brymer found that nature relatedness was significantly correlated with lower levels of anxiety with respect to both passing states of anxiety and anxiety as an ongoing trait.[294] In using the scale they created, Nisbet and Zelenski, found nature relatedness is connected to overall happiness. They specifically assessed whether it was a sense of connection in general that controlled happiness, but found that feeling connected to nature appears to adds a layer of happiness distinct from our connection to friends, loved ones, or other aspects of life.[295]

Within the last few years, some healthcare researchers have characterized nature as an "upstream health promotion intervention." [296] Scholars affiliated with the School of Health and Social Development at Deakin University, Melbourne, Australia, suggested "too much artificial stimulation and an existence spent in purely human environments may cause exhaustion and produce a loss of vitality and health."[297] Drawing on a wide range of research, these authors concluded that natural spaces "provide a fundamental setting for health promotion and the creation of well-being for urban populations that to date have lacked due recognition."[298] From a public health perspective, they argue "natural areas can be seen as one of our most vital health resources."[299] Their final assessment: "In the context of the growing worldwide mental illness burden of disease, contact with nature may offer an affordable, accessible and equitable choice in tackling the imminent epidemic, within both preventative and restorative public health strategies."[300]

Since certain communities (e.g., public agencies, schools, health care) grant "reality" status to evidence-based research conducted in the scientific model, one can applaud the growth of "evidence" about our human need for nature. But I cannot help noting the irony of living in a culture that has so removed itself from nature—and constructed analytical, objective ways of assessing "reality"—that we discuss immersion in nature as a "health promotion intervention." Granted, from present academic and institutional perspectives, this is the language necessary to gain the attention of people with power to implement change. Yet it is strange, and to me kind of hilarious, to envision "science" coming up with the idea of "nature" as a healthcare strategy. From the perspective of a species evolving within nature for hundreds of thousands of years, descended from other species living *as* nature for millions of years, we might chuckle with our scientific "discovery" that we can now "intervene" in our health through using the "variable" of nature.

Our Ecological Selves

In earlier chapters, we considered various conceptions of an internal self through which our psychologies operate in the world. We now consider what it might mean to develop an "ecological self." Arne Naess, a Norwegian philosopher and mountaineer, first talked about an "ecological identity" or "ecological self" to describe our internal sense of identification with nature. [301] He invented the term "deep ecology" to suggest study of the underlying reasons for human disconnection from nature and abuse of the natural world. Since Naess, several other deep ecologists and psychologists have considered what it might mean to have an ecological self. Clinical psychologist Sarah Conn describes a way of being that explores all the connections between "the inner and outer landscapes within which we live" and looks "for diversity, interconnectedness and flows of nourishment."[302] Conn distinguishes this form of understanding oneself from what is prevalent in our culture:

> In our Western Euro-American culture, the dominant psychology of the self is still based on the Cartesian worldview. Humans are seen as separate from and hierarchically superior to the non-human world. Individual humans are seen as separated from each other, and some humans are thought to be superior to other humans. Most of us describe ourselves by our occupational, family, gender, racial or ethnic roles. Most of our descriptions of ourselves are nouns preceded with an "a." "I am a woman, a psychologist, a mother, a wife, a WASP." This way of describing ourselves emphasizes separateness, boundedness, fixedness, reification, non fluidity. We think we can locate ourselves as a "thing" in space and time, separate from other "things" in other spaces and times. This is the dominant version of reality: the world is a collection of separate entities that are related mechanically if at all. We have narrowed the experience of connectedness to dominance, manipulation and control.[303]

Conn envisions an ecological self as fluid, a process of becoming more than a static identity. She draws on the nuances of the word for "insanity" in the Native American language Okanagan. Each of the nuances of insanity involves an element of static separation. The first is "the tendency to 'talk, talk inside your head.'"[304] This involves separation from sensations and emotions. Development of an ecological self would include attending to the "ecology of experience, to look at how our feelings and sensations fit together with the talk inside our heads."[305] The second element involves "being 'scattered and having no community.'"[306] Developing an ecological self, according to Conn, eases out of this separation by "recognizing the communities of which we are a part, developing rituals which enliven and maintain those communities, and practicing citizenship in new, more direct ways."[307]

The third separation coming from the Okanagan word for insanity involves "having no relationship to the land."[308] The fourth is being "disconnected from the whole-earth part."[309] The process of becoming an ecological self moves us toward understandings ourselves as part of the ecosystems around us and the larger life of the earth. Conn writes: "As parts of the larger air, water, soil, meaning and feeling systems around us, both biosphere and culture, nature and nurture, this means to know ourselves as wholes in our constant partness."[310] Conn recognizes this process as learning to harmonize with the ever-changing ecology around us. As with evolution on a macro scale, the environments around us are constantly changing, adapting. In developing an ecological self, in Conn's understanding, "a healthy individual's identity changes continually, expanding and contracting according to the context of the moment" and potentially moving "beyond the family, the neighborhood, the country or even the planet, to include the sense of being a part of the evolving ecological universe at the same time that one's sense of coherence, uniqueness and connectedness are sustained."[311]

In developing an ecological self, we may find we are shifting our identification into someone who is a participant within nature, even if most of our time is spent within civilization. This entire book could be considered a description of my particular process of developing an ecological self. For some of us, this begins with deconstruction of identification solely within culture—moving past the many separations Conn and others describe. Since much of that identification with culture is unconsciously held, increasing our awareness of the exclusion of nature from consensus trance is part of the process. This is not necessarily a straightforward process since our internal sense of self involves layers of our psyche that are not completely accessible to conscious processing. Layers and layers of emotions, memories, habits, and conditioning may be tied up with a sense of self separate from nature.

It may be useful to write down how we each understand ourselves in connection with nature. I will go first. I have come to understand myself as someone living now within twenty-first century American culture, with increasing participation in an international community, as the descendent of billions of earthly life forms that have produced Homo sapiens in our current form, one of which is me. I understand myself as related to all those other life forms, those now living, and those who are now extinct. I am trying to move into more and more comfort with that understanding, including eventual contact, to the extent possible, with more and more of my relatives. As Conn described, for me, there is a simultaneous draw to the particularities of manifestations of the natural world around me, as well as a "taking within myself" of the world and even universe as a whole.

This brings us to what many of our indigenous cousins have known all along, but for those of us in Western Culture, I think it is helpful to get there in a way that incorporates our intellectual and scientific traditions about evolution, psychology, neuroscience, anthropology and history. Otherwise, there is the danger we take wisdom from indigenous cultures as myths in the sense of not real and keep those understandings split off from how we hold material science. This brings us back to the divides many people unconsciously hold between "stories" that involve connection and spirituality and "science" which includes dissection and separation. When I write that my sense of an ecological self includes my non-human ancestors and cousins, that is a realistic assessment of who I am in embodied form and who my ancestors have been as something that really happened, not something that is symbolic, though of course the symbolic is also generated. I *am* the descendant of creatures that were like monkeys, and before them the ancestors included creatures halfway between mammals and reptiles, and before that were reptiles, and on and on backwards. Any creature now living is my cousin, in fact, though I will concede the consanguinity is often as cousin many times removed.

I will say more about my understanding of an ecological self, but let me first turn to what some others have said about developing an ecological self. Joanna Macy was among the first to describe a process of "greening of the self," an incorporation of planetary ecology into an experience of oneself. [312] In the chapter on grief, we looked at how grief may emerge as we release repressions and unfreeze traumatic experiences that may have become frozen within us. Macy was among the first to realize our lives as separated from nature and threatening each other with annihilation based on technology is a frozen trauma for many people. As part of a "greening of the self," Macy believes, facing this trauma is necessary. This means allowing the surfacing of grief, even despair. As we open ourselves to experiencing the world inside us, particularly an experience of nature, it tends to hurt. "Far from being crazy," she writes, "this pain is a testimony to the unity of all life, the deep interconnection that relates us to all things."[313] Macy and her colleagues believe "profound existential changes" become possible "when we own and use, rather than repress, our pain for the world."[314]

As Macy writes, healing the split in the psyche cutting us off from the material world involves dismantling the experience of ego-self as separate from the natural world.[315] To develop an ecological self we need to face the feelings that arise if we release our sense of self as protected encapsulated civilized beings. To face the feelings, we need to make conscious what has happened to us with respect to nature. To assist a dismantling of that separate ego-self, I developed the narrative about how we humans arrived at our current predicament which forms the first three chapters of this book. On a more personal level, Macy and her colleagues have offered workshops that assist people in finding ways to release their sense of separation from nature and the world.

Interestingly, the concept of an ecological self emerges from a place where psychology and ecology meet. The ecological movement began several decades ago to incorporate psychological understandings in order to reach the root causes of environmental degradation. The environmental movement initially gained force in the 1960s and 1970s with mostly social, political and biological perspectives, but some ecologists began to realize it was necessary to look deeply within the human psyche. As noted above, Arne Naess created the concept of "deep ecology" in order to distinguish a movement looking into the inner workings of humanity from one concerned with more "shallow" solutions.

Depth psychology and deep ecology meet at the place where both seek to understand the structures underlying contemporary human alienation from a healthy relationship between self and surroundings. George Sessions, a leading voice in deep ecology, describes a goal of encouraging "a major paradigm shift—a shift in perception, values, and lifestyles—as a basis for redirecting the ecologically destructive path of modern industrial growth societies."[316] Ultimately, this is a psychological issue, involving what prevents each of us from understanding harm to the natural world as harm to ourselves, our families, and our communities. As far as I am concerned, any paradigm shift includes individual people shifting how they understand themselves.

Warwick Fox, an Australian philosopher, encourages a blending of deep ecology and transpersonal psychology. In *Toward a Transpersonal Ecology*, Fox advocates "psychologizing" deep ecology and "ecologizing" of transpersonal psychology. [317] The psychologizing of deep ecology would require more conscious concern with an individual's "opening to ecological awareness; with realizing one's ecological, wider, or bigger Self."[318] Toward this goal, deep ecology would attempt to conceptualize, and then study, the experience of self as inclusive of the natural world. From the other direction, the ecologizing of transpersonal psychology would broaden the locus of study from the human individual to the matrix of relationship in a natural context, a stance viewed by Fox as less anthropocentric. Anathema to environmentalists, anthropocentrism has been defined as "the position that human beings are the central or most significant species on the planet (in the sense that they are considered to have a moral status different to that of other animals), or the assessment of reality through an exclusively human perspective."[319]

A broadening of transpersonal psychology beyond a human perspective was encouraged by Jose Ferrer in what he describes as a "participatory turn." [320] In *Revisioning Transpersonal Theory: A Participatory Vision of Human Spirituality,* Jorge Ferrer explains:

> The basic idea underlying the participatory turn, then, is not that an expansion of individual consciousness allows access to transpersonal contents, but rather that the emergence of a transpersonal event precipitates in the individual what has been called a transpersonal experience. Thus understood, the ontological dimension of transpersonal phenomenon is primary and results in the experiential one. Transpersonal experiences do not lead to transpersonal knowledge, but rather transpersonal participatory events elicit in the individual what have been commonly called transpersonal experiences.[321]

Essentially, Ferrer moves the "reality" status of transpersonal experience from individual human consciousness into a transpersonal realm. While not focusing on nature, Ferrer avoids anthropocentrism by opening the possibility that other life forms within the natural world might "participate" in transpersonal events as much as human consciousness. Ferrer illustrates his conception of spiritual phenomenon with "the visionary transfiguration of the world that occurs in nature mysticism." He writes:

> In nature mysticism, as well as during certain ritual uses of entheogens [substances enhancing consciousness, like psychedelics], the natural world can be drastically transformed and unfold with an exalted quality of depth, pregnant meaning, profound numinosity, luscious Life, and sacred Mystery. In the context of the participatory vision, *this transfiguration of the world is not seen as a mere change in our individual experience of a pregiven world, but as the emergence of an ontological event in reality in which our consciousness creatively participates.* In other words, it is not so much our experience of the world that changes, but rather our experience-and-the-world that undergo a mutually codetermined transformation.[322]

Ferrer's expansion of transpersonal experience into participatory events is helpful in realizing that individual human consciousness may not be the best focal point in assessing experiences that seem to involve transpersonal realms. We can apply this general idea to developing an ecological self including the understanding that our consciousness now as processed through the "television set" of the Homo sapiens brain is not necessarily the only "television set" that has ever existed or ever will exist. In other words, my sense of self shaped at least in part by my current anatomy and cultural training is participating at this moment in historical time in a life in the material world. All the other beings who have emerged from the natural world—living now and living in the past—were participants in the same unfolding history of life. We should remember at this point what I have said several times already: that I have come to believe there is some aspect of our consciousness which participates in non-material realms that exist outside of historical time and material space.

Putting this together into an experience of an ecological self, I am my consciousness as evolving now, one member of billions of the species Homo sapiens, expanding myself to include within my sense of self all other life forms that have existed and may exist in the future as equal partners in whatever it is that is happening in our corner of the universe. We are all participants. It is interesting to note that David Abram also likes to describe us as participating in nature, as noted in Chapter 3. The reason for my narrative of deconstructing our "thinking" self as conveyed in the early chapters of this book is that it seems to me, as it has seemed to Shepard, Berman, and others, that even with our civilized, analytical, conceptualizing, thinking, habits of being, we retain within us the ability to resume a participation in nature through a state of consciousness that knows how to disperse itself into nature. In the language of Abram and phenomenologists, this would be a state of awareness that participates in nature through the body, including most importantly sensations. David Levin wrote about an "elemental body-self" with the ability to integrate into "the elements" through a "bodily belonging to the earth."[323] This possibility feels to me a most important component of a developing ecological self.

My conceptualization of an ecological self takes into account this embodied, non-thinking, way of experiencing nature. Whether this is called participation or by any other name does not matter a great deal to me. For me personally, I move toward an ecological self by retaining memory of the ways that I have felt when deeply connected to nature, which is why my experience meditating in the rain has framed this book. What matters is holding onto memory of that state of being and increasing the possibility of acting from that state of being in ordinary life. During those numinous moments when I have experienced deep connection with the natural world, mostly I am feeling an overwhelming sense of gratitude for a physical-emotional-sensory opening into myself. We shall return to the experience of gratitude in response to nature in Chapter 11, Sensing God in Nature, but for now, let us understand that this orientation of gratitude in connection with nature is a trajectory of the evolving ecological self.

Humility about our human position in respect to the panoply of evolution and nature, as well the unfolding evolution of the cosmos in addition to our one planet, is an important experiential component of what feels like an emerging ecological self. With respect to anthropocentrism, I have never considered humans central to the universe, perhaps because of my awareness of the severe limits of humans. This is not humility in the sense of being a good boy by being humble but is experience-based. I would even say, evidence-based. The tragic limits of human awareness and understanding have been clear to me for as long as I can remember. One of the reasons I enjoy science fiction, including the various incarnations of *Star Trek*, is to envision the possibility of not only humanity growing up, but humanity coming into contact with some other beings with a bit more perspective than we have yet developed. Mr. Spock, when did you say the Vulcans are coming? And, yes, I know the Vulcans control their emotions but they do this so they do not act them out unconsciously, an improvement over how most of us roll on the planet.

Having known a fair number of non-human animals fairly intimately (admittedly most of them domesticated, though there was my wild raven friend, several wild rabbit acquaintances, and a brief summer with a few coyotes), I have a deep respect for our cousins on the planet. Many of them seem wiser than us. Indeed, perhaps sadly, sometimes I am more inclined to respect animals more deeply than humans. When I read about self-consciousness existing in humans and not in non-human animals, I find myself looking around for those self-conscious humans. I will confess to great sympathy with Lemuel Gulliver's decision to live with horses rather than flawed humans on his return from *Gulliver's Travels* in Jonathan Swift's great work of fiction. This is not to say that I lack compassion for us humans—to the contrary. But with respect to how I hold an ecological self, I hold all of us Homo sapiens as works in progress.

I will now more overtly add a transpersonal component to the concept of an ecological self. My version of a transpersonal-ecological self includes awareness that we humans at present are biological creatures embodying consciousness at certain stages of biological and consciousness evolution. My understanding emphasizes the dynamic nature of earthly evolution over the few billion years our planet has been around. We have no choice but to view our participation in transpersonal realms as emerging from what the phenomenologists would call the *Dasein* of our particular historical lens. It is my hope that our *Dasein* as a collective will increasingly include recollection of where we have been, where we are now, what we have lost and what it seems we are about to lose.

This becomes significant in the conception (and description) of a transpersonal-ecological self. For me, that ecological self includes remembering—from the increasingly inclusive level of psychospiritual development emerging in our global culture—all that has happened in our biological evolution, including all the ways of being through which we, our ancestors, and our cousins, all the other life forms, have evolved. In another writing project, tentatively titled *Remembering All the Way Back*, I imagine myself—and our species—back through history and evolution. In our time, through evolutionary biology, anthropology, archeology and many other disciplines, we can piece together a story of our origins based on what actually happened. Others have undertaken similar imaginings. For instance, Brian Swimme and Thomas Berry have written *The Universe Story: From the Primordial Flaring Forth to the Ecozoic Era—A Celebration of the Unfolding of the Cosmos.* [324] Swimme narrated the highly acclaimed documentary *Journey of the Universe,* described by musician Paul Winter as the "saga of the 14 billion year journey of the universe…the greatest story ever told…the context of the vast perspective of time and space that we need to orient and reconcile our personal journeys on this tiny speck called Earth."[325]

As I imagine my way backwards in *Remembering All the Way Back*, first back to our parents, then our grandparents, etc., and then a hundred-thousand years back to when we became Homo sapiens, then six-million years back to our common ancestor with chimpanzees, and then millions more years back as primates, then mammals, then reptiles, and fish, and eventually, going backwards, single celled organisms, and biological life beginning at a hot fissure at the bottom of the ocean, I identify with every aspect of awareness in which life has taken form during the history of our planet. My sense of self and being expands through this imagined journey, allowing me to understand all of us as nature. I am grateful for an increasing sense that I am one participant—albeit for a very brief moment in time—in unfolding evolution on earth and in the cosmos.

Moving toward this sense of a transpersonal-ecological self, it seems to me, is deeply healing. As a template for becoming, there is little that I cannot take within myself and see how it feels. It is important yet again to remember that my sense of a transpersonal-ecological self includes ways of being and knowing more inclusive of all of the possibilities for experiencing the world around me than my thinking, conceptualizing mind. The integral vision of Ken Wilber is helpful in articulating a stage of awareness in human evolution in which all prior stages of consciousness are incorporated.[326] Through nonordinary states available in Holotropic

Breathwork and other modalities, ways of being and states of awareness held by our ancestors and cousins in the animal, even plant, kingdoms are included within my conception of a transpersonal-ecological self moving towards wholeness.

From a Jungian perspective, my evolving transpersonal-ecological self would include all levels of my personal psyche and the collective psyche. Some of those levels are unconscious but become accessible to me through symbolic mechanisms that often include an involvement or recollection of nature. Within my transpersonal-ecological self are thus all the real and imaged, actual and archetypal, conscious and unconscious, representatives of nature that appear in my dreams and manifest in the mythology, arts, and practices of all of our cultures. From such an evolving sense of self, the various parts of myself that I project out onto nature, or bring back within my internal sense of self from nature, are parts of my evolving transpersonal-ecological self. As I move into becoming the next versions of myself in the world, and leave behind any limitations from my civilized self that I no longer admire, then I am becoming nature in ways that are increasingly conscious and whole.

Nature as Therapy

Julie Longhill wrote to me when she was living in Cleveland, Ohio, near a twenty mile stretch of parks. *I was always attracted to nature. When I was growing up, I would run out into the woods, climb trees, and just sit there and watch. I loved the animals. As an adult, my love for nature re-emerged when I started to recover from my psychological hurts. When I moved to Cleveland, I found the Metroparks. Then I found an apartment close to the parks so I could walk. Around the same time that I started therapy, I began painting outdoors. Painting was meditative for me—I became one with the trees, the water, and the flowers. This was nature's therapy. I felt safe in nature, calm, and inspired. I truly felt loved—and I loved nature back.*

I have engaged in many therapeutic practices, particularly those involving my body. Before I began this healing, I was disconnected from my physical self. I was numb. I believe my body had been traumatized. Nature played an important role in my healing. The healing presence of nature helped me feel connected to something larger than myself. My body feels the wind—my body even feels the birds and the trees. When the river overflows its banks and rushes with great fury, I feel that energy. Yesterday I felt the energy of high winds—it was invigorating, rejuvenating. My body feels this and I feel cleansed.

The silence and the beauty allow me the space to feel my emotions. When I am in nature, I am not judged, or dismissed, or shamed for feeling. Nature even helps my anger. I recently took a walk in the park when I was very angry. I felt safe enough to kick the snow and rant and rave at the sky. The truth is: humans are not as good as nature in witnessing pain and emotions and allowing them just to be.

I took a walk one spring day when I was feeling quite down about myself and the world. My relationships weighed heavily on my mind. I couldn't shake my funk. As I walked, I began to cry. I was very aware of nature all around me—my trees, the sky, the birds, even the air. Crying felt good and rejuvenating. I felt as though nature was nurturing me, holding me in its arms. The further I walked, the more serene I became, and the tears turned into humming, and the humming became a song: A black crow in a blue sky, it doesn't get much better than that, like a rainbow and a butterfly, it doesn't get much better than that. The song came from a time that day when I was lying in the grass, looking up at the sky, and a beautiful crow flew overhead. It was so black, and the sky was so blue: in that moment, I had never seen anything so beautiful. I realized that nature is the ultimate healer, if we only embrace it, let ourselves merge into its glory.

Years later, when I reconnected with Julie, she told me she left Cleveland not long after she wrote to me about her experiences in the Metroparks. *We left with the soul mission of un-plugging from society, reconnecting with nature, in order to feel and heal our inner emotional selves. For over a year, we lived in a tent in Florida . . . and wrote songs about our experience. After we left Florida, we found ourselves in South Carolina (foothills of the Smoky Mountains). We have been here for seven years; surrounded by waterfalls and National forests . . . it has allowed more grief to surface . . . wow! I had no idea how much grief my soul was carrying. The Cherokee in this area said the "mountains have water eyes" . . . (waterfalls). We have led healing circles here, and continue to dedicate our lives to healing in nature.*

Taking in Julie's story once again after many years, I am reminded that nature acts for Julie, for me, and I imagine for many other people, like the "good enough mother" who affirms our hopes and holds our fears as we create the selves we want to be in the world. She is not an omnipotent mother with whom we want to fuse to avoid our need for separation, she is a familiar place where we can connect with our sensations and emotions, remembering ways of being that are our heritage. She activates our growth and healing rather than stifles it. She holds us while we separate from those things, and people, in our lives who we realize are not good for us. Granted, anyone can project onto nature as onto anything else, or avoid facing problems by going into nature as in thousands of other ways. But if we connect with nature as Julie has, she is more likely to offer us reality than almost anything we can find in civilization. As many people are discovering, nature is an ally in therapy.

Within the last few decades, a number of therapists have developed therapeutic styles involving nature, including recognition that nature helps us process our grief. We now have eco-therapy, nature-guided therapy, wilderness therapy, and adventure therapy, among other nature-related therapies. Many of these therapies are designed to assist behavioral changes, foster empowerment, or help emotional processing of personal issues. Underlying the therapies is an experiential understanding that alignment with nature assists many people in healing from personal psychological wounds and suffering. The proponents of these methods share the goal of breaking down psychological barriers between our experience of ourselves and nature—in part to take advantage of the healing potential of nature, in part to help us become people who remember we are part of nature. One of these proponents, Howard Clinebell, puts it this way: we need both education and therapy based on "an understanding of human growth and healing that includes the deep earth-rootedness of all aspects of our species."[327]

In *Ecotherapy: Healing Ourselves, Healing the Earth*, Clinebell describes various techniques to assist this transformation. The first involves *consciousness-raising* because "many people are so out of touch with the natural world that they are unaware of both the deep pain and healing energies of the biosphere."[328] He recommends people complete an *ecological wellness checkup*, a questionnaire for assessing our relationship to nature and our awareness of ecological issues. Ecotherapy focuses on *nature-issues* through discussion of a client's personal relationship with nature. Clinebell invites sharing of stories about nature and learning facts about the ecological crisis. Ecotherapy examines both personal and collective issues through noticing the inter-relationship of all things, offering nature as a healing presence, and breaking through our collective denial surrounding our loss of nature.

Clinebell encourages "increased nurture by nature."[329] Even when immersion in nature is not possible, guided imagery techniques involving the natural world encourage movement toward wholeness and recovery from psychological problems. Corollary techniques focus on images of the natural world appearing in dreams and creative expression (arts, photography, or writing) to bring the energy of nature into one's life. Consistent with research regarding the healing impact of nature within institutional settings, Clinebell suggests an ecological "greening and cleaning" of the places we conduct counseling, education, and life, recognizing that healing the individual, and healing the earth, can be "mutually reinforcing processes."[330]

Like Joanna Macy, Clinebell understands grief to underlie our collective disconnection from nature. Since psychological healing often involves accessing repressed grief, Clinebell's Ecotherapy uses nature as a fulcrum for exploring grief in the hope of healing both personal and social wounds. "Among earth-loving people," Clinebell writes, "grief is an often-hidden component of the reality-based feelings triggered by the day-to-day evidence of our deteriorating environment."[331] Accessing our grief "can help identify amorphous feelings of discomfort, loss, depression, and sadness about the environmental crisis, and facilitate movement toward using that energy for earth-caring action."[332]

Nature may help us release repression against experiencing grief around losses in our personal life. Clinebell recalls a story shared by one of his clients:

> The man mentioned the death of his father and was about to pass over this huge loss quickly, when he said he had cried just once. After his father's death, he was camping with his current girlfriend near a rushing creek with a tiny island of granite boulders. He told of being able to cry as he sat alone on one of the rocks, surrounded by rushing water. When asked how that felt, he said, "It was so good to just let go."[333]

While nature can feel psychologically healing for many people, for others, it may trigger unhappy memories, fear, or even a post-trauma response. Nature-related trauma must be healed before nature becomes therapeutic. As Clinebell notes, this might include gradual exposure (real or imagery-based) to the natural phenomena associated with the trauma or simply visiting nature in safe outings if the fear is more general. Revisiting the source of a particular trauma in nature may invite exploration of other aspects of the negative experience. When nature is the source of trauma, healing will likely require recognition that nature *is* dangerous, even murderous. As discussed in a later chapter, realizing that nature is both the giver and taker of life may assist existential shifts in understanding and worldview, relieving not only negative associations with nature, but opening an easier path for psychospiritual transformation. Some spiritual teachers, as well as existential philosophers and psychologists, maintain that acceptance of the reality of death is a prerequisite, and harbinger, of psychological and spiritual maturity. Accepting that nature brings death as well as life strikes me as necessary for eco-psychological maturity. This also cures any tendency we may have to project "all-good" into nature. Perhaps paradoxically, taking into our souls the harsh realities of nature is not contradictory with experiencing nature as a healing force.

Ecopsychotherapy developed by George W. Burns is another therapeutic model drawing on nature as "an initiator of health, healing, and well-being."[334] Burns understands well-being to include living in a healthy environment while experiencing "a harmonious connection with that ecology."[335] He encourages his clients to develop their unique sensory orientations toward nature based on sight, sound, smell, taste, and touch. The therapist may provide "sensory awareness directives" to encourage deepening of sensory experiences in nature. Such directives "are not about simply being *in* nature," but suggest "being *with* nature . . . being part of the process.[336] Burns describes this as an *ecocentric* approach to therapy, with the client encouraged to move his identification of self out into the natural world.

Burns suggests the potential value of *nature ordeals*. Drawing on the success of paradoxical therapeutic techniques, as advocated by Fritz Perls, Jay Haley, and others, the therapist instructs the client to "go ahead" with problematic behavior, as long as the behavior is followed by some endeavor in nature. The therapist assigns a task in nature the client will likely view as difficult, time-consuming, or otherwise burdensome. For example, a client who wishes to stop overeating, but has been unsuccessful with dieting or exercise, may be asked to walk an hour in nature following every diet lapse. While the walk may at first seem onerous, once in nature the client may find pleasure not previously experienced. At the same time, the client obtains exercise and may release any consuming self-focus involved with many problematic behaviors.

Working in Israel, Ronen Berger described another version of nature-based therapy. He describes his practice as an "interdisciplinary and experiential approach which draws from disciplines such as Drama Therapy, Narrative Psychology, Adventure Therapy, Anthropology and Ecopsychology."[337] He views "the therapeutic process as a journey allowing the client to work on relevant emotional, physical, spiritual, [and] cognitive issues" through direct contact with nature. In Berger's nature therapy, the "self" is understood not only in relationship with other people, "but also by relationships and interactions with the culture and environment that the person lives in."[338] Nature is considered a partner in the therapy, forming a triad with the client and therapist, providing "sacred space" or a possible "home" to facilitate sharing and healing.

Sarah Conn, mentioned in the preceding section for her understanding of an ecological self, suggests that any sense of personal pain, whether physical or psychological, can be understood by a therapist as "both unique to the person *and* as a signal from a larger context, as 'the earth speaking through us.'"[339] She draws on Don Mazer's idea that therapists might become "naturalists of the psyche."[340] This would involve "learning to hear, see, feel the 'earth speaking through' the symptom and developing ways it might be pointing towards the symptom-holder's fuller, more mindful participation in the larger community."[341] Conn provides an example of working with a client she calls Mary Lou, a single professional woman in her forties. When Mary Lou referred to "the pit" of her depression, Conn invited her to "take an imaginal walk through the pit, paying attention to the ecology of the landscape."[342]

Mary Lou first described "a psychic monoculture, with no diversity, no sense of connectedness, and no nourishment flow."[343] When Conn asked her to focus "on her bodily sensations, her direct sensual awareness of the pit," Mary Lou was initially stuck "in that thought, that way of 'talking, talking inside her head.'"[344] Then she reached a feeling of fear, and as "the numbness began to differentiate," Mary Lou was able to connect her feelings to her relationship history and family background. The therapy then considered Mary Lou's experience of separation from others as well as from her community and the earth. Honoring "the diversity and complexity" of Mary Lou's inner experience was aligned with noticing the diversity and complexity of the natural world all around her. Conn finds it important at this stage of therapy to look for "flows of nourishment" for the client in ever-expanding circles of inclusiveness. She asks: "What forms of interactions with the more-than-human world and to the land might provide support for sustaining psychological growth and aliveness?"[345]

Many therapeutic approaches involve immersion in the natural world as a means to encourage psychological healing or growth. Wilderness therapy is considered particularly valuable for youth, women, and abuse survivors. Wilderness programs assist development of self-esteem, positive motivation, and the ability to cooperate with others.[346] In the wilds, people work on communication skills, discipline, and the gradual release of the aggressive and self-destructive tendencies experienced by many people, particularly youth, in our "civilized" culture. In *Breaking through Barriers: Wilderness Therapy for Sexual Assault Survivors,* Deborah Levine describes the propensity of wilderness to "promote team building, trust, self-esteem, confidence, intimacy and personal growth" for assault victims.[347]

Other wilderness programs for women seek transformation of negative body-image or problematic self-assumptions and behaviors. Ellen Cole, Eve Erdman, and Esther Rothblum share their experience in wilderness work:

> [W]omen together in the wilderness, taking risks, become empowered in a way that enables them to break through gender barriers—and therapeutic barriers—by facing the basic unforgiving state of nature together. The stark metaphors of uncertainty and daring allow women to rekindle their natural spirits in ways that cannot be achieved in a traditional therapeutic setting.[348]

Irene Powch finds "two distinct components of wilderness therapy—the healing effects of specific therapeutic activities in a novel environment, and the more elusive, spiritual healing effects of a newly found, or renewed sense of connectedness with the powers of the earth and the creative life cycle in the wilderness."[349] In nature, Powch emphasizes, feedback in challenging experiences is immediate and concrete.[350] She finds this empowering, particularly for women, because the response of the wilderness is even-handed, not preferential to men. Nature rewards concrete mastery, regardless of gender or background.[351] Describing her sense of the spiritual component in nature, Powch recalls an experience while rock-climbing in Zion National Park:

> I looked out over the horizon at an endless stretch of red rock, white rock, sage—and suddenly everything was different. I no longer just felt the warmth of the sun, smelled the scents of earth and sage, saw the rock and sky—these were no longer just sensory experiences—a moment had crept upon me where everything transformed. I was enveloped by a sense of belonging and being "in place" that I had never known before.[352]

Powch compares this feeling to the deep intimacy occurring when two people "open up" to each other. "Magnify this a thousand times," she writes. "Imagine this emanating not from one focus, one person, but from every rock, every breath of air, every pore of earth. Imagine strongly feeling the power of the universe, and taking your place in it, knowing it is within you."[353]

Merry Coburn studied the experience of psychospiritual transformation by twelve women in mid life who walked over two thousand miles on the Appalachian Trail in the southern-central United States.[354] From listening to the women's stories, reading their writing, and viewing artwork or images related to their experience, Coburn discerned the following themes relating to the wilderness experience: "encountering the embodied feminine, dissolving boundaries between the self and the wild, experiencing acceptance, being in relationship, everything as it should be, connected, challenging, trustworthy, sensual, vast, timeless, ever changing."[355] She concluded wilderness experience encouraged the emergence of a more integrated and expansive level of psychospiritual development, as well as an increase in service to others and creativity in self-expression.

David Cumes, a medical doctor who trained with indigenous shamanic healers, believes the energies of nature activate a healing force inside us. In *Inner Passages, Outer Journeys: Wilderness, Healing and the Discovery of Self*, Cumes suggests nature connects us with "the place of inner peace, calm, harmony, and at oneness."[356] From his shamanic training, Cumes experiences connection with nature as literally bringing personal life force, dissipated for a variety of reasons, back into the body. In *The Spirit of Healing*, he remembers an insight from one of his early travels: "One day, while adjusting to the effects of high altitude on my first morning at 11,000 feet in Peru, a sense of knowing or a small voice crept into my consciousness as I rested on the bed. It said, 'You need to translate your life into your physical body. This is your route to inner peace.'"[357] Through the physical body, as I have been saying, nature comes alive and heals.

In Nature…

After many years of city life, Linda Carroll Hassler moved to rural Arkansas. Recalling her urban life, Linda writes: *There was a time when I had anxiety attacks. During my first experience of this kind of panic in my body, I rocked back and forth indoors, but then something told me to go outside and lay on the grass, spread-eagled. This felt* right. *After a while, the panic eased from my body. A few years later, I had an experience of feeling weak after a medical procedure. I was in a concert hall and followed my intuition into the outdoors. I lay down on the ground, spreading my arms and legs. I needed something the earth could give me, and I knew this instinctively.*

When I am feeling distraught, nature seems to embrace me, to comfort me, to allow me. I have experienced nature like a giant bed, where I could feel safe, protected by the sheets and blankets, the softness underneath. Nature is so enormous; I feel as if God and the Great Ones are there, and they are on my side.

In western Canada, I have marveled at the loons singing in the trees, often a mile away from each other, calling and answering as the evening sets in. Their sounds are perfect for entraining all who can hear, human or other animal, bringing us into the same harmony. I hear them saying, "Day's over, relax together, let us quiet down, time to sleep and dream." The same message is brought by the wind, whether it is breeze or gale, refreshing the air we breathe, bringing change, yet consistency, safety in the rhythms.

I have often said that I want to die outdoors. I'll be so much more comforted and assured. Put me under a tree in the sunshine or under the night sky. Even in the rain, cover my head and body, but get me outside. If we approach nature with a tad of reverence, she can produce feelings of awe that wipe away petty thoughts and worries. Nature sweetly offers sounds that are not too loud or jarring; the murmurs of nature reassure me.

When I'm in nature, I feel secure, at home, because I feel how many living things are all around me. Most of them are small, not even visible, but they are life. We are related; we are the same; I am not alone. In nature,

I am surrounded by life and, intuitively, I feel that all is right with the world. None of the living things around me are complaining about their lot in life; they do not appear to be suffering; they are accepting of what they are. Nature just is.

Janet Taylor lives in Victoria, on Vancouver Island. For many years, she worked as coordinator of the Spiritual Emergence Service, a Canadian organization offering therapy referrals for people involved in spiritual emergency. Janet grew up in the Okamagan Valley, another part of British Columbia, near warm lakes and superb beaches. *When I was twelve,* she writes, *my brother and I voluntarily joined the United Church, which is similar to the Episcopal Church in the United States. Two years older than me, my brother believed in God, but I listened to the minister and decided I did not believe what he was saying. Still, I wanted to participate in the church group with my friends, and decided that if there was a God, he probably wouldn't mind.*

It was the summer between seventh and eighth grades. Life was difficult at home. There were long periods of conflict with my father when the only time I was allowed to leave home was when I was involved in church activities. I was allowed to attend camp for two weeks, a welcome break from my home life. We traveled to Cultus Lake, British Columbia. It was evening vesper services, just as the sun was setting. We were gathered on the shore of the lake. I was slightly away from the others, leaning against a tree trunk. It was a warm evening. The water of the lake was lapping gently against small rocks and pebbles on the shoreline. There were small ripples in the lake.

Suddenly I was overcome with the impact of the beauty around me. Tears came to my eyes. There was illumination: the lake and sky were brilliantly lit. Behind me was the soft voice of the leader. I was overcome with the combination of light and the feeling of camaraderie with my peers. This brought understanding that this was how it can and should be. While I still considered myself an atheist, I understood there was unity and harmony in the natural world. When I remember this experience from the viewpoint of age, what I recall is relief. All the pain I felt at home seemed to disappear into the light reflected from the lake and experience of belonging.

Another time, I was visiting my two aunts, who lived in Moose Jaw, Saskatchewan. Moose Jaw is on the flat Canadian prairie. I was in my twenties and I rose early. They stayed in bed until late morning. I left the quiet house and walked on the road north of town. I came to a field of oats. Remembering times playing in oat fields with my brother, I walked out into the crops. There was so much space, so much sky. The prairie horizon stretched as far as I could see. I felt very small in the middle of all that space. But suddenly everything was put into perspective. I had a small part in this universe, but I was part of everything. For the first time, all the pain in my family seemed to blend into the crops, dissipating into the distance toward the horizon. This was not the bright illumination of the Cultus Lake experience, but more of an inner illumination, an overwhelming feeling of peace and happiness. I just stood there with tears streaming down my face. It was so beautiful.

CHAPTER 9

Ecological Grief

In this chapter, we feel into experiences I am calling ecological grief. In our times, many people are grieving *for* or *about* nature. Our tears are in response to harm to the natural world. There are so many reasons to grieve what is happening to nature on the planet, small and large. Sometimes seeing trash in weeds on the side of the road is enough to hurt the heart. Development is all around us, sometimes taking down trees on a mountain we knew as children or changing a coastline we knew as empty. Every few years a major environmental disaster grabs the attention of the world. Environmental campaigns for protection of particular animals or lands keep our attention on the steady onslaught against the natural world by our global civilization. I have already written about our times being known as the Sixth Extinction Event.

Often it hurts more when something about it feels personal. I suspect many people, like me, were impacted by scenes of black sticky oil on the waters and shores of the American Gulf Coast after the 2010 explosion of the Deepwater Horizon Rig. Photographs and videos of egrets and seagulls coated with dark slime spoke volumes, more poignant when framed against the background of a beautiful Gulf of Mexico sunset. Some of the best times of my youth were spent on the white sand beaches of Mississippi, Alabama, and the Florida panhandle. An environmental disaster on those shores touches not only ecological grief but reaches into the depths of my personal history. That particular oil spill was an unfortunate accident, with responsible clean-up and quicker recovery than I could have imagined. Even so, the steady onslaught against the environment hurts.

When people hear about my interest in grief and nature, usually they assume this is what I am talking about: grieving destruction of the environment. Ecological grief is an important part of what I am talking about, but by now you will know that I am interested in how everything is related to everything else. From a behaviorist psychological perspective, awareness of harm to nature would be called the stimulus for a weeping response in ecological grief. From a depth psychological perspective, ecological grief would be respected as grief about harm to the environment—and would also represent an invitation to consider associations that may lead into discovery of other areas of grief. In Chapter 6, we considered how any experience of grief tends to reverberate with other experiences of grief, perhaps all pointing back towards an original experience of loss. When I saw those images of oil on those birds on the Gulf Coast, I had an immediate lump in my throat. That is grief for those birds and all the life on the coast, and even for the water and the sandy beaches, but there was an invitation to feel back into my past. I have precious memories of times on the coast with my family, and then with my high school friends, that bring up some longing. If I moved into grief about that coast in therapy, I would move though many personal as well as collective issues.

While the depths of grief interest me, in this chapter we focus on the experience of ecological grief, which is an experience unto itself. Ecological grief feels different than some of the other experiences discussed in this book. The focus is on nature rather than on oneself. Even for me, it is a relief to let the grief be only about nature. Grief emerges in deep authentic compassion for other life forms, often animals, sometimes just nature itself. Sometimes people grieving the destruction of nature realize their grief almost feels like bereavement. They may be mourning a personal loss of something in nature they loved or found particularly beautiful. Sometimes the grief is more general, involving the seeming disappearance of nature from the planet. Sadness may emerge when considering what will be left of the natural world for our grandchildren and their grandchildren and on down the line.

If you wake up to what is happening, it is hard not to grieve. Almost invariably in our times, when we grieve *for* or *about* nature, we are aware of the social, political, and economic aspects of environmental degradation. With an outer focus, this form of grief sometimes blends with anger and blame directed towards those perceived as destroying nature. It is easy to layer grief with anger at the industrial-technological development machine chewing up nature. Hazards or hurts to the health of ourselves and those around us may come into the picture. As discussed in the previous chapter, this is the entry point into grief emphasized by Joanna Macy when she observed many people recognize planetary distress at some psychological or somatic level, including sensing, even if dimly, threat to personal safety and health. As noted, she finds "anguish and anxiety in the face of the perils that threaten us is a healthy reaction."[358]

With ecological grief, we are usually aware of the collective human responsibility for destruction of nature. Even when blaming the industrial machine, many people include themselves in the assessment of fault. Anger and blame may then shift into guilt and remorse. This takes ecological grief into terrains that may feel religious. As we shall experience through some of the stories shared in this chapter, ecological grief often includes awe or a sense of the sacred in nature. It is thus natural for ecological grief to shift into penitence or longing for redemption, as described in Chapter 7 with respect to these elements in sacred tears. While longing for change in our habits, we may feel helpless with respect to environmental destruction. We may feel abused and violated, yet know we are part of the collective having responsibility. A sense of needing a higher power to help may arise. If we seek penitence or forgiveness, it is often not just for each of us individually, but for all of us as a species. From such experiences we may vow to assist the environmental movement, or simply take small steps on our own—for instance, cleaning up a littered beach.

Reflecting on the ecological sins of the collective may recall the timeless religious urge for restoration of the human community to the sacred. Etymology of the Latin word *religio* (which becomes *religion* in English) is not entirely clear, but early Christian writers, including St. Augustine, suggested derivation from the verb "religere," meaning "to bind back." After citing this derivation in *City of God,* St. Augustine wrote: "Being attached to Him, or rather let me say, re-attached,—for we had detached ourselves and lost hold of Him,—being, I say, re-attached to Him, we tend towards Him by love, that we may rest in Him, and find our blessedness by attaining that end."[359] Ecological grief can be felt as the desire to restore our human community to a sacred balance with nature. We may want in some ways to "rest finally" in nature, not unlike the desire of Linda Carroll Hassler expressed literally in her story in the last chapter, to die *"under a tree in the sunshine or under the night sky,"* where she feels she would be *"so much more comforted and assured."* Not just in death, but in life, many of us desire a healthy nature in which to repose ourselves, whether in life or imagination.

When It All Comes Down...

Ralph Litwin grew up in New Jersey. After high school, he spent eight years attending college and bumming around the country as a carpenter and street musician. After earning a degree in fine arts, he attended law school. Ralph made his life in his home state with his wife and three children. Along with continuing to play music, he built custom cabinets and hosted an award-winning regional cable show featuring a wide variety of entertainers. Ralph wrote:

In the 60s and early 70s I took psychedelics a few times and tripped in the great outdoors, engendering a very strong feeling of love for Life Force expressed through nature, which I still feel to this day, especially when outdoors. I was very active in the safe energy movement in the mid to late 70s, and worked with Public Interest Research Group in the early 80s while I was in law school. I have kept well-informed about many irresponsible acts of insensitive profit-motivated exploitation of the environment, and have studied more benign alternatives.

During the early 80s, I made a regular practice of running about an hour a day around a local golf course in the green rolling hills of northwestern New Jersey. Around that time, I had been reading some particularly alarming reports of environmental devastation. One gorgeous, sunny, blue sky day, I was running across the golf course, surrounded by lush green trees waving hypnotically in the breeze. Halfway down an open fairway, the grief hit me suddenly. From out of nowhere I was overwhelmed instantly by strong emotions and wept profusely in sorrow.

I wept as I ran, not only for the environmental and animal devastation, but also for humanity's immense spiritual vacuum, ignorance, and stupidity, which allow the devastation to occur. I kept running as I began feeling more and more released from the repressed sorrow by the huge sobs, tears streaming down my face.

A related experience some years later: I had been performing the song "Mother Earth" by Memphis Slim as part of Earth Day activities and in other concerts. It contains the refrain, "I don't care how great you are. I don't care what you're worth. When it all comes down, you got to go back to Mother Earth." When I sang the song I was investing the line with a great deal of negative emotion: hatred for all those hard-hearted bastards, the captains of industry, financiers, politicians, and so forth, who justify ecological destruction with self-aggrandizing rationalizations.

Not sensing any relationship between this activity and the tight feelings in my neck and shoulders, I made an appointment for a massage. I hadn't had a massage in quite a long time. When Mary-Rose started to work on me, I began to cry just a little at first. She asked why I was crying and it came into my mind that all those negative emotions were caught in me, and served no practical purpose. During that massage I had a good hard cry and released much of that anger. I resolved not to involve myself any further in that kind of negative energy. And, now I get massages regularly.

Rosie Kuhn was one of my classmates at the Institute of Transpersonal Psychology. After growing up in the American Midwest, she spent several years in Nova Scotia, where she learned to sail on the rough north-Atlantic seas. Sailing as a transformative experience became her primary research topic while at ITP. The author of several books on the "real life" of psychospiritual transformation, Rosie lives in northern California where she works as a life coach for individuals, couples, and businesses.[360] Rose wrote:

As a sailor and student of transpersonal psychology I am conscious of, and deeply connected with, the natural environment. I cannot help but experience layers of despair and disbelief, dismay and depression, as I reflect upon the striations and variations of cloudless sky with industrial pollution and car emissions. Smog is everywhere.

My heart is often overwhelmed with grief for what the human population has done to our home, our Mother Earth. At times I despair more than others, but I am in a state of despair a great deal of my life due to my sense of responsibility and my own influence in the situation. I feel guilt and shame, humiliation, embarrassment for the lack of conscious action on my part and that of Western "civilization."

A number of years ago, during a retreat at Pajaro Dunes, south of Santa Cruz, California, I felt an overwhelming need to pay the ocean an intentional visit. My heart needed to make an act of contrition in order to express my true feelings for how we as a species continue to devastate the planet. I felt silly and embarrassed for creating a conversation with the Ocean. I was afraid someone would see me or hear me cry. And, simultaneously I was compelled to be fully present in this confession. I sobbed and asked forgiveness. The sobbing was bigger than I could hold. It was a request for mercy. Prostrating myself before the illimitable creator, I asked for forgiveness and assistance to reverse the present trend of world destruction.

I was overwhelmed with my sense of inadequacy to change myself or this world to make a difference in healing the planet. This quest came from my soul, from an integral part of my body. My ego struggled with the emotional exposition. It was irrational, trivial, childish behavior to cry and talk with the Ocean, as if she were my mother, as if she would forgive me and compassionately comfort me. The ocean waves rolled in unmoved by my outpouring. I watched them come in, the eternal rhythm, the eternal motion, undaunted, unmoved by one human's insignificant cry of despair.

The crying began again. I wondered, am I being heard? Is there significance to this existence I am presently embodying? A profound sense of insignificance again enfolded me. The grains of sand I sat upon reminded me that any one of us sentient and non-sentient beings is insignificant, but the collective provides a foundation of substance. This one individual grain of sand is needed in order to form this beach.

I watched the ocean, waiting for the next wave of emotion to move through me. I watched my anger rise as the dauntless sea remained unmoved by my outreaching. I laughed at my arrogance, that I would get a personal response, perhaps like a visitation from the Blessed Virgin Mary. The Ocean was no more likely to acknowledge and console me for my expression of remorse than the man in the moon. Purging my regrets, my mistakes, my grief and guilt would not move the mountains under the sea. I was moved to consciously express with clarity my own human response to the devastation of the Earth.

An act of contrition is only that: "Oh my God, I am heartily sorry for having offended thee. . . ." I wanted some response, some acknowledgment that I made a difference if for only an instant. But I could only sit with my humility, my humiliation, my humanity. That's all there was to do. While the ocean was unmoved by my grief, I have made a practice of finding that place inside me that knows what we humans have done to the earth. Acknowledging that place puts me in better relationship to all that we have here on the planet.

Roseann Seryak grew up in Ohio, married John in 1973, and together they raised six children. Many years ago, amidst personal spiritual and psychological transformation, Roseann was drawn to movement. In 1996, she earned a degree in dance performance. When she shared her experiences in nature with me, Roseann was living in Wadsworth, Ohio, teaching dance. A convert to Reform Judaism, Roseann speaks of the importance of Tikkun Olam, which means "repair the world." As she shares, she has *always been deeply touched by nature. It is only in the past few years that I have experienced waves of grief. As my connection with the Earth increases, I feel more physical pain. Sometimes I have urges to find a cave. It seems I want to escape and be protected from the vibrations that are destroying nature.*

Cancun, Mexico. December 1998. It is my 25th wedding anniversary. My husband and I have traveled to Cancun to celebrate this marital milestone. I am excited with the opportunity to experience Cancun. The people are friendly, the air invigorating. Just walking on the beach renews my tired soul. I feel the warmth of the sun as it kisses my skin. As I face the ocean, I feel a pulse. It is strange, somewhat mysterious. It creates discomfort. I fidget. The pulse seems to be coming from the ocean. I am not sure I like it. I push the feeling into a memory box. A twinge of sadness engulfs me. I don't understand. I only remember. Sadness. I push it away, I am on vacation.

We make our plans. The hotel is wonderful. The ocean breeze moves smoothly through the open hallways. I seem to hear a whisper, faint. I stop. I listen. I hear. I feel sad.

Tourist trips seem the easiest way to spend our time here. We sign up for a trip to Tulum. I am eager to view the ruins with my own eyes. Our tour bus is quite comfortable. The guide is informative. We arrive and enter the park. Once past the souvenir stand it happens. Sadness again. I feel funny, sort of nauseous, as I do upon entering a funeral home. The guide is speaking but I am not listening to him. I seem to hear another voice in the background. Where is it? Who is it coming from? What are they saying?

"Pay attention to the guide," I tell myself. It is hot. I move on. Others don't seem to notice what I do. I feel as though I am in a dream.

The tour finally comes to an end. We are given an hour to wander around by ourselves before returning to the bus. I don't know where to go first. I am looking for something, but what? Suddenly, I see a high point. I run up to this point. The view of the sea is quite stunning. I look and I feel my heart cry out to the ocean. I hear an answer, like an echo, "Tu sabes." Tu sabes? What does that mean? "You know, you know." I cry. What do I know? I cry.

December, 2000. Grand Bahama Island. John and I are taking a few days rest from the winter blues of Ohio and enjoying the warmth of the Bahamas. Shortly after checking into the hotel we decide to tour the island. We rent a car. The road seems to carry an uneasy stillness, like something from the Twilight Zone. Tree after tree of something not quite right. I cannot put my finger on it, but it is not pleasant. I smell death and I don't know why. We find a restaurant at the end of the island. The beach front is deserted. I have never seen so much empty beach. But it isn't really empty. It is cluttered with trash. Broken bottles, tires, oil cans, plastic containers, pop cans, and shoes cover this beach, like a bad case of pox. No people around, only their trash.

I start to ache all over. Why? Why is this happening? My grief begins to swell in my body. I look out to the ocean. I pray . . . why? An answer comes back, "Save me. I am dying." I must be crazy, overly sentimental. I walk, feeling downtrodden, beaten. "My beach is so dirty." I start to gather the trash. John watches as I make my little pile. "Clean it up. Clean it up." I do my best. It is not enough. I leave a note in a bottle right in the middle of the trash pile. Will someone read it? I write notes on stones. Will they be read? Not sure. "Clean me. Love me. Protect me." It is the ocean that speaks. "Tu sabes . . . you know . . . what to do."

Back to Ohio, return to work. Ocean songs still with me. I shall dance it. Extinction is its title. Cello music with waves in the background. Slow, heavy, emptying, full stage to empty stage. In my dance, I hear grandmother ocean crying. Is she taking her last breaths? I don't know. I only weep, and feel the poison from within. As she dies, it seems that I too am dying. My body is wracked from pain. My joints are stiff and my muscles tight. Doctors cannot find a reason. All medical tests come back normal.

I seem to hear Mother Ocean. "Please stop," she says. "Stop the noise, stop your fighting, stop your building, stop pouring concrete on my skin. I can't breathe." My body aches. I collapse. I too have trouble breathing. Asthma. I understand her and I cry. "I am sorry my mother. I don't know how to stop it. Forgive me. Forgive us." I sit quietly for awhile and I thank her for my life. "Thank you, Mother Earth. I am here."

After the events of September 11, 2001, Roseann wrote to me: *A group of ladies, mostly strangers to each other, gathered at a house which has a labyrinth in the back yard. We gathered to pray for the healing of the crisis that has recently attacked our country. The labyrinth is simply a grass path. We walked the path during the evening hours in pouring rain. My body sometimes cries to be exposed to the elements full force. For example, I have urges to lie in snow, roll in mud, submerge myself under a waterfall. I usually restrain these urges. But last night I allowed the pouring rain to fall on my head uncovered.*

As I walked this path of grass, I feel a new surge of energy and connection. With that surge also comes grief and sorrow, yet I am not overwhelmed. I feel like I am sighing, groaning, with Mother Earth. I share this with all those walking this labyrinth and all similar paths. We who feel the pain must pay attention to the solution. It is there as well. We come equipped to handle the problem. We must use our skills well to find solutions. I just needed to share that.

Ecology as Relationship

Ecology was long ago defined as "the science of the relationships between organisms and their environments," including "the relationships between human groups and their physical and social environments." [361] Ecological grief concerns relationship. For some of us, moving into ecological grief is analogous to waking up to an abusive relationship between our species and the planet. Certainly humans have been abusing nature in various ways for most of our history. But in our times, our industrial capacities blending with our propensity to ignore long term consequences has created a collective assault of our civilization on nature. In my lifetime, the primary definition of ecology shifted into "the study of the detrimental effects of modern civilization on the environment, with a view toward prevention or reversal through conservation."[362]

There is an iconic scene in the television show *Mad Men* that allowed my children a glimpse into the level of ecological consciousness in the United States when I was a child. In an early episode of the long-running series, advertising superstar and classic American anti-hero Don Draper, in the form of actor Jon Hamm, is spending some rare family time with his wife and two children in Connecticut, away from his Madison Avenue work and Manhattan haunts. Looking like a proto-typical early 1960s family, the Drapers are picnicking in a public park, with paper plates and cups, perhaps even some take-out from one of the fast-food franchise restaurants popping up in cities and suburbs. In this much-talked-about television moment, with their nature-in-the-park time complete, the Drapers just get up and leave, not picking up anything, their trash left to blow around in the breeze. I told my children, and I am not sure they believed me, that when I was a kid and we ate fast food in the car driving around New Orleans, I was told to just throw the trash out the window.

There was nothing malicious about this behavior. It was more or less normal. There were surely always responsible people picking up after themselves in parks, not throwing trash outside the window of a running automobile, but the world was less crowded and people were not aware we were, literally, starting to trash the planet. There are roughly twice as many people in the United States now as when I was a child. A similar statistic exists for the world as a whole. The capitalist economic model requires expansion—constant expansion, meaning more and more building, more and more industry, and this is all necessary to feed, clothe, house, and entertain more and more people. The pressures on nature in the last fifty years have become staggering. Returning to one of my favorite movies, *The Matrix,* agent Smith, an enforcer for artificial intelligence, gives the following assessment of how humanity has operated on the planet:

> I'd like to share a revelation that I've had during my time here. It came to me when I tried to classify your species and I realized that you aren't actually mammals. Every mammal on this planet instinctively develops a natural equilibrium with its surrounding environment, but you humans do not. You move to an area and you multiply and multiply until every natural resource is consumed, and the only way you can survive is to spread to another area. There is another organism on this planet that follows the same pattern. Do you know what it is? A virus. Human beings are a disease, a cancer of this planet. You are a plague. And we are the cure.[363]

I would not say we have exactly woken up, but a great deal has changed in my lifetime. By the time I was in middle school, Rachel Carson's *Silent Spring* was required summer reading.[364] Cultural anthropologist John Paull considers this single book, published in 1962, to have started the environmental movement as a cultural force. *Silent Spring*, and the cascading publicity surrounding the book, "ignited a national, and eventually, an international furor and debate."[365] Paull explained: "Silent Spring attracted fans and infuriated foes. It was a critique, especially of dichlorodiphenyltrichloroethane (DDT), and, more generally, of our relationship with the natural world." [366]

According to Paull, those in the orthodox scientific community did not all react well to the entry of environmentalism into science. Paull quoted a 1967 article in *Science* lamenting "the plague of Rachel Carson's *Silent Spring* [which] continues to infest the minds of scientists."[367] But, as Paull continued, "half a century after it first appeared, *Silent Spring* is still in print and continues to engage and recruit fresh advocates and detractors."[368] Like many others, Paull believes the "U.S. Environmental Protection Agency (EPA) was founded in December 1970, largely in response to *Silent Spring*."[369]

During the 1970s, in the midst of other widespread social change, ecology became a social and political movement gaining more and more momentum. This happened through awareness of the increasingly negative impact of pollution, dwindling natural resources, and the spread of concrete and buildings. The adjective "ecological" began to suggest practices intended to protect the natural world.[370] Those of us around the United States in the early 1970s may remember a stirring advertising campaign involving a single tear rolling down the face of a Native American man. This was ecological grief waking up a nation. On television commercials and billboards around the country, in response to environmental degradation of open lands, Iron Eyes Cody stood stoic, except for one tear rolling down his weathered face. This was a cogent moral statement in favor of "Keeping America Beautiful"—much more powerful than any amount of exhortation through words.[371]

During the 1980s and beyond, changes in the United States became noticeable. Recycling became standard in thousands of communities, public areas, and homes. Through the hard work of many educators, writers, social activists, concerned citizens, and politicians, various laws had been passed allowing interested citizens or groups to challenge practices or planned development that may endanger animals or the environment. The protection of particular species provided leverage to fight against development in some places. Battles between environmentalists and interests of industry and development became common. Accidents at the Three Mile Island Nuclear Power Plant in Pennsylvania in 1979, and at Chernobyl in the Ukraine in 1986, fueled protests against nuclear power that became part of the environmental issue for many people. When I graduated from law school in 1984, a good number of my friends and acquaintances were interested in environmental law.

Just as important were the continuing shifts in education and public awareness. The concept of an "ecological footprint" was coined in 1990 by Mathis Wackernagel and William Rees at the University of British Columbia.[372] An ecological footprint is the amount of land, water, and natural resources the lifestyle of a person, community, nation, or other collective consumes. The notion of leaving no footprint became a goal for many people and communities. By the time my children were in middle school, they knew all about ecological footprints and how to practice "no trace" wilderness camping. I love the "no trace" camping image as a general ecological attitude, the idea of visiting nature but leaving the natural world just as it was before you arrived, a leap forward from the Draper family leaving their trash in the park. More realistic, and perhaps even possible, is to create ways of living where nature at least has the possibility of recovering from us in a reasonable period of time.

In many places, a significant recovery has already happened. When I first drove back and forth from Louisiana to California for college, passing through Los Angeles was an encounter with dense smog. My eyes hurt and that bright southern California sunshine was diffused through a city where you were not sure you were going to see the tops of big buildings or even billboards. It was hard to see the Hollywood sign. Somewhere during those times we drove the kids down to Disneyland from San Jose I realized the smog was essentially gone. Now when I drive around L.A., I see the hills and that sunshine dazzles, though the devil in me sometimes misses that hazy vision of palm trees in pollution. Air quality in many cities in North America is one sure sign that environmental laws can make a difference.

Some deep ecologists complain we should not become smug because the air in some American cities is better. Problems continue all over the world and the real issue is gaining a handle on environmental standards internationally. At least the battle is engaged in political bodies from world organizations to national congresses to local commissions considering issues of zoning and community environmental regulations. Recently, the ongoing political fight in the United States between the voices of industry and environmentalism manifested in debates in the United States Congress about completing an oil pipeline from Canada to the southern United States. Regardless of the merits of that particular issue—and it may be that a pipeline would have less deleterious impact on the natural world than business as usual—the power of the environmental political lobby in the United States is now what might be called "a force of nature."

We have come a long way in envisioning possibilities for "green" societies. Ecological viewpoints and ecologically themed courses are now common in the curriculums of many schools, from grade school up to the graduate level. Colleges and universities are full of ecologically related majors. Ecological perspectives often enter into consideration of almost any subject regardless of academic department. Eco-psychology courses are among the most popular in contemporary psychology schools. I recently sat on a plane next to a young man who studied environmental architecture at Yale University. He now works as an architect in a firm specializing in environmentally consciousness designs. The airplane trip was not so great for my personal ecological footprint but listening to him vastly increased my optimism for the future.

In general, within many segments of mainstream culture in the industrialized-technological countries has emerged a cultural value of conservation and consideration of environmental impact. In the last few years, many of the newer buildings I have visited in my law work are "green buildings" designed by people like my airplane seatmate to minimize use of environmental resources. At the homeowner level, where I live now, I see frequent advertisements encouraging us to renovate our houses with environmental consciousness. Sometimes we even get a tax break to help us. In a growing number of places, trash cans are now labeled "landfill" suggesting that recycling is the norm and sending something to "landfill" should be your last option. In many parts of the industrialized world, building projects go forward only with studies about environmental impact and, sometimes, with required protections or give-backs to the environment.

Many people are working for international standards to protect the environment, proposing mechanisms to bring a measure of ecological footprint into our economies through laws and treaties. Responsible economics now understands the structural problem in free market economies from the absence of the "cost" of environmental degradation in the operation of the invisible hand. Laws and treaties are proposed to build these "costs" into economies, but resistance remains great: after all, the economy is what keeps us moving individually and collectively. At the international level, the choice of "the economy" over nature by power interests in places such as the United States may be one of the larger problems, but it is impossible to discount the role of developing nations desiring to provide for their people the things we take for granted in technological-industrial countries. Pressures on the natural world are increasing with the growth of bustling economies in South America, Asia, and other previously less developed places.

I have thought for many years that a desire to protect nature might become an international force uniting peoples in distant lands, across cultural divides. I hope this is more than a wish. Granted, problems of survival continue for many people and threats from terrorism trump concern about nature. Conflicts and problems around the world seem to continue as always, creating the impression among some that concern about nature may be an indulgence. Nor should we forget the backlash among many in the public. Despite a scientific consensus that global warming is occurring as the result of our carbon emissions, some business, political, and media interests contend the phenomenon is an invention of environmentalists. Many people believe this and have become antagonist towards ecologically-minded people. Being labeled an environmentalist in most parts of Montana can still help you to lose an election. This is not particularly unusual and blends into the general "cultural wars" in the United States between groups with disparate values.

Sometimes, it is hard for me to imagine a shift into choosing nature over "the economy" without decades of more "in-your-face" environmental disasters bearing an increasingly undeniable impact on daily life. Being from planet Earth as well as the American South, I was not surprised to hear many people along the Gulf of Mexico, only a year or so after the largest oil spill in recent memory, already pushing back at environmentalists as interfering with their jobs and businesses. And, you know what, they probably were. Still, there are reasons for optimism, particularly with younger generations raised on ecological values and practices as normal and necessary. We have come a very long way in my lifetime. Practically speaking, we may be just one or two game-changing inventions away from releasing our dependence on fossil fuels, now worsening given developing economies. These possible future shifts in energy generation could make a big difference.

Until that happens, we remain immersed in the Sixth Extinction Event, this one our making. Even with all the progress made in many parts of the world for protection of nature, the onslaught still feels hard to stop. In a doomsayer scenario, the coming losses loom larger than what has already been lost. In *The Human Nature of Unsustainability,* ecological economist William Rees, one of the creators of the concept of ecological footprint, observed "the average world citizen has an eco-footprint of about 2.7 global average hectares while there are only 2.1 global average hectares of bioproductive land and water per capita on Earth."[373] Rees believes "humanity has already overshot global biocapacity by 30 percent and now lives unsustainably by depleting stocks of "natural capital" (e.g., fish, forests, and soil) and eroding critical life-support functions."[374] He observed:

> Humans may pride themselves as being the best evidence for intelligent life on Earth, but an alien observer would record that the (un)sustainability conundrum has the global community floundering in a swamp of cognitive dissonance and collective denial. Indeed, our alien friend might go so far as to ask why our reasonably intelligent species seems unable to recognize the crisis for what it is and respond accordingly.[375]

I have some friends whose response to nature is similar to mine, but who have stopped recycling because "ain't nothin' gonna save us...the recycling thing just lulls people into believing it's all under control." I still recycle, but I sympathize with those who suggest we may be lulled into believing we have nothing to worry about as long as we separate out our glass, cans, paper, plastics, and "landfill," putting them in the right bin. On the individual level, more and more of us can do our part, but global political action is likely necessary for the real shift to occur. In the meantime, there is nothing wrong with everyone doing our bit, staying optimistic, and searching for solutions. And yet the feelings of imminent loss remain for many people. When I step back and take a broad view, it is hard to imagine how we will turn the psychological, social, and political corner in order to make sustainability work for over 7 billion people and counting. No wonder some people are suffering ecological grief.

My Little Piece of Earth in Harm's Way . . .

A retired emergency room nurse, Terry Taylor was living in the mountains of North Carolina, with her husband, three dogs, four pot-bellied pigs, and two mallard ducks, when she saw my request for stories about grief in response to nature. She wrote to me immediately. *I don't believe this! I was sitting in the woods today with my friends . . . the trees, and other animals and plants, and cried over the paint can in the stream. I ache from head to toe at the repercussions of acid rain, noise pollution, litter bugs, and my little piece of earth that is in harm's way. I feel so connected with nature that I often merge with it. You know what I mean?*

I do transcendental meditation. I think it helps me realize we are all one . . . we are all in God and God is in us, God being divine energy, highest awareness, cosmic consciousness, or whatever you like to call it. The greeting Namaste means the place in me honors the place in you where we are one. I say that to everything in nature. No words but I commune and connect in the silence.

When I was about ten years old, I was sitting by a stream and watching a friend of mine, an adult banded water snake. I knew all the snakes and their favorite sitting rocks. A boy in the neighborhood sneaked up on us and, with a huge limb, smashed the snake. I had projected myself on the rock and felt as though I had been sitting beside the snake, or was him somehow, and the blow made me almost faint. I felt very nauseated, in a type of physical shock. I was more than just upset he had been killed. I felt as though I couldn't breathe.

In the woods I have a knowing that a tree is in trouble and I will look around and there will be a huge limb leaning, crushing a smaller tree or weighing down its branches. I will remove it and I feel the appreciation of the tree. I bend down all the time after a rain and move earthworms that are trapped on the pavement, close to drying out, and I put them back in the grass, and I know of their gratitude. Do unto others as you would have them do unto you, because they are you: we are all spiritually one.

Hailing from the Twin Cities of Minnesota, Raymond Voet describes himself as a retired "dishwasher" (he worked in metallurgical chemistry for thirty years), a "listener" (he acquired a degree in psychology), and a "troublemaker" (he wants people to think and he says that is usually trouble). He wrote to me: *I am the son of a Kansas farmer. My father cared about the soil and worked to improve it by appropriate fertilizing, crop rotation, terracing fields, and building dams in gullies and other appropriate places. I learned from my father, and also from my mother. She only had an eighth grade education, but she spent her life learning, observing, and teaching about our communion with Mother Earth.*

I have driven to Kansas, through Minnesota, Iowa, and Nebraska, and observed the farms and environment along the way. I have cried during drought years when I saw the grass in the highway ditches being harvested for livestock feed. It hurts me to see the land in pain, a pain that I am aware of. There is loss of topsoil from erosion. In Iowa and Wisconsin, where the ground water has been contaminated with excess nitrogen, i.e., nitrates, deep wells are needed. People have become separated from the land, the soil. We get our food from the Co-op or the grocery store and we are not aware of sources. There is a great movement towards "organic foods" by people who worry about contaminates and health, but who know nothing about agriculture and the biosphere. The soils are depleted, Cu, Zn, Mg, Mn, Co, and so on, and we think because something looks good or bad, it is healthy.

People are ignorant of our connection to the land and believe what is promulgated by "authorities" who often have hidden agendas, mostly financial or fear mongering. Perhaps I am wrong, but I fear, and I cry.

Ruth Beane Davis lived most of her life in Maine, where she had a long career in psychiatric nursing. When she wrote to me, Ruth was remembering a time she was mourning a series of losses in her life. She had retreated to a home in nature, where she was able to smell the first wildflowers of spring, listen to a robin sing at twilight, and look up into the clear night sky to watch the Big Dipper and Cassiopeia appear. Her time in nature brought forth vivid and moving dreams, helping access her feelings about nature. Ruth wrote:

I remember a startling dream which just came out of the blue. I dreamed I was offered the opportunity to be part of a crew of a half-dozen people who were leaving Earth to colonize a distant galaxy. Our once-beautiful planet was a blackened, smoldering, uninhabitable ruin. Human greed, ignorance, and disrespect had destroyed the Earth and the planet was not able to recover. There were no animals, trees, or plants. The skies were lifeless, the oceans empty and full of waste. As I considered this offer to start a new life, an opportunity only available to a few people, I thought about how it would be to live without animals, or flowers, or birds, to never hear the peepers in spring or feel soft grass under my feet.

How could I never see a baby animal again? Or never hear the wind rustle through the trees on a soft summer night? Without a moon to shine across still waters or the sun to turn the evening sky into a thrilling display of color, what would be my inspiration and meaning for living? Even though I knew these things were gone from the Earth, I realized I could never, ever, live without them. I replied aloud: "I will stay here, and die with them."

I did not remember this dream upon awakening, but it returned to me that afternoon when I was walking in the woods. Initially, my memory was pure cognition, no emotions. I was bewildered. Why, I wondered, would I have such a strange and powerful dream about Earth being destroyed and me being offered a chance to colonize a distant planet? I had not been ruminating about planetary destruction and entertained no fantasies about being one of a "chosen few" to populate other galaxies.

I next remembered the feelings I had in the dream and re-experienced terrible grief and sadness, which still return when I remember the dream. I felt utter desolation at realizing that what I loved more than anything else—the natural world and its creatures—had been annihilated and there was nothing I could do to bring them back. I felt grieved beyond my capacity to endure it. I fully felt the consequences of human greed and ignorance. I felt as though I were carrying the feelings of a living population of non-humans which could not speak for themselves. Hopeless grief was a very heavy feeling in my chest.

I then felt my grief whip into a pure, unadulterated fury at the way this innocent race of beings had been wiped out by a race that I happened to have been born into. We should have been using our sophistication to protect these more vulnerable beings! Instead, we thought we could do as we pleased because living creatures could not speak "our" language. I was deeply ashamed and furious.

As I recall my outrage and grief in this dream, there is nothing about it that I find surprising or unusual. It was not news to me that I would react so strongly in a dream or another situation where creatures were harmed. I was born with an extremely strong love for animals and all nature. It was part of my lifeblood. In retrospect, I also understand that the dream occurred in the context of my being comforted by the natural world upon my retreat to the woods.

I was still deeply bereaved from the death of my mother a few years earlier, which had been followed by additional losses: the sale of my old and beloved family home, the end of my relationship with my fiancé, the death of my three-year-old border collie from cancer, separation and divorce among my siblings, deaths of old family friends and close neighbors. All my education and experience in the mental health field could not assuage my emotional and spiritual suffering. My religious upbringing as a Protestant Baptist could not answer the extremely specific and compelling questions I had about life after death, nor tell me how to navigate through the challenges presented by my overwhelming recent losses. It was nature that helped me begin to heal from my losses.

Three years later, I understand that my dream has helped me acknowledge the reverence and love that I have for animals. The Marines talk about mountains you would die for. My dream showed me my mountain. In reconnecting with my dream, I realized that I was being asked to take a deeper look at my love for animals and to accept this love within my life. I had been reluctant to do this because of the pain and helplessness I inevitably felt when animals were harmed. I have learned to stay with these feelings and have noticed a transformation. When I re-enter that pain in my dream, it SPRINGS, becoming what feels like an incandescent blue laser. I become this laser as it leaps out of my eyes and the center of my chest. I have no words which adequately describe the intensity of this light, which is simultaneously blazing and icy. I can only describe it in terms of these qualities: "It cuts to the chase." "It is capable of self-launch on an instant's notice." "Woe to those who get in the way." "One blow from it is like a sledgehammer to a block of ice." "It scorches a straight-arrow path to the heart of things." "It's as soft as it is sharp." "It has a mission and will not stop halfway."

Since I have learned to stay with these feelings, I feel the grief transformed into a laser-love. Love has power in my grief now. As the result of going back into my own painful feelings toward animal suffering, I have found that the animals themselves are there to guide and assist me. I had been suspecting this for awhile because of some very touching animal experiences. Then, around six months after my dream, I obeyed a sudden and unusual inner prompting to go into a bookstore I was driving by. A well-known intuitive was giving psychic readings there, which I did not know until I walked in. I signed up for the next reading, which is even more unusual as I knew nothing about this person. She looked up as I walked in, and said to me, "You are surrounded by guardian spirits and they are animals who are grateful to you."

I have been part of a dream group in Helena, Montana, for several years. We meet most Wednesday nights except during the brief summer. Following the "if it were my dream" model articulated by Jeremy Taylor, we comment on other people's dreams not as a matter of objective analysis, but as a discussion about what the narrative and symbols would mean to us personally, "if it were my dream."[376] We start with everyone sharing a recent dream if they have one; then we gravitate to one dream for discussion in our two hour gathering. The dreamer tells the dream again, this time from memory, not reading from a dream journal. People ask questions for clarification, talk about where they feel the most energy in the dream, and suggest the meanings and associations that come up for them around particular images. Eventually someone asks something like, "What were your feelings in the dream" or "What feelings do you have now around the dream?" Through the feelings, the transformational possibilities of the dream often open up. Sometimes, near the end of a session, we will ponder what actions the dreamer might take to bring the transformational possibilities out into the world.

Ruth worked her own dream walking in the woods. She began with "cognition," moved into emotions, and then found an intention to take the emotional charge of the dream out into her world. As sometimes happens with dream work or any psychological endeavor, grief shifted into anger as a possible spark for speaking a truth or taking an action. Through staying with her dream, Ruth realized she had been numbing her feelings about nature in the midst of a sense of helplessness. By staying with her feelings, she moved into an anger that felt like a transformation into action. Ruth then felt the world came into her life to support her awakening, including a stranger seeing the presence of animal spirits around her. Whether or not we all believe in animal spirits, this was a remarkable synchronicity for Ruth to hear. As noted by Jung, synchronicities tend to occur in life when we delve deeply into our unconscious through dreams or other imagery. For some of us, the synchronicities feel like support from the universe to empower us through overcoming any sense we are helpless to change our lives.

When awakening to ecological grief, a sense of helplessness to halt the destruction of the natural world is not uncommon. Several of the people relating their experiences of ecological grief have touched upon feelings of helplessness, such as Rosie Kuhn's feeling of being "overwhelmed with my sense of inadequacy to change myself or this world to make a difference in healing the planet." Near the beginning of this chapter, I suggested that waking up to ecological grief can feel like waking up to an abusive relationship. Helplessness is a particularly common experience for those suffering an abusive relationship. If our collective human relationship with nature has become abusive, it makes sense that many of us feel trapped and helpless. Numbing to the feelings is a common component of helplessness, as Ruth realized.

In the last few decades, an understanding of "learned helplessness" has emerged in the psychological literature. Several experiments with dogs were undertaken by a research team including Martin Seligman, Steve

Maier, and Christopher Peterson. From the perspective of those with compassion for animals, like Ruth and many people reading this book, these experiments might be considered cruel. In the future one hopes ways to develop understandings about biology and psychology will rely less on inflicting pain to animals. Nevertheless, as seminal experiments about the experience of helplessness, I find this research illuminating. Seligman and Peterson described a condition, similar to chronic clinical depression in humans, in which dogs "learned" that nothing could be done to stop a painful condition from occurring. Many of the dogs stopped trying to avoid pain. Even when returned to situations in which they could impact their condition, they remained stuck in malaise, a condition all too recognizable by many people in contemporary life.[377] Returning to the example of an abusive relationship, we learn that nothing we do or say changes the circumstances, so we stop trying.

But, one of the important discoveries in this research was that not *all* dogs in the experiments became helpless. About one-third of the canines in Seligman's later experiments continued trying—and through *trying* found a way out of the painful situation. In later research Peterson and Seligman focused on humans. They found some individuals avoid "learned helplessness" with an "explanatory style" realizing the negative condition is neither permanent, nor personal to them, nor pervasive. This is not naïve denial of reality, but the ability to understand that conditions could be different. One of the gifts of my experiences of embeddedness in nature, including experiences in Holotropic Breathwork, has been an embodied awareness that my relationship to nature could be different—maybe even *has* been different if I start to believe in prior lifetimes. I have learned that our current loss of nature is not necessarily a permanent condition—it may simply be one stage in our evolution. Can we imagine future stages in which we return to nature?

Understanding learned helplessness led to the development of techniques for assisting people in moving through depression. Many of these therapeutic techniques fall into the category of "cognitive therapy." We learn to release limiting beliefs. Releasing a pessimistic "explanatory style" has been shown important for physical as well as psychological health. Some studies indicate people with "helpless" views of the world have weakened immune systems, increased minor and major illnesses, and increased difficulty in recovering from illness.[378] If we are feeling helpless in our ecological grief, we can help ourselves and the planet by knowing there is nothing inevitable about exclusion of nature from civilization. We can look around us and begin to notice the possibilities for creating a global culture respecting nature and understanding ourselves as part of nature. As a believer in allowing our emotions to transform us, I suspect that finding our grief—and the anger layered into our grief—might be exactly what fuels transformation of enough of us to make a difference.

In an earlier chapter, I referenced Chellis Glendinning's *My Name is Chellis and I'm in Recovery from Western Civilization*. Glendinning considers "earthgrief" part of the recovery process, an initial stage. Some of her words sound almost sacramental. "To open our hearts to the sad history of humanity and the devastated state of the Earth," she writes, "is the next step in our reclamation of our bodies, the body of our human community, and the body of the Earth."[379] As a therapist, she knows the practical impact of entering into grief. She describes "feeling the pain and knowing its source" as the "crucial turning point." In her view, this is the "healing crisis" described by homeopathic healers. In more common language of contemporary spiritual practitioners, Glendinning writes, this shift clears "negative patterns so that life-affirming patterns may arise. As formidable as the task may seem, to feel our pain is to come alive."[380]

From her mouth to God's ears. In closing this chapter, I am reminded of one of my favorite quotes. Aldous Huxley, a man familiar with nonordinary states of consciousness as well as idealistic political movements, once said: "I wanted to change the world. But I have found that the only thing one can be sure of changing is oneself."[381]

CHAPER 10

Psychological Immersion in Nature

In 1953, Carl Jung wrote:

> Through scientific understanding, our world has become dehumanized. Man feels himself isolated in the cosmos. He is no longer involved in nature and has lost his emotional participation in natural events, which hitherto had a symbolic meaning for him. Thunder is no longer the voice of god, nor is lightening his avenging missile. No river contains a spirit, no tree a man's life, no snake is the embodiment of wisdom, and no mountain harbors a great demon. Neither do things speak to him nor can he speak to things, like stones, plants, and animals. He no longer has a bush-soul identifying him with a wild animal. His immediate communication with nature is gone forever, and the emotional energy it generated has sunk into the unconscious.[382]

If we have lost emotional participation in nature, and the emotional energy around our communication with nature has sunken into our unconscious, we might expect that energy to seek outlet in various ways. When emotional energy sinks into the unconscious, it is often projected out unconsciously onto aspects of the outer world. Without having much conscious awareness of what is happening, we might find some of our attitudes, beliefs, actions, attractions and repulsions intertwined with strong emotional energy connected with nature. Esther Harding, one of the first Jungian analysts to work in the United States, described projection in this way:

> When we find ourselves the victim of an emotional reaction that is out of proportion to the situation, or where we have such a reaction in regard to some situation that is not really within the range of our concern but is strictly someone else's business, we should suspect that we are reacting to something of our own that we have not recognized as ours.[383]

In this chapter, we consider some of the ways some of us, in our times, may be playing out a strong desire for deep psychological connection with nature other than through embodied grief and longing. Most of this book, of course, has looked into the longing for intimate connection with nature that is expressed through grief and/or weeping in response to nature. Here, we consider what may be similar mechanisms, not necessarily involving grief, through which the deeper layers of our psyche manifest a desire for return to immersion in nature—or sometimes seem to fear that return and fight against it. We begin with consideration of wolves, the animals in nature I believe carry more projections from humans during our times than any other wild animals. We move to bears, a species representing for many of us, including myself, the last representatives of the truly magnificently wild (and deadly) in nature. Bears help us look into what may lie at the basis of our removal from nature: the actual terror of descent into a dark chaos where we may fear the depths of our unconscious in a way that is simultaneous with our fear of the depths of nature.

The chapter then shifts into consideration of the desire (and experience) many people now have for communication with representatives of nature, principally animals and plants, either through encounter in the external world or through internal contact in nonordinary states. This takes me into imagining ways to be with nature—experienced both externally and internally—that includes a return to "symbolic meaning" that Jung described as having been lost as we moved out of nature. I call this dreamwork in nature. While possibly similar to how Jung imagined our ancestors (and perhaps some contemporary indigenous people) communicating with nature, the way I hold this relationship with nature retains the kind of separation from "object' that allows us to work through our personal and collective projections into nature so that consciousness may emerge about the complicated personal and collective psychologies we now inhabit in our postmodern world. As noted throughout this book, I believe consciousness about who we have become opens possibilities for imagining who we might still become. The chapter concludes with my sharing about the way this kind of psychological immersion in nature has felt deeply healing, and restorative, for me and some others.

Wolves

Every November, the Helena Education Foundation hosts an event called Great Conversations. People gather to participate in an evening discussion at one of approximately forty tables focusing on a topic hosted by someone with experience or interest in the subject. One year I went to the wolf table. The host was a young woman who worked for a state agency with responsibility for management of the highly politicized issue of returning wolves to the wild in Montana. Just before I sat down at the table, a friend with insider knowledge informed me that my host had recently been removed from a position involving the wolf issue. My impression was she had been perceived as too "pro-wolf" by someone or some group vocal on the issue.

About eight of us sat down around the table and began introducing ourselves. After the initial pleasantries, our host opened the discussion by holding up a drawing of a wolf, which could be seen as either a friendly wolf or a menacing wolf, depending on how your vision took in the image. It worked like the various other drawings floating around that can be seen in two ways, like the one that seems to shift between a hag and fashionable young woman. Our host asked us what we saw in the image. I saw the good wolf. As I sat there, I had to work hard to see the other image, but that often happens to me with those shifting images in these drawings. By easing up on myself, eventually a snarling wolf came into view.

We found that most of us at the table could see both images but there were a few locked into the good wolf or the bad wolf. With all of us living in Montana, we readily understood the metaphor: what you make of wolves depends a great deal on what you see in them, whether you see something good or something menacing. Often this has little to do with factual reality. Our host asked us to go around the table and say what had brought us to this particular discussion. When my turn came—about halfway around—I said that I was interested in the way so many people seem to get very riled up on the wolf issue. I said it seemed people project good or evil into wolves. I was also interested in how the wolf issue seems to bring out the animosity of some people who live near nature for other people they see as "out of state" environmentalists or bureaucrats without much actual experience with nature. Our host joked that I had taken away some of her punch lines, but said she was interested in these things as well.

The evening continued and people asked questions and expressed opinions, mostly "pro-wolf." I became a bit of a devil's advocate. I mentioned the incident a few years earlier where a man said he was walking in the woods near Macdonald Pass and found himself surrounded by a pack of wolves. He said they were threatening to move in on him. "Maybe it's dangerous to have a wolf pack so close to town," I said.

The table was quiet. I added, "It was also kind of weird to me how so many people refused to believe him, practically called him a liar. I wonder why that was."

"Because wolves don't do that," somebody said. "It's just not possible."

"Really," I said, "so you know this man was definitely lying? Why would he do that?"

"Maybe he wanted attention," somebody said. "Maybe he doesn't like wolves." This was still polite conversation, but some nerves had been touched.

"Well maybe he was just mistaken," somebody else said, trying to soften things up.

Near the time of the incident on MacDonald Pass, I had a discussion with a young woman environmentalist, a transplant to Montana, who was quite forceful in her opinion that it was completely impossible that wolves had menaced this man. Eventually, I politely eased out of the discussion because I saw she was angry and not comfortable being angry with me. I was not so comfortable either.

Around that same time, I found myself in a mirror-image discussion while sitting in a barber chair having the little hair on my head trimmed. It was an old style barber shop, the kind with the spinning red and blue barber's pole outside the door. During any given haircut, the clientele at the barber shop invariably include a good many hunters and military men from nearby Fort Harrison. Having nothing to do with me, the conversation turned to how finally maybe the environmentalists will believe how dangerous it is to have wolves back near town given that this guy was almost attacked on MacDonald Pass. No doubt about it: people see different things in the picture of a wolf.

I knew the barber, so I said, "Come on, Jack, isn't what you're really worried about that you think the wolves are thinning out the elk population so much that you can't fill your elk tags." In hunter's talk, "can't fill your tags" means you are not able to kill the animal the state has given you permission to kill in a hunting season based on your application and payment of the appropriate fee. "Oh, I'll fill my tags," said my barber friend. "Don't you worry about that." I felt a little bit of an edge.

Interesting, this wolf issue. At the rational level, the issue is an interesting example of navigating the realities of attempting to bring "the wild" back near civilization. Excellent science-based strategies were used in the Northern Rocky Mountain reintroduction of wolves, as well as extremely skillful public relations and community service. The issue is particularly interesting to me in considering the sources of the strong emotional energy, not much based in reason, seeming to surround wolves for a good many people. There seem to be different emotional sources for different people, intertwined with nature in different ways.

First, let us consider some reality. The concern about wolves taking down animals in which humans have an interest is completely legitimate. In Montana and Idaho, where wolves were reintroduced beginning in the 1980s, ranchers and farmers were rightfully concerned about livestock loss. "Although wolves feed primarily on big game animals," explains the website of the Montana Department of Fish and Game, "they occasionally do kill livestock and other domestic animals such as domestic dogs or llamas."[384] The issue of losing big game is real to many Montana hunters, and to the tourist industry, but the livestock issue involves the livelihood of hardworking citizens.

I think the legacy of homesteading western ranchers and farmers is also invoked. If we are bringing back wolves, maybe the morality of killing them off to begin with is questioned. Maybe wolves should never have been driven out of this territory. I think this touches the deeply rooted but mostly unconscious question of whether European descendants have a right to this land—whether or not we were right to drive out the wild, which at some level implicates what was done to Native Americans. Lest anyone think I am completely insane, I have heard well-educated compassionate mainstream Euro-American people make comments such as, "Well, the Indians weren't really using the land anyway, so it was okay that we took it." "Not using it" means the natives were not ranching and farming. I heard that as rationalization around guilt. I imagine something like this: "If we let the wolves come back, maybe we should never have taken the land and maybe we cannot hold onto it." Western civilization itself is implicated.

Between 1987 and 2004, there were a total of 429 cattle and 1,074 sheep confirmed as killed by wolves in Montana, Idaho, and Wyoming. The role of the Montana Department of Fish and Game includes working "with livestock producers to reduce the risk of wolf-caused losses and resolve conflicts through a combination of non-lethal deterrents and lethal control." [385] Between 1987 and 2004, the Department or its agents killed 292 wolves in the tri-state area to resolve wolf-livestock conflicts, with 166 of those wolves killed in Montana.[386]

On the issue of big game, the Department acknowledges wolves impact populations of deer, elk, and moose, on which they feed. "How much of an impact," states the website, "varies in space and through time and most importantly, it varies with other environmental factors such as drought, severe winter, overall carnivore density, or general habitat conditions."[387] On human-wolf interaction, the Montana Department of Fish and Game takes the position:

> Like many wild animals, wolves are capable of posing a threat to human safety, but such occurrences are rare. In the past 100 years, there have been several published accounts of human injuries due to wolves. In almost all cases where healthy wolves have attacked people, the wolf or wolves have been habituated to people and food conditioned prior to the attack. These factors also frequently contribute to bear attacks on people. It is unusual for a wild wolf to associate or interact with people, linger near buildings, livestock or domestic dogs for extended periods of time. This behavior is more typical of a released captive wolf-dog hybrid, a wolf habituated to a domestic food source, or an unhealthy animal.[388]

Settlers in the Americas killed off wolves because of their fear, to some extent based on experience, of wolves taking down their livestock and posing a danger to people. Because wolves have carried projections of evil in some cultures for centuries (remember Little Red Riding Hood?), it is likely this projection, predating our industrial and technological times, was intermixed with a reasonable desire to protect livestock, livelihood, and families. While many wild animals can pose a danger to humans and animals in which we claim an interest, I believe wolves are unique in that we hold them in our awareness as possessing the danger we have domesticated out of dogs, our loyal, mostly friendly companions. In Jungian psychology, the "shadow" is the repository of rejected or feared elements of the psyche, including instinctual urges. It is easy to project the "shadow" of dogs onto wolves—and to some extent this is true, as we bred the wild out of most dogs. If we identify with dogs at some level, then at some level our own shadow is projected onto wolves. Wolves carry this projection because they remain wild and can be ruthless carnivores, perhaps more frightening to us because they look like dogs so we want to believe they are friendly—again, remember Red Riding Hood and the wolf pretending to be Grandma.

In 2009, there was an incident widely reported in Montana of a wolf "thrill kill." A rancher near Dillon, Montana, found 120 of her buck sheep killed in what appeared to be one incident of wolf mayhem. [389] Kathy Konan said she had lost guard dogs to wolves previously, but had never seen anything like this. She said dead sheep "were in the sagebrush, on the creek bottom—just all over the pasture." A Montana Fish and Wildlife representative confirmed eighty-two sheep had been killed by wolves in the incident, with another forty carcasses classified as probable kills. There was some evidence of scavenging by bears. "That's a lot all in one incident," said Carolyn Sime of the Fish and Wildlife Department. "The sheep were just killed and yet the carcasses were almost all intact," Konen added, leading to the media description of thrill kill. There was speculation the attack had been by "adolescent wolves," which seemed consistent with the fear some of us carry about the wildness of teenagers.

With sympathies to the rancher, not to mention the poor slaughtered sheep, it is easy for me to feel into the thrill that surely helped sell media coverage of the "thrill kill" by wolves. If you mention wolves to my kids, one of the first things you hear is, "remember that 'thrill kill'?" I will confess to the existence of a dark place inside me awakened just a bit by the notion of running amok and killing randomly for no reason. Perhaps this is shocking, but I think this is a part of our heritage, which continues to play itself out in wars and genocides. "Thrill kill." Shadowy, even evil, but part of our human repertoire.

There is also a separate place inside me that "thrills" to sensing a dark, dangerous force "out there" that may swoop in at any time with devastating impact. With this mirror image of thrill, the sense of the wild, instinctual and dangerous is projected out as an enemy looming at the gates. Wolves in the forest, menacing, out to get us.

Then of course there is that more peaceful, reasonable place where I have nothing but sympathy for the animals needlessly killed and resonance with a hard-working rancher trying to make a living and protect her animals. Having raised some animals on my gentleman-farmer ranchette, I would take that loss very personally. From that place of reason, I can also "understand" the wildness in wolves as something that can be managed in order to walk the line between competing interests. And yet, I would be kidding myself if I did not own up to some buzz from "thrill kill" and acknowledge, at least to myself, that part of the picture.

I have very limited personal experience with wolves. Once, I stood early one morning with my wife and daughter on the side of a road in Yellowstone, trying to see wolves through binoculars. This is quite a ritual in Yellowstone. Just about every morning when the road is open, wolf groupies congregate to look through telescopes and binoculars for the latest in what is happening in the wolf packs. They know particular animals and you hear things like, "his tail is looking a lot better today." A second incident I remember, which I much preferred, was seeing a proverbial "lone wolf" running in a ditch near the Blackfoot Reservation in northwestern Montana. Possibly it was just a dog that looked like a wolf but there was something about the steady intensity and confidence of the run that made me think "this is a wolf."

The third incident involved becoming convinced a dog my father adopted from the pound in Helena was part wolf. Wolf hybrids might be born through nature taking her course when dogs and wolves meet, but usually result from intentional breeding by humans looking for a taste of the wild or some toughness in their dogs. These unfortunate hybrids are sometimes killed or discarded because they turn out to be dangerous as pets. We gradually began to suspect there was some wolf in the dog my father adopted because of her erratic behaviors and inability to "settle" in the house. I became more convinced when the dog, named Stella, suddenly and for no discernible reason ripped open the belly of my dad's other dog, a German Sheppard. Poor Stella was taken back to the pound. Poor Pal was stitched up. I still think Stella was part wolf, but maybe I had just fallen victim to the projection of danger onto wolves. Stella turned violent; she must be a wolf.

For me, wolves are a particularly good example of how our psychologies are projected into nature. As we shall feel into more deeply with bears, some people imagining the "good wolf" seem to have little experience with carnivore reality. A friend told me a story about a woman living in one of our larger communities where wolf packs were starting to thrive just on the outskirts. The woman had been actively "pro-wolf," wholeheartedly and vocally supporting the wolf recovery program. Then one day, as fate would have it, a wolf took down an elk in her front yard. The wolf was devouring the elk. The woman called one of the state agencies, practically frantic, asking them to come stop the wolf from devouring the elk. It was horrible to see. Nature had suddenly become real.

The dividing line on the wolf issue may tend to fall quite similarly to the dividing line on many other issues in United States politics. But with wolves, there is something clarifying about the divide. I think it comes down, at least to some extent, to whether you, metaphorically speaking, sees the menacing wolf or the friendly wolf in that picture held up at the Helena Education Foundation dinner. Another part of the energy seems to involve your position—or your social group's position—on whether there is any value to bringing the wild back into contact with humans in its own right, or whether that is naïve as well as detrimental to humans. As suggested above, to some extent, I think your position on "civilization" may even be implicated. Perhaps some of us want to ease up on that dominance of nature we have managed to create over the last several thousand years, whereas others do not want to give any of that up. I doubt this is thought through consciously by most of us. Rather, I suspect our position on issues like wolves involves how our particular personalities and enculturation mingle with unconscious energies surrounding nature and emerge as outlook and viewpoints.

From one perspective, the wolf issue is one of the innumerable social and political issues on which people simply have different values, and might disagree on what should happen in our communities based on actual information. And yet my experience has been—and that experience was echoed to me by those in leadership roles in wolf management—that emotional charges run high on the wolf issue, so high that sometimes the facts seem to be irrelevant. At the very least, the emotional charge is so high that it becomes a struggle for those managing wolves to be heard from a place of reason. This suggests to me that wolves, a part of nature, are carrying some of our emotional charges around nature, some of the energies that exist in our unconscious, perhaps both personal and collective. The emotional charges are not necessarily exclusively *about* nature, but nature is involved, such that we might consider the wolf situation an example of our unconscious psychological immersion in nature.

Back in that barber shop conversation, I started to have the sense that some people wanted me to be scared. Somebody said, "Up where you live, there's wolves now. I'm surprised you haven't seen them. I would be careful if I was you." Somebody else said, "I hope you can shoot." I was waiting for, "You have kids?" Nobody said it clearly, but we were back to that terrain my neighbor had entered when we first moved to Montana: "Better not let your kids play in them woods, there's a bear in there." Though no one in the barber shop was nearly this heartless, I also remembered some of the energy that came toward my family and me a few years earlier just a few blocks down the street from the barber shop.

On several Friday afternoons in the spring of 2003, just after the United States and the United Kingdom invaded Iraq, our family stood with others in protest, just a few people on a street corner with some signs. My wife and I did not believe the information being disseminated about the necessity for invasion and found a strong coincidence between an alleged need to occupy Iraq, an American administration with ties to the oil industry, and the presence of an enormous amount of undeveloped oil in Iraq. This is not to say I am against all military action, as sometimes it is necessary, just as police functions are necessary in any civilized society when actual imminent dangers are presented. In this case, judging the evidence, we felt it was our civic duty to protest, which was also a way for us to educate our children. I also thought a little protesting that particular "shock and awe" invasion might separate me out from the pack and protect my karma.

Most people passing by on a Friday afternoon did not seem to care about a few people standing on a street corner with signs. Many honked horns in support, but there was a fair amount of animosity directed our way. The most troubling was the guy who rounded the corner fast in his pickup and shouted at me, while I was standing between my 13 and 9 year old girls, "Wait 'til they rape your daughter." I have always wondered who was meant by "they?" Iraqis, Arabs, or maybe just basically foreigners? Could this be a "they" existing at the same unconscious level as wolves? It is interesting to note how rapacious men are sometimes called "wolves." And that rapacious men thing is no joke. I was close during college with a German woman who hid in a kitchen cupboard when Russians came through her Berlin neighborhood looking for women as the allies occupied Berlin at the close of World War II, the Russians being the first to arrive. Historians believe some two million German women were raped by Red Army soldiers as Hitler's Third Reich Fell.[390] That is not to start an argument blaming Russians; we are all part of humanity. There is violence within us, particularly when we are amassed in packs: wolves in the woods, even as we sit with our families by the hearth with our trusted domesticated dogs.

I have had the pleasure of several conversations with Ed Bangs, who for 23 years led the effort to reintroduce wolves into the northern Rocky Mountains. He worked as the wolf recovery coordinator for the United

States Fish and Wildlife Service. When Ed retired in 2011, an article in the Missoulian (Missoula's daily newspaper) observed:

> At various times, depending on the stage of the reintroduction, he was heralded as a hero while simultaneously being denounced as a wolf lover or hater, depending on people's perspective. Yet somehow he managed to charm many on both sides of the wolf wars, with a mix of humor tinged with a reputation for fairness.
>
> "He would get in front of a group trying to ridicule and criticize him, and Ed would beat them to the punch," recalled Carter Niemeyer, a former Wildlife Services supervisor who worked closely with Bangs for decades. "One time, we were in Grangeville, Idaho, in front of a hostile crowd, with one guy leading the charge. He said, 'Tell me what the hell good the blankedy-blank wolves ever did.' Ed chimed up and said, 'They gave me this cushy job' and the whole audience cracked up. The man got up and left because he was so angry.
>
> "He would win the crowd over, because they thought he was kind of funny, and that would get things going."[391]

After his retirement, Ed continued to travel around the world on invitation from groups interested in hearing about the reintroduction of wolves into Montana, Idaho, and Wyoming. His trips were likely great for Montana tourism, as we see a fair number of foreign visitors every summer. Some people might be interested in wolves just as they are interested in any other aspect of nature, or any other controversial issue. But I believe there is something about wolves that pulls at that place inside us where we know we have lost contact with the wild—just as our dogs, those descendants of wolf-like ancestors, literally lost their wildness when throwing their lot in with humans. Recent DNA research indicates this transition from wolf-ancestor to dog-ancestor happened eleven to sixteen thousand years ago, in Europe, before agriculture, when our own ancestors were hunter-gatherers.[392] Presumably, some ancient wolf-relatives were hanging around carcasses or campfires and a lasting friendship developed with some wolf-curious humans.

Bangs says one of the biggest issues he faced from the public was the feeling that out-of-state bureaucrats and environmentalists were forcing wolves on a locale where they did not live. This might explain some of the strength of the feelings expressed during the early years of wolf recovery, a form of territoriality or irritation that others with no business in an issue think they know better. While everyone's reasons for having energy on the issue might be unique to them, I suspect there is something in our human collective, something in our collective unconscious, giving rise to the energy on both sides. Within those passionately wanting the return of wolf populations to the lower 48 states, I suspect there is an individual and emerging collective need for an internal sense of nature, an intimacy with nature, since that intimacy has been mostly lost through a few thousand years of civilization.

Along with many other animals of the Rocky Mountains, certainly including bears, wolves are very popular among a good number of people I have encountered at experiential personal growth workshops and educational opportunities in the United States and Europe. I once had a conversation about wolves with a young woman from Maryland at a California retreat. She asked for my address and not long afterwards there arrived a gift from her, a poster of a gray wolf. I hung it on the wall of my basement so I could see it when I exercised on the treadmill. I looked at that wolf most mornings for years. A great sympathy for my acquaintance from Maryland would cross my mind. I suspect there was something healing for her in knowing she had a connection to a guy who lived in Montana and that there were wolves around where he lived. The poster she sent connected us to each other and through wolves to the wild.

Equally interesting to me is the animosity to wolves which Bangs so skillfully handled. He joked with the Missoulian "that wolves are actually kind of boring," referring to them as "just big dogs that have been studied to death." But he found people fascinating, which is one reason he didn't hesitate, wrote the Missoulian, "when walking into rooms filled with angry people."[393] Given my own conversations with some anti-wolf folks, I suspect there is more happening inside many of these folks than a clean response to actual danger to livestock or humans. Some of the energy is likely rural animosity toward big-city-know-it-alls. But I suspect there is something than runs even more deeply. When our wild instincts are repressed into the unconscious, personal or collective, then wolves, those "wild" dogs, are a perfect hook for projecting our fears around unleashing all that chaos and violence of our animal instincts. When there is some actual danger involved, all the easier. For me, finding and somehow processing that violence within nature is a lurking issue within the return to nature so many of us crave.

There is possibly some danger in denying our dark side—we are then more likely to project it out and act dangerously in unconscious ways. One of the topics studied by transpersonal psychology is "spiritual bypass." This happens when we identify with "the love and light" of spirituality and neglect to notice our instinctual sides, the darkness within us, whether that is trauma, violence, anger, or simply suffering. Those of us seeing only the "good wolf" in nature might not just be naïve about nature, but a bit naïve about ourselves. And for this reason, I suspect it may help us to find the actual emotions and instincts that exist deeply within our psyches with respect to nature.

"...and Bears"

A few years ago my friend Sally told our dream group a story of a bear encounter in Glacier National Park. Every year, Sally and her husband hike in the park, some years all the way up the mountains from Many Glacier Lodge, past Swift Current Lake, along Grinnel Lake, into some of the most beautiful country on the planet. It is grizzly country. It is also tourist country. On this occasion, Sally rounded a bend and there was a grizzly just alongside the main hiking trail. There were also about a dozen hikers—some of them naïve tourists—stopped in their tracks by the presence of the bear. Some of the tourists were actually moving closer to the bear to take pictures, despite the fairly relentless warnings given in the parks against such human behavior. I mean, at the trail heads in Glacier, there are signs reading, "Danger of death."

Sally, whose father was a forest ranger, took out her bear spray and quietly told everyone they needed to stay together, make some noise but not too much, and move past the bear without disturbing him. When Sally told this story in our dream group, she reported feeling a mixture of grief and rage about this experience, which she had not completely understood until she began telling the story. As we talked, she said things like, "They didn't seem to understand this was real." Everyone in dream group other than Sally is a transplant to Montana; we all shared a love for living in one of the few places left in the lower forty-eight states where some areas are wild. Sally said, "They didn't seem to understand bears are actual, real animals. They're not just something you take a picture of. It feels the same as something bigger. Like nobody seems to understand that our destruction of the planet *is real*. It's not just an idea. These bears and all these other animals will be gone if all this craziness doesn't stop."

In one of our first summers in Montana, my family took a fairly stupid hike in the mountains near Lincoln, very much grizzly country. We had been camping with some visitors from California. It rained overnight, thoroughly drenching the campsite. The next morning, we decided to get away from the soggy tents and make a hike to a nearby lake described in a guide book. We set out with nine of us. We took the wrong trail. Eventually, my wife and I started to realize we might be on the wrong trail, but our friends kept saying, "Let's just keep going." The woods were dense, but I kept thinking we would round a bend any minute and find the lake described so gloriously in the guide book. Just as men do not like to ask for directions, we do not like to admit we have taken the wrong trail. As we walked down the path—some of our California friends actually in flip-flops—I started to notice what looked like bear scat on the trail. From the dense woods, I heard what sounded like low growling, a rumbling. At first, I pretended to myself it could not be a bear. Then I saw claw marks on trees.

I suggested we were in grizzly territory. Having read some books about bear attacks, some part of me was aware of danger, but my friends seemed to think we were in Disneyland, where danger is constructed, pretend, and not real. I kept hearing, "the lake has to be just around the bend." Finally, I looked at my wife and nodded toward the claw marks on the tree. She insisted we turn around. I still remember that growling off in the woods, and more importantly I remember the way I had such difficulty believing there could be real danger in nature. I knew and yet I would not believe. Or was it the draw to danger that kept me walking? That scares me, embarrasses me, and yet pulls at me. If I am honest with myself, it was probably, in part, my own draw to the *idea* of danger of nature that kept me walking on that trail longer than I should have. I suspect that was not just naiveté, but unconscious need for immersion in the deadly reality of nature. Pity I was unconscious enough to let other people keep walking with me for as long as I did.

In the fascinating film *Grizzly Man*, German filmmaker Werner Herzog tells the tragic story of Timothy Treadwell, a man who spent thirteen summers camping in grizzly country in Alaska. Each year, Treadwell managed to coexist with the bears in close proximity. The last summer, he was joined by his girlfriend Amie Hugenard. They packed up camp as summer ended, always Treadwell's practice, but a frustrating experience at the airport caused them to return to the wilds, rejecting civilization. This was a different time of year, with different bears in proximity. Exactly what happened is not known, but Treadwell and Hugenard were both killed. Parts of their bodies were found in the digestive system of a bear.

Herzog constructed a narrative of the summer with use of video taken by Treadwell, interwoven with his own footage, including interviews with people who either knew Treadwell or were involved in the tragic aftermath. Listening to some of Treadwell's narration in his videos leaves an impression of a sadly unbalanced individual. Treadwell recorded: "I'm in love with my animal friends. I'm in love with my animal friends! In love with my animal friends. I'm very, very troubled. It's very emotional. It's probably not cool even looking like this. I'm so in love with them, and they're so fucked over, which so sucks."[394] He said: "I will die for these animals; I will die for these animals; I will die for these animals." Even more strangely: "Oh my gosh! The bear, Miss Chocolate, has left me her poop! It's her crap! It was just in her butt and it's still warm! This is a gift from Miss Chocolate!"

Herzog understood Treadwell as having projected a benign view of nature onto grizzlies. He suggested Treadwell naively viewed bears through his own lens of nature as a beneficent wonderland, with civilization as the root of all evil. Most people would understand Treadwell as tragically descending into some form of mental illness. Even so, some of us may sympathize with his desire to merge with nature through coexistence with one of the most dangerous creatures on the planet. I am inclined to believe Treadwell had some capacity to mingle with bears arising from his sincere desire for restoration of the wild. Yet I am right there with Sam Egli, a helicopter pilot who helped transport the remains of Treadwell and Hugenard. "My opinion," Egli says on film, "I think Treadwell thought these bears were big, scary looking, harmless creatures that he could go up and pet and sing to, and they would bond as children of the universe or some odd. I think he lost sight of what was really going on." Then Egli got to the point: "That bear, I think, that day, decided that he had either had enough of Tim Treadwell or that something clicked in that bear's head that he thought 'Hey, you know, he might be good to eat.'"

Herzog saw more in what happened—or perhaps he saw less. His voice narrates:

> And what haunts me, is that in all the faces of all the bears that Treadwell ever filmed, I discover no kinship, no understanding, no mercy. I see only the overwhelming indifference of nature. To me, there is no such thing as a secret world of the bears. And this blank stare speaks only of a half-bored interest in food. But for Timothy Treadwell, this bear was a friend, a savior.

Going even more deeply, Herzog shared: "I believe the common character of the universe is not harmony, but chaos, hostility, and murder." It is interesting to me that Herzog used the word "universe" rather than "nature." This speaks a dark vision of not just the natural world, but of the cosmos, practically an existential proposition. When I have talked with others about this nihilist vision in the context of nature, often someone quotes the famous line from Joseph Conrad's novel *Heart of Darkness,* "The horror...the horror."[395] Some of us will remember reading the novel in high school or college. In 1979, it was adapted by Francis Ford Coppola into *Apocalypse Now,* involving the horrors of the Vietnam War. The novel is a tale within a tale, told by one of the most famous narrators in English literature, Marlow. On a sea voyage, Marlow captivates fellow travelers with the recollection of his journey upriver into the Congo. He was in search of the infamous Mr. Kurtz, who had rejected civilization and descended into a form of mayhem and madness. In *Apocalypse Now,* Kurtz is recreated by a calmly crazed-looking Marlon Brando.

In the novel, Marlow describes his reaction when he finally encountered Kurtz: "I tried to break the spell—the heavy, mute spell of the wilderness— that seemed to draw him to its pitiless breast by the awakening of forgotten and brutal instincts, by the memory of gratified and monstrous passions."[396] Marlow continues: "But his soul was mad. Being alone in the wilderness, it had looked within itself, and, by heavens! I tell you, it had gone mad."[397] Marlow tells us what he saw in Kurtz: "His was an impenetrable darkness." Then he describes how he felt when coming upon Kurtz nearing death:

> I was fascinated. It was as though a veil had been rent. I saw on that ivory face the expression of sombre pride, of ruthless power, of craven terror—of an intense and hopeless despair. Did he live his life again in every detail of desire, temptation, and surrender during that supreme moment of complete knowledge? He cried in a whisper at some image, at some vision—he cried out twice, a cry that was no more than a breath—"The horror! The horror!"[398]

Like many a high school and college student before me, I am going to wonder what it was that Kurtz saw. Was it death that brought horror to Kurtz? Madness? Having lost civilization? Literary critic and Conrad biographer Leo Gurko considers Marlow, like Kurtz, having been "tempted by the wilderness," noting the "darkness of Africa embraces both demoralizing savagery and burgeoning life."[399] Quoting Conrad, Gurko describes Marlow as feeling the "'fascination of the abomination,'" but considered Marlow, unlike Kurtz, saved by his ability to glimpse "his own hidden self without falling over the precipice or 'kicking himself loose from the earth' as Kurtz has."[400] *Heart of Darkness* is so powerful because the external journey into the depths of the Congo mirrors an internal journey into the depths of the unconscious. There is something about immersion in wilderness that seems to parallel immersion in the unconscious for some of us—and sometimes that immersion becomes a form of madness. I suspect part of the naiveté some of us hold around nature is a naiveté about the way in which civilization might be keeping us together in an individual psychological sense. A walk in the woods may not take us into insanity, but there is something about fully letting go into the wilds of nature that may be psychologically dangerous for some of us.

My family's hike to the unfound lake near Lincoln took place not far from where Ted Kaczynski, the Unabomber, once lived in a woodsy cabin, an anonymous recluse until his capture in 1996. Highly intelligent, and highly unstable, Kaczynski had a short-lived career as a mathematician, including teaching on the faculty at the University of California, Berkeley. Then he retreated to the woods near Lincoln, where he began to learn survival skills. Over a period of eighteen years, he mailed homemade bombs to officials he associated with development and technology. He killed three people and maimed many others. While the nuances of his motives have been debated, one of his journals described a desire to murder "snowmobilists, motorcyclists, outboard motor users or the like," those people who ruin the solitude of those of us who like to commune more peacefully with nature.[401] Another of his journals included:

> I believe in nothing . . . I don't even believe in the cult of nature-worshipers or wilderness-worshipers. (I am perfectly ready to litter in parts of the woods that are of no use to me - I often throw cans in logged-over areas or in places much frequented by people; I don't find wilderness particularly healthy physically; I don't hesitate to poach.)[402]

It seems to me the form of madness experienced by Kaczynski—and I am not talking about the merits of an insanity defense, but a common sense understanding of madness—is inextricable from his desire to immerse himself in the wilderness. Kaczynski is an extreme example of the pull nature has for some people experiencing what most of us would call mental illness. People familiar with trekking into the mountains through dirt roads and private trails realize that some remote cabins are occupied by people who seem fearful, paranoid, and angry enough to be dangerous to strangers. Sometimes a "No Trespassing" sign encountered on an exploratory trek in the mountains can indicate more real menace than those "Danger of Death" signs at the base of trails in grizzly country.

When I first watched *Grizzly Man,* I heard Herzog's nihilism as a healthy corrective to the romantic vision of nature held by many people, including me. Then, over time, as this settled into me, I concluded that Herzog's dismal view might be too fearful, a projection of a brilliant mind—with vivid access to the unconscious—more than a grounded assessment of either nature or the universe. There is violence in nature but I do not find the sort of chaos that suggests no meaning to existence. Many of us have our moments of existential wonderings in nature, but my experience suggests that if we stick with what is arising, we may find our own order and cohesion. In such existential moments, nature may reflect back to us some of our deepest fears about existence and non-existence, about the nature of the universe, about the purpose or lack of purpose of our own lives. Yet if we reach the other side, we might find comfort in addition to the possibility of despair and madness, meaningfulness as well as meaninglessness.

Perhaps paradoxically, nature may call forth our fear and then assuage it. Gayle Abbott, a mental health counselor living in New Mexico, shared her experience looking out at the ocean at night. *I feel that I could easily become lost in the vastness of the sea, the relentless pounding of the waves. I feel very much alone and insignificant. My heart quickens with fear and chills spread over my body. I may then be comforted by the rhythm of the waves, which may take me into sleep. The vastness of the night sky can also produce feelings of insignificance and loss in me. I sometimes cry for the people who have passed on, perhaps because I miss them, or perhaps because I question whether we remain connected. Then the feelings of sadness seem to give way into the expanse of the darkness, leaving me with a feeling of hope.*

Many years ago, John Bullaro faced a crossroads in his personal and professional life. His marriage was breaking up, which meant he would no longer live full time with his children. His career felt stifling. He wrote: *In those early adult years, I was consumed with the goal of being accepted into groups I cared little for: churches, service clubs, social clubs, political action committees. I guess I thought that membership in the "right" group meant I was successful. Even my career as an insurance executive was bought by supporting the dreams of a company for whose mission I felt, at best, indifference.*

The attempt to succeed in a world I found irrational exhausted me in time. By achieving success I surrendered any attempt at personal control over my destiny. Success was built on the ideas of other people, ideas I thought would make me successful in this mystifying world. This lack of control, these compromises, dishonored me. On the outside, I looked successful; on the inside, I felt lost, hopeless. Still, I dreamed of a personal resurrection.

It was at this time I became familiar with the Native American practice of vision questing. I happened to meet a mixed blood Native American/ Anglo man who explained to me the dynamics of going into an uninhabited area, without distraction, and sitting with the big questions. On a sunny, cool fall day, I packed my motorcycle bags with water, clothes, two blankets, matches, a drinking cup, and a broad brimmed hat. Leaving the San Fernando Valley for Death Valley, I began what I expected would be a three-day vision quest. I envisioned little more than a holiday to sort things out. Being an experienced outdoors-person, I did not expect the emotional experiences that awaited me.

I found an isolated spot in the desert, at the foot of what could only be called a large hill. I noticed a ring of rocks from an old campfire, so I made this place my camp. It was late in the afternoon and the shadows were long. Few plants grew in the area and a strong steady breeze was blowing, common on the desert. I walked some distance from my camp and secured a load of firewood from dead blown Mesquite brush dotting the area.

As night closed in, I began to experience strong feelings of loneliness. The fire offered warmth but no companionship. Since I had no distractions, I sat staring into the fire about my big questions. In no time the darkness closed in all around me. Despite myself, I was afraid. In the distance, I heard coyotes yipping as if playing games with each other. I envied them for having a group they belonged to. As night wore on, my sense of isolation from family, friends, and all my old-life connections became a profound and frightening feeling. I found myself talking to the coyotes, asking them to come and join me. Of course, they didn't.

The night was long and terrifying. I felt as if I were the last person alive on the planet. I managed to get through the darkness. Around an hour after day break, with my fire once again offering warmth and some comfort, I saw in the distance a man walking toward me. When he arrived at my camp, he asked if I was okay, if I needed anything. I told him I was here on a vision quest and started to explain what this was. He interrupted me to say he knew what this was about and had himself done a similar thing four years earlier, when he was an aero-space engineer for a military aircraft production company. He told me how, as a result of his vision quest, he left the war business and became a park ranger, which is what he was doing at that time. I was blown away by his story. Later, I even thought I might have imagined the whole interaction. It was as if I had seen myself resurrected, just as I asked. After returning to school, I became an instructor in outdoor recreation, which became a long, productive and fulfilling career.

In John's story, I imagine the expanse of Death Valley, the darkness, and the indifference of nature having brought to the surface the emotions John needed to face. While he felt alone, even terrified, nature held what was happening to him, and allowed John to experience a new dawn, just through staying present to the night. Perhaps there is an emptiness in nature, beyond good and evil, a blankness not the same as evil chaos but connected to a deep source of psychological equilibrium, the opposite of madness yet perhaps somehow right next door.

Rosemarie Anderson describes an experience of the wild in nature, which she realized reflected an internal experience of blankness, perhaps important to human spiritual wholeness. *Some years ago,* she writes, *I was camping along the Klamath River in northern California just south of the Oregon border. The river valley is remote and river wild. I decided to drive across the Siskiyou Mountains to Oregon on a country road. At the summit, I got out of the car and walked along a ridge, knowing that I could easily follow the ridge back to the car. However, as I bushwhacked my way, I was frightened. There was nothing human here; nothing familiar to my knowing; nothing that reflected back to me humanness as I knew it. "No human has walked this ridge before," I wondered. I scurried back to the car. Later, I knew that I had experienced the correspondence of the wilderness with the Buddhist understanding of Sunyata, Emptiness. I knew then in a way that I could never explain adequately in words that the human psyche depends on the wild for nurturance.*[403]

As descendants of the natural world, perhaps we can remember the indifference of nature, even the violence, without loss of our conscious, human selves. If we are the most conscious products of earthly evolution (a big if in my view), our consciousness, I believe, involves our ability to appreciate meaning. But meaning is not the same as benevolence, peace, or even compassion. Harsh as it may seem, as I move more maturely into an understanding of my ecological self, I do not experience myself as whole only when I am benign and caring. While I am far from condoning the expression of murderous instincts, I am interested in making conscious all aspects of being human, and all aspects of being pre-human, including the parts we consider horrible. These parts include what we know as cruelty, violence, and indifference to life and death. This does not mean I want terrifying experiences for myself or those in my life; to the contrary, I pray otherwise. But I do want to understand that our heritage contains death as well as life, murder as well as nurturing, harshness as well as comfort. Ultimately, it is this systemic wholeness that wants to live in my body: the dark as well as the light—even a sense of wholeness beyond dark and light as separated manifestations.

In our dream group, my friend Sally recently described a dream involving bears, which she has permitted me to share. Sally and her husband Richard were walking up a Montana stream bed in a place called Bear Trap Canyon. The rocks in the stream bed were polished to a numinous glow. The water was too warm for the season, a worrisome sign of global warming, but felt good on the feet. As Sally and Richard continued uphill, they were suddenly in a truck, as can happen in dreams, driving up a rutted dirt road into a high, narrow canyon. Before them appeared a plywood tree house on a pole, reminding Sally of the many tree houses of her youth. Her father's work as a forest ranger graced the family with many years living in or near wilderness. I did not share this projection of mine in dream group, but my own association with tree houses includes our evolutionary heritage as primates living in trees—tree houses take me into our instinctual heritage.

In the tree house in Sally's dream were a number of bear carcasses. They were piled on top of each other. Dead bears, killed by humans, kept for skins or as trophies. To the right of the tree house, Sally saw a "creepy" man camping, not unusual in the woods. He had vicious looking dogs, along with various tools and machines that one might associate with twentieth or twenty-first century machismo of a certain brand. To the left was her father as he is now, in his nineties, breaking camp, saying he was ready to move on. Through some emotion, shared by others of us in the room, Sally described her sense that people like her father, who knew how to be in the woods peacefully, but realistically, may be becoming scarce.

I asked Sally if she could describe more what she meant. "It has to do with control and not control," she said. "Not judging the horror and the aggression, just being with it, and being happy." Synchronistically, I had checked *Heart of Darkness* out of the library that afternoon; it was sitting in my truck, but neither I nor anyone else had yet mentioned the word "horror" that evening. I asked Sally what she felt from the other campsite in the dream. She responded: "Deprivation, harshness, meanness, resentment." Projecting into Sally's dream, I recognize the creepy guy in the next campsite as one of those many people with animosity for us naïve nature lovers, a hater of tree-huggers, an anti-environmentalist. In *Grizzly Man*, Herzog read from a letter someone had written in response to the tragic deaths of Treadwell and Hugenard. The hateful letter said: "A bear diet consists of liberals and Dems and wacko environmentalists that think the spotted owl is the most important thing in the world. We need to somehow drastically increase the number of bears in America, especially in such key spots as the Berkeley campus."

I asked Sally if she had any insight into the source of the "deprivation, harshness, meanness, resentment." I asked, "Is this about fear?" Sally thought for a moment, and then nodded her head, but her affirmative struck me as half-hearted. I was not completely convinced the "deprivation" and "resentment" part of us is just about fear. It seems darker to me than fear. A few days later, another idea occurred to me when I was watching the television show *The Fall*, a 2013 series produced by Netflix. Set in Belfast, Northern Ireland, a place that has seen a large share of violence, *The Fall* takes us into the life of a darkly charismatic fictional serial killer. Played skillfully by Jamie Dornan, the character Paul Specter suffered a horrible childhood, including the loss of his mother to suicide, followed by shuffling back and forth through foster homes, including one run by a sexually abusive priest.

At the time of the story, Specter, interestingly enough, works as a grief counselor. He is married with two children and, strangely, he is powerfully impactful in assisting people suffering from grief and trauma. But, he rapes and kills beautiful young women. He does this right alongside an apparently sincere love for his young daughter, who adores him. After several episodes, Chief Inspector Stella Gibson, played by Gillian Anderson of *X-Files* fame, closes in on him in a cat and mouse game where it is not clear who is cat and who is mouse, though the game is deeply psychological. With the police on to him, Specter elicits the help of a 16-year-old babysitter who has a sexually-charged crush on him. He asks her to destroy evidence that might implicate him. Even though she realizes he is the serial killer, she helps because she is powerfully pulled to him by those dangerous adolescent instincts.

To nail her into him, Specter asks her to feel into her dark side. She says she does not know how to do that. He asks her to think about her friend, a blond and healthy-looking teenager we have seen several times, and to imagine how good it would feel if the friend began to lose everything she wanted. Boys would no longer be interested, her grades would be falling, her life in general would be turning dim. Specter tells her to imagine how good it might feel to throw acid in the face of her friend, a further step in his direction. The babysitter gets this in a visceral way and it becomes possible to imagine a connection between sexuality, death, and taking the life force of other beings.

Later, when confronted about his murders by Chief Inspector Gibson, Specter explains how all his senses are aroused, the colors more vivid, his skin on fire, sounds more intense, when he is about to take a life. This darkness feels to me like it comes from the realm of "deprivation, harshness, meanness, resentment," to return to Sally's words about one side of the campsite in her dream. Deprived of his childhood, Specter was thrust into a world where people used other people, including a priest using adolescent boys for his own gratification. Specter explains to Inspector Gibson the freedom that arises from throwing off all morality (all civilization) and just taking what you want. To me, this seems to be touching a dark and unconscious instinct for survival, perverted in Specter's case. I find myself into terrain that is inexplicable in words. Perhaps this is the "impenetrable darkness" Marlow saw in Kurtz. Taking, killing, and dominance, because tomorrow I may not have anything to eat, no way to gratify my other instinctual urges. The fear might be fear of death, fear of hunger, fear of dominance by others. Interestingly enough, after portraying Specter, actor Jamie Dornan played Christian Grey in the film version of the popular *Fifty Shades of Grey* books, about sexual dominance and submission.

"Why the bears in the dream?" someone asked Sally. She wondered if bears remind us that human dominance is an illusion—nature in the end will come for us all, from inside ourselves, as our biological selves pass into death. Maybe it is a relief for some of us to come face to face with nature as an animal stronger than us, as a potential killer. Yet Sally also considered bears "like humans"—and another dream group member found a reference in one of our symbolism books to a native tradition in which bears are the ancestors of humans.

Sally said she likes being around bears in part because "then we're not at the top of the food chain…there's somebody else up there." She recalled an outing a few years ago in the Cabinet Mountains. She took her dad, her nephews, and a great-nephew into the woods to pick huckleberries. The nephews were quiet but the great-nephew talked non-stop, repeatedly hoping for a bear to come along. My sense was that Sally conveyed to him to be careful what he wished for. On their drive home, on a mountain gravel road, suddenly there crossed in front of them a mother bear with three cubs behind her. "Three cubs," Sally repeated. "That's every unusual." When Sally stopped the car, the mother bear stopped right in front of them. "She reared up," Sally said. "On two legs." Sally described her father's reaction. "He just sat there in the truck and said, 'Whoa.'"

Sally said her dad knew better than any of them that you're in trouble when a bear rears onto two legs. It's a sign of aggression. Her father's "whoa" included an urgency to back off, even if they were in a car. When I asked Sally what else was in the "whoa," she said, "reverence, danger, beauty, vulnerability, and, ultimately, knowing our place in the order of things."

Christmas Trees

Emily Squires lived most of her life in New York City. In her later years, she spent long periods of time with her husband in their country home. An Emmy-Award-winning writer and director of *Sesame Street*, Emily also worked on cable television productions about the Dali Lama, Buddhist writer Frederick Franck, and Hiroshima. Emily and her husband, Len Belzer, authored a book called *Spiritual Places In and Around New York City.*[404] A decade before her 2012 passing, Emily described for me some of her experiences of grief in response to nature. She wrote:

I have many experiences of crying with nature as you put it. It is often of a global nature when I see what we are doing to our planet. But I think you might be interested in a very personal sadness I feel every Christmas. At Christmas time in New York, as everywhere else, millions of evergreen trees are shipped into the city. We see huge open trucks with trees smashed down on top of one another and lashed to the sides with ropes. Outside every deli and 24-hour store, stands are erected where the trees are laid out for sale. People actually sleep in their cars and trucks so they can tend their wares twenty-four hours a day.

When I walk past these tree stands, I seem to hear a high-pitched scree emanating from the near-lifeless beings leaning helplessly against one another. I think of how they were just alive and well in a place where they belonged, even if it were only a Christmas tree farm. I imagine their being summarily hacked down, slung atop one another and transported to this dirty, noisy, cement world, the life oozing out of them. Yes, I cry as I pass them by. Sometimes I touch them trying to offer solace, but they are too far gone to hear me.

Recently I bought a house in the country. It's on thirty-seven acres. The prior owners planted way too many evergreens, too close together for room to grow. So, last Christmas, I invited a family to come out with me and cut two trees down for Christmas, thinning out the herd at the same time. I explained to the trees that they were too close together and this was going to help them. I also tried to explain how we silly human beings yearned for a connection with Nature in the deep of winter and that was why we brought trees indoors. But, as Richard cut my tree down, I felt this real pain in my chest. It was as if they had believed me when I told them I would never hurt the land, never use pesticides, never intrude on Nature as I had found it here. And here I was cutting one of them down. I was devastated. I have finally come to the conclusion that I can no longer cut a tree down for Christmas. It is like the sacrifice of a living being. Think of all the beings we could save, all the trees left alive, if we didn't have this silly ritual of cutting down trees at Christmas.

Just last night I went to a screening of The Secret Life of Plants. After the film, twenty people, all of us just having come through a major snow storm, talked about our connection to the plant world. As a child in Virginia, I did not exactly talk with the plants, but I definitely felt more secure and happy in nature than anywhere else. Over the years we have all seen what's happening to the Earth. I belong to at least fifteen environmental and animal rights organizations. And I eat organic food and care about farm animals and on and on.

New York City is a dirty, noisy, cement world, but we have all chosen to live here, those of us who do. We stuff our apartments with plants and animals to make it feel more like country. That does make the air fresher and we have green life near us. Counting them, I have twenty plants and trees in my two-bedroom apartment and I'm not particularly unusual. There are places to go here that offer respite—my husband and I described some of them in our book. Are we crazy to live here? It's more of a love-hate thing, really. My husband and I hate all the negatives, but can't live without the action, the brio, the pace. I guess you could call it a drug. We have a beautiful house in the country and stay there for long periods of time, especially in the summer. But the thought of not being umbilically connected with NYC is unthinkable for me.

I feel my connection to Nature mostly in my heart. Seeing a little blade of grass pushing its way mightily up through a crack in the sidewalk overwhelms me. Such energy, such determination, even in the middle of concrete. Last night at the film, I was astounded to find that others feel the way I do—exactly the same way. I could call it a deep respect and closeness. We honor nature and how it gives to us constantly, never asking for anything in return.

Crying in response to nature is painful for me. It happens often and naturally. When it does, it takes a lot out of me.

Like Emily Squires, I have finally come to the conclusion that I can no longer cut down a tree at Christmas. I personally cut down Christmas trees for many years. I grew up, like millions of Americans, picking out Christmas trees with my parents from a Christmas tree lot. In my case, these were lots alongside Veterans Highway in Metairie, Louisiana and it always seemed to be raining. Years later, in California, we realized you could drive into the Santa Cruz Mountains and cut down your own tree from amidst trees planted and grown for years for that purchase. It was not cheap, but it was fun. Then, in Montana, for fifteen years, we paid five dollars every year to the National Forest Service for a permit to cut down a tree from public land. We drove across the dam over Canyon Ferry Lake, turned onto Jimtown Road into the Helena National Forest, parked and climbed up some steep mountain looking for the perfect tree.

A couple of years ago, I told my family I cannot do it anymore. As I did so, I thought about Emily Squires. I had come to the place she had come. I knew I would miss the ritual of hiking up the slope, dragging the tree down the mountain with my daughter helping, loading it on the back of the truck, managing to get it into the house, smelling pine for the weeks of the holiday season. But I knew I would not miss the part where I was on the snow on my stomach, sawing at the trunk of a living tree. It was starting to hurt my heart and I just could not do it again. The last family Christmas I spent in Montana, I bought a fake tree at Wal-Mart, adding the justification that I was helping the economy by buying.

I do not begrudge the growing and killing of trees in this holiday tradition. I just cannot saw down any more myself. In the larger scheme of things, with respect to all those trees sold in cities and suburbs, the holiday tree business may well have relatively mild impact on the natural world given that trees are grown for the purpose, produce oxygen while they grow, and are transported into cities in ways not likely creating any more ecological footprint than many other products. People in this industry have as much right to a living as anyone. I have a friend who financed his transpersonal education by selling Christmas trees in San Francisco for a few weeks every holiday season. That was one lucrative gig. If I am not against the practice or the industry, it is interesting to consider why I just cannot cut down another tree.

I wonder about whether, in my case, there is more going on within me than concern for the tree. I eat meat, so it stands to reason that if my compassion for animals does not make me a vegetarian, then why should I have trouble killing a tree someone has given me permission to kill. In other words, I reach the question whether my personal psychological process is being projected, at least in part, onto Christmas trees and their cutting down. Putting myself down on that snow on the mountain in the national forest, about to saw through the trunk of a living tree, I experience a desire not to harm the tree that feels similar to weariness of hurt on my own part. If I process through the simple hurt, I come up against the reality that I am no longer a young man. Perhaps I am grieving the passage of time and want to ease out of the hurting and being-hurt game. Because Christmas trees helped take me here, this grief is textured with the rich smell of Christmas inside the house, limber branches that bend through door frames, that deep green of the tree. Then we reach the reality of children grown up, long past the miracle of believing in Santa, now forming their own families and family traditions. Then I am into territory rife with loss, as are many of us. The easy love of the holiday season ends, families disperse. Everything in life is impermanent.

If I keep going inside the burning in my chest, there is grief for the end of my time in Montana. My family created a Christmas tree tradition of driving to that particular section of the Helena National Forest on the other side of the Missouri River. We made the outing on Thanksgiving weekend, hiking up the mountain, most years in snow, once or twice on dry ground, sometimes in very deep snow. Each of us would branch out separately in search of our version of the perfect tree. In the early years, I was jazzed that I was more rugged than those poor saps buying trees from lots in the cities or cutting them down on tree farms in places like California. Something has changed in me. If I move my attention into my new reaction against cutting down living trees, I find a desire not to interfere with the life of the tree wrapped up with the need to redefine myself in myriad ways. My desire not to harm the tree has emotional reality with respect to trees but, if I am honest with myself, the shift in my stance emerges in large part from shifts within me. This emotion exists simultaneously with and yet distinct from actual love and respect for the tree.

Moving into these thoughts and feelings is a form of psychological immersion in nature. I could call this projection of myself into the tree, and it is surely that in some respects, but it feels more like a blending with Christmas trees and feeling into what they have to share with me. Emily had her own unique blending with Christmas trees, involving her life in New York City and in her country home. Christmas trees gave her a story to tell. They gave me my own story. If I feel into all that Christmas trees have meant to me, keeping close to my emotions and sensations (touch of the branches, sticky pine on my hands, smell in the house, needles on the floor), then that one Christmas tree aspect of nature has richly blended with the story of my life. Then I could add elements of culture, such as the Christmas story, and nature would become laced within civilization.

Unlike Emily and some of my friends and acquaintances, I do not experience myself as having literal dialogue with trees or the spirit of trees. This is closer to what Jung ascribed to our ancestors when he wrote they could speak to things, "like stones, plants, and animals." I am inclined to believe that is possible. I have not experienced communicating with plants or rocks, though I did once encourage my children to "ask the rock" before they took souvenirs from a stream, to which my son Max responded, "Dad, it's a rock." On the other hand, I have experienced myself as having mental communication at times with my paint mare, in which she sends picture images and I communicate back with images and language. This was not something I sought. In fact, it surprised me.

The first time this happened I was about to move the horses from a corralled area near our house to a pasture across the dirt road. It was late summer and most of the grass in the pasture was eaten down. The horses would get hay I would carry to them twice a day across the road, so they would not be grazing the pasture, but the pasture was large and I thought they might like a last few weeks with more open space for running around. When I approached the mare with a halter, she resisted with her body, not running away but not her usual moving toward the halter. Suddenly a visual image appeared in my mind of the dusty scrub now covering the pasture. There was an underlying negative emotional tone of "do not want that." Conveyed to me through the image was the statement from her: "it is depressing over there." Apparently for a horse, or for this particular horse, it does not feel good to be on a pasture that once had grass that felt relatively abundant and now had scrub that feels desolate. I said aloud, "Okay, you don't need to go over there; I see it's depressing."

There have been other times. Once recently, while she is staying at the home of a friend of mine, I went to visit her and my other horse. When I walked up to the mare, it was kind of like, "hey, what's new" between us. I received an image, which felt like it was coming from her, of an older girl riding her, along with an assurance from her, "I did not expect that but I did not act up." Later, my human friend told me some relatives had been visiting and her niece had ridden the mare. My friend said the mare did just fine. Knowing the mare, and knowing she had rarely been ridden by anyone other than me, I think even my friend was surprised the mare did not give her niece any trouble. Interestingly enough, I had received the same report from one human and one horse friend.

On another occasion, more recently, when the mare had probably realized something had shifted long term in where I was living, I visited and saw images of times we had ridden in fields near the Missouri River. In the images, we were riding at full gallop, both of us exhilarated. Again, it was a felt sense along with visual pictures. Sure, that might have come just from my mind. But it struck me as coming from her. I communicated back that I missed those times but that things had changed. "You're safe here," I told her aloud. I nodded to my friend's big dun gelding, standing right next to her, hardly allowing me a minute with her without butting in. I told her,

"And this guy is in love with you." She agreed and I sensed that she wanted me to know she enjoyed being with him. She flashed an image to me of Little Joe, the old gelding who had been her great-uncle-paramour for several years until he passed away. I understood that she remembered him and that this was different but once again she had someone. She never quite had that same kind of relationship with other horses that lived with us.

You might notice that I believe these were communications with my horse, but I hold that belief very lightly. I am not offended that most people I know would think this was coming solely from me, a projection of my thoughts and emotions into a conversation with a horse. On the other hand, there are many people these days experiencing these types of communications, with plants as well as animals. In *Plant Intelligence and the Imaginal Realm: Into the Dreaming of Earth,* Stephen Harrod Buhner rejects the belief that only humans can engage in intelligent communication.[405] "What is actually true," he writes, "is that once self-organization occurs the capacity for analysis, innovation, and response all occur contemporaneously."[406] To meet the intelligence of plants, Buhner encourages "loss of the human orientation."[407] Though not using the word *transpersonal,* Buhner speaks transpersonally: "Foundationally, the thinning of boundary between self and other is crucial. The complete elimination of it is, at times, a necessity. It is only then that it is possible to experience the other inhabitants [of the Earth] from inside their own lives."[408]

I have a friend who is sorting through myriad difficulties with medication issues for her aging father, including expense, side-effects, and conflicting properties between various chemicals. She was recently telling me how frustrated she felt because she believes "there are plants out there which would just tell us 'use me to help' if we knew how to hear them." Buhner writes about the potentially healing "oscillating" properties of plants. Buhner believes "all open, non-linear, self-organized systems" move electromagnetically around a point of equilibrium. "On one side is chaos, on the other self-organization."[409] Like many indigenous peoples, Buhner calls these electromagnetic dynamics "songs, possessing melody, movement, communicative interiority. They *speak* of the life of the self-organized system, of how it feels, of the interior struggles it undergoes and the impact of the exterior world upon it, and its responses to those struggles, those touches."[410]

It is easy to wonder if those of us experiencing communication with plants and animals are projecting our desire for intimacy with nature into another life form, imagining a conversation taking place only in our own heads. From the perspective of scientific materialism, this would be imagination no different from a child imagining a conversation with her stuffed teddy bear. I would like to encourage a middle ground. I do not dismiss the possibility of literal communication between humans and animals or plants—or the less dramatic sense of feeling something meaningful but not entirely specific from the non-human realm of life, such as good will from a particular tree in your courtyard or from the raven hanging around your yard. But I would always examine what I was "receiving" from a transpersonal contact with any representative of nature for projections from my own psychology. This need not derogate the "reality" of intelligence or even individuality within nature, but encourages not only learning from nature but increasing our own psychospiritual evolution.

In *Walking Shadows: Archetype and Psyche in Crisis and Growth,* psychiatrist Tim Read articulates the concept of a *cispersonal* realm of the psyche, a meeting point or mixture of transpersonal and personal psychological realities.[411] The prefix *cis*, meaning "on the near side of," suggests a realm of the psyche just beyond the personal. Read draws on the analogy of the lands outside ancient Rome to explain the cispersonal realm. In the days of the Roman Empire, there was Cisalpine Gaul, a mountainous part of northern Italy closer to Rome, and Transalpine Gaul, a more foreign, more dangerous land on the other side of the mountains. "Using the ancient Roman world as a metaphor for the psyche," Read explains, "we can cast modern man as a Roman. Rome represents the personal psyche, our ego, our perception of our environment as mediated by our organs of perception, our cognitive apparatus and the prevailing ideas and paradigms."[412] Transpersonal terrain, analogous to the distant, foreign lands from Rome, contains images, experiences, communications or archetypal energies with reality separate from the individual perceiving human consciousness. Our consciousness can participate in the transpersonal but there is a closer realm, the cispersonal, which, Read writes, may open "to material from the deeper layers of the unconscious but this material is rooted predominantly in the personal or the psycho-social layer of the psyche. It is not obviously a transpersonal experience although there may be elements of the transpersonal."[413]

The concept of the cispersonal is useful to me in considering the *scree* heard by Emily Squires from Christmas trees on New York pavement and the images I thought I was receiving from my mare. I do not discount the reality of either, but I also examine what is involved in my own psychology, as Emily did implicitly by talking about her relationship to both nature and New York. The cispersonal concept facilitates discussion of the possibility that much of what we tell ourselves is transpersonal lies very close to manifestations of our personalities. On the other hand, in terms of healing us by creating intimacy with nature, whether the experience is "real" is irrelevant, as long as we do not get ourselves all inflated with the idea we are magical or avoid self-reflection and self-examination.

Like Read, I have deep respect for cispersonal experience as important for psychospiritual insight and growth. The cispersonal may be seeded with energies or images from a transpersonal realm, yet those energies or images manifest through personal content. Similar to images that appear in important dreams, cispersonal experiences may be laden with symbolic complexity. Exploring these symbols and their association to our biographical lives and future trajectories may form the means for integrating transpersonal experiences in ways that facilitate growth and increased health, well-being, creativity, and enthusiasm for life. Manifestations within the cispersonal might be described as aspects of Grofian COEXs or Jungian complexes, with roots in archetypal or transpersonal realms, yet wrapped around personal wounds or transformational trajectories.

I understand the cispersonal as different from the elements of a COEX articulated by Grof because the cispersonal provides a way of considering whether what appears as a transpersonal reality is infused with personal content. For instance, if I have a breathwork experiences in which I feel I have been in contact with the Gorgon Medusa, and the contact feels transpersonal, I need not discard the transpersonal reality, but can also ask myself what parts of my personal psyche are tied up with this image. This is a fruitful middle ground between a position of "it's only a projection" and a position of "it is real separate from me." The fruitfulness comes in the ability of the cispersonal elements to take us even more deeply into ourselves, where we are increasingly likely to meet that which is more pristinely transpersonal.

I believe it is important not to dismiss or negate the reality of the transpersonal energy appearing, as this energy is useful in bringing intensity to the elements of the experience and, I think, is undeniably "real" in that sense. Treating as cispersonal our experiences from nonordinary states of consciousness, or from extrasensory contacts in ordinary consciousness, strikes me as consistent with how many of us routinely work with what comes to us, particularly if the images or experiences are taken into the body and emotions. If I *feel* what my mare has given me, then it does not matter whether she has *really* sent me an image as our connection is deepened. If I *feel into* Medusa and allow her to take my body, emotions, senses, and life where she takes me, then whether she is "real" in a transpersonal sense or resides in a cispersonal realm is not relevant. What would be relevant would be identification with Medusa as a transpersonal consort who authorized actions or states of being *without* self-examination through sensations and emotions. That would lead into an avoidance, I think, that would not serve the interests of growth.

It is in this way that we may begin to feel we are psychologically immersed in nature but from a perspective of contemporary people who have developed a sense of self separate from our surroundings and other people. Very important to this process is allowing connections to develop and grow through sensations and emotions, through the body, and not simply as mental concepts creating realities. In the most recent mental communication with my mare, it was all about feelings. As I stood near her, my personal memories of our past years galloping in the mountains were surely reaching for the surface. Maybe she felt this and sent me what she sent me. Maybe I just imagined it all. Holding the memory as a dialogue between us helped me access the grief around changes in my circumstances in a way that felt as though I was being held by one of the best friends of my life, this gorgeous black and white paint mare.

Perhaps in an actual energetic sense, she *did* help hold that emerging grief—helped move it toward an acceptance, a lasting memory of those years of riding that would always live in my body, always shared between us, timeless and always present even though completed and necessarily released. Perhaps we just said to each other, "those were good times, back in the day." Even if it was all in my head, she was there for me, a living ambassador from not just the natural world but from those thousands of years of our history closer to nature, all those years of our ancestors riding, reminding me it was all just as it was meant to be, my life passing just like all the billions of lives passing before me.

Not long ago, a friend told me about a conversation he had with a seagull on San Francisco Fisherman's Wharf. My friend had just experienced a psychologically intense weekend in San Francisco. His sense of himself had shifted and opened into terrains considered almost demonic by much of the mainstream culture. He wandered to the Aquatic Park on the Bay and sat on a low stone wall dividing the beach from the sidewalk. We had sat together on that precise spot a few months before. The Golden Gate Bridge was over to the left, opening to the Pacific Ocean. Alcatraz was out in the bay to the right. Slow almost miniscule waves lapped the beach. A steady stream of tourists, bikers, skaters, runners, moved along the sidewalk just behind the low stone wall.

My friend called me on his cell phone and said he had just been telling a sea gull about what had happened. He said he was not yet ready to tell any humans. We talked for a few minutes about nothing much. With the sea gull still near him, he began sharing a bit of his story with me. It felt as if my friend believed the sea gull had listened to him and was waiting around for him to integrate his experience a little bit more. He took comfort in his impression the sea gull did not judge the way we humans judge. The conversation between him and me was slow, nothing rushed. Eventually my friend said, "Wait a minute, the sea gull is leaving, I need to say goodbye." Because I had felt the intensity of his mood and the way the sea gull had helped him, that departure almost made me cry.

My friend was not asserting to me that the sea gull had in fact listened to him or needing me to believe the sea gull had any intentionality in the encounter. The mood struck me as too sacred for any pretense or power trips. What I heard was simple gratitude for a helpful conversation with a sea gull. When he said goodbye to the gull, it sounded like the kind of "good luck" you say when you have a nice conversation with a stranger and then take your leave, knowing you will probably never see each other again, but grateful for the encounter. What if that was the attitude we had to all of nature we meet in passing?

Dreamwork in Nature

This chapter began with Jung's observation that humankind "is no longer involved in nature and has lost his emotional participation in natural events, which hitherto had a symbolic meaning for him." Jung believed our "immediate communication with nature is gone forever, and the emotional energy it generated has sunk into the unconscious."[414] I do not believe our psychological immersion in nature is necessarily lost forever, although our communication with nature from postmodern times must likely be different from what we assume was experienced by our ancestors.

One of the ways we can understand the possibility of symbolic communication with nature is through considering our interactions with nature as we consider our dreams. Many people consider dreams nonsense, accidentally triggered images our brains pieces together into narratives as neurons fire randomly during sleep to clear residue from the day or the past. Those of us working with dreams know better—if we pay attention to our dreams, we find layers and layers of meaning, a meeting between our conscious attitudes and our unconscious yearnings, a settling back into the deepest parts of ourselves from which we connect to all that is. On the subject of people insisting to me that dreams are meaningless, on occasion I have had one of those people tell me one of their recent dreams as evidence of the nonsense happening at night, and I knew them well enough to think to myself, "whoa, you just summarized a whole bunch of your issues and you have no idea."

When working with dreams, I come back again and again to the images in the dream and stay close to the felt sense, including emotions, emerging from the dream images. I learned this in working with Hillevi Ruumet at ITP and from other teachings such as those by Jungian analyst Robert

Bosnak in *Tracks in the Wilderness of Dreaming.*[415] Staying close to the body and emotions helps avoid our tendency to "colonize" the meanings and even emotions of the dream into narratives desired by or habitual to our conscious minds. This is not the same as saying that dreams are meaningless and we piece together any sensibility. Rather, I am making the point made by dream worker Jeremy Taylor that dreams never come to tell us what we already know, but sometimes we resist learning something about ourselves we do not already know, so our conscious habituated minds might "take over" the symbolic growth-encouraging message and transform it into a message with which the conscious mind is comfortable.

Staying with a felt sense and emotions in the dream tends to keep this from happening. In staying with the felt-sense emerging from dream images, I ease away from habitual mental processing of information, just as I eased away from habitual mental chatter to stay with the embodied sense of the rain as described in the opening of this book. I do not immediately jump in what I want from the dream, but rather I feel into the deeper and deeper layers of unconscious material made accessible by the dream. Many dreamwork teachers suggest you are on to something if your body registers an "aha" experience. Depending on the circumstances, finding grief may be another signal that a layer of important psychic substance has been reached.

I have the same approach to experiences of connection with nature that seem to give us information or impact us deeply. Staying close to the body and emotions allows the experience to work through our psychologies and all the resonances invoked. Moving into symbolic associations with aspects of nature then begins to feel like a psychological immersion in nature at the level of dreams, where everything is connected to everything else and we are all one.

Around the same time I had the rain experience, I sometimes sat for meditation near a mostly unnoticed creek running through Willow Glen, our neighborhood in San Jose. You walked down an embankment constructed of small concrete bags hardened into a lumpy wall creating something like erratically placed steps. Los Gatos Creek was down there hidden amidst bushes and tall thin-trunked trees. I would sit in a sunny spot in the dirt next to a boulder. One afternoon, when I opened my eyes after a meditation session, I noticed a small green lizard lying in the sun on the boulder, less than two feet from me, not moving. I kept still like the lizard. Eventually I moved and the lizard moved. When I returned on other days and sat, the lizard was often present when I opened my eyes. This was an increasingly emotional experience, as I found myself hoping the lizard would be there when I opened my eyes. When he was there, I would feel graced, filled with gratitude.

Eventually, I began to sense what felt like the experience of the lizard. It felt binary, a life of forward or backward, go or stop. Stillness was absolute stillness, interesting because through meditation I was trying to move toward an experience of stillness. I do not claim to know this was the experience of the lizard and I resist people who suggest that I allow myself to make that claim. But I imagine through my body and emotions what arises with a felt-sense of connection to the lizard. My embodied associations primarily involved an orientation toward stillness. Feeling into the lizard felt like a dream. That the lizard appeared in person and not in a dream felt a bit miraculous, perhaps usefully framed as a synchronicity, but my experience has been that if you stay with these representatives of nature in this way, the boundary between dreams and waking life begins to ease, as does the boundary between me and nature, between inner and outer, between body and mind, and everything starts to feel sacred.

If the lizard appeared in one of my dreams, I would feel into my body and find this same stillness. Then I would reach more deeply into and beyond the stillness, in this case into memory. I move into my associations with lizards from my youth in New Orleans. This would begin with mild pleasant memories of similar small green lizards in the rock garden outside the front door at the house where I grew up. With a lizard being a reptile, and having placed my memory-attention near the front door of that house, a separate fear-based memory arises. Maybe I am three or four years old. Milk in those days would be delivered by the "milk man" in glass bottles left on a ledge just outside the front door. Immediately to the right of the front door was a large plate glass window, from floor to ceiling, the same size as the door. On the mornings when the milk would come, my mother would ask me to look and see if the milk was there. I would push aside the curtain and see hard and beautiful glass bottles full of white milk. This would viscerally associate with the taste of cold milk from the refrigerator, which in those days we still called an ice box.

On one particular morning, I pushed aside the curtain to see if the milk was there and instead of sweating glass bottles of cold milk in the New Orleans heat and humidity, there was a large coiled dark snake. There was the window between me and the snake but the reptile was within inches of me. Terror shot through me. The snake was still, very still, but brought forth an entirely different reaction in the pre-school me than the green lizards in the front rock garden or the lizard next to me on a rock in my mid-thirties. What is that? Instinct? My horse jumps sideways in panic when seeing dried branches on trails looking like snakes. Hard wiring in some of us mammals? I could go down the road of all our Judeo-Christian baggage around snakes and evil, but that feels like it takes me away from the felt-sense. Back with snakes in Louisiana, I am then remembering in my body how it felt that time I was swimming in a bayou on a camping trip and a snake swam right past me. Part of me is still terrified. If "snake" comes to me now, he offers a way to feel into fear, perhaps into mammalian instinct.

If I am feeling fear and sensing myself located in that part of the house, the sense of terror forms a bridge into the first nightmare I remember, the first dream I remember, where a man who now vaguely reminds me of the strange high falsetto singer Tiny Tim from the 1960s was trying to break through the perforated metal door that stood between my bedroom and the stairs leading to the darkness downstairs. Now deep into my own heart of darkness, the image of an immobile snake on the other side of glass seems almost a relief. Perhaps in defense, I allow in images from Judeo-Christian mythology and my awareness of reptiles as our distant pre-mammalian ancestors, then from the dream of stillness from the lizard into memories emerges a richly textured (partly with fear) journey back through the ages into the evolutionary depths, before the Garden of Eden in a mythological sense, before mammals in an evolutionary sense, a place that I often, and increasingly, seem to visit. Perhaps I could get back to these evolutionary depths through free association from a toothbrush, but I will spare us all from that particular journey.

Is this merely projection from my free-associating mind into a reptilian lineage? Or do these feelings have something to do with the actual reptiles? In a time and geography-shifting sense, is that coiled snake from early 1960s Louisiana communicating with me? Do the snake and the lizard know each other? Do we all know each other? If it were a dream, what is the meaning of finding a snake where nurturing mammalian milk was expected? Even if I am projecting onto a snake, the projection works because there is something about snakes that calls forth the projection. The lizard would be a helper in this regard, but a helper appropriate for us sophisticated psychological types in postmodern times. The help would involve an invitation for me to take the feeling-based image or association inside myself and allow the arising of whatever arises. Moving from felt-sense and emotions into symbolic understanding is important. Perhaps considering cultural and mythological associations with reptiles might help. In other words, I work with the images, feeling them inside me, learning what I need to learn.

Sometimes when I have told people about my interest in an internal experience of nature, I hear back, "Oh, you're talking about shamanism." If I told this story about the lizard in some circles, a few people might suggest to me "lizard" was my power animal. I might even hear that "lizard" was a transitional helper to bring me to "snake," who holds the actual gift for me. These friendly observations would be based on their experience in contemporary personal growth workshops of "shamanic journeying" or perhaps from a trip or two to South America or the American southwest to work with an indigenous "shaman." Following the 1951 book by historian of religion Mircea Eliade, *Shamanism: Archaic Techniques of Ecstasy,* and the 1981 book by anthropologist Michael Harner, *The Way of the Shaman,* "shamanism" has become popular among many people as a means to journey into a nonordinary state of consciousness, usually through induction with drumming or a substance, often to find a power animal to provide assistance with personal growth or healing of others.[416]

Deriving from the Asian language Tungusic, the words *shaman* and *shamanism* originally referred to a role and practices within Siberia and Central Asia. In contemporary times, the words usually reference ways of communicating with the energies of nature through nonordinary states of consciousness. My experience with shamanism—or what I prefer to call neo-shamanism—suggests to me that many people drawn to "shamanic" practices offered in workshops or adapted for personal psychospiritual work are manifesting a strong desire to bring an experience of nature into their body-mind-souls. I understand this, at least in part, as a quest for psychological immersion in nature.

While not a particularly important frame for my personal path, neo-shamanism has brought thousands of people a deeply meaningful internal experience of the power of nature. Similar to what I wrote about the possibility of communicating with actual animals, I believe it is possible to communicate with an essence of animals or particular spirits through shamanic practices. Harner provides an example of such a communication in describing his initiation into shamanism. Conducting anthropological research, Harner lived alongside the Jivaro Indians on the eastern slopes of the Andes in Ecuador in 1956 and 1957, then with the Conibo in the Peruvian Amazon in 1960 and 1961. After realizing he was not gaining much information from the Conibo about their religion, Harner accepted their invitation to drink a hallucinogenic liquid made from *ayahuasca,* the "soul vine."[417] In this way he made the transition from learning about shamanism to experiencing shamanic realms.

Harner describes a deeply impactful experience, beginning with immersion in a huge fun house with a supernatural circus of demons, presided over by a "gigantic, grinning crocodile head, from whose cavernous jaws gushed a torrential flow of water." Then he moved into a sea-faring vessel "with a huge dragon-headed prow," where he became conscious of "the most beautiful singing I have ever heard in my life, emanating from myriad voices on board the galley."[418] I associate the singing described by Harner with the vibration of particular life forms, perhaps in their collective spirit manifestations, similar to Stephen Harrod

Buhner's description of the "songs" emerging from the vibration of plants, "possessing melody, movement, communicative interiority," speaking of "the life of the self-organized system, of how it feels."[419]

In the shamanic world, spirits are real and possess powers, sometimes accessible to the shaman. The shamans described by Eliade were experts in finding helping spirits, often nature spirits. They were able to see them, talk with them, and ask for their aid. Some helping spirits might come under a shaman's control, becoming his "familiars." Although nature spirits were not always in the form of animals, the appearance of animal helpers was typical, sometimes understood as the spirit of a particular animal, sometimes felt as the spirit of a species. Eliade listed common healing spirits for Siberian shamans as including "bears, wolves, stags, hares, all kinds of birds (especially the goose, eagle, owl, crow, etc.)…great worms," and also "phantoms, wood spirits, earth spirits, hearth spirits, and so on."[420] Whether due to Eliade's book or the mythic presence of the North American mountain west (as in Montana) in the psyche of many people, neo-shamanism often seems to involve, in my experience, woodland animals, particularly those still considered wild and powerful.

When someone suggests to me I am talking about shamanism, I usually say something like, "you're probably right…it's all the same in the end, isn't it?" I have had a number of positive experiences with this form of journeying, sometimes very similar to my experiences in Holotropic Breathwork. And yet, there is a part of me that feels like I am pretending to be indigenous in neo-shamanic practice when I am postmodern. This makes me uncomfortable. I can remember, yes, but it is easy for me to feel I am getting lost in contemporary reverberation of images—essentially entering a realm of performance—if I imagine myself as shamanic. Several years ago, my son told me one of his anthropology classes at Lewis and Clark College hosted a "shaman" for an experiential taste of shamanic techniques. I asked him if the visitor was an indigenous tribesperson of some kind. His response: "No, just some middle-class white lady."

Meaning no disrespect to this particular middle-class white lady, I have learned to be circumspect about the designation "shaman." The term *shamanic practitioner* works slightly better for me. A woman I greatly respect who, over several decades, has studied indigenous practices in many countries, as well as nonordinary states of consciousness, encouraged my circumspection about Westerners holding themselves out as shamans. I think her exact words were, "I would not trust any Westerner identifying himself as a shaman."

So that I do not get lost in civilized issues of performance, power, and control, I prefer to "get there" through rigorously insisting on consideration of my own psychology before I move into the assumption I am in contact with an animal spirit. In my experience, if I move through my own psychology, the question of the reality of the animal spirit seems to disappear. I also avoid the possibility I am imagining a Disney version of an animal helper.

Jung is well known for distinguishing between symbols and signs. He described signs as denoting particular objects to which they are attached, such as trademarks standing for commercial products. Symbols, in contrast, imply something more than their most obvious and immediate referent, something ultimately broader than can be contained within particulars, something ineffable. In *Man and his Symbols,* he described symbols as having "a wider, 'unconscious' aspect that is never precisely defined or fully explained."[421] In his view, one should not expect to fully explain symbols: they are to be explored, given life. "As the mind explores the symbol, it is led to ideas that lie beyond the grasp of reason."[422] For instance, he writes, a wheel "may lead our thoughts toward the concept of a 'divine' sun, but at this point reason must admit its incompetence; man is unable to define a 'divine' being."[423]

Jung confesses it is not easy to understand this point, but he found an understanding of symbolism essential for understanding the human mind. Interestingly enough, *Man and His Symbols* was one of the few books in my family home in New Orleans that would also exist on my own bookshelf for several decades. I have no idea how it found its way into our house, but the Tibetan mandala on the hardback cover caused me to open the book many times in my pre-teen years. I would need adulthood, some reading in psychology, and, most importantly, experience with what emerges from the unconscious body-mind before I would begin to understand Jung's meaning about symbols. I am thinking of the distinction between signs and symbols now as a way to convey the difference between how I feel many of us are conditioned to experience nature in postmodern times and what I am calling dreamwork in nature. I am talking about how the creatures, plants, and lands of nature may greet us from the natural world as conduits into a symbolic inter-connected world in which we too have a home.

A bear on a commercial for Coca-Cola may be fun and interesting, but he remains a sign directing us toward Coca-Cola, pulling on associations we have for bears, but mostly locked in a realm of commodity. A bear on a trail in Glacier, or standing on two legs rearing up toward a truck on a warm Montana afternoon, or dead with comrades in a tree house, seems closer to bringing us into a symbolic realm inviting psychological immersion in not only the actualities of nature, but also the depths of nature inside us. If we meet a bear or a wolf in a shamanic journey, she may well be a particular bear or wolf who has come to find us, or she may be a representative of the energy of "bear" or "wolf" at a species level. Or we may be so conditioned into postmodernism that we cannot help using the image as a sign based on an prior expectation or an existing narrative of our conscious minds. There is nothing wrong with this side of experiencing. Perhaps this is just what we need at any given time. But I imagine something more from living dreams in nature. Something that may be surprisingly effortless once we get in the habit. But just remember what Jeremy Taylor says about dreams: they never come to tell you what you already know.

Releasing into Nature

In Montana, nature helped me turn off the television set. The closer presence of nature allowed my moods to spread out into my natural surroundings. Take the seasons, their rhythms. As I first wrote these pages, it was September, and the days were shortening. After being with the light all summer, the darkness begins to return. The darkness comes every year, stark in the northern Montana latitudes. I start to sleep more, remember more dreams. I move more slowly, conserving myself, in some way preparing. Some sadness arises, and it eases out into the change of the seasons. Some introspection emerges, with feelings like depression. If I allow myself to blend out into nature, then the lack of light *is* my mood. This is not seasonal affective disorder to be cured, but an invitation to live inside myself and experience that internalization as reflected in what is happening outside. The difference between my mood and the change of seasons is subtle if existing at all. If I can learn to experience my turning within as a season of nature, similar to animals slowing down or hibernating in the winter, then I understand I am not alone, but part of the cycles of nature. If all my emotions start to find places of residence in the natural world, then my internal structures align with the earthly eternity of natural life. I just exist within it.

It is not only so with the dark or difficult emotions. When I have joy, if it is shared with the birds in the sky, then my joy expands into the air around me. I can understand implicitly that joy is well shared with the open sky. If I am shy, then the reticence of the deer, and her stillness as she ventures near me to nibble at grass, is a normal characteristic, not a defect making me less capable in business. If I am loud and abrasive, then I can laugh at myself as I laugh at the two geese that honked and hissed and raised ruckus when someone went near our barn. It all blends out into nature. It all seems normal. I am immersed in nature, psychologically.

Years ago, Susan Gray was the mother of three young children, herself young. She was, in her words, *tired, and a little resentful that I never had time to do my own thing. One day I went with my husband, his friend, and the children on a fishing expedition on the Blackfoot Reservation in northern Montana. The two men were teaching the children how to bait the hook and cast the rod. Left with nothing to do, I walked up a gentle prairie swelling to a small lake. I sat looking at the spring flowers and marveling how they could survive a "Browning" winter. (Browning is the main town on the Blackfoot Reservation.) I walked a short way over the crest of the hill so I could be alone and out of sight of the fishing party.*

It was a beautiful day. The sun was shining, not a cloud in sight. The wind was just a breeze and kept the mosquitoes at bay. There wasn't a sign of civilization. No roads to be seen, no barbed wire, jet streams, or engine noise from the highway. Just me and the prairie. I sat down to stare at the great expanse of wild, never touched by the plow, virtually the same as when the Blackfoot warriors hunted buffalo and Meriwether Lewis trudged north to check out the origin of the Marias River.

I sat there a long while enjoying the silence, the smells of spring, and the aloneness. Guilt, another frequent companion to a young woman with children, finally forced me up and started me back to the pond to check on the kids. As I reached the crest of the little hill on the return trip, I was startled by a shadow passing over me. I looked up and saw seven white pelicans gliding over my head, down the hill to the prairie pond. I was in awe. I hadn't seen them coming and didn't hear them. It was as though I had received a sign that all was right in my world, that I was giving enough, that my alone time would come. I looked to the scene below. The kids were having fun. My husband and his friend were having fun. My guilt was gone. The flight of those pelicans remains burned in my memory. It awakens in me an intense interest in nature and an awareness of life that surrounds us all the time.

Another time, Susan and her husband were driving south along Flathead Lake in northwestern Montana. *It was the time of evening when the sky is light and all other things are black. Our kids were asleep in the back of the station wagon. We had been listening to classical music on the radio and enjoying the evening. I was not thinking about anything in particular when I looked out the window and saw a V of ducks, perfect silhouettes against a silver sky. I instantly felt that when I die I will fly with the ducks and, somehow, know all I need to know. That memory has been a great comfort to me during tough times. It has greatly reduced my fear of death.*

Susan makes a great deal of sense to me. The natural world is there to blend with all aspects of our psychological being. Sometimes this feels like taking nature inside me; sometimes it feels like easing myself out into nature. Sometimes there is no difference. No matter where I am, I can find nature intentionally when I need this. If I am lacking peace, then I may notice the silent snowfall and bring it into my soul. Even in cities, I can find birds or squirrels, trees and bushes, even grass pushing up through the sidewalk or weeds on the side of the highway. Sometimes nature appears on her own, a seeming synchronicity. Last year, in a time of confusion, with our children grown and my marriage ending, I was walking in the mountains, under a bright blue summer sky, and noticed two hawks flying toward me from different directions. They met twenty yards above me and flew in a circle directly above my head. Their circling formed an invisible circumference; they brought wholeness into me—it was a miracle, a gift.

This works with all manifestations of the natural world, including geographical forms, weather, seasons, and all that lies beyond the Earth—the moon, sun, planets and stars, out into the universe. I have been flirting with the moon for several years now. Living in Montana, she is much more present to me than she was in California or New Orleans, mostly because of the darkness that comes with this territory. Prior to living here, I paid very little attention to the moon, though I recall my older children's fascination with the moon if we drove any distance at night. Both of them reported, separately, years apart, that "the moon is following me." Not understanding what they meant, I tried to look at the moon as they were seeing her. Then I realized, with it coming to me all at once, that if you were moving and looking at the moon in a certain way, she seemed to move with you. She followed you. It was very personal, intimate.

I am embarrassed to admit that until I moved to Montana, I did not fully understand the relationship of the moon, earth, and sun. A few years ago, my friend Mike McCarter finally explained it to me in a way that I understood. While some of you may have always understood this, here is an explanation for the rest of you, as I have met few people who really get this in our times. Ease out of a passive reading mode and use that complicated brain we developed to create a mental representation. Getting this image of the earth, sun, and moon can be tough because you need to hold two perspectives at the same time: one is the perspective of someone standing on earth and looking out at the moon and the sun; the second is the perspective of someone looking from outer space at our solar system and observing what is really happening with the sun, earth and moon. If anyone notices an analogy to the psychospiritual endeavor of holding our own perspective while also observing it, then you have me.

To get how we see the phases of the moon, the key is to bring into your spatial reality the fact that we see a full moon rising at dusk because that is the time the moon is behind the earth in relation to the sun. The moon appears full because she is behind the earth and we are able to see the full face of the moon lit by the sun on the other side of us. When the moon, in her monthly cycle, is behind the earth, she "rises" as the part of the earth on which we are standing reaches the edge of the sun's rays hitting our planet, that is, nightfall. From our perspective standing on earth, the sun goes down behind us (so to speak) while the full moon rises in front of us. From the perspective of outer space, the moon has moved into a place in her monthly cycling around the earth where she is furthest from the sun as she is on the other side of the earth from the sun. Half of the moon is always lit by the light of the sun. It is just that when the moon is on the other side of the earth from the sun, the full face of the moon always lit by the sun faces us on earth.

Don't get confused with eclipses, those rare occasions when the earth actually blocks the light of the sun from striking the moon because the earth comes directly between the sun and the moon. Every full moon, the moon is on the other side of the earth in relation to the sun, but it is rare that the earth actually comes directly between the sun and the moon so as to block the sun's light from the moon. Not so rare, but rather every month, the moon reaches that far point where her placement behind us in relation to the sun means we see her full bright face. If she were not at that far point, the light from the sun would still be hitting a full half of the moon, but from our perspective on earth, we would see only a segment of the moon lit by the sun. This is hard to explain in words: you need to create a mental image, use that talent we developed as Homo-sapiens. Sad to think Neanderthals might not have gotten this even if they lived in post-Galilean times. On the other hand, I did not get it until I was in my forties.

Where the moon is at any time in relation to the sun explains what phase of the moon we see (how much is lit up) *and* what time of day or night the moon rises on the horizon. These things are linked, essentially the same process. From the perspective of outer space, we see a new moon when the moon is between the earth and the sun, the exact other point in her monthly cycle from a full moon. From outer space we would see that the half of the moon lit by the sun is facing away from earth. From our place on earth, when the moon is "new," we see no light on the part of her facing us, though we can generally see her outline in the sky. The sun is behind her, so lights up the side we cannot see. The new moon rises at dawn because our part of the earth is turning into the sun's rays at the same moment we can first see the moon, that is, when she rises from our perspective.

Do not be confused by a solar eclipse. This happens only rarely, but a new moon happens every month. Every new moon involves the moon being between the Earth and the sun, but Solar Eclipses occur only when the moon is directly between the Earth and the sun so as to block the sun's rays from falling on a portion of the Earth. Once I understood this, I was surprised at the number of times I read references in novels to a "new moon" rising at dusk. Many people without thinking assume the moon always "comes up" at dusk no matter her phase. We may first notice her at dusk because it is becoming dark enough to see her easily, but she does not always "come up" at dusk. She is much more complicated.

I devoted these paragraphs to this explanation because, in my experience, if you get this into your body, then you may find yourself more securely planted on the planet somewhere deep inside yourself. The solar system, even the universe, may start to feel more real. Do not go too far with the reality of the universe as it can be terrifying to fully accept you are on a planet hurtling through black space, maybe even worse than fully accepting you are in a metal shell thirty-five thousand feet in the air when you travel by flight. By comparison, the sun and the moon are easy companions.

The sun and the moon are personal. If you know them, you may feel their energies deeply within each of us, masculine and feminine, shining and receiving, giver of life and teacher of change. The moon may even become one of your familiars, though she is fickle, she loves billions of us. Not just the billions of us humans now on the planet, but all of our earthly cousins, not just those now living, but all who have lived over billions of years. Sun and moon rising, doing their dance, month to month, though time is meaningless on these scales. One of my favorite moments in the last many years was walking on the beach in Santa Cruz, California, with a friend I was just getting to know, when, to my surprise, I turned from looking at the sun setting on the ocean and saw an enormous full moon rising over the mountains. I think I actually gasped.

It is a pity city lights obscure the way in which the full moon transforms the night world into a landscape of diffuse black and white, an invitation to consider the gray areas of life, and to notice change. Among the things I loved about our first house in Montana, where much of this book was written over a period of years, was the way the full moon traversed across our huge bedroom window in winter, when I most needed her. Sometimes I woke up from a dream and she was there, not following me, but watching me. Sometimes she was so bright we had to shut the curtains in order to sleep. She is particularly bright with snow on the ground. For me, the moon is a holder of secrets, a compassionate and yet passionless creature. You can tell her your troubles, and she will hear them, and hold them, but she will not cry for you. If you give your troubles to her when she is full, and let her hold them, then as her fullness wanes, your troubles may wane as well, or they may come back into your body for you to resolve. In either case, you may see that an emotional relationship with the moon is offered to you. Despite what some contemporary shrinks may have to say, this is not madness, though the moon may bring you close to madness, that is one of her ways. This is the way you live if you allow your psychology to disperse into the elements, to communicate with the elements.

Having a deep sense of psychological participation in nature might be diagnosed by mainstream psychiatrists as a regression of ego function. The trick is consciousness, which is why understanding projection can be helpful. Jung advocated incorporation of unconscious material into the conscious personality, but recognized the possibility of unconscious identification with objects, including aspects of nature, without the separate sense of self characteristic of conscious, rational beings. Drawing on the writings of sociologist Lucien Lévy-Bruhl, who studied the so-called primitive mind, Jung used the term *participation mystique* to describe "a peculiar kind of psychological connection with objects, [which] consists in the fact that the subject cannot clearly distinguish himself from the object but is bound to it by a direct relationship which amounts to partial identity."[424]

Like many others, Jung believed primitive peoples experienced a more collective sense of self, lacking the individuality we believe has arisen in mature, contemporary consciousness. He wrote: "The further we go back into history, the more we see personality disappearing beneath the wrappings of collectivity. And if we go right back to primitive psychology, we find absolutely no trace of the concept of an individual."[425] Without debating the accuracy of this observation, we can note, even from contemporary experience, the lack of differentiation between personal needs, desires, and behaviors that sometimes exists in close community. Many people use the term *co-dependence*—originating in Alcoholics Anonymous communities—to indicate unconscious blending with the behaviors and needs of others. Without needing to label people who lived before us, we can recognize the value in experiencing ourselves as separate people with our own wants and needs, but people who are able to connect with each other, and with nature, at deep levels of experience.

Participation mystique is often used to describe an experience of merger with nature. Lévy-Bruhl described the "primitive mentality" as experiencing connection with aspects of nature (including nature-connected spirits or demons) without differentiation between individual experience and the external attributes of the natural world. The related concept of "magical thinking" describes the belief and experience of causal interplay between a person and something in the environment, as in, for instance, an ability to cause rain to fall or an animal to appear. Attention to experiences of synchronicity may be considered "magical thinking" from a mainstream clinical perspective, particularly if the individual finding meaning in the coincidence believes she or he has "magically" caused the occurrence or has been specially graced by the universe with the synchronicity due to a particular worthiness. In my experience, synchronicities can feel magical and yet over time, with ruthless self-examination, that feeling eases into a deep gratitude rather than a sense of grandiosity or alignment with power.

Those identified with a materialist paradigm may consider psychological immersion in nature a form of *participation mystique*. From my perspective, this assessment might involve some level of defense against intimate experience of nature. Imagining into this, is there fear of loss of the self? Perhaps even some fear of that dissolution of the structures of self that may lead to dissolution of the structures of civilization? The type of psychological "dispersion" into nature that I am describing, and that has been described to me by many people, has no loss of ego consciousness. To the contrary, those describing this form of return to nature generally strike me as less unconsciously blended with consensus reality and the needs, desires, and addictions of others than most of the rest of us. Allowing oneself to merge out into nature holds the potential of increasing consciousness. We are offered a resumption of sensing ourselves as part of the earth, a restoration of health. Divides between body and mind, and between humans and nature, seem to dissolve. A sense of wholeness seems to emerge.

Through all of my experiences, I know who I am and remain aware of an experience happening to me, knowing that I am a subject perceiving something. I may allow subject and object to blend, but I retain my status as subject, at least for this lifetime. When I felt the rain on the roof as described in the opening of this book, I knew water was falling on shingles of the roof because it was raining and I knew that I was experiencing something in my nervous system. Indeed, some part of me was observing my nervous system having the experience and opening to an intimate sense of connection to the rain. Similarly, when I write about waking up and finding the moon "watching me," I do not believe that the moon is a personified goddess who is purposefully connecting with me, but I allow myself to project my desire for holding and care on that beautiful distant white body in the dark, cold Montana night.

At no point am I deluded into thinking the Moon is under my control, or controls me, nor do I believe I have been made special by a body of rock in the sky. And yet emotionally, psychologically, I allow myself to experience what my body, heart, mind, and soul long to experience— intimate connection with this beautiful reflective Moon, seen by virtually every creature with eyes that has lived on our planet for billions of years.

Richard Tarnas, a professor of philosophy and cultural history at the California Institute of Integral Studies in San Francisco, authored *The Passion of the Western Mind*, an illumination of the movements in Western thought and history from a depth psychological perspective. Although not describing psychological immersion in nature in the terms I have used, Tarnas envisions the re-immersion of Western consciousness in nature as part of a great cultural shift and healing taking place in our times. He writes:

> As Jung prophesied, an epochal shift is taking place in the contemporary psyche, a reconciliation between the two great polarities, a union of opposites: a hieros gamos (sacred marriage) between the long-dominant but now alienated masculine and the long-suppressed but now ascending feminine. And this dramatic development is not just a compensation, not just a return of the repressed, as I believe this has all along been the underlying goal of Western intellectual and spiritual evolution. For the deepest passion of the Western mind has been to reunite with the ground of its being.
>
> The driving impulse of the West's masculine consciousness has been its dialectical quest not only to realize itself, to forge its own autonomy, but also, finally, to recover its connection with the whole, to come to terms with the great feminine principle in life: to differentiate itself from but then rediscover and reunite with the feminine, with the mystery of life, of nature, of soul. And that reunion can now occur on a new and profoundly different level from that of the primordial unconscious unity, for the long evolution of human consciousness has prepared it to be capable at last of embracing the ground and matrix of its own being freely and consciously. The telos, the inner direction and goal, of the Western mind has been to reconnect with the cosmos in a mature participation mystique, to surrender itself freely and consciously in the embrace of a larger unity that preserves human autonomy while also transcending human alienation.[426]

CHAPTER 11

Sensing God in Nature

As I was nearing completion of this book, I moved out of our house in the south Helena hills and started a sojourn on the west coast of North America. After a Holotropic Breathwork workshop in Joshua Tree, just north of Palm Springs, I drove south to San Diego and then, eventually, all the way up to the coast to Vancouver, British Columbia. I stopped to visit friends, did some teaching work, and saw two of my children. Even with finding myself back in California, I did not feel I had come full circle from my years in Montana as my ties to Montana would continue—and I would settle, at least for a time, on the east coast.

While in Berkeley, I reconnected with a friend from ITP who works as a therapist and is training as a Jungian analyst. Originally from New Brunswick, Canada, Guy Albert has lived on the west coast of the United States for most of his adult life. He invited me for a walk in Tilden Park, high in the East Bay hills. There were views of San Francisco, Marin County, the bay, three bridges, all sparkling in the early March sun. California had been in severe drought during the winter but hard rains had fallen in the last week. Parts of the trails were muddy wet, sloppy, practically sucking in your shoes. The mud was black. The reservoir behind the park was full, a deep blue. Brown hills had turned to green.

Knowing what I have been writing about, my friend told me about his first encounter with enormous redwood trees in the Montgomery Woods State Reserve, a park up the California coast. Following a trail, he walked over a mild rise and down into an ancient grove. He was drawn to one particular huge redwood. As he stopped before the massive trunk, his knees gave way. He fell to the ground weeping. All these years later, I asked him if he could describe the experience. "I felt so small in comparison to this tree," he said. "It must have been hundreds of years old. I thought about all it had seen, all the time that had passed."

I asked Guy if he could put words to the emotions that led to his weeping. *Awe* was one that worked for him. *Gratitude*. Even better was *reverence.*

Guy was describing an experience that has been described to me by a number of other people. This involves being moved to tears through experiencing the sacred in nature. Perhaps we could put this the other way: being moved to tears in nature and having the experience feel sacred. For some people, this is not far from the experience of beauty or joy that often brings tears, but perhaps these experiences push just a little bit further. Often they seem to come out of nowhere, like what Guy described in the Redwood trees. Sometimes, nature becomes suddenly, spontaneously sacred. Often we weep. It is hard to put into words.

Some people say they feel God's presence. When the word *God* is used in such contexts, it is typically not a matter of belief or dogma, but simply the best way for some people to describe a deep level of connection and reverence—a sense of the divine in and through nature. For other people, nature does invoke a spiritual presence they associate with an experience of God they have encountered through religion. Others do not use the word God but refer to the presence of the divine or spirit. Some people describe their experience simply by narrating what they saw, heard, smelled and felt. Their recollection is invariably sensory and emotional. Often they describe an experience feeling outside of time or as though everything from one's entire life has come together into one sacred moment.

These experiences need to be heard in the voice of the people having them, so we will soon turn to several experiences. Each story is unique but we begin to notice certain commonalities. Among them is the presence of a deep sense of gratitude, not just for nature, but for all of one's life. As Guy said, there is a reverence. From this reverence sometimes emerges an acceptance of the inconsistencies and paradoxes in life, the coming in and the going out. There may be an acceptance of death and an embracing of life. People tend not to forget these experiences.

All I Could Do Was To Cry

Several years ago, a young man named Ryan wrote to me as follows:

On a small holiday with my wife and a close friend of ours, sitting on a cliff in southern central Missouri, I began to cry (and by returning to that moment in my mind, will likely do so again before I am finished). These were not really tears of sorrow, nor of joy. As I sat there alone, what was one moment just some trees, pastures, and a small river came together and revealed themselves for what they truly were. I was taken aback. The first instant was realization, the second was a complete assessment of everything I had ever done in all my life, which only took the time of one inhalation of breath.

After that moment, being in that place, mindful of the presence of friends, accompanied by the two people I love most on Earth, the only thing I could feel was gratitude. This was a gratitude so sublime, so powerful, so unlike any other emotion I have encountered, that my body could not contain my mind, heart, and spirit as they swelled and transcended the bounds placed by physical experience. No words can truly describe this experience, nor could anything spoken be enough to express this gratitude.

As I sat crying, our friend joined me. I did not know her then as well as I know her now. I have always been very guarded with my tears. Only a scant few trusted friends have seen them. I was so comfortable in the presence of this friend that I didn't stop crying, which was unprecedented for me. As I cried even more than before, she held me. My wife soon joined us and we sat looking at the river, trees and pastures. As a man in North American society, I was indoctrinated from youth that a crying man is a vulnerable man, a weak man. I now realize this is patently false.

My tears were recognition of the miracle all around me. This gift, this happenstance, whatever you believe nature to be, is the most pure form of innocence to which one may bear witness. This beauty exists and welcomes me without regard to what I have done wrong in life, whether the wrong was to myself, to others, or to the planet. Consistently, nature provides comfort, and sustenance. All the necessities of life are here with us—and although nature should be tended and nurtured, the earth requires little and asks for nothing.

Nature has provided all that makes our lives possible, offers the blessed encounters we have every day of our lives, and does so without judgment and without requirement. Nature is responsible for all of our experiences. I've had some bad and I've had some good. I've had experiences that cause me to fill with such utter joy that the difficult times become easy to manage. For those moments of joy, I am grateful beyond words.

So I have no words of thanks, I have tears. All my thanks, my tears— full to the brimming with the love, fear, anger, sadness, joy, and pain, and with gratitude for all of my life, and for the lives of those who made my life possible, from beginning to end—fall to the ground. Those seemingly insignificant drops of water sink into the soil, disappearing from sight, rejoining nature, that which made it all possible.

I believe that nature feels my gratitude, though perhaps not in the way we feel emotion. I sense that life feels itself and nature knows my gratitude because I am part of the whole. Someday, my body will nourish the earth as the earth nourishes me now. Until that day, my tears and my actions, small as they may be, will give back what precious little that seems possible. I like to think that tears of this kind are the articulation by spirit of what the mind and body cannot express alone. Perhaps the mind and body are tools of something more sublime, which I will call Spirit for lack of a better term. My spirit is connected to the spirit of all things, if we are even separate at all. Spirit has a common language beyond words; this force is ever-present, though in this day and age, few know how to listen. If you listen with your spirit, you will understand.

Ana Ines Avruj is an Argentinean psychotherapist active in the transpersonal movement in South America, and worldwide, for many years. She and her husband Julio cofounded the Transpersonal Association of Argentina and an organization called Consciousness without Barriers, focusing on research and development in consciousness studies. Active for many years in the Spiritual Emergence Network, Ana helped develop criteria for distinguishing between spiritual crisis and psychological conditions requiring more traditional assistance. In addition to offering workshops in many transpersonal activities, such as mandala-making and a program called *Labyrinths for Peace*, Ana supervises the clinical training of transpersonal psychotherapists. Several years ago, she wrote *Chronicles of a Journey of Death and Rebirth, or Story of an Initiation.* Ana shares with us the following excerpt:[427]

Day before the full moon of Gemini. Reclining on a flat rock, with the caresses of the sun on my skin, I am filled with the beauty of the place. I give thanks to Mother Nature for her gifts. I sense her messages of love in the form of a funny squirrel and two delicate blue birds who silently keep me company. The waters of a mighty cascade fall in a rushing torrent, forming a river that aims directly toward me. Energetic wind splashes ice-cold drops on my body. The power of this place comes from the profusion of energies around me: imposing mountains, gushing water, ancient trees, pure air. My heart is full of pleasure and admiration. In this fire, alchemy is produced.

I breathe deeply, exchanging my energies with those of the waterfall. I inhale its vigor, beauty, and force. I exhale my gratitude and love. Everything around me begins to disappear—or does it all converge and integrate? My connection with the waterfall intensifies. As I breathe in the power of the rushing water, I am now breathing out my own openness and surrender. Each breath carries more excitement, more exhalation. I feel the waterfall entering my body and I mix with her. The moment is magic. There is no time, no friction, almost no separation. I am making love with the waterfall. She is in my flesh, in my breath. The two become one. All is one. There is union, an in-love-ness.

Another time, I am near Curitiba, known as the "ecological capitol of Brazil." In one of the most serene places I have ever known, surrounded by mountains and dense vegetation, lies an absolutely still lake. Like a perfect mirror, the water of the lake reflects everything that comes there to rest. As reflection pairs with substance, the world becomes a waking dream, every object with its perfect double: swans, rocks, trees.

Sitting near the water, my soul finds reflection in the lake. Gratitude rises from the greatest depth. I feel hand-in-hand with life—that life has given to me and I have given to life; that my thirst for mysteries has been quenched and I have brushed harmonies without equal. I have known deep pain and all the subtleties of the emotions, from the most hurtful to the most exquisite. I have had the courage to live several lives in one, and the accompanying fatigue, from an internal motor that rarely let me rest. I have had the privilege to meet wise men and women, loving teachers. As I have opened to all that exists in this world, life has hurt me through its intensity. I have felt within me the children without a home, the grandparents who are hungry, the men and women moving through life suffocated by resentment and wracked by violence born in suffering. At the same time, life dazzles me with its beauty and unlimited wisdom.

I can no longer remember all the images passing through the mirror of the lake of my soul. I only remember the uncontainable cry that flowed from within me, a mix of pain, gratitude, and purification. I knew this would be a beautiful place in which to die, to leave the body where the body belonged. These were not tears of shame nor of pain, though I have shed many such tears in my life. These were tears of a different quality, a grateful farewell for all that I had received, a recounting. These tears bring integration: the celestial and earthy, masculine and feminine, body and spirit; to leave nothing outside, to realize that all can co-exist in the present. Differences are erased. There is no longer "this is yours, this is mine," or "this is from here, this belongs over there." All can be joined together, included, and that causes an explosion of energy. With every barrier dissolved, explosions of energy circulate once more through the unified system.

I wonder about the relationship between grief and gratitude. I wonder if weeping connects them. I wonder if grief and gratitude describe emotional experiences on a continuum. If grief involves longing, is gratitude an experience of longing satisfied? When we are grateful, has something for which we have longed, perhaps unconsciously, been provided to us? Might deep gratitude always involve an element of the unexpected? Most of us say "thank you" quite often by rote. Deep gratitude may involve a sense of humility, the far side of entitlement, nothing routine about it. Perhaps there is something even beyond gratitude in these experiences: recognition and acceptance, the sense of a blessing, witnessing a miracle in life.

Miracles are unexpected. The element of surprise can be felt as a shock in the body. This is well expressed by Jenny Lee, who wrote to me from her home in North London, where she embraces painting, music, poetry, and movement. She wrote: *Walking due west on a cold winter's day in London, along the street where I live, the sight of a winter-flowering cherry blossom hit me in the chest. The sudden awareness of the pale pearl-like blooms against the black bark of the trunk came as a physical blow to my body. The sheer perfect beauty of the tree revealed itself to me as a physical experience, simply present, with no thought or effort on my part. In the physicality of the experience was a sense of gratitude. For a single moment, the tree and I shared in its creation. As we become aware that we are not separate, we find a delicate offering of beauty, free, available at any moment. I find this challenges our sense of values, opens us to other dimensions.*

You can feel it in your heart, almost like heartbreak, a blow to the chest as Jenny Lee described. Something unexpected. We may walk around with an unconscious sense of not receiving, not realizing what is all around us. Then suddenly, bam, a winter-flowering cherry blossom hits you in the chest. As we discussed in the chapter on Joyful and Sacred Weeping, this seems to involve an opening of the heart. Gratitude is the word that best fits. Brother David Steindl-Rast, a Catholic Benedictine monk, describes gratefulness as flowing naturally from the heart when the body, mind, spirit is clear. He considers the heart "our whole being, not one or another part of it; rather the center, the source, the taproot of our being."[428] For Brother Steindl-Rast, the heart "stands for the fact that I can gather myself together and give myself away in that give-and-take which we call life."[429] He continues: "As long as the heart is alive, it constantly sends forth and takes in."[430]

That sending forth and taking in lies within many stories of weeping in recognition of the sacred in nature. It feels as though our very heartbeats become aligned with the pulse of energy in nature. An energetic give and take, life gives to me, and takes from me, I have known great suffering, and I have known great joy. It comes and goes, I live and I die. I am grateful, surprised and grateful. In describing "Surprise and Gratefulness," Brother Steindl-Rast calls forth an example from nature:

A rainbow always comes as a surprise. Not that it cannot be predicted. Surprise sometimes means unpredictable, but it often means more. Surprising in the full sense means somehow gratuitous. . . . Our eyes are opened to that surprise character of the world around us the moment we wake up from taking things for granted. Rainbows have a way of waking us up. A complete stranger might pull your sleeve and point to the sky: "Did you notice the rainbow?" Bored and boring adults become excited children.[431]

Valerie Becker wrote to me about rainbows. Born and raised in eastern Pennsylvania, she made most of her life in Ohio, where she has been drawn to almost everything—colors, the outdoors, the arts, friends and acquaintances, her job for the local police department, her gardens, collecting antiques. Valerie wrote: *I have always had an emotional feeling when outside in nature. Rainbows are the most overwhelming part of nature for me. Right up there with rainbows is the sun; and that first day of spring, when the color of the air is different and there is a particular smell. An overall feeling hits me right in the sternum. I breathe in real deep; then I get the chills, shut my eyes, and feel transported back in time, perhaps to when I was a child, or perhaps to some other time when spring had great meaning. These feelings are very tender, very loving. It is some type of connection.*

When I am in the sun, I feel connected; that's the only way I can describe it. I feel connected to God. Sometimes I practically cry because I want so badly for God to know my soul. I want the sun to wrap itself around me. I have been around people in the workplace for a very long time, but I rarely connect with them. I adored my parents, but did not connect with them. Now rainbows, that's another thing. Sometimes I feel in my gut that there is going to be a rainbow. I get in my car and drive around looking for the rainbow, my heart beating a thousand times a minute. If I find one, it takes my breath away and I almost cry out—from the amazement, from the beauty going right through me, right to my heart. I get that strange feeling as though I am taken by surprise, a funny empty feeling, right there at the sternum. Sometimes on my way home from work I see a tiny rainbow near the sun. There is a cloud, and some moisture, and a faint rainbow. The beauty takes my breath away and I keep saying to myself, "Thank you, thank you!"

The smell of the earth, dirt, gives me a similar sensation, but not exactly like the sun or rainbows. I love being in the dirt, getting muddy, planting things and replanting, planting and replanting, just getting my hands in the dirt. It simply makes my heart feel so good; it is so comfortable.

Oh, and then there was tonight when I got home, around seven in the evening, and it was cold, winter. I looked up and it was snowing, but the sky was clear and the moon was out, hazy, but it was out, and this bright, bright star, was close to the moon.

There have been a few occasions when I felt as though I were being cradled, taken to a spiritual place, that God could hear my thoughts. I never get answers or have those "out-of-body" experiences that people talk about. I just get a wonderful feeling, like walking through the woods blind, but safe.

Adam Butler lives in Austin, Texas, where he is "father to three boys, a brother to four siblings, a husband to one wife and a slave to the bicycles." Adam describes his "deep interest in public health issues and how entrepreneurs, cause organizations and for-profit companies can innovate offerings that create wellness and profits simultaneously." With his brother, he cofounded a "creative communications company that is hell bent on making the world a more sustainable place."[432] He is active in the Fearless Revolution, an organization advocating a "new consumer revolution . . . founded on the principles that we have the power and the tools to reshape the world again."[433] Adam shared the following recollection of his visit to Northern California many years ago:

I arrived at Muir Woods around eight-thirty on a Sunday morning. I had spent most of the previous three weeks in hotel rooms and editing commercials in dank buildings. I was long overdue for some time outside. Muir Woods are 295 acres of uncut, old growth redwoods, just north of San Francisco. Some of the trees are more than a thousand years old. I had never beheld such majestic trees. As I entered the canopy of this ancient forest, I felt like a child headed for the base of a Christmas tree on the morning of December 25.

I hiked briskly to warm myself from the cool morning temperatures. The cathedral-like quality of the forest only made the place feel colder. Yet inside the coldness was warmth I cannot explain. As I climbed uphill, my heart began to beat hard. I could hear it. I could feel the artery in my neck throbbing against my skin, just inside the collar of my raincoat. My lungs filled with air, and then I breathed out. I began to perspire. With my heart pounding in my chest, I was very aware of my temporal body. All at once I was struck by how fast I was walking, though I had no schedule to keep. At that moment a poem arrived. I pulled pen and paper from my shoulder bag and wrote:

As I walk, I breathe the old air of these woods,
A glutton in such a giving place;
I walk faster to speed my breath;
Tomorrow I will not breathe here.

Inside this poem is my knowledge of the temporal nature of my very human existence. I may never make it back to these woods; and, moreover, the next beat of my heart could quite possibly be the last. The natural world reminds me to be thankful for my life. The lack of human-made noise allows me to examine my thoughts from a critical distance. Sometimes the sheer magnitude of nature humbles me. On more than one occasion, the enormity of the Rocky Mountains has brought on feelings of panic. Yet always around the corner is a sense of empowerment. I am bolstered by the knowledge that I was made to walk in such places. The natural world gives me context in which to view matters of the heart and soul. I extrapolate a plan for living: be prepared, know the terrain, stop and smell the roses, rest when tired, be alert.

I am a seeker. I believe in Jesus Christ, not as an end, but as a beginning. I love talking to other people about what they believe and why they believe what they believe. I try to notice how it makes them feel. When I'm alone in nature, I am carrying on a conversation with the Creator himself. I am amongst his works. I can learn more from touching, feeling, and smelling than from merely seeing. Nature is full of experience. I believe nature is a gift of experience.

Michael Leas is a professional artist. He grew up in Nebraska and was living in San Diego when he wrote to me: *I was climbing Mt. Rainer with my two brothers and my dad. We were witnessing the sun rise up at 13,000 feet. My senses could not take in all the splendor of this experience, but I felt it inwardly, beyond what I knew was real. Tears came to my eyes to feel such connection with life. We were roped together with ice axes in our hands, and crampons on our boots. I felt the true power of the mountain. We had started climbing around midnight to reach the top by sunrise. While strapped to the mountain, and seeing the sun kiss the edge of the world, I sensed the roll of the earth beneath me.*

Another time, I was in the Sequoia Forest with my wife. The massive trees filled me with awe. I felt love within the forest and filled with emotion. I knew this was the essence of life; these were the roots of the human. My experiences in nature have breathed life into me; and it grows and grows. I can even appreciate a blade of grass, and get the same feelings all over again.

After growing up in Denmark, Louis Nielsen lived and worked in many places around the world. He writes about an experience on a wilderness trail in the Umfolozi Nature Reserve in Natal, South Africa: *Most of the wild animals of the region inhabit the Umfolozi, including lion, hyena, hippo, crocodile, and rhinoceros. On the trail excursion, you walk four to six hours every day then set up camp for the night. You sleep under the stars, near the fire. Team members take turns keeping watch during the night.*

One morning I walked away from the camp alone (against the rules) and before long found myself standing within thirty feet of a large male waterbuck. He had not noticed me. I stood completely still and watched him. Soon he must have caught my scent. He looked up and saw me. I expected him to run away, but he stood there looking at me. I felt a deep wish that he should not run away. I tried to communicate my friendly feelings toward him. Perhaps he sensed that I was no danger.

Within a few moments, he returned to grazing, which filled me with happiness. I felt accepted in spite of the danger humans normally pose to wild animals. I felt a part of the nature around me, part of the earth beneath me, part of the sky above. I felt connected to the universe, as though I merged with the world around me. Strong emotions welled up inside me. Time seemed to stand still. I felt a gratitude for my existence. I felt complete and deep inner peace. The meaning of this experience is difficult to express in words. Perhaps in that moment I was embraced by the universe—by universal consciousness, by God.

Beth lives in St. Joseph, Missouri. She writes: *In approximately 1992, a terrific ice storm left thousands of trees broken, power lines down, and other examples of the destructive power of nature. Yet amidst all the hazards, there was great beauty. In our town, there is a very graceful system of boulevards, where for miles and miles the focus is trees. The morning after the storm, I ventured down one of the boulevards. I found a stunning city of ice. Trees bent over the street from both sides. As the sun shone brightly on the trees, they burst into an all-encompassing crystalline radiance. I felt such depth and communion with nature, crying and thanking God were all that I could do. I talked to God in gratitude. These moments were transient in some sense, but live forever in my soul.*

When she first wrote to me, Jaene Leonard was an actor and writer living in New York City. She has since moved across country to Oakland, California. Jaene always felt connected to nature. *Growing up in the suburbs, there were many summer evenings coming home in the car with my family. I always liked the window down. I loved the wind rushing into the back seat and rustling through my hair. I would watch the moon frolic along with us all the way home. Gazing at the stars, I would feel a profound sense of wonder.*

When I was about seven or eight, a magical experience led me into even deeper connection with nature. I was leaving for school out the back door, and just as I stepped outside the gate and into the road, I turned back to wave at my mother, who always watched and blew kisses from the kitchen window. It was a late summer morning, and the sun was rising, although her direct light had not yet reached our block. The shade from the swaying trees in our neighborhood—tall pines, oaks, and in our yard a lovely mid-dle-aged sugar maple—cast a lazy chill that spilled into the yard and into the street. All of my senses were enticed—the air smelled deliciously of morning dew and fresh cut grass. The blue sky pierced through the green canopy in a commanding, comforting way. Through our screen door, carried on a sweet breeze, wafted a barely audible melody from the console stereo my mother always had playing. And the birds—robins, sparrows, bluebirds, cardinals, blackbirds—all sang hymns in the delicate branches of the trees.

A propeller plane moved through the sky with a soft hum. I looked up, closed my eyes, and breathed the day into my soul. I was aware for the very first time that I was alive. I was filled with bittersweet joy and a sort of remembrance of the connectedness of everything. The moment was new and yet ancient. I felt a birth of gentleness inside me. I believe that moment shifted my entire perception of life.

Since that morning, I have relived that moment over and over again, tying to label it. Recalling it is easy; describing it is difficult. The words fall short in conveying the magnitude I experienced in that one tiny moment. I could go on writing for pages and never get to the sacredness of it. I do know that my heart broke wide open that day, for that was the day I was introduced to God.

The Paradox of the Broken Heart

What do we find when our heart breaks open? We may find poignancy, thankfulness, gentleness, beauty, maybe mixed with a deep sadness, with literal physical sensitivity in our chest. We may feel fragile, raw; ready to love but remembering hurt. Sometimes there is grief; or something like grief: awareness of the nature of earthly life, so beautiful and perfect, so full of suffering, so finite. I think there is paradox in a broken heart, awareness of suffering mixed with gratitude for the beauty of life. We come here to love and yet nothing is permanent. We can close off our hearts or we can open them, and then feel it all.

When Lisa Graiff wrote to me about her experience in nature, she was living in Dallas, working as an architect, a designer of "big ole skyscrapers." She loved to paint, dance, read, and write. She reflected on her experiences of weeping in nature: *Quite often when I'm sitting quietly and observing nature I find myself crying. I wouldn't call it grieving, but more like an overwhelming mixture of conflicting emotions that rise to the surface all at once bringing me to tears. I would say the main conflicting emotions are great joy and great sadness. Each of these emotions seems to incorporate many others. The joy is an awareness of wonder, love, amazement, security, peace and contentment. The sadness is an awareness of hate, insecurity, turbulence, and discontent. I believe longing is also a part. For me, this has to do with the awareness that everything is happening as it should, and yet, from where I sit, so much seems so wrong. I long to know why and yet I feel that doing so would somehow lesson my part in the whole process.*

From Lisa's journal: *December 29. I am sitting at White Rock Lake. It is a wonderfully bright day, the kind of bright that seems to happen when the air is crisp and cool and the sky is that crystalline lightest blue color with only the occasional billowy cloud passing by and the winter sun shines and everything is just a little bit brighter and more clear. There is a slight breeze, my hands are cold, and I am crying. I think because on days like today, sitting in nature, I can almost feel God's presence and the feeling overwhelms me. A mixture of conflicting emotions rises to the surface all at once—wonderment and joy tinged with great sadness—and the tears start flowing.*

For a moment I feel as if I am aware of all that's right and all that's wrong in the world. I came here to think about next year, to make resolutions. I feel this is going to be a year of breakthroughs for me after the turbulence of last year. I have been sitting here on the root of a tree watching a squirrel building a nest out of twigs in the crook of the branch of a neighboring tree. She scampers down to the end of one of the branches, chews off a twig and then struggles with it back to the nest, looking to find a place for it. Sometimes her twigs are just too big. She'll struggle to get one back to the nest only to drop it at the last minute, but no matter—off for another. She's taking a break right now. She took a good look at me then inspected my car and is now off running around. It occurred to me that I should learn a lesson from this little squirrel and just drop those things that don't fit in my life and go on to find others that do.

Now I'm sitting out on the pier. I scared off all the birds. It's a little warmer out here in the sun. The water is softly glittering and the steeple of a church stands proudly among the rooftops in the distance. I'm reading the graffiti on the planks and notice that someone has written a prayer to God. It makes me think of the Buddhist tradition of writing prayers on flags and then putting them up in a high place where the wind can take the prayer to God. The flag stays there until it disappears. I'm wondering if I had to write down one prayer to God, what that would be.

Why: why am I crying? Because I feel your closeness and my distance at the same time; because everything is right and yet everything is wrong; because I feel all and nothing together; because love escapes me and yet is me; because of the wind and the rain and the moon and the stars; because the earth cries through me; because I seek an answer to a question that doesn't have one; because I am both the cause and the solution; because of all that is and all that was, isn't and wasn't; because time means nothing in the end and everything right now; because of the past, the present, and the future; because of family and friends and strangers and enemies.

Deeply resonating with Lisa's words, I asked if she could say more. She responded: *Nature in its constancy, its cyclical nature, its relationship to the whole (interrelatedness) reminds me of both the amazing potential and the great failings of mankind. Nature does seem more perfect as it is, with its natural cycle, nearly devoid of the negative human traits of greed and selfishness and hate and so many others. On the other hand, nature is almost devoid of some of the positive human traits like kindness and charity and even love. I think, for me, the feeling of God's presence in nature leads to tears because in sensing God's absolute love and perfection, I am more acutely aware of my failures and imperfections. It is that opposites thing again—in being aware of one, I am, at the same time, more aware of its opposite.*

Just as I was finishing this chapter, a friend, Amber Balk, wrote to me about a recent experience that sounded similar to what Lisa was describing. Amber put it this way: *a direct experience of the sacredness of the Universe...brought another paradoxical insight—the two (painful separation/existential loneliness and blissful union/merging with the Whole) are the same energies in opposition yet bound to one another.* Perhaps this is that breathing in and breathing out. Inhalation is only possible because you exhaled; you can only exhale because you have filled your lungs with breath. Awareness of suffering is only possible if you open your heart and love. If you open your heart and love, you will know suffering. Knowing God is only possible if you have been separated. Out of separation comes longing for connection which brings you back to love. Breathing in and breathing out. Your heart pumping blood around your body, pulsing squeeze and letting go: beating only for as long as your heart beats.

When our daughter Tess was seven, during the summer after her first grade year, she attended a day camp near Canyon Ferry Lake. She came home one day and quietly told us about watching a snake eat a shrew. Her group, along with their camp counselor, had come upon a bush where there was some slight rustling. They kneeled down to look. A bull snake had its mouth and jaws around a still living shrew, pulling it forward, into its body. Tess told us the campers watched quietly, not a sound, no one turning away. Tess has always been mostly matter-of-fact, no drama. But even for Tess, there was an undercurrent of extraordinary calm in what she was sharing: a stillness that let you feel the quiet struggling of the shrew, the slow automatic action of the snake, the inevitability of it all. There was a sense Tess was sharing something sacred. Life dying for life: a cycle, with the small mammal losing this time.

For reasons I still don't completely understand, when I heard this story, I thought, "this is God." This would not be the anthropomorphized God of many people, nor would this be the God we expect to hold only goodness, even while using his name and image to inflict cruelty on others. Rather, this would be a God encompassing all things just as they are, including death and the dank, murky processes that we usually pretend are not actually happening. This may be the God some people find in nature, when they find themselves crying for all that is, for all sides of all that is. Perhaps some of us recognize this God as reflecting our capacity to hold all that exists, just as nature is capable of holding all the contradictory, messy, broken pieces of ourselves. In the end, perhaps nature teaches acceptance—what the eastern religions might call release of attachment, a free falling. Things rise into complexity and then break into chaos; and then something rises anew.

Linda Carroll Hassler wrote about her fascination with how nature breaks things down. *To shovel manure and hay, to smell pines, these are the smells of Nature, far more seductive than perfume. When the sun, the wind, the rain are allowed to get to things, the nature of things changes. The microbes come in and change smelling things to sweet, bacteria are eaten by microbes needing that bacteria, things break down. Last year, I removed a just-killed medium sized dog from the edge of the highway, pulling it down a grassy slope out of the line of sight of cars. A few days later, I pulled my car over to where I thought the dog would be and looked at what was happening. Tiny animals were finding their way in, through the holes natural to the dog...mouth, nose, eye sockets. A week after that, I visited the dog again. This time, his skin was still over his ribs, but it was breaking up; the fur had fallen out of much of it; the carcass was bereft of insides now. This was impressive.*

In the midst of sacred experiences in nature, some of us find ourselves becoming comfortable with death. Something changes, something moves. I remember very clearly the first moment I truly understood and accepted that someday I would die. This happened sleeping on a beach in Mexico, twenty yards from the Caribbean Sea. Somewhere in the early nineties, my parents took care of our children while my wife and I spent a week in the Yucatan. One night we slept in a palapa, a thatched hut on the beach, screened with mesh. The darkness was dense. Clouds blocked the stars but there was an eerie dim yellow light from a single lamp outside the open-air restaurant where we had paid to sleep in the hut. Margee and I were in the same hammock, pushed together. Her breathing was close. We were sweaty. The surf was endless and loud. It was hot and humid, but air moved through the hut, gently, now and then. I kept falling asleep and waking up. Sand creatures scurried beneath us all night. My dreams seemed as dense as the humid air, with images just out of my reach creeping through me like the creatures creeping through the sand.

Eventually, everything changed into sharp clarity as I breached into full waking awareness. I knew, fully and completely, as if it were real, that someday I would die. Of course, I had known this intellectually for as long as I could remember. What arrived that night was a different form of knowing, involving my physical animal self and what felt like my soul. I accepted it—and it seemed to have something to do with those creatures scurrying all night in the sand, with the darkness, the dim yellow light, the salt in the air, the sounds of the surf, the damp pressing of my wife against me. It could be no other way. Unless I would die, none of this would exist. I hesitate to unpack that knowing, not wanting to lose the mystical in the rational, but the intellectual piece is that without death in the animal kingdom, diversity in evolution could not have occurred. I only reasoned that out later.

That night, I returned to sleep, but I woke up very early, just as the sun was cresting the water. I climbed out of the hammock and walked down the beach to sit alone. After all, now I *knew* I was going to die. My body was not completely sure what to do with this information. As it turned out, I did not want to cry—my body wanted to worship. Not because I thought worship would save me, but because that is what bodies who know they will die gravitate toward doing. Perhaps we do not actually worship in our culture because we deny death.

On that side of the Yucatan, the coast faces east. The sun was rising over the Caribbean Sea. There was a man awake before me, sitting in a lotus position in the hard sand not far from the light surf. I had never done any yoga myself at that point, but when he stood up, I recognized he was forming yoga postures in connection with the emerging sun. This was three or four years before ITP, just as spiritual experiences were starting to come my way. Yoga was not yet in my repertoire, but something in my body understood exactly what was happening and why I was seeing it.

Even at this early hour, in the Yucatan, the rays of the sun felt thick and hot. I kept my distance from him but could not stop myself from watching. As the sun grew higher, his positions changed but he always seemed in connection with the dawn and the surf. I think I fell somewhat in love with him. I wanted to know how to do what he was doing. I wanted to know how to worship the sun and the sea. My body would someday die, but this man's body was moving as the rays of the sun hit us, as the waves ran up on the beach. The man's motions, the quickly rising sun, the increasingly stickiness as I began to sweat, the sand on me and around me, the waves, the sand gnats, the sea stretching outward, all existed together as one moment of pure physicality. To say the least, it was sacred.

Taking the Steps We Can Take

Like many of us, Amber Balk is deeply connected to the natural world. She loves rivers, particularly the Upper Iowa River near her home in Decorah, Iowa, where she runs and knows the birds, bushes, and trees. She shared: *Today I went hiking and then dipped in the super cold springs— first time this year. As I have mentioned before, I consider that action to be a highly significant cleansing/clearing ritual. I feel it aligns me with the wild energies of the land, and that helps me remember myself and what I am doing here, in this life, at this time. And it feels deeply nourishing. I just can't get over the rich bounty of this land in the summer. Absolutely enchanting. Such a blessing that I still sometimes cry for no reason other than awe and pure gratitude.*

Through ITP, which is now Sofia University, Amber conducted a form of transpersonal action research into the desires among some people in her community for different ways to celebrate the death passages of their loved ones. [434] Drawing on the work of Stanislav Grof, she described her way of working with information as holotropic, meaning she considered insights coming from nonordinary as well as ordinary channels and looked for the "movement toward wholeness" in group discussions with her community members. Green burial—putting our loved ones back into the dirt without the trappings of the funeral industry—was one of the discussion topics that arose. More generally, the group talked about how to "do death differently" than what they were experiencing in our culture. This was grass roots, beginning with the yearnings of people for new-old ways to experience the sacred in death. Not surprisingly, the discussion included the intimations of many people of a sacred realm beyond the material world. Also not surprisingly, one of the action items some people hoped to pursue was creating a green cemetery, where the living can feel they have returned their dead directly into nature.

It was important to Amber to start from the ground up, to gather a community of people and talk about what was important to them on a particular topic. She wanted any action, as well as research findings, to arise out of community. In Chapter 4, I quoted David Strong, who wrote about the Crazy Mountains in Montana, as noting what I believe is the most realistic thing we can say about "returning to nature." Strong realized this reform cannot be "masterminded," but must flow from "communities of people who are able to speak and convey to each other what things matter in the way they matter." [435] From such communities, if there is to be change, "It will be the result of people working together and taking a few deliberate steps at a time, as possibilities open up." [436] This is because the "true frontier" is no longer external wilderness, but what exists inside ourselves.

I have made a case throughout this book for going inside ourselves, recovering nature intimately from the inside out. As we do this, if we communicate to others what we find, and work on particular projects with particular people hearing a similar calling, then the world will continue to evolve and nature might just return to us on the outside as well as the inside. Within psychology, more and more researchers are documenting the positive impact of intimate experience of nature. Joan Snyder sought to answer the question, "What is it like to feel really connected with nature?" She began with her own realization that she felt most "real" when connected with nature. She wrote:

> At first, I experienced connection to nature in the natural world, in the trees, plants, rocks, animals, clouds, sky, ocean and in the lakes, hills and mountains. Then came a feeling of being connected with nature in a fuller, deeper sense. My experience put me in touch with the energy of nature, with creation itself, a sense of tie to the universe, and, ultimately, to the Goddess/God that permeates spiritual life. Faced with such realness I have but one answer— yes, yes, I am tied to this awesome totality. I must take my place as a responsible counterpart of this creative force of nature. I begin to spin in rhythm and harmony with all, loved and loving. There is meaning here, purpose here, and work to do. I am committed to remain open, to stay connected, and to learn from nature.[437]

Snyder found four repeating themes in her discussions with other women who felt deep connection with nature: "The perception of nature as sacred and/or as a spiritual inspiration; a sense of oneness and unity with nature; need fulfillment through nature; and a desire to reciprocate for the gifts given by nature."[438] She summarized:

> They speak of awe or wonder; they speak of God; they feel as if they are in a church; they experience ego-transcendence; they experience energy from nature; they experience a sense of presence through words, touch, or sensation from nature; they experience the power of nature; they feel that they are healed by nature; they sense that nature blesses them; and they speak specifically of the spiritual or soul dimension of experience in nature.[439]

Those experiencing "oneness and unity with nature" described feeling "a part of nature and the universe; they feel that they are made of the same substance; they experience nature as a friend; they feel that they belong; and they feel that they are at a reunion or are at home."[440] This happens in the body, not just the head. Kira, one of the women with whom Snyder spoke, lived "in a neighborhood with older trees, in abundance, visible through the many windows in her apartment on the second floor." Connecting with the trees mirrored "the images and feelings that are alive in her body. She continues to feel warmth in her body. She exclaims, 'It keeps happening,' and she touches her solar plexus."[441] Another woman told Snyder when she is nature, "My senses are filled. . . I see, hear, smell, feel and taste what the earth and universe offers."[442] From another woman: "There are times when I experience a spinning energy within my center which feels connected to the unceasing energy of the universe."[443]

Research of Patricia Martyn and Eric Brymer into the relationship between nature relatedness and lower levels of anxiety was mentioned in

Chapter 8. Their study included a qualitative component based on reflections from research participants as to what nature means to them. Martyn and Brymer reported common themes of "relaxation, time out, enjoyment, connection, expanse, sensory engagement and a healthy perspective." [444] The theme of connection involved "being connected to something larger and revolved around feeling immersed, being part of something bigger, at one with, or connecting with what was important."[445] For those who mentioned sensory engagement, nature was considered a source of beauty and was "deeply and beneficially engaging of the senses."[446] Martyn and Bremer noted this often included "a spiritual aspect or a sense of flawlessness of nature," as well as "an expansive sense of space."[447]

Janet Ruffing, a Sister of Mercy and Professor in the Practice of Spirituality and Ministerial Leadership at Yale Divinity School, talked with people about contemporary Christian mystical experience in nature. She described three characteristics: "a sense of oneness or communion with nature, reasoning to the Creator from an element in nature, and a sense of the presence of God in nature."[448] From her discussions with Roman Catholics and Episcopalians drawn to nature in their spiritual practice, Ruffing found the "utter sacramentality of the natural world deepened their sense of themselves in the universe, in the human community, and in a larger faith community." [449] For most of the people with whom she spoke, the experience of God through nature involved "oneness with their earthly home; a oneness with the elements of which we are fashioned; [and] a perception that human reality is made from the same material elements and processes of the earth itself; all of which emerge from the Creator Spirit."[450]

Ruffing identified several "wholeness-making" characteristics of contemporary Christian nature mysticism. Regardless of whether they sensed the presence of God in nature, most people described "a process of reconnection with themselves physically, spiritually and emotionally."[451] Many people with whom she spoke gave examples of their sensory engagement, such as "hearing bird songs, smelling the air and the flowers, hearing the sound of the sea and the wind, tasting fruit, feeling the earth beneath their feet or the texture of bark and leaves." People wanted more and more to get out into nature. They "walked, they swam, they worked the earth, they collected some treasure from the day and brought it home."[452]

Several people described tears in their experience. One man recalled a pilgrimage to Israel, during which he was largely unmoved by the shrines, but found God in a sunrise. "About six o'clock in the morning, I was on the roof, alone, facing Yeshiva University, and the sun was coming up. And I went right down to my knees. It was such a powerful. . . . You talk about tears, I mean I was sobbing. It was sunrise. It was God."[453] Tears came to someone else when she was speaking to Ruffing about her experience in nature. She recalled: "It was rather chilly; the wind blows off the river up that street. And I stopped because the trees there had just the smallest, freshest, greenest buds and I stood there and. . . I just said, ah. . . And I began to pray. (tears while speaking.)"[454]

Similar experiences in nature are sometimes described as "peak experiences," using the phrase originated by psychologist Abraham Maslow, one of the founders of transpersonal psychology.[455] Kevin Krycka and Ryan DeMares spoke with several people about their "felt sense" of connection with dolphins and whales.[456] They described five feelings arising from peak experiences with cetaceans: harmony, aliveness, connectedness, intention and reciprocity of process. There was a "sense of aliveness in the process of experiencing awe, elation, deep joy, or unconditional love." This contributed to reconnection with one's inner being and a sense of wholeness. Tears came to some people during such experiences. Krycka and DeMares quoted the story of a mother who went whale-watching with her son in the context of disharmony in their relationship:

> as we first went out, we encountered . . . a mother [whale] and adolescent son named Slick and Mike [who began] breaching in tandem off the bow of the boat. . . . And [my son] and I were both in tears, and we felt very much that these whales were responding to our process . . .

> And it didn't take but a couple of seconds before I started to have a feeling that I've never had before at this level. It was love, exponentially enhanced to a point that I can't describe. . . . I just stood there and realized that tears were falling off my chin. . . . My blouse was wet. The feelings were so powerful and so filling.[457]

In *Religions, Values and Peak Experiences,* Maslow observed that "the very beginning, the intrinsic core, the essence, the universal nucleus of every known high religion . . . has been the private, lonely, personal illumination, revelation, or ecstasy of some acutely sensitive prophet or seer."[458] In our times, moments of experiencing the sacred in nature may point us toward (re)organizing ourselves into communities that may be able, in our current culture and context, to bind enough of us together into lasting structures for developing lasting new ways. This might even function in ways similar to "high religions" in the past yet within the ways of our time. As we move together into one global community, some common core of meaning seems necessary as we learn to solve conflicts without wars and to moderate economic growth with sustainable practices. Moments of experiencing the sacred through nature might provide cohesion for a movement that may unite us as children of the earth and responsible stewards of our collective future.

James Swan, ecology advocate, author, and educator, suggests that people "who experienced early positive encounters with nature, usually in the presence of loved adults, and later experienced 'transcendental' moments in nature as adults, are those most likely to engage in, and remain committed to, protecting the environment."[459] In the last few decades, several researchers have found support for this awareness. In research conducted through ITP, Samantha Dowdall observed statistically significant relationships among measures of the following five attributes: (1) ecologically supportive actions; (2) positive environmental attitudes; (3) exceptional and mystical/unitive experiences in nature; (4) spirituality; and (5) well-being. In other words, as Swan predicted, people who reported spiritual experiences in nature also tended to be ecologists and to experience personal well-being. [460]

When describing meaningful nature experiences, Dowdall used the phrase "exceptional human experiences" coined by Rhea White, whom we met in Chapter 2 through her recollection of growing up near nature. Dowdall noted common themes from people describing exceptional human experiences in nature: connectedness, unity, spirituality, noetic (inner knowing), quiet connection with nature, heightened senses and body sensations, ecstasy, transcendence, and connection with a divine presence. Dowdall found greater degrees of positive ecological action were especially strongly related to a greater density of exceptional human experiences in nature. Put more simply, the more sacred experiences we have in nature, the more committed we become to taking action to protect the natural world. People who undertake positive ecological action also enjoyed greater psychological well-being, reflected in reduced stress and increased positive attitudes toward life.

A growing number of researchers have investigated the relationship between ecological attitudes and intimate experience in nature. Elisabeth Kals, Daniel Schumacher, and Leo Montada found attitudes and behaviors favoring environmental protection tend to emerge from the combination of two responses to nature: *interest* in understanding natural phenomenon and *emotional affinity* leading to sensory contact with nature.[461] More generally, they found that positive experiences in the wilderness seem to change perceptions of the relationship of people and the environment encouraging of ecological attitudes.[462] In research conducted through ITP, Barbara Dawn Drake investigated whether using cameras to record images in nature increases human connection with nature.[463] While further research is necessary, the information received from participants is promising.

Even with rampant "nature deficit disorder" in our culture, many programs exist to get us out into nature, including programs for children. Like many of their peers, my children took benefit of many wilderness camps in Montana, across the American West, even in other parts of the world. At their best, such programs provide more than vacation activities, offering a glimpse into life in the natural world. The summer she was researching the desire of some in her community to "do death differently," Amber Balk wrote to me about her efforts to guide campers into an internal experience of nature.

I volunteered as a camp counselor for a nature-based summer camp for about fifty of our local kids, including my daughter. First time I've ever done that. The kids' ages ranged from six to twelve. It was so clear to see the increased sense of separation and cultural indoctrination with each older age group. The general sense of entitlement with the surrounding wildlife was astonishing—mindless grabbing and destroying of plants, swatting at insects, digging up moss, etc. By the end of the second day, I was overwhelmed with feelings of hopelessness. How are things going to change with such mindless disregard for the environment? A pair of red-tail hawks circled overhead, and a rush of emotion flowed through me. Luckily, the camp elders understood my concerns, held me with knowing hearts, and encouraged me to address things in whatever way felt best and right.

So, I created a nature awareness curriculum and introduced the kids to contemplative exercises combined with high-energy physically demanding tasks. The idea came from a dream incubation. As I drifted off chanting a request for guidance, I had a hypnagogic vision of a kiddy nature boot camp. I adapted the vision and added inward-focused exercises. I'm not sure some of the kids had ever been asked to tune into an inward focus before. It was fascinating to witness them trying it out.

In one of the exercises, we did a sort of shared inner/outer journey. We crossed a rickety wooden bridge high above the swollen Upper Iowa, trekked deep into the woods, and then basically did something kind of like a super-mini breathwork session (without the actual breathing technique though). I brought along my iPod and a speaker and played a very tribal song, getting them to dance and yell and let out animal cries. Then, a slower song played, and I had them all lie on the moss, close their eyes, and see what they could see with their eyes closed. Some joked about not seeing anything or seeing black. Many immediately accessed beautiful visions, such as those associated with Grof's first perinatal matrix, an oceanic holding by nature. Many others (especially the boys) began describing things that sounded an awful lot like the second and third birth perinatal matrices, such as being stuck inside some part of the natural world or struggling violently with some animal or fighting for survival in nature.

I think some of them thought it would be fun to test my boundaries with violent imagery, but in that space they were free to see and speak whatever came up, so it flowed and eventually shifted. SO FASCINATING!!! By the end of the week, we were all barefoot, singing, playing, and more respectful of the world around us. I returned home feeling like I'd been on another planet, totally wiped out, and also feeling the same type of clearing out or re-centering that I felt after my first Holotropic Breathwork session in Taos. I drove home soaking up the rich green of trees and plants, which felt wide-open from recent rains. Funny how the rain opens things up, like weeping—definitely another micro/macrocosm. I wonder how the galaxy weeps/rains.

The river these days is silty brown and flowing wild. The mere sight of it makes my heart beat faster. I feel renewed, more open and permeable and simultaneously more solidly flexible and strong. Probably being outside non-stop for a week was healing. Waking with the rising sun, up and running non-stop, and crashing when the bats and lightnin' bugs emerged. . . . I could live like that.

These kinds of spontaneous projects in nature, emerging from our insides, captivating the attention of others, rejuvenating, give me hope for the future.

Falling Water

A few years ago, while in the New York area visiting relatives, we took my father on a road trip to Niagara Falls, probably more our idea of a good time than his. We stopped along the way in New York's finger lake country. It was late March, the landscape still sparse from winter. At Niagara Falls, we stayed on the Canadian side, in a high-rise hotel perched above the river, packed within tourist attractions and restaurants. I had been to Niagara Falls once before, almost thirty years prior, on our honeymoon (we have a sense of humor). In those intervening three decades, a mini-Las-Vegas had grown up on the Canadian side, but no amount of hyper-real glitz could interfere with the impact of watching all that water move toward the edge, fall into space, and crash onto the rocks below.

My favorite spot is just upriver from Horseshoe Falls. An enormous expanse of turbulent river flows endlessly, relentlessly, toward the broad, curved ledge. There is a viewing spot where you can see the expanse, with Goat Island out in mid-river. In the distance, there is the horizon. To the left is the edge. Mist rises up from below and moves with the wind. Standing there, I feel as though my heart, soul, and essence are being pulled with the torrents of water toward that edge, into the unknown, into fate, into the endlessly passing moments of life. Strangely enough, I am glad to have the hyper-real glitz of Vegas-style civilization right there behind me. Maybe it is good to know nothing can minimize the majesty of nature—or maybe McWorld just feels comforting at my back.

We walk along the path at river's edge and the depth of the falling water comes into view. It looks like a deadly drop down to the river, though I know several daredevils have survived the plunge. Mostly, I feel an incomprehensible amount of water, endlessly falling over the edge into the air. We stop and take it in. I tell my daughter Tess, then in High School, that the last time I was there, mom and I were twenty-three. Tess wonders if I had any idea that someday I would be back in this place, three kids and all these years later. At the same time she is talking, my 84-year-old father is standing alone, leaning on part of the chain link fence protecting us from falling into the river. He looks cold in his windbreaker. My mother has been gone ten years already, I think. Time passes quickly.

I look back toward the expanse of water still heading for the falls. A boat is scuttled out in the middle of the river, stuck for decades amidst boulders, the river rolling endlessly around it. I breathe into myself: what was I feeling? It was not exactly grief, more like awe at the steady flow of life, awareness of the brevity of any single expression, yet the flow of life continues tumultuously. Niagara Falls is particularly grand at hitting you right in the heart if you're open for it. But this can happen anywhere, from the air touching your skin as a train pulls into an underground subway station, to the sight of weeds at the side of the highway, the flutter of pigeons in big cities, even the rats that have adapted better than most humans to civilization. In my older years, in subways in various parts of the world, I take strange comfort in those dark scurries at the corner of my eye in the early morning or late at night: survivors.

No matter where you are, you can find the sacred in nature and know all you need to know. My teacher and friend Hillevi Ruumet describes a simple experience meditating in nature:

> Some time ago, as I was meditating in the forest, away from "civilization," I suddenly knew, without words but as simply so, that I could sit right there on that spot for the rest of my life and learn everything essential there is to know simply by blending into my surroundings. Life was pulsating all around and through my body, waxing and waning in the trees, clouds, insects, birds, critters seen or only sensed, wind—everything! No difference, simply so. I don't know for how long, because this was out of time. Then I noticed my watch, abruptly returning to the world of sequential time and the need to not be late for an appointment. But the experience stayed with me and imbued my subsequent moments of relaxing in nature with a touch of pure Being.[464]

If you feel it, no matter where you are, go with the feeling. In Holotropic Breathwork, when an experience is emerging through the body, a facilitator may encourage: "That's it, make it bigger. Stay with it." A whole new way of life may emerge from willingness to live on the planet.

CHAPTER 12

Intimations of the Future

In *The Great Work: Our Way into the Future,* Thomas Berry, a Catholic priest and eco-theologian, wrote:

> The mission of our times is to reinvent the human—at the species level, with critical reflection, within the community of life-systems, in a time-developmental context, by means of story and shared dream experience. I say *reinvent the human* because humans, more than any other living form, invent themselves.[465]

Berry's dream summarizes many of the themes of this book. If we find and move through our grief of separation from nature, we find not only nature, but ourselves, our own bodies, and the "community of life systems" from which we arose. This is not entirely a rational "head" experience. Rather it is manifestation of a story and a dream. A dream of ourselves, where we come from, who we have been, who we might become, together, the diverse and compassionate expression of the heart and mind of the earth.

At the personal level, after fifteen years in Montana, I have left the ranchette for a return to city life. The plan is New York City, first stop suburban New Jersey. As with my family's move to Montana fifteen years ago, there are many reasons in the mix, but most fundamentally I am following intuition and instinct. Our children grown, my wife and I want to create separate lives. I want to see what might happen if I look for ways to "reinvent the human" from the insides of dense civilization outwards. Mostly, the "human" in question is myself. I am staying with my elderly father, helping out, and once again—after a lapse of many years—getting up early most mornings to meditate. The space inside me is very different than it was all those years ago when I sat on my zafu and finally heard the rain. Now it feels like endless space, a legacy of Montana. Emotions still arise, but they are more likely to pass through. The mind-language chatter comes now and then, but it is quieter, easier to release.

Outside, externally, there is a busy street right in front of our flat, where commuters line up every morning at a stop sign, waiting for their chance to dart out onto another connecting avenue. In this part of New Jersey, most streets you turn down end in a neighborhood without egress. They call the ones that go through the "connecting" streets. I like that. I like living at the cross-section of two connecting streets. The noise and presence of the energy of traffic comforts rather than bothers me. A few blocks away is the New Jersey Transit train station for Ridgewood. Thirty-five minutes give or take and you are in Secaucus, change trains, ten minutes under the Hudson River and you enter one of the hubs of the world, New York City, through Penn Station. I have always been fascinated with this city, no less at present. I suspect there is something about the melting-pot nature of the place, walking, and subways. I like rattling around in the subterranean of things. I like seeing people from all over the world. I like people playing music in the subway stations.

Fortunately, my ties to Montana will continue and yet I am meeting new people and reconnecting with those from my past. A good friend from my youth lives not far from Union Square in the city. A few weeks ago we were up on the roof of his building, where you can see the Empire State Building in midtown and the new Freedom Tower downtown. Knowing he has lived in this building for years, I said, "You must have been able to see the Towers burning." He said he had gone up to the roof after he heard the news of the first plane crashing into the World Trade Center. Through binoculars, from less than two dozen blocks, he watched the first tower burning. "It was a beautiful bright clear morning, just like today," he said. Initial media reports talked about an accident with a small plane, but he knew immediately it was a terrorist attack. One of his neighbors arrived on the roof with his young daughter, who also started watching through binoculars. My friend saw people jumping from the building and told his neighbor not to let the girl watch. The neighbor said, "That has to be just debris or something."

My friend said, "No, it's people." Then he saw another plane flying low toward the city and realized what was about to happen. He followed the plane with his binoculars and watched it explode into the second tower. The field of his binoculars filled with flames. The story shared by my friend felt sacred to me. Horrible, unthinkable, but sacred. In the days after I was up on his roof, it was hard for me not to get choked up when remembering him watching up close the event introducing our new century. After all these years, I am still a cry-baby, though now the grief is mainly about people. The pull is toward civilization. New York City pulls at me for many reasons, including its connection to the world—all that it holds not just for Americans but for all of us. Just as I wanted to feel nature inside me, I yearn to feel the world inside me, all of us separate peoples yet all of us expressions of life on the planet, descendants of those same single-celled organisms making the jump into life processes those several billion years ago, down there at the bottom of the ocean.

When I told my Montana dream-group friends my move to New York involved a need to return to civilization, they all laughed. I am still not sure whether they laughed because they thought Montana *was* civilization or because they thought New York City was not. One thing I have noticed from moving around is that many people seem to have pretty strong opinions about the places they live and the places they do not live. Many people here seem to think Montana is full of crazy red necks. Of course, when national media picks up thing like the Montana Legislature considering one bill legalizing spear-throwing as a hunting technique and another instructing the Governor to follow state but not federal laws, you can see where they get that impression. On the other hand, many people in Montana seem to think New York City is full of snobs and hoods. The accents and attitudes might be different, but I have found about the same spread of kindness and meanness, authenticity and foolishness, no matter the groups of humans into which I have thrown my lot.

One thing I have finally learned is that nature is everywhere. The wind blows; it rains. Grass grows, birds fly, rodents dig underground or burrow into city walls. It all seems like one planet to me now, concrete or grass, though I really like the grass. If Montana has nature, so does the big city. When I am riding the train to New York, I love the wetlands around Secaucus, the stop just before you go into the tunnel. People around me are playing on their cell phones while I am content to look at weeds growing out of water. Then I am always surprised when we enter the tunnel, hurtle under the river, and ease into Penn Station. I ride the escalator up onto Seventh Avenue and dig the buzz around me. No bears to worry about, but probably some wolf energy if I look for it.

Although this move was nowhere on the horizon when I started this book, it strikes me that New York City has been a character in this story from the outset. Right now, finishing up this work of ten or twelve years, I am listening to JAY Z rap his way through *Empire State of Mind*. Different Jay than me, but I feel him. "Statue of Liberty, long live the World Trade, New York, concrete jungle where dreams are made of . . ." This song feels like a world dream, not just about New York. One of my favorite books is *Lonesome Dove*, about a late 1800s cattle drive from Texas to paradise imagined in Montana. As preface to the story, author Larry McMurtry quotes T. K. Whipple: "Our forefathers had civilization inside themselves, the wild outside. We live in the civilization they created, but within us the wilderness still lingers. What they dreamed, we live, and what they lived, we dream."[466] A century and a half later, I want both dreams inside me.

Perhaps longing for nature will return as my time is spent on concrete, though the space inside me now feels in harmony with nature no matter where I am. Cities are just part of what is. A trick for changing perspective on city life was shared with me by Marie McLean, a teacher living in Toronto. One evening, Marie suddenly realized she was *always* in nature, even in the midst of urban life. She wrote: *I was walking to a beautiful garden near City Hall, where I had done a nature-connecting activity for a course I was taking in my doctoral program. I remembered the experience of the activity and wanted it again. When I was a block away, I came upon barricades, a St. John Ambulance emergency treatment vehicle, canopies, a sound system, and an Elvis impersonator* (!) *booming out that it's Saturday night and time to party.*

I caught myself groaning and thinking a wrangled thought about how people would "ruin" my contact with nature. I wondered if anyone had asked permission from this spot to use it as a stage. But, trying to ease out of my attitude, I thought to myself, "It will be an interesting opportunity to integrate this." I went to my spot in the garden to visit my old friends (the plants), asking for communion with them. There was a (fake) stream running through this little ecosystem and I was attracted to it immediately. Elvis couldn't drown out the babbling of this little brook—and my mind went straight to "love flowers." I was startled by how quickly this came to me. I then spotted a grouping of flowers that riveted my eyes. It was the blending of their colors that captivated me.

I moved away from the area to get a quick peek at what Elvis was wearing. As I stood there, a shaft of the setting sun came out from behind me and fell directly on the middle of my back. I had the sensation with no label attached to it and that made me smile. I almost felt the sun on my back was solid enough to lean into. I closed my eyes and the words "love is warmth in the heart" came up. God, I felt so good. I didn't want to leave, but I had promised to bring home a pizza. I thanked the area and, as I stepped back into the street, I felt my senses were assaulted. The street was barricaded and there were all manner of carnival things happening. I decided to focus on all the nature things the city had either preserved or planted. I went from tree to hanging flowers to dogs. When no greenery was near I looked at the sky and the clouds and the few shafts of light cutting through the low buildings.

As I looked into the distance I could see tree tops that were several blocks away. With the sky as a backdrop, all of a sudden I had a "symphonic" experience. It was as if many energies were coming together, distinct, perhaps discordant, but one whole experience. I got a bigger picture feeling. It hit my senses that whereas before I used to feel remorse and hunger that cities had taken over the earth and kept meager pockets and pots of nature around for decoration, I now had the macro sense that earth keeps pockets of cities!!!

Earth and nature are everywhere, popping up and even breaking through concrete. Earth surrounds us and engulfs us and supports us and will never leave us and will, somehow, endure our madness. I had a curiously satisfying vision of nature, hundreds of years from now, somehow thriving quietly, and intelligently, and over the centuries mulching up all the buildings and reestablishing itself with love. "Nature creates no garbage and recycles ours." I felt inured to the commotion around me and, more important, I felt lovingly enveloped by nature in the middle of the street while on a pizza mission.

On another occasion, I wanted to walk to the store, which takes 45 minutes down one of the busiest streets in Brampton. It is one of the ugliest sights, I think, to have six lanes of traffic lying between horrendous strip malls, golden arches, and other such places. It gets really discouraging for me to expose myself to that. The traffic creates so much white noise that I always strap on music and try to make the best of it. As I walked along, once again, I got that macro thing happening. As I scanned the horizon, I could see the tops of trees above all the housing for a few blocks and again got that feeling of "cities in nature" rather than "nature in cities." It felt soothing and reassuring, and the walk began to feel better. I could shrink down the effect of the traffic and ugliness. I began to feel happy.

The sidewalk dipped down into a depression (no jokes, please) while the road kept going straight. Despite the music in my headphones, the song of a bird grabbed me and I stopped. There to my right were the most unusual flowering "weeds." They had spiky purple blossoms and were about six feet tall. I asked permission to touch them and they felt wonderfully and firmly fuzzy. I looked past them and there was the lushest area! I sat down on a stone wall and just stared. It was then that I caught sight of a brilliant little yellow and black bird. I had a sharp intake of breath to see that shot of color.

When we learn to release the trance of civilization, nature becomes a "bigger picture" solace all around us, always. I would not say my grief around nature has disappeared entirely but I would say it has blended out around the planet. Nature and her ways now seem as real to me as humans, so I am increasingly interested in what we humans will do in response to what we have done. How will we cope with this level of technology and globalism? How will we act as fewer and fewer people have any sense of the natural world? What will happen as more and more species disappear? Will it be enough to watch nature on television? Is the natural world destined to become Disneyland in reality as well as in our minds? Are we headed for an environmental Armageddon as some doomsayers predict—or is that doom-saying just our contemporary version of the apocalyptic predictions that have always been with us?

No matter how it flows, I suspect the wave of grief in response to nature may rise up for more and more people. If so, I hope we move through it rather than deny it. Laurel Smith, a retired marine biologist living in Houston, described her way of coping with grief surrounding the environmental crisis. *I have felt profound sadness upon reading that some researchers believe some dolphins and other mammals deliberately beach themselves in protest to the pollution of their marine environment. I wonder what dolphins breaching the surface of the water think when they see cities and suburbs on the horizon instead of trees and beach sand. Are they amazed, disgusted, and angry? To even think that dolphins might be committing suicide in protest, when most of their human audience cannot begin to grant them the respect to believe they would be capable of such an act, is deeply moving. It fills me with remorse, powerlessness, awe, and shame.*

Sometimes when I am driving alone, I can achieve a feeling of connectedness to this planet with a ritual I have devised. I imagine my car like an ant on a large beach ball. I'm chugging along, with buildings, signs, trees, marshes, water rushing by. The freeway is like a tiny asphalt ribbon on which I am moving. I think of the immensity of the planet and how we all exist sharing its gifts of sustenance. I can frequently reach a place where I feel connected to everything on this planet. I remember that every living thing shares common biochemical pathways and similar DNA sequences. Do we need more to prove our connection to nature?

I live in Houston, a metropolitan area of four-million people. I love this thriving, improving city. Sometimes I feel disconnected from nature here. However, outside I see myriad trees and green spaces. I work in my flower and vegetable gardens. Digging in the dirt makes me feel better. When I stroll down my street, I admire the beautiful yards. In the distance I hear the freeway, not half a mile away. The speeding cars and trucks sound like a rushing river. I imagine an immense flow making the noise. I accept that this flow of energy—cars? water?—is alright. It can even be soothing if I let it.

Once we have the sense of one contiguous world, all within nature, the dividing line between us and nature disappears. So much is in the mind, the constructs we make. Just as I constructed cities and suburbs in California as oppressing me, so I imagined a pristine Montana where I could hide out with nature. That illusion died one day when I was driving north from Helena on Interstate 15 with people from work. I happened to ask about those low concrete buildings I kept seeing not far out in the prairie. Turns out they were silos for nuclear bombs. Things became even more interesting when I was teaching transpersonal psychology at a seminar in California and ran across a young guy from Montana. "Oh, where do you live?"I asked.

"Great Falls."

"What do you do up there?"

"Well, actually, I'm in the military" he said. "I'm one of those guys sitting in the silos with my finger on the nuclear bomb trigger." Turns out the government pays for those guys and gals to take online courses to help them stay focused and awake while they are sitting down in the bunkers. This particular fellow chose to take courses in transpersonal psychology. I had to find a quiet spot to take that in. Once I did, it made all the sense in the world.

While I sought and relied upon Montana as a place where nature still roams, the state is also home to some of our worst ecological disasters. Understanding this reality helped me release any pretense about nature preserved in some places, destroyed in others. For instance, asbestos contamination haunts the town of Libby in northwest Montana. This is a legacy of mining. Between 1919 and 1990, seventy percent of all the mineral vermiculite sold in the United States came from a mine near Libby, which also contained asbestos. Used extensively in insulation, vermiculite is a composed of shiny flakes which, when heated, expand into a light-weight, fire-resistant material.[467] People who grew up in Libby describe the piles of vermiculite that were everywhere in town, particularly around athletic fields, where the substance was used to mark boundary lines. Kids played in the piles, particularly in the 1950s and 1960s. Unfortunately, asbestos contaminated much of the vermiculite. Scores of people from Libby and its environs are suffering from asbestosis or have already died from the breath-depriving disease.

Another infamous Montana eco-disaster is known as the Berkeley pit. My wife tells the story of a friend from Butte, who casually remarked one day that the house where she grew up was no longer there. Having lived through the tear-down and rebuild movements in various cities and suburbs, Margee asked if someone bought the lot to build something else. "No," explained her friend. "The house is not there anymore because the whole neighborhood is not there anymore. It all fell into the pit."

When I first saw the Berkeley pit, I was struck more by amazement than grief. One mile long, half a mile wide, one-third of a mile deep, the pit is a sea of brownish, yellowish liquid looking like nothing I have ever seen—well, maybe something like the ooze brought by aliens in a bad sci-fi movie. Here is how it happened. When the mine under this part of Butte closed in 1982, the water pumps were removed. Groundwater filled the tunnels. Then the earth above the tunnels started to collapse and settle to the bottom of what became the Berkeley pit. From the remains of heavy metals and chemicals, including arsenic, cadmium, zinc, and sulfuric acid, a toxic lake emerged. As more and more empty mining caverns collapsed, the pit expanded, claiming homes and businesses.

Neighborhoods disappeared, but a tourist attraction emerged, fittingly postmodern. You can walk out onto a platform extending over the yellowish "water" for proper viewing. There are pay-binoculars-on-a-stand for a closer look, and a gift shop.[468] "Hey, this is something to see, let's see it." Not just scenery, but history, a moment in time, our moment: a Montana moment. Some people with macabre humor tell me they used to stand by the pit and watch birds land on the sludge. Tragic mistake for those poor birds; they soon succumbed, whether to gas or the sheer toxicity, falling into the lake, adding their organic matter to the chemical mix. Horrible situation, but not twenty minutes in any direction and you are in some of the most beautiful mountains I have ever seen. The drive through the canyons up to Helena from Butte is stunning, sometimes winding and craggy, sometimes open fields where snow blows steady in the winter. One of those fields is named Elk Park. A guy I know wrecked his van hitting an elk in the dark there early one morning, so the name is apt.

Several years ago I had occasion to lead a discussion on grief in response to nature. Similar to the narratives shared in this book, many people told deeply personal stories involving their intimate relationship with nature, others of their dismay at our collective and relentless assault on the natural world. Eventually one young woman who had not previously spoken raised her hand and waited to be acknowledged. She said, "This is not really about nature, it's about us. Nature is going to be fine if she has long enough. To the earth, a million years is no big deal. Mother Nature will repair herself. But we humans may not be around. We ought to be grieving for ourselves, because we could be about to make ourselves extinct."

This was not exactly a bombshell, but the room went quiet for a moment. You could feel the discussion deepen. We had moved into the deeper silence that sometimes happens with a shift in group awareness. Imagining one's own death is challenging enough. Extinction of our whole species takes a different kind of imagination. That threat happens in science fiction movies but we always prevail in the end, don't we? If you let in the possible demise of all of us, no more people on the planet, no more descendants, it is quite breathtaking. I am not talking polemics, but deep internal understanding, as when I woke up in the palapa in Mexico and knew that I would die. Transfer that certainty to a possibility for our species. No more humans; the voice goes silent, no more human thoughts, no more human emotions. No more planning, no more construction, no more hopes and dreams. No more peace, no more wars: well, maybe there is an advantage to getting rid of the silly monkey if the wars and pollution stop.

Consider the world without us. Alan Weisman, a journalist, teacher, and radio producer, did just that. In *The World Without Us*, Weisman invites us to imagine what would happen if humans were suddenly removed from the Earth. He recognizes the difficulty of this "creative experiment." As he notes, "Any conjecture gets muddled by our obstinate reluctance to accept that the worst might actually occur. We may be undermined by our survival instincts, honed over eons to help us deny, defy, or ignore catastrophic portents lest they paralyze us with fright."[469] While most of us may not want to go there, envisioning the world without us seems practically an act of worship—or at the very least, a respite from our hubris. Weisman asks:

> How would the rest of nature respond if it were suddenly relieved of the relentless pressure we heap on it and our fellow organisms? How soon would, or could, the climate return to where it was before we fired up all our engines? How long would it take to recover lost ground and restore Eden to the way it must have gleamed and smelled the day before Adam, or *Homo habilis,* appeared?[470]

Weisman and many others suggest our actions have changed the planet irreparably. Thousands of species have become extinct as the result of our economies. They will almost certainly never again exist in the exact same combination of DNA. On the other hand, while some miracles of evolution are permanently gone, plastics are apparently here to stay, filling not only landfills but our oceans. One scientist told Weisman, optimistically, that the Earth may be able to process our fifty-years-worth of plastics in around 100,000 years.[471] That was a short five decades since Dustin Hoffman in *The Graduate* listened to his parent's friend instructing him the future for a young man with ambition was "plastics." Interestingly, one possibility for creative imagination is that evolution will produce species of microbes able to digest and process our plastics, something no species on Earth can currently do. Why not? That seems quite a reasonable ecological niche needing to be filled. Evolutionary forces, like marketers, are always looking for a niche.

So what if it takes the Earth 100,000 years to degrade our plastics? That is nothing compared to four-and-a-half-billion years of planetary history. Weisman's creative experiment in envisioning the world without us leads, for the most part, to an understanding that Gaia will indeed move on—as people do from a relationship that just didn't work. Our houses will be gone like nothing flat, an extended slow-motion version of descent into the Berkeley pit. Weisman explains this humorously, drawing on our awareness of just how easily nature creeps into our dwellings, through water, insects, even small mammals. Then it is just a matter of time until all the trappings of civilization are broken down. He estimates no more than 50 years, maybe 100.

Even the steel and concrete structures of our modern cities will succumb more quickly than we might imagine. Depending on the particular city, water will likely lead the way, just as happened with the Berkeley Pit. Without power and human maintenance, pumps fail and water rises in the cities near oceans or rivers. Even without water, heat and cold over time bring cracks to the strongest structures. If an ice age comes, glaciers wipe the urban slates clean. Even without glaciers, the lands we farmed will return to forests, while more densely inhabited lands will turn to deserts, at least initially. What a pity, deserts with no one left to build swimming pools.

If we become extinct soon enough, before more wild animals succumb, Weisman predicts wildlife would soon make prey of domesticated animals, except perhaps in isolated spots (such as Hawaii) where there are few predators. At least that will be the situation until new predators evolve. If we last long enough to destroy all but the most resilient species (think rats, insects, snakes) then only our imaginations can predict what evolution may produce given enough times. Weisman shares the scenario offered by Peter Ward in his book *Future Evolution*,[472] where "rats evolve into kangaroo-sized hoppers with saber tusks, and snakes . . . learn to soar."[473]

Soaring snakes may seem like fantasy until we remember that dinosaurs roamed the Earth before us, which is unimaginable in its own way. Even while mindful of the diseases carried by some city-dwelling rodents (remember the plagues?), I feel a kinship for rats, the carriers of much of our civilized projected fears. One of my favorite books in the last many years is Robert Sullivan's *Rats: Observations on the History and Habitat of the City's Most Unwanted Inhabitants.*[474] The focus is New York: the thing to remember is you are never more than a few feet away from a rat when in the city, though you rarely know it. If we become extinct, I say, good luck to all you rat descendants. I say that with the same good will borne by my daughter Audrey when she said, "Good luck, chickens" as we drove out of our Montana driveway leaving the chickens scurrying away from the fox. You rats, with a few billion years under your evolutionary belt, maybe you'll come up with your own civilization. See how much you like hearing some other creature rattling around in your walls.

When I first practiced imagining the world without us, I did not feel much sadness. I told myself I had more confidence in the life force than in our particular species, that extinction would basically serve us right. And then, just as I neared writing the last sentences of this book, the breathtaking nature of the possibility of human extinction started to hit me. Wow, could that really happen? The grief started to arise, almost making me throw up.

All the struggles of all our ancestors, billions of parents protecting billions of offspring, sometimes successfully, sometimes not, all those creatures before us, and this is what happens? Grim as things sometimes look, I refuse to believe it.

In the next chapter of my life, I am making myself available for service to our species in the interest of making our role in evolution work out. I have very little idea what this means or how it looks. As for grief in response to nature, it does not press on me as much as when I began this journey. Now I understand grief as a vehicle—an expression of longing, pulling us toward something. Even if grief involves a permanent loss, something comes next. That is, if we remain open to what is possible and do not cling to the past. We need to look to the future, but my God what a mess! On the other hand, I suppose it was always this way in this messy ooze of a planet.

Brother David Steindl-Rast believes we humans "can learn to understand some of the mystery of the heart—our own mystery— by looking at the image of home and journey. Only with reference to a home is our journey truly a journey: otherwise we would merely be drifting."[475] He believes "out-pouring and ingathering, journey and home, are inseparably united in its dynamic reality." Drawing from "Four Quartets" by T.S. Eliot, Steindl-Rast observes home is where we begin and where we end up. "What we call the beginning," Eliot writes, "is often the end, And to make an end is to make a beginning."[476] Surely saying the same thing said by countless humans before him, but saying it beautifully, Eliot wrote:

> We shall not cease from exploration
> And the end of all our exploring
> Will be to arrive where we started
> And know the place for the first time.[477]

Assisting in the Holotropic Breathwork movement, I have traveled to India twice in the last year. Father K. C. Thomas, a priest in the Don Bosco Order, asked the Grof Transpersonal Training program to prepare groups of Indian priests and nuns to facilitate Holotropic Breathwork in their country. Responding to the call, my friends Holly Harmon and Marianne Murray invited me to apprentice in some of the two-week trainings. As Stan Grof observed in a video greeting to the group, it seems strange to have been asked to bring a newly designed spiritual practice to the heartland of many of the world's sacred traditions. And yet, it makes so much sense: an interweaving, a return, West meets East, East meets West, inner and outer, outer and inner, now all one planet. So much for all of us to learn, and unlearn. As with many of the spiritual practices arising on the Indian subcontinent, Holotropic Breathwork is an invitation to find our source from inside ourselves, to bring whatever we find back out to the world.

On my last trip to India, after two weeks in the field of Holotropic Breathwork, I spent a few days with my friend Ryan Westrum on the beach at Kovalam, a tourist town on the Arabian Sea. One morning we ate a late breakfast at *The Beatles Café*. Yes, this was India in 2014 and mention of the Beatles still helped draw a crowd. To avoid the hucksters and beggars, we had found this second story café, where no one could accost us from the street. Grateful for a decent cup of coffee, we lingered at a table on the edge of the balcony, looking out at the cove, watching the endless surf. The waves looked calm enough, but everyone was telling us about the undertow, something about the monsoons only a few weeks away. Down on the beach, people ventured out into the surf, then lifeguards blew whistles and ordered them back in.

I was telling Ryan that when I got home, I absolutely, positively needed to finish this book. It had gone on long enough. I needed it out of my life. He knew the book was about nature and grief, but he did not know details. In his way, he paused, giving me space to explain, giving me space not to explain. We looked out at the beach. A few dozen men and women were pulling in ropes attached to an enormous net stretched out across the large cove, extending way out into the sea. They were pulling in fish. It looked like all the fish in the ocean would be pulled in and harvested. Ryan said something like, "Wow, how are there going to be any fish left in the sea?" I shrugged. He asked, "Does this upset you—pulling in all these fish? I mean, with your nature and grief thing?"

"Not at all," I said. "These people need to eat. I'll be eating one of those fish for dinner." From the days just passed, I knew that by afternoon there would be women with metal tubs on their heads wandering along the pavement bringing the daily catch to the restaurants. The night before, I had picked out my own fish from a display on ice at our night-time balcony restaurant.

Ryan looked at me and took a sip of his coffee. Then we started to smell what you smell throughout much of India, garbage burning. We looked to the promontory at the end of the beach: a group of people milling around, colorful clothes, some men stirring a fire, gray smoke rising, blowing our way. This is not criticism or affluent Western judgment. Rather, this is reality about the world out there. Over a billion people in India and hard for ecological infrastructure to emerge while people are trying to better themselves and their country. Garbage needs burning, including at both ends of a beautiful beach. Not a big deal if the choking smell gets in your throat when you are sitting at *The Beatles Café* and trying to imagine a new world.

On the other hand, even with the smoke in your chest, your heart is full with all the people you have met in this glorious crowded country, including friendly young people standing with you as far out in the surf as the lifeguards with their whistles would allow, striking you as more sensible, spiritual, and capable of creating a new world than most of the dazed hyper-reality people back home. And you are still processing your emotions from being deeply touched by the service and spirituality of the priests and nuns you encountered. Like a good postmodern intellectual, you imagine saying to everyone back home, "Now I realize how everything in the West is all about power dynamics," but you know deep down you are all image and projection, imagination into the next thing, like everyone else. You know the world will take care of itself; all you have to do is feel what you feel.

In a lull in the conversation, Ryan asks me, "How does the book end?"

I pause for a moment, breathe in a bit of smoke on a salty breeze. Then I know. I answer, "It ends like this. Sitting right here. Just like this."

Endnotes

1. Ramakrishna, Sri (1997). In *The teachings of Yoga* (Georg Feuerstein, Trans. & Ed.) Boston, MA: Shambhala, p. 140.

2. Scally, Aylwyn & Durbin, Richard. (2012). *Nature Reviews Genetics, 13,* 745-753.

3. Dufrechou, Jay. (2002). Coming home to nature through the body: An intuitive inquiry into experiences of grief, weeping and other deep emotions in response to nature. Unpublished Doctoral Dissertation, Institute of Transpersonal Psychology, Palo Alto, CA. The research method for the study was Intuitive Inquiry, a methodology developed by Rosemarie Anderson, particularly appropriate for researching experiences of personal and cultural transformation. See, Anderson, Rosemarie. (1998). Intuitive inquiry: A transpersonal approach. In William Braud & Rosemarie Anderson (Eds.), *Transpersonal research methods for the social sciences: Honoring human experience* (pp. 69-94). Thousand Oaks, CA: Sage, p. 73; Anderson, Rosemarie. (2004). Intuitive inquiry: An epistemology of the heart for scientific inquiry. *The Humanistic Psychologist, 32*(4); Anderson, Rosemarie. (2011). Intuitive Inquiry: The ways of the heart in human science research. In R. Anderson & W. Braud, *Transforming self and others through research: Transpersonal research methods and skills for the human sciences and humanities.* Albany, NY: SUNY; Rosemarie, Anderson. (2011). Intuitive inquiry: Exploring the mirroring discourse of disease. In Wertz, Frederick J., Charmaz, Kathy, McMullen, Linda M., Josselson, Ruthellen, Anderson, Rosemarie & McSpadden, Emalinda, *Five ways of doing qualitative analysis: Phenomenological psychology, grounded theory, discourse analysis, narrative research, and intuitive inquiry.* New York, NY: The Guilford Press.

4. http://newswatch.nationalgeographic.com/2012/03/28/the-sixth-great-extinction-a-silent-extermination/

5. http://www.spacequotations.com/earth.html

6. Ibid, quoting Frank Borman, Apollo 8, 'A Science Fiction World—Awesome Forlorn Beauty,' Life magazine, 17 January 1969

7. Ibid, quoting Frank Borman, Apollo 8, Newsweek magazine, 23 December 1968.

8. Ibid.

9. http://www.worldbeyondborders.org/quotes.htm

10. http://www.spacequotations.com/earth.html, quoting Edgar Mitchell, Apollo 14 astronaut, People magazine, 8 April 1974.

11. Rumi, Jalal al-Din. (trans. 1995/2004). *The essential Rumi.* (Coleman Barks,Trans.). New York, NY: Harper Collins.
12. Bacon, Francis (1597/1986). *The essays.* New York, NY: Penguin Classics.
13. See http://www.ehe.org/display/ehe-menu36be.html?sectid=4
14. Louv, Richard. (2005). *Last child in the woods: Saving our children from nature-deficit disorder.* Chapel Hill, NC: Algonquin Books of Chapel Hill.
15. Ibid, p. 3.
16. Ibid, p. 1.
17. Ibid, p. 97.
18. Ibid, p. 2.
19. Ibid.
20. Tart, Charles. (1987). *Waking up: Overcoming the obstacles to human potential.* Boston: Shambhala, p. 88.
21. Ibid, p. 87.
22. Ibid, p. 88.
23. Ibid.
24. Gurdjieff and his work are described in Ouspensky, P.D. (1949). *In search of the miraculous: Fragments of an unknown teaching.* New York, NY: Harcourt, Brace and Company.
25. Tart, *Waking Up,* p. 197.
26. Ibid.
27. Ibid, p. 85.
28. Ibid.
29. Ibid, p. 184.
30. Ibid, p. 190.
31. See Sparks, Tav. (2009). *Movie yoga: How every film can change your life.* Santa Cruz, CA: Hanford Mead.
32. Jung, Carl Gustav. (2010/1952). *Synchronicity: An acausal connecting principle.* Princeton, NJ: Princeton University Press; Koesler, Arthur (1973). *The roots of coincidence.* New York, NY: Vintage Books.
33. Gendlin, Eugene, Beebe, J., Cassens, J., Klein, M., & Oberlander, M. (1968). Focusing ability in psychotherapy, personality, and creativity. In J. M. Shlein (Ed.), *Research in psychotherapy: Vol. II.* Washington, D. C.: American Psychological Association.
34. Gendlin, Eugene. (1981). *Focusing.* New York, NY: Bantam, p. 11.
35. Ruumet, Hillevi. (2006). *Pathways of the soul: Exploring the human journey.* Victoria, Canada: Trafford.
36. See, e.g., Wrangham, Richard & Peterson, Dale (1996). *Demonic males: Apes and the origins of human violence.* Boston, MA: Houghton Mifflin
37. http://www.actionbioscience.org/newfrontiers/eldredge2.html   (retrieved 6/9/13).
38. Ibid.
39. Shepard, Florence R. (1997). Preface. In Shepard, Paul, *Coming home to the pleistocene.* Washington, D.C.: Island Press/Shearwater Books.
40. Shepard, Paul. (1996). Preface. In Shepard, Paul (Ed.), *A Paul Shepard Reader: The only world we've got.* San Francisco, CA: Sierra Club Books.

41. Ibid, p. ix.
42. Ibid, p. x.
43. Ibid.
44. Ibid, p. xiv.
45. Berman, Morris. (2000). *Wandering God: A study in nomadic spirituality.* Albany, NY: SUNY, p. 17.
46. Ibid, p. 6.
47. Ibid, p. 3.
48. Ibid, p. 6.
49. Ibid, p. 3.
50. Ibid, pp. 3-4.
51. Ibid, p. 223.
52. Shepard, Paul. (1978/1998). *Thinking animals: Animals and the development of human intelligence.* Athens, GA: The University of Georgia Press; Shepard, Paul. (1996). *The others: How animals made us human.* Washington, D.C.: Island Press/Shearwater Books.
53. Ibid, p. 182.
54. Ibid.
55. Wrangham, Richard & Peterson, Dale (1996). *Demonic males: Apes and the origins of human violence.* Boston, MA: Houghton Mifflin
56. Shepard, Preface to *A Paul Shepard Reader: The only world we've got,* p. xv.
57. Ibid, p. xx.
58. Nietzsche, Friedrich. (1882/1974). *The gay science: With a prelude in rhymes and appendix in songs.* (Trans. Walter Kaufmann). New York, NY: Vintage.
59. See Eden, Amnon, Moor, James, Søraker, Johnny, & Steinhart, Eric (Eds.) (2013). *Singularity hypotheses: A scientific and philosophical assessment.* New York, NY: Springer.
60. Compare Kurzweil, Ray. (2006). *The singularity is near.* New York, NY: Penguin Group; and Vinge, Vernor. (1993). The coming technological singularity: How to survive in the post-human era. In Landis, G.A. (Ed.) *Vision-21: Interdisciplinary science and engineering in the era of cyberspace,* pp. 11–22.
61. See Braud, William & Anderson, Rosemarie. (1998). *Transpersonal research methods for the social sciences: Honoring human experience.* Thousand Oaks, CA: Sage; Anderson, Rosemarie & Braud, William. (2011). *Transforming self and others through research: Transpersonal research methods and skills for the human sciences and humanities.* Albany, NY: SUNY.
62. http://www.oxforddictionaries.com/definition/english/epiphenomenon
63. See, e.g., Storm, Lance & Thalbourne, Michael A. (2006). *The survival of human consciousness: Essays on the possibility of life after death.* Jefferson, NC: McFarland & Company; Lachman, Gary (2003). *A secret history of consciousness.* Great Barrington, MA: Lindisfarne Books.
64. Capra, Fritjof. (1975). *The tao of physics: An exploration of the parallels between modern physics and eastern mysticism.* Boston, MA: Shambhala.

65. Le Grice, Keiron. (2010). *The archetypal cosmos: Rediscovering the god in myth, science and astrology.* Edinburgh, Scotland: Floris Books.

66. See, e.g., Wilber, Ken (1996). *The Atman project: A transpersonal view of human development.* Wheaton, IL: Quest Books; Wilber, Ken (1993). *The spectrum of consciousness.* Wheaton, IL: Quest Books; Wilber, Ken. (1983). *A sociable God: Toward a new understanding of religion.* Boston, MA: Shambhala.

67. Mumford, Lewis. (1966). *The myth of the machine: Volume one: Technics and human development.* San Diego, CA: Harcourt Brace Jovanovich, p. 3.

68. Ibid.

69. Ibid.

70. Ibid.

71. Ibid.

72. Mumford, Lewis (1966). *The myth of the machine: Volume two: The pentagon of power.* San Diego, CA: Harcourt, Brace, Jovanovich, p. 51.

73. Ibid.

74. Ibid.

75. McKibbin, Bill. (1989). *The end of nature.* New York, NY: Anchor Books, p. 64.

76. Ibid.

77. Ibid.

78. See, e.g., http://www.postnatural.org/, the website for the Center for Post-Natural History; and, for instance, Asoka Bandarage writing on "A Post-nature, Post-human World?" in the Huffington Post, http://www.huffingtonpost.com/asoka-bandarage/a-post-nature-post-human-world_b_3451865.html, discussing predictions that the "technological singularity" in which artificial intelligence becomes "conscious" and exceeds human intelligence will become reality.

79. Baudrillard, Jean. (1994). *Simulacra and simulation. The precession of simulacra.* Ann Arbor, MI: University of Michigan Press; see interviews and film clip in http://www.youtube.com/watch?v=e3tr0gSNBx4, titled, *Philosophy and the Matrix.*

80. Baudrillard, Jean. (1976/1988). *Selected Writing.* Stanford, CA: Stanford University Press, p. 128.

81. Ibid.

82. Ibid, p. 127.

83. Barber, Benjamin. (1995). *Jihad v. McWorld.* New York, NY: Ballantine Books.

84. See http://consumerist.com/2007/03/21/mcdonalds-mcfights-mclanguage-in-mcdictionary/; http://www.academia.edu/151543/McDeconstruction; Bowman, Paul. (2006). *McDeconstruction:* (Rochampton Univeristy, http://www.academia.edu/151543/McDeconstruction).

85. Ibid, p. 4.

86. Ibid, p. 1.

87. Mander, Jerry. (1978). Four arguments for the elimination of television. New York, NY: Quill.
88. Ibid, p. 24.
89. Ibid, p. 24.
90. Ibid, p. 113.
91. Ibid, p. 155.
92. http://www.nydailynews.com/entertainment/tv-movies/americans-spend-34-hours-week-watching-tv-nielsen-numbers-article-1.1162285
93. http://www.huffingtonpost.com/2013/08/01/tv-digital-devices_n_3691196.html
94. *See* Chomsky, Noam. (2008). *The essential Chomsky* (Anthony Arnove, Ed.) New York, NY: The New Press.
95. Mander, p. 224.
96. See, e.g., Grof, Stanislav (1985). *Beyond the brain: Birth, death and transcendence in psychotherapy.* Albany, NY: SUNY, p. 22.
97. Miller, E.K. & Cohen, J.D. (2001). An integrative theory of prefrontal cortex function. *Annual Review Neuroscience, 24*, 167-202.
98. Ibid.
99. Schlain, Leonard. (1998). *The alphabet versus the goddess.* New York, NY: Penguin Group.
100. Ibid, p. 19.
101. Husserl, Edmund. (1936/1970). *The crisis of European sciences and transcendental phenomenology.* (David Carr, Trans.). Evanston, IL: Northwestern University Press.
102. Heidegger, Martin. (1926/1962). *Being and time.* (John Macquarrie & Edward Robinson, Trans.). New York, NY: Harper & Row.
103. Merleau-Ponty, Maurice. (1964). *The primacy of perception* (William Cobb, Arleen B. Dallery, Carleton Dallery, James M. Edie, John Flodstrom, Nancy Metzel & John Wild, Trans.). Evanston, IL: Northwestern University Press.
104. Levin, David. (1988). Transpersonal phenomenology: The corporeal schema. *The Humanistic Psychologist, 16*(2), 282-313.
105. Lame Deer, & Erfoes, R. (1972). *Lame Deer: Seeker of visions.* New York, NY: Simon & Schuster, p. 157.
106. Levin, p. 282.
107. Ibid.
108. Levin, pp. 301-302.
109. Ibid, p. 303.
110. Abram, David. (1996). *The Spell of the Sensuous.* New York: Vintage Books.
111. Ibid, p. 57.
112. Ibid, p. 65.
113. Ibid, p. 65.
114. Abram, David. (2010). *Becoming animal: An earthly cosmology.* New York, NY: Vintage Books.
115. Ibid, p. 4.

116. Ibid.

117. Ibid, p. 3.

118. Ibid, p. 3.

119. Wasowski, Andy & Wasowski, Sally. (2006). *Building within nature: A guide for home owners, contractors, and architects.* Minneapolis, MN: University of Minnesota Press.

120. Ibid, p. 3.

121. Ibid.

122. Mollison, Bill. (1988). *Permaculture: A designer's manual.* Sister's Creek, Tasmania, Australia: Tagari Publications; Mollison, Bill. (1997). *Introduction to permaculture.* Sister's Creek, Tasmania, Australia: Tagari Publications.

123. http://www.pricklypearlt.org/easements/

124. Glendinning, Chellis. (1994). *My name is Chellis and I'm in recovery from Western Civilization.* Boston, MA: Shambhalla,

125. Ibid, p, ix-x.

126. Ibid.

127. Ibid.

128. Ibid.

129. Ibid, p. x.

130. Strong, David. (1995). *Crazy Mountains: Learning from wilderness to weigh technology.* Albany, NY: SUNY, p. 6.

131. Ibid, p. 3.

132. Ibid, p. 205.

133. Ibid, p. 205.

134. Ibid, p. 205.

135. Ibid, p. 205.

136. Ibid, p. 206.

137. Stevens, Anthony. (1990). *On Jung.* New York, NY: Penguin, p. 44.

138. Jung, C.G. (1928/1971). Relations between the ego and the unconscious. In Joseph Campbell (Ed.), *The Portable Jung* (pp.70-138). New York, NY: Penguin, p. 121.

139. Ibid, p. 105

140. Jung, C. G. (1938). *Pyschology and religion.* New Haven, CT: Yale University Press, p. 100.

141. Stevens, p. 41.

142. Jung, C. G. (1968). *Analytical psychology: Its theory and practice.* New York: Random House, pp. 137-138.

143. Ibid.

144. Sabini, Meredith. (Ed.) (2002). *C.G. Jung on nature, technology & modern life.* Berkeley, CA: North Atlantic Book.

145. Ibid, p. 9.

146. Ibid.

147. Ibid, p. 4.

148. Ibid, pp. 7-8, quoting from C.G. Jung Letters, Vol. II, p. 607.

149. The actual origin of the saying is apparently unknown. See, http://www.answers.com/topic/there-is-nothing-so-good-for-the-inside-of-a-man-as-the-outside-of-a-horse .

150. Glendinning, pp. 4-5.

151. Ibid, p. 5.

152. Hofmann, Albert (1979/2005). *LSD, my problem child: Reflections on sacred drugs, mysticism and science.* Sarasota, FL: MAPS, p. 47.

153. Ibid, p. 47.

154. Ibid, p. 29.

155. Ibid.

156. Ibid, p. 30.

157. Ibid, p. 31.

158. See, http://www.maps.org/research/psilo-lsd.

159. Grof, Stanislav (2006). *When the impossible happens: Adventures in non-ordinary realities.* Boulder, CO: Sounds True, pp. xxix-xxxv.

160. Ibid, p. xxxiii.

161. Ibid, p. xxxiii.

162. Ibid.

163. Ibid, p. xxxiv.

164. Stanislav Grof. (1985). *Beyond the Brain: Birth, Death, and Transcendence in Psychotherapy.* Albany, NY: SUNY, p. 192.

165. Grof, Stanislav (2012). *Healing our deepest wounds: The holotropic paradigm shift.* Newcastle, WA: Stream of Consciousness Productions, p. 11, citing Sutich, Anthony (1976). The emergence of the transpersonal orientation: A personal account. *Journal of Transpersonal Psychology, 8,* 5-19.

166. Grof, *Healing our deepest wounds,* p. 13.

167. Grof, Stanislav & Grof, Christina (Eds.) (1989). *Spiritual emergency: When personal transformation becomes a crisis.* Los Angeles, CA: Tarcher, p. 2.

168. http://www.realitysandwich.com/spiritual_emergencies; see also, Grof, Stanislav (2000). *Psychology of the future: Lessons from modern consciousness research.* Albany, NY: SUNY, p. 137.

169. http://en.wikipedia.org/wiki/Spiritual_crisis

170. Ibid, p. xv.

171. http://www.holotropic.com/about.shtml

172. Ibid.

173. Ibid.

174. Malcolm, Janet (2013, September 23). Profiles: Nobody's looking at you: Eileen Fisher and the art of understatement. *The New Yorker,* p. 60.

175. Ruumet, Hillevi. (2006). *Pathways of the soul: Exploring the human journey.* Victoria, Canada: Trafford Publishing.

176. Smirnova, Marina. (2013). *Atonement with the dreadful manifestations of the sacred in Holotropic Breathwork: Interpretive phenomenological analysis of the breather's embodied experience and the meaning arising within and out of it.* Unpublished doctoral dissertation, Sofia University, formerly Institute of Transpersonal Psychology, Palo Alto, CA.

177. Ibid, p. 8, quoting Otto, Rudolf. (1923/1958). *The idea of the holy*. New York, NY: Oxford University Press, p. 16, 62.

178. Smirnova, p. iii.

179. Ibid.

180. Ibid.

181. Peter Levine. (1997). *Waking the tiger: Healing trauma*. Berkeley, CA: North Atlantic Books.

182. Ibid, p. 19.

183. Ibid.

184. On the question of being good, see Mary Oliver's poem, *Wild Geese,* which advises one need not be good, "You only have to let the soft animal of your body love what it loves." http://www.rjgeib.com/thoughts/geese/geese. html; Oliver, Mary (1992). *New and selected poems: Mary Oliver.* Boston, MA: Beacon Press, p. 110.

185. See https://www.google.com/?gws_rd=ssl#q=Words+to+song+rocket+man

186. Jacobson, Bertil, Nyberg, Karin, Gronbladh, Leif, Eklund, Gunnar, Bygdeman, Marc, & Rydberg, Ulf (1990). Opiate addiction in adult offspring through possible imprinting after obstetric treatment. *British Medical Journal, 301*,1067-1070.

187. Jacobson, Bertil, Nyberg, Karin, Eklund, Gunnar, Bygdeman, Marc, & Rydberg, Ulf. (1988). Obstetric pain medication and eventual adult amphetamine addiction in offspring. *Acta Obstet Gynaecol. Scand., 6,* 677-682.

188. See http://gnosis.org/Evans-Jung-Interview/evans2.html

189. http://gnosis.org/Evans-Jung-Interview/evans2.html

190. Stanislav Grof. (1988). *The adventure of self-discovery: Dimensions of consciousness and new perspectives in psychotherapy and inner exploration.* Albany, NY: State University of New York Press; Stanislav Grof, with Hal Zina Bennet. (1993). *The holotropic mind: The three levels of human consciousness and how they shape our lives.* San Francisco: HarperSanFrancisco.

191. Grof, Stanislav & Grof, Christina (2010). *Holotropic Breathwork: A new approach to self-exploration and therapy.* Albany, NY: SUNY, p. 15; see also, Grof, Stanislav. (1975). *Realms of the human unconscious: Observations from LSD research.* New York: Viking Press, republished in 2009 as *LSD: Doorway to the numinous: The ground-breaking psychedelic research into realms of the human unconscious.* Rochester, VT: Park Street Press; and Grof, Stanislav. (2000). *Psychology of the future: Lessons from modern consciousness research.* Albany, NY: SUNY.

192. http://www.naap.nl/Bronnen/Artikelen/complexen/main.htm   (retrieved 10/13/13).

193. Grof & Grof, *Holotropic breathwork*, p. 15.

194. Grof, Stanislav. (1985). *Beyond the brain: Birth, death and transcendence in psychotherapy*. Albany, NY: SUNY.

195. Grof, Stanislav, *Beyond the brain*, p. 191.

196. Grof & Grof, *Holotropic breathwork*, p. 15.

197. Grof, Stanislav, *Beyond the Brain,* p. 127.
198. Ibid, p. 191.
199. Ibid. p. 192.
200. Ibid.
201. Ibid.
202. Ibid.
203. Ibid.
204. Ibid.
205. Ibid, p. 222.
206. Ibid.
207. Marzluff, John & Angell, Tony (2012). *Gifts of the crow: How perception, emotion, and thought allow smart birds to behave like humans.* New York, NY: Simon & Schuster.
208. Ibid, p. xi.
209. http://www.saveourlake.org/
210. Grof, Stanislav. (2006). *The ultimate journey: Consciousness and the mystery of death.* Ben Lomond, CA: MAPS.
211. Shakespeare. *The tempest,* Act IV, Scene 1.
212. Grof, Stanislav (2000). *Psychology of the future: Lessons from modern consciousness research.* Albany, NY: SUNY, p. 218.
213. Ibid.
214. Ibid.
215. Ibid.
216. Bache, Christopher M. (2000). *Dark night, early dawn.* Albany, NY: SUNY, p. 257.
217. Ibid.
218. Ibid, p. 256.
219. Grof, Stanislav (2012). *Healing our deepest wounds: The holotropic paradigm shift.* Newcastle, WA: Stream of Consciousness Productions, p. 191.
220. McKenna, Terrence (1992). *Food of the gods: The search for the original tree of knowledge.* New York, NY: Bantam Books, p.
221. Grof, *Healing our deepest wounds*, p. 191.
222. See, http://www.webexhibits.org/colorart/mood.html; http://www.people.vcu.edu/~djbromle/modern04/paulh/
223. Swan, James A. (1990). *Sacred places: How the living earth seeks our friendship.* Santa Fe, NM: Bear & Company, p. 221.
224. Gates, Robert. (2014). *Duty: Memoir of a secretary at war.* New York, NY: Knopf.
225. Transcript: Former Defense Secretary Robert Gates' Interview with NPR. http://www.npr.org/2014/01/11/261711869/transcript-former-defense-secretary-robert-gates-interview-with-npr
226. Rothschild, Babette (2000). *The body remembers: The psychophysiology of trauma and trauma treatment.* New York, NY: W. W. Norton & Company, p. 63.

227. Cosgrove, Mary Catherine. (1973). *Breathing, crying, and gestalt therapy.* Unpublished Doctoral Dissertation, University of South Dakota, Vermillion, South Dakota.

228. Weiss, Joseph. (1952). Crying at the happy ending. *Psychoanalytic Review, 39*(4), 338.

229. http://www.wikihow.com/Cry-and-Let-It-All-Out

230. Sadoff, Robert L. (1966). On the nature of crying and weeping. *Psychiatric Quarterly, 40*(3), 490-503.

231. Sparks, supra.

232. Romanyshyn, Robert (2002). *Ways of the heart: Essays toward an imaginal psychology.* Pittsburgh, PA: Trivium Publications, p. 55.

233. Freud, Sigmund (1989). Mourning and melancholia. In *The Freud Reader* (Peter Gay, Ed.). pp. 584-589. New York, NY: W. W. Norton & Company.

234. Kubler-Ross, Elizabeth. (1969). *On death and dying.* New York, NY: Macmillan.

235. Maciejewski, Paul K., Ph.D., Zhang, Baohui Zhang, M.S., Block, Susan D., M.D., Prigerson, & Holly G., Ph.D. (2007). An empirical examination of the stage theory of grief, *Journal of the American Medical Association, 297*(7) 716-723.

236. Tatelbaum, Judy (1980). *The courage to grieve: Creative living, recovery and growth through grief.* New York: Harper & Row, p. 9.

237. E.g., Klein, Melanie. (1935). A contribution to the psychogenesis of manic-depressive states. *Interntaional Journal of Psycho-Analysis, 16,* 145-174; Klein, Melanie. (1940). Mourning and its relation to manic-depressive states. *International Journal of Psycho-Analysis, 21,* 125-153.

238. See Wilber, Ken. (1981). *Up from Eden: A transpersonal view of human evolution.* New York, NY: Quest Books*; and The Atman project, supra.*

239. Masterson, James F. (1988). *The search for the real self: Unmasking the personality disorders of our age.* New York, NY: The Free Press.

240. Ibid, p. 23 (emphasis in original).

241. Ibid.

242. Ibid.

243. Wolfe, Thomas. (1934/1990). *You can't go home again.* New York, NY: Scribner, p. 39.

244. Masterson, pp. 218-219.

245. Milloff, Ina C. (1997). *Loss at the heart of our being: Core Issues in separation-individuation and the process of becoming.* Unpublished doctoral dissertation, Prescott College, Tucson, AZ, p. 5.

246. Ibid, pp. 91-92.

247. Edwards, Mark. (1997). Being present: Experiential connection between Zen Buddhist practices and the grieving process. *Disability and Rehabilitation, 19*(10), 442-451.

248. Ibid, p. 446.

249. Ibid.

250. Ibid, p. 445.

251. Bernstein, Jerome S. (2005). *Living in the borderland: The evolution of consciousness and the challenge of healing trauma.* New York, NY: Routledge, p. 73.

252. Ibid.

253. Ibid.

254. See Chevalier, Tracy. (1999). *Girl with a pearl earring: A novel.* New York, NY: Plume.

255. Borgquist, Alvin. (1906). Crying. *The American Journal of Psychology, 17*(2), 149-205.

256. Flescher, Joachim (1955). A dualistic view on anxiety. *Journal of the American Psychoanalytic Association, 3,* 415-446.

257. Braud, William G. (2001). Experiencing tears of wonder-joy: Seeing with the heart's eye. *Journal of Transpersonal Psychology, 33,* 99-111.

258. Ibid, p. 100.

259. Ibid, p. 101.

260. Ibid, pp. 103-104

261. Ibid, p. 105.

262. Ibid, p. 103.

263. Ibid, p. 104.

264. Ibid, p. 103.

265. Ibid, p. 107.

266. Ibid.

267. Ibid, p. 106.

268. Ibid, p. 109.

269. Anderson, Rosemarie. (1996). Nine psycho-spiritual characteristics of spontaneous and involuntary weeping. *Journal of Transpersonal Psychology, 28*(2), 167-173.

270. Ibid, p. 167.

271. Ibid, pp. 168-171.

272. Ibid, p. 170.

273. Ibid.

274. Ibid.

275. Van Heukelem, Judith F. (1979). "Weep with those who weep": Understanding and helping the crying person, *Journal of Psychology and Theology, 7*(2), 83-91.

276. Ibid, p. 87.

277. Vingerhoets, Ad (2013). *Why only humans weep: Unraveling the mysteries of tears.* Oxford, UK: Oxford University Press, p. 237, citing Lutz, Tom (1999). *Crying: a natural and cultural history of tears.* New York, NY: W.W. Norton & Company.

278. Vingerhoets, p. 237.

279. http://www.saintbrigid.net/column07/post.01.21.07.html.

280. Pagels, Elaine. (1979). *The Gnostic gospels.* New York, NY: Vintage Books, p. xv.

281. Moore, Ernest O. (1981) A prison environment's effect on health care service demands. *Journal of Environmental Systems, 11,* 17–34.

282. Ulrich, Roger S. (1984) View through a window may influence recovery from surgery. *Science, 224*, 420–421.
283. http://www.scientificamerican.com/article.cfm?id=nature-that-nurtures
284. Ibid.
285. Wilson, Edward O. (1984). *Biophilia.* Cambridge, MA: Harvard University Press.
286. Berman, Marc G., Jonides, John, & Kaplan, Stephen. (2008). The cognitive benefits of interacting with nature. *Psychological Science, 19*(12), 1207-1212.
287. Ibid, p. 1207.
288. Ibid.
289. Kaplan, Rachel & Kaplan, Stephen. (1989). *The experience of nature: A psychological perspective.* Cambridge, UK: Cambridge University Press.
290. Pretty, Jules, Peacock, Jo, Sellens, Martin, & Griffin, Murray (2005). The mental and physical health outcomes of green exercises. *International Journal of Environmental Health Research, 15*(5), 319-337.
291. Kuppuswamy, Hemavathy. (2009). Improving health in cities using green infrastructure: a review. FORUM Ejournal (December 2009): 63-76. Newcastle University.
292. Wells, Nancy M., & Evans, Gary W. (2003). Nearby nature: A buffer of life stress among rural children. *Environment and Behavior, 35*(3), 311-330.
293. Nisbet, Elizabeth K., Zelenski, John M., & Murphy, Steven A. (2009). The nature relatedness scale: Linking individuals' connection with nature to environmental concern and behavior. *Environment and Behavior, 41*(5), 715-740.
294. Martyn, Patricia & Brymer, Eric. (2014). The relationship between nature relatedness and anxiety. *Journal of Health Psychology,* 1-10.
295. Zelenski, John M. & Nisbet, Elizabeth K. (2014). Happiness and feeling connected: The distinct role of nature relatedness. *Environment and Behavior , 46,* 1, 3-23.
296. Maller, Cecily, Townsend, Mardie , Pryor, Anita, Brown, Peter & St. Leger, Lawrence. (2005). *Healthy nature healthy people: 'contact with nature' as an upstream health promotion intervention for populations.* Oxford, UK: Oxford University Press, p. 46.
297. Ibid.
298. Ibid, p. 51.
299. Ibid, p. 52.
300. Ibid.
301. Naess, Arne (1973). The shallow and the deep ecology movements. *Inquiry, 16,* 95-100.
302. Conn, Sarah A. (1998). Living in the Earth: Ecopsychology, health, and psychotherapy. *The Humanistic Psychologist, 26,* 1-3, 179-198, p. 196.
303. Ibid, p. 181.
304. Ibid, p. 183.
305. Ibid.

306. Ibid.
307. Ibid.
308. Ibid.
309. Ibid, p. 184.
310. Ibid.
311. Ibid, p. 197.
312. See Macy, Joanna & Brown, Molly Young. (1998). *Coming back to life: practices to reconnect our lives, our world.* Gabriola Island, Canada: New Society Publishers; Macy, Joanna. (1991). *World as lover: World as self.* Berkeley, CA: Parallax Press.
313. Macy, Joanna. (1983). *Despair and personal power in the nuclear age.* Philadelphia: New Society Publishers, p. 21.
314. Macy, Joanna. (1998). Preface. In Joanna Macy & Molly Young Brown. (1998). *Coming back to life: Practices to reconnect our lives, our world.* Gabriola Island, Canada: New Society Publishers, p. 5.
315. Ibid, p. 77.
316. Sessions, George. (1995). Preface. In George Sessions (Ed.), *Deep ecology for the 21st century: Readings on the philosophy and practice of the new environmentalism.* Boston, MA: Shambhala, p. ix.
317. Fox, Warwick. (1995). Toward a transpersonal ecology: Developing new foundations for environmentalism. Albany, NY: SUNY.
318. Ibid, p. 198.
319. http://en.wikipedia.org/wiki/Anthropocentrism, citing Merriam-Webster dictionary definition.
320. Ferrer, Jorge N. (2002). *Revisioning transpersonal theory: A participatory vision of human spirituality.* Albany, NY: SUNY.
321. Ibid, p. 116.
322. Ibid, p. 118.
323. Levin, p. 301, 302.
324. Swimme, Brian & Berry, Thomas. (1994). *The universe story: From the primordial flaring forth to the ecozoic era—a celebration of the unfolding of the cosmos.* New York, NY: HarperOne.
325. See http://www.journeyoftheuniverse.org/testimonials/
326. See Wilber, Ken. (2007). *The integral vision: A very short introduction to the revolutionary integral approach to life, god, the universe and everything.* Boston, MA: Shambhala.
327. Clinebell, Howard. (1996). *Ecotherapy: Healing ourselves, healing the earth.* New York, NY: The Haworth Press, p. 25.
328. Ibid, p. 189.
329. Ibid, p. 194.
330. Ibid.
331. Ibid, p. 206.
332. Ibid.
333. Ibid, p. 109-110.
334. Burns, George W. (1998). *Nature-guided therapy: Brief integrative strategies for health and well-being.* Bristol, PA: Brunner/Mazei, p. 20.

335. Ibid.

336. Ibid, p. 56.

337. Berger, Ronen. (2007). The therapeutic aspect of nature therapy. *Therapy through the Arts—the Journal of the Israeli Association of Creative and Expressive Therapies, 3,* 60-69.

338. Ibid.

339. Conn, p. 179.

340. Ibid, p. 182, citing Mazer, Don. (1996). *Ecopsychology and psychopathology: Contributions of a nature-based psychology for understanding human problems.* University of Prince Edward Island Department of Psychology, Unpublished manuscript.

341. Conn, p. 182.

342. Ibid, p. 186.

343. Ibid.

344. Ibid.

345. Ibid, p. 188.

346. Davis-Berman, Jennifer & Berman, Dene S. (1994). *Wilderness therapy: Foundations, theory & research.* Dubuque, IA: Kendall Hunt.

347. Levine, Deborah. (1994). Breaking through barriers: Wilderness therapy for sexual assault survivors. In Ellen Cole, Eve Erdman, & Esther D. Rothblum (Eds.) (1994). *Wilderness therapy for women: The power of adventure.* New York, NY: The Haworth Press, p. 175-185.

348. Cole, Ellen, Erdman, Eve, & Rothblum, Esther D. (Eds.) (1994). *Wilderness therapy for women: The power of adventure.* New York: The Haworth Press, p. 2.

349. Powch, Irene. *Wilderness therapy: What makes it empowering for women?* In Ellen Cole, Eve Erdman, & Esther D. Rothblum (Eds.) (1994). *Wilderness therapy for women: The power of adventure.* New York, NY: The Haworth Press, pp. 12-13.

350. Ibid, p. 17.

351. Ibid, p. 18.

352. Ibid, p. 19.

353. Ibid, p. 19

354. Coburn, Merry J. (2006). *Walking home: Women's transformative experiences in the wilderness of the Appalachian Trail.* Unpublished Doctoral Dissertation, Institute of Transpersonal Psychology, Palo Alto, CA.

355. Ibid.

356. Cumes, David, M.D. (1998). *Inner passages: Outer journeys.* St. Paul, MN: Llewellyn Publications, p. 37.

357. Cumes, David, M.D. (1999). *The spirit of healing: Venture into the wilderness to rediscover the healing force.* St. Paul, MN: Llewellyn Publications.

358. Macy, Joanna. (1983). *Despair and personal power in the nuclear age.* Philadelphia: New Society Publishers, p. 21.

359. St. Augustine. *City of God,* X.3.

360. See http://www.theparadigmshifts.com/

361. American Heritage Dictionary of the English Language (1973); http://www. thefreedictionary.com/ecology.

362. http://www.thefreedictionary.com/ecology.

363. See http://www.teemingbrain.com/2009/05/09/its-official-the-human-race-is-earths-disease/

364. Carson, Rachel (1962). *Silent spring*. New York, NY: Houghton Mifflin.

365. Paull, John (2013). The Rachel Carson letters and the making of *Silent Spring*. *SAGE Open, 2013, 1-12,* p. 1; *see http://orgprints.org/22934/7/22934.pdf.*

366. Ibid.

367. Ibid, p. 1, quoting Marvin, P. H. (1967). Pesticides: Overstated dangers, *Science, 156*(3771), p. 14.

368. Ibid.

369. Ibid, p. 2.

370. http://www.thefreedictionary.com/ecological .

371. http://en.wikipedia.org/wiki/Keep_America_Beautiful

372. http://www.ehow.com/about_5090820_definition-ecological-footprints. html; Rees, William E., Wackernagel, Mathis, & Testemale, Phil (1996.) *Our ecological footprint: Reducing human impact on the earth.* Gabriola Island, Canada: New Society Publishers.

373. Rees, William (2010). The Human Nature of Unsustainability. In Heinberg, Richard & Leich,Daniel. *The post carbon reader: Managing the 21st century sustainability crisis.* Santa Rosa, CA: Post Carbon Institute; http://www.postcarbon.org/publications/human-nature-of-unsustainability/

374. Ibid.

375. Ibid.

376. Taylor, Jeremy (1983). *Dream work: Techniques for discovering the creative power in dreams.* Mahwah, NJ: Paulist Press; Taylor, Jeremy (2009). *The wisdom of your dreams: Using dreams to tap into your unconscious and transform your life.* New York, NY: Jeremy P. Tarcher.

377. Peterson, Christopher, Maier, Steven F., & Seligman, Martin E. P. (1995). *Learned helplessness: A theory for the age of personal control.* New York: Oxford University Press.

378. Bennett, K.K., & Elliott, M. (2005). Pessimistic explanatory style and cardiac health: What is the relation and the mechanism that links them? *Basic and applied social psychology, 27,* 239–248.

379. Glendinning, p. 160.

380. Ibid, p. 170

381. http://www.huxley.net/ah/aldous-quote.html

382. Jung, Carl (1986). *The collected works of C.G. Jung: Symbolic life: Miscellaneous writings,* ¶ 585. Princeton, NJ: Princeton University Press.

383. Harding, M. Esther (1965). *The I and the not I.* Princeton, NJ: Bolingen,

384. http://fwp.mt.gov/fishAndWildlife/management/wolf/history.html

385. Ibid.

386. Ibid.

387. Ibid.

388. Ibid.

389. See http://www.city-data.com/forum/politics-other-controversies/751264-wolves-kill-over-100-sheep-one.html

390. See, e.g., http://www.npr.org/templates/story/story.php?storyId=106687768. National Public Radio story on "Silence Broken on Red Army Rapes in Germany."

391. http://missoulian.com/news/state-and-regional/adventures-in-wolf-recovery-ending-for-ed-bangs-as-he/article_87e7bc68-6e2a-11e0-b553-001cc4c03286.html

392. Freedman, Adam H., Gronau, Ilan, Schweizer, Rena M., Ortega-Del Vecchyo, Diego, Han, Eunjung, Silva, Pedro M., ... Novembre, John (16 January 2014). Genome Sequencing Highlights Genes Under Selection and the Dynamic Early History of Dogs, *PLOS Genetics (PLOS Org) 10* (1).

393. Ibid.

394. http://www.imdb.com/title/tt0427312/quotes

395. Conrad, Joseph. (1899/1980). *Heart of darkness.* Norwalk, CT: The Easton Press.

396. Ibid, p. 99.

397. Ibid., p. 100.

398. Ibid, p. 105

399. Gurko, Leo. (1980). An introduction. In Conrad, Joseph. (1980/1899). *Heart of Darkness,* Norwalk, CT: The Easton Press, p. xvi.

400. Ibid, p. xvii.

401. See http://www.sfgate.com/news/article/Kaczynski-motive-Rage-not-politics-3092255.php

402. Ibid.

403. Rosemarie Anderson (personal communication, January 17, 2014)

404. Squires, Emily & Belzer, Len. (2000). *Spiritual places in and around New York City.* New York, NY: Paraview Press. For a description of Emily's work and life, see http://en.wikipedia.org/wiki/Emily_Squires.

405. Buhner, Stephen Harrod (2014). *Plant intelligence and the imaginal realm: Into the dreaming of the earth.* Rochester, VT: Bear & Co., p. 84.

406. Ibid, p. 84.

407. Ibid, p. 360.

408. Ibid., p. 360.

409. Ibid., p. 384.

410. Ibid, p. 384.

411. Read, Tim. (2014). *Walking shadows: Archetype and psyche in crisis and growth.* London, UK: Muswell Hill Press.

412. Ibid, p. 261.

413. Ibid, p. 261.

414. Jung, Carl (1986). *The collected works of C.G. Jung: Symbolic life: Miscellaneous writings,* ¶585. Princeton, NJ: Princeton University Press.

415. Bosnak, Robert. (1996). *Tracks in the wilderness of dreaming.* New York, NY: Delacorte Press.

416. Eliade, Mircea (1951/1964/1972). *Shamanism: Archaic techniques of ecstasy.* Princeton, NJ: Princeton University Press; Harner, Michael (1980/1990). *The way of the shaman.* San Francisco, CA: HarperSanFrancisco.

417. Harner, p. 2.

418. Ibid, p. 3.

419. Buhner, p. 384.

420. Eliade, p. 89.

421. Jung, Carl G. (1964). *Man and his symbols.* New York, NY: Doubleday, p. 20.

422. Ibid, p. 21.

423. Ibid, p. 21.

424. Jung, Carl Gustav. (1921/1971). *Collected Works of C.G. Jung.* Princeton, N.J.: Princeton University Press, ¶781.

425. Ibid, ¶12.

426. Tarnas, Richard. (1991). *The passion of the western mind: Understanding the ideas that have shaped our world view.* New York, NY: Ballantine Books.

427. Translated from the Spanish by Vicki Capestany.

428. http://www.gratefulness.org/readings/dsr_AboutTheHeart.htm

429. Ibid.

430. Ibid.

431. Steindl-Rast, David. (1984). *Gratefulness, the heart of prayer: An approach to life in fullness.* Ramsey, NJ: The Paulist Press, p. 9.

432. http://fearlessrevolution.com/adam-butler/.

433. http://fearlessrevolution.com/about/.

434. Balk, Amber. (2015). *Doing death differently: An integrative-holotropic community action research project.* Unpublished doctoral dissertation, Sofia University, formerly Institute of Transpersonal Psychology, Palo Alto, CA.

435. Strong, p. 206.

436. Ibid.

437. Snyder, Joan. (1989). *The experience of really feeling connected to nature.* Unpublished doctoral dissertation, Union Institute Graduate School, Cincinatti, OH, p. 1-2.

438. Ibid, p. 110.

439. Ibid.

440. Ibid.

441. Ibid, p. 106.

442. Ibid, p. 100.

443. Ibid, p. 101.

444. Martyn & Brymer, p. 1.

445. Ibid, p. 7.

446. Ibid.

447. Ibid.

448. Ruffing, Janet. (1997). "To have been one with the earth...": Nature in contemporary Christian mystical experience. *Presence: The Journal of Spiritual Directors International, 3*(1), 40-54, p. 44.
449. Ibid, p. 42.
450. Ibid, pp. 42-44.
451. Ibid, p. 44
452. Ibid, p. 45
453. Ibid, p. 48.
454. Ibid, p. 47
455. See, Maslow, Abraham. (1970). *Religion, values and peak experiences.* New York, NY: Viking; Maslow, Abraham. (1970). *Religious aspects of peak experiences: Personality and religion.* New York, NY: Harper & Row; Maslow, Abraham. (1971). *The farther reaches of human nature.* New York, NY: Viking Press.
456. DeMares, Ryan, & Krycka, Kevin. (1998). Wild-animal triggered peak experiences: Transpersonal aspects. *Journal of Transpersonal Psychology, 30*(2), 161-177.
457. DeMares & Krycka, p. 175.
458. Maslow, *Religions, values and peak experiences*, p. 19.
459. Swan, James. (1992). *The power of place.* Wheaton, IL: Quest Books.
460. Dowdall, Samantha. (1998). *Roots of the spirit: Interrelationships among ecological actions and attitudes, nature-related exceptional human experiences, spirituality, and well-being.* Unpublished Doctoral Dissertation, Institute of Transpersonal Psychology, Palo Alto, CA.
461. Kals, Elisabeth., Schumacher, Daniel, & Montada, Leo (1999). Emotional affinity toward nature as a motivational basis to protect nature. *Environment and Behavior, 31*, 178-202, p. 182, cited and quoted in Drake, Barbara Dawn (2012). *Nature photography and the ecological self: An exploration of college students' experience of an environmental photography assignment.* Unpublished Doctoral Dissertation, Institute of Transpersonal Psychology, Palo Alto, CA.
462. See, e.g., Coburn, *supra;* Nisbet, Elizabeth K. (2005). *The human-nature connection: Increasing nature relatedness, environmental concern, and well-being through education.* M.A. Thesis, Carleton University.
463. Drake, *supra.*
464. Ruumet, p. 136.
465. Berry, Thomas (1999). *The great work: Our way into the future.* New York, NY: Bell Tower, p. 159.
466. McMurtry, Larry. (1985). *Lonesome Dove.* New York, NY: Simon & Schuster.
467. http://www.epa.gov/asbestos/pubs/verm.html
468. See, http://en.wikipedia.org/wiki/Berkeley_Pit
469. Weisman, Alan. (2007). *The world without us.* New York, NY: St. Martin's Press.

470. Ibid, p. 4.
471. Ibid, p. 128.
472. Ward, Peter. (2001). *Future evolution.* New York, NY: Times Books.
473. Weisman, p. 232.
474. Sullivan, Robert (2006). *Rats: Observations on the history and habitat of the city's most unwanted habitants.* New York, NY: Bloomsbury.
475. http://www.gratefulness.org/readings/dsr_AboutTheHeart.htm
476. http://www.gratefulness.org/readings/dsr_AboutTheHeart.htm
477. Elliot, T.S. (1943). *Little Gidding.* See http://www.columbia.edu/itc/history/winter/w3206/edit/tseliotlittlegidding.htm

Bibliography

Abram, David. (1996). *The spell of the sensuous.* New York, NY: Vintage Books.

Abram, David. (2010). *Becoming animal: An earthly cosmology.* New York, NY: Vintage Books.

Anderson, Rosemarie. (1996). Nine psycho-spiritual characteristics of spontaneous and involuntary weeping. *Journal of Transpersonal Psychology, 28*(2), 167-173.

Anderson, Rosemarie. (2004). Intuitive inquiry: An epistemology of the heart for scientific inquiry. *The Humanistic Psychologist, 32*(4).

Anderson, Rosemarie. (2011). Intuitive inquiry: Exploring the mirroring discourse of disease. In Wertz, Frederick J., Charmaz, Kathy, McMullen, Linda M., Josselson, Ruthellen, Anderson, Rosemarie & McSpadden, Emalinda, *Five ways of doing qualitative analysis: Phenomenological psychology, grounded theory, discourse analysis, narrative research, and intuitive inquiry*. New York, NY: The Guilford Press.

Anderson, Rosemarie & Braud, William. (2011). *Transforming self and others through research: Transpersonal research methods and skills for the human sciences and humanities*. Albany, NY: SUNY.

Bache, Christopher M. (2000). *Dark night, early dawn.* Albany, NY: SUNY.

Bacon, Francis. (1597/1986). *The essays.* New York, NY: Penguin.

Balk, Amber. (2015). *Doing death differently: An integrative-holotropic community action research project.* Unpublished doctoral dissertation, Sofia University, formerly Institute of Transpersonal Psychology, Palo Alto, CA.

Barber, Benjamin. *Jihad v. McWorld.* (1995). New York, NY: Ballantine Books.

Baudrillard, Jean. (1976/1988). *Selected writing.* Stanford, CA: Stanford University Press.

Baudrillard, Jean. (1994). *Simulacra and simulation. The precession of simulacra.* Ann Arbor, MI: University of Michigan Press.

Bennett, K.K., & Elliott, M. (2005). Pessimistic explanatory style and cardiac health: What is the relation and the mechanism that links them? *Basic and Applied Social Psychology, 27*, 239–248.

Berger, Ronen. (2007). The therapeutic aspect of nature therapy. *Therapy through the Arts—the Journal of the Israeli Association of Creative and Expressive Therapies, 3*, 60-69.

Berman, Morris. (2000). *Wandering God: A study in nomadic spirituality.* Albany, NY: SUNY.

Berman, Marc G., Jonides, John, and Kaplan, Stephen. (2008). The cognitive benefits of interacting with nature. *Psychological Science, 19*(12), 1207-1212.

Bernstein, Jerome S. (2005). *Living in the borderland: The evolution of consciousness and the challenge of healing trauma.* New York, NY: Routledge.

Berry, Thomas. (1999). *The great work: Our way into the future.* New York, NY: Bell Tower.

Borgquist, Alvin. (1906). Crying. *The American Journal of Psychology, 17*(2), 149-205.

Bosnak, Robert. (1996). *Tracks in the wilderness of dreaming.* New York, NY: Delacorte Press.

Braud, William G. (2001). Experiencing tears of wonder-joy: Seeing with the heart's eye. *Journal of Transpersonal Psychology, 33*, 99-111.

Braud, William & Anderson, Rosemarie. (1998). *Transpersonal research methods for the social sciences: Honoring human experience.* Thousand Oaks, CA: Sage.

Buhner, Stephen Harrod. (2014). *Plant intelligence and the imaginal realm: Into the dreaming of the earth.* Rochester, VT: Bear & Co.

Burns, George W. (1998). *Nature-guided therapy: Brief integrative strategies for health and well-being.* Bristol, PA: Brunner/Mazei.

Capra, Fritjof. (1975). *The tao of physics: An exploration of the parallels between modern physics and eastern mysticism.* Boston, MA: Shambhala.

Carson, Rachel. (1962). *Silent spring.* New York, NY: Houghton Mifflin.

Clinebell, Howard. (1996). *Ecotherapy: Healing ourselves, healing the earth.* New York, NY: The Haworth Press.

Chomsky, Noam. (2008). *The essential Chomsky* (Anthony Arnove, Ed.) New York, NY: The New Press.

Cole, Ellen, Erdman, Eve, Rothblum, Esther D. (Eds.) (1994). *Wilderness therapy for women: The power of adventure.* New York, NY: The Haworth Press.

Conn, Sarah A. (1998). Living in the Earth: Ecopsychology, health, and psychotherapy. *The Humanistic Psychologist, 26,* 1-3, 179-198.

Conrad, Joseph. (1899/1980). *Heart of darkness.* Norwalk, CT: The Easton Press.

Cosgrove, Mary Catherine. (1973). *Breathing, crying, and gestalt therapy.* Unpublished Doctoral Dissertation, University of South Dakota, Vermillion, South Dakota

Cumes, David, M.D. (1998). *Inner passages: Outer journeys.* St. Paul, MN: Llewellyn Publications.

Cumes, David, M.D. (1999). *The spirit of healing: Venture into the wilderness to rediscover the healing force.* St. Paul, MN: Llewellyn Publications.

Davis-Berman, Jennifer, & Berman, Dene S. (1994). *Wilderness therapy: Foundations, theory & research.* Dubuque, IA: Kendall Hunt.

DeMares, Ryan, & Krycka, Kevin. (1998). Wild-animal triggered peak experiences: Transpersonal aspects. *Journal of Transpersonal Psychology, 30*(2), 161-177.

Dowdall, Samantha. (1998). *Roots of the spirit: Interrelationships among ecological actions and attitudes, nature-related exceptional human experiences, spirituality, and well-being.* Unpublished Doctoral Dissertation, Institute of Transpersonal Psychology, Palo Alto, CA.

Drake, Barbara Dawn. (2012). *Nature photography and the ecological self: An exploration of college students' experience of an environmental photography assignment.* Unpublished Doctoral Dissertation, Institute of Transpersonal Psychology, Palo Alto, CA.

Dufrechou, Jay P. (2002). *Coming home to nature through the body: An intuitive inquiry into experiences of grief, weeping and other deep emotions in response to nature.* Unpublished Doctoral Dissertation, Institute of Transpersonal Psychology, Palo Alto, CA

Eden, Amnon, Moor, James, Søraker, Johnny, & Steinhart, Eric (Eds.) (2013). *Singularity hypotheses: A scientific and philosophical assessment.* New York, NY: Springer.

Edwards, Mark. (1997). Being present: Experiential connection between Zen Buddhist practices and the grieving process. *Disability and Rehabilitation, 19*(10), 442-451.

Eliade, Mircea (1951). *Shamanism: Archaic techniques of ecstasy.* Princeton, NJ: Princeton University Press.

Ferrer, Jorge N. (2002). *Revisioning transpersonal theory: A participatory vision of human spirituality.* Albany, NY: SUNY.

Flescher, Joachim. (1955). A dualistic view on anxiety. *Journal of the American Psychoanalytic Association, 3,* 415-446.

Fox, Warwick. (1995). *Toward a transpersonal ecology: Developing new foundations for environmentalism.* Albany, NY: SUNY.

Foxe, Arthur N. (1941). The therapeutic effects of crying. *Medical Record—New York, 153,* 167-168.

Freedman, Adam H., Gronau, Ilan, Schweizer, Rena M., Ortega-Del Vecchyo, Diego, Han, Eunjung, Silva, Pedro M., ... Novembre, John. (16 January 2014). Genome Sequencing Highlights Genes Under Selection and the Dynamic Early History of Dogs, *PLOS Genetics (PLOS Org) 10* (1).

Freud, Sigmund. (1989). Mourning and melancholia. In *The Freud reader* (Peter Gay, Ed.). New York, NY: W. W. Norton & Company.

Gates, Robert. (2014). *Duty: Memoir of a secretary at war.* New York, NY: Knopf.

Gendlin, Eugene, Beebe, J., Cassens, J., Klein, M., & Oberlander, M. (1968). Focusing ability in psychotherapy, personality, and creativity. In J. M. Shlein (Ed.), *Research in psychotherapy: Vol. II.* Washington, D. C.: American Psychological Association.

Gendlin, Eugene. (1981). *Focusing.* New York, NY: Bantam.

Glendinning, Chellis. (1994). *My name is Chellis and I'm in recovery from western civilization.* Boston, MA: Shambhala.

Grof, Stanislav. (1975). *Realms of the human unconscious: Observations from LSD research.* New York, NY: Viking Press, republished in 2009 as *LSD: Doorway to the numinous: The ground-breaking psychedelic research into realms of the human unconscious.* Rochester, VT: Park Street Press.

Grof, Stanislav. (1985). *Beyond the brain: Birth, death and transcendence in psychotherapy.* Albany, NY: SUNY.

Grof, Stanislav. (1988). *The adventure of self-discovery: Dimensions of consciousness and new perspectives in psychotherapy and inner exploration.* Albany, NY: SUNY.

Grof, Stanislav. (2000). *Psychology of the future: Lessons from modern consciousness research.* Albany, NY: SUNY.

Grof, Stanislav. (2006). *The ultimate journey: Consciousness and the mystery of death.* Ben Lomand, CA: MAPS.

Grof, Stanislav. (2006). *When the impossible happens: Adventures in non-ordinary realities.* Boulder, CO: Sounds True.

Grof, Stanislav. (2012). *Healing our deepest wounds: The holotropic paradigm shift.* Newcastle, WA: Stream of Consciousness Productions.

Grof, Christina & Grof, Stanislav. (1992). *The stormy search for the self: A guide to personal growth through transformational crisis.* Los Angeles, CA: Jeremy Tarcher.

Grof, Stanislav & Grof, Christina. (Eds.) (1989). *Spiritual emergency: When personal transformation becomes a crisis.* Los Angeles, CA: Tarcher.

Grof, Stanislav & Grof, Christina. (2010). *Holotropic Breathwork: A new approach to self-exploration and therapy.* Albany, NY: SUNY.

Grof, Stanislav , with Hal Zina Bennet. (1993). *The holotropic mind: The three levels of human consciousness and how they shape our lives.* San Francisco: HarperSanFrancisco.

Gurko, Leo. (1980). An introduction. In Conrad, Joseph. *Heart of Darkness,* Norwalk, CT: The Easton Press.

Harding, Mary Esther. (1965). *The I and the not I.* Princeton, NJ: Bolingen.

Harner, Michael. (1980/1990). *The way of the shaman.* San Francisco, CA: HarperSanFrancisco.

Heidegger, Martin. (1926/1962). *Being and time.* (John Macquarrie & Edward Robinson, Trans.). New York, NY: Harper & Row.

Hofmann, Albert. (1979/2005). *LSD, my problem child: Reflections on sacred drugs, mysticism and science.* Sarasota, FL: MAPS.

Husserl, Edmund. (1926/1970). *The crisis of European sciences and transcendental phenomenology.* (David Carr, Trans.). Evanston, IL: Northwestern University Press.

Jacobson, Bertil, Nyberg, Karin, Gronbladh, Leif, Eklund, Gunnar, Bygdeman, Marc, & Rydberg, Ulf. (1990). Opiate addiction in adult offspring through possible imprinting after obstetric treatment. *British Medical Journal, 301,* 1067-1070.

Jacobson, Bertil, Nyberg, Karin, Eklund, Gunnar, Bygdeman, Marc, & Rydberg, Ulf. (1988). Obstetric pain medication and eventual adult amphetamine addiction in offspring. *Acta Obstet Gynaecol. Scand., 6,* 677-682.

Jung, C. G. (1928/1971). Relations between the ego and the unconscious. In Joseph Campbell (Ed.), *The Portable Jung* (pp.70-138). New York, NY: Penguin.

Jung, C. G. (1938). *Psychology and religion.* New Haven, CT: Yale University Press.

Jung, Carl Gustav. (1952/2010). *Synchronicity: An acausal connecting principle.* Princeton, NJ: Princeton University Press.

Jung, C. G. (1968). *Analytical psychology: Its theory and practice.* New York: Random House.

Jung, C. G. (1986). *The collected works of C.G. Jung: Symbolic life: Miscellaneous writings,* ¶ 585. Princeton, NJ: Princeton University Press.

Kals, Elisabeth., Schumacher, Daniel, & Montada, Leo. (1999). Emotional affinity toward nature as a motivational basis to protect nature. *Environment and Behavior, 31,* 178-202.

Kaplan, Rachel & Kaplan, Stephen. (1989). *The experience of nature: A psychological perspective.* Cambridge, UK: Cambridge University Press.

Klein, Melanie. (1935). A contribution to the psychogenesis of manic-depressive states. *International Journal of Psycho-Analysis, 16,* 145-174

Klein, Melanie. (1940). Mourning and its relation to manic-depressive states. *International Journal of Psycho-Analysis, 21,* 125-153.

Koesler, Arthur. (1973). *The roots of coincidence.* New York, NY: Vintage Books.

Kubler-Ross, Elizabeth. (1969). *On death and dying.* New York, NY: Macmillan.

Kuppuswamy, Hemavathy. (2009). Improving health in cities using green infrastructure: a review. FORUM Ejournal (December 2009): 63-76. Newcastle University.

Kurzweil, Ray. (2006). *The singularity is near.* New York, NY: Penguin Group.

Lachman, Gary (2003). *A secret history of consciousness.* Great Barrington, MA: Lindisfarne Books.

Lame Deer, & Erfoes, R. (1972). *Lame Deer: Seeker of visions.* New York, NY: Simon & Schuster.

Le Grice, Keiron (2010). *The archetypal cosmos: Rediscovering the gods in myth, science and astrology.* Edinburgh, Scotland: Floris Books

Levin, David. (1988). Transpersonal phenomenology: The corporeal schema. *The Humanistic Psychologist, 16*(2), 282-313.

Levine, Peter. (1997). *Waking the tiger: Healing trauma.* Berkeley, CA: North Atlantic Books.

Louv, Richard. (2005). *Last child in the woods: Saving our children from nature-deficit disorder.* Chapel Hill, NC: Algonquin Books of Chapel Hill.

Maciejewski, Paul K., Ph.D.; Zhang, Baohui Zhang, M.S.; Block, Susan D., M.D.; Prigerson, Holly G., Ph.D. (2007). An empirical examination of the stage theory of grief, *Journal of the American Medical Association, 297*(7) 716-723.

Macy, Joanna. (1983). *Despair and personal power in the nuclear age.* Philadelphia, PA: New Society Publishers.

Macy, Joanna & Brown, Molly Young. (1998). (1998). *Coming back to life: Practices to reconnect our lives, our world.* Gabriola Island, Canada: New Society Publishers.

Martyn, Patricia & Brymer, Eric. (2014). The relationship between nature relatedness and anxiety. *Journal of Health Psychology, 1-10.*

Masterson, James F. (1988). *The search for the real self: Unmasking the personality disorders of our age.* New York, NY: The Free Press.

McKenna, Terrence (1992). *Food of the gods: The search for the original tree of knowledge.* New York, NY: Bantam Books.

McKibbin, Bill. (1989). *The end of nature.* New York, NY: Anchor Books.

Malcolm, Janet. (2013, September 23). Profiles: Nobody's looking at you: Eileen Fisher and the art of understatement. *The New Yorker.*

Maller, Cecily, Townsend, Mardie , Pryor, Anita, Brown, Peter and St. Leger, Lawrence. (2005). *Healthy nature healthy people: 'contact with nature' as an upstream health promotion intervention for populations.* Oxford, UK: Oxford University Press.

Mander, Jerry. (1978). *Four arguments for the elimination of television.* New York, NY: Quill.

Marzluff, John & Angell, Tony. (2012). *Gifts of the crow: How perception, emotion, and thought allow smart birds to behave like humans.* New York, NY: Simon & Schuster.

Maslow, Abraham. (1970). *Religion, values and peak experiences.* New York, NY: Viking.

Maslow, Abraham. (1970). *Religious aspects of peak experience: Personality and religion.* New York, NY: Harper & Row.

Maslow, Abraham. (1971). *The farther reaches of human nature.* New York, NY: Viking Press.

Merleau-Ponty, Maurice. (1964). *The primacy of perception* (William Cobb, Arleen B. Dallery, Carleton Dallery, James M. Edie, John Flodstrom, Nancy Metzel & John Wild, Trans.). Evanston, IL: Northwestern University Press.

Miller, E.K. & Cohen, J.D. (2001). An integrative theory of prefrontal cortex function. *Annual Review Neuroscience, 24,* 167-202.

Milloff, Ina C. (1997). *Loss at the heart of our being: Core Issues in separation-individuation and the process of becoming.* Unpublished doctoral dissertation, Prescott College, Tucson, AZ.

Mollison, Bill (1997). *Introduction to permaculture.* Sister's Creek, Tasmania, Australia: Tagari Publications.

Mollison, Bill (1988). *Permaculture: A designer's manual.* Sister's Creek, Tasmania, Australia: Tagari Publications .

Moore, Ernest O. (1981) A prison environment's effect on health care service demands. *Journal of Environmental Systems, 11,* 17–34.

Mumford, Lewis. (1966). *The myth of the machine: Volume one: Technics and human development.* San Diego, CA: Harcourt Brace Jovanovich.

Mumford, Lewis. (1966). *The myth of the machine: Volume two: The pentagon of power.* San Diego, CA: Harcourt, Brace, Jovanovich.

Naess, Arne. (1973). The shallow and the deep ecology movements. *Inquiry, 16,* 95-100.

Nietzsche, Friedrich. (1882/1974). *The gay science: With a prelude in rhymes and appendix in songs.* (Trans. Walter Kaufmann). New York, NY: Vintage.

Nisbet, Elizabeth K., Zelenski, John M., & Murphy, Steven A. (2009). The nature relatedness scale: Linking individuals' connection with nature to environmental concern and behavior. *Environment and Behavior, 41*(5), 715-740.

Otto, Rudolf. (1923/1958). *The idea of the holy.* New York, NY: Oxford University Press.

Ouspensky, P.D. (1949). *In search of the miraculous: Fragments of an unknown teaching.* New York, NY: Harcourt, Brace and Company.

Pagels, Elaine. (1979). *The Gnostic gospels.* New York, NY: Vintage Books.

Paull, John. (2013). The Rachel Carson letters and the making of *Silent Spring. SAGE Open, 2013, 1-12.*

Peterson,Christopher, Maier, Steven F., and Seligman, Martin E. P.. (1995). *Learned helplessness: A theory for the age of personal control.* New York, NY: Oxford University Press.

Pretty, Jules, Peacock, Jo, Sellens, Martin, & Griffin, Murray. (2005). The mental and physical health outcomes of green exercises. *International Journal of Environmental Health Research, 15*(5), 319-337.

Ramakrishna, Sri. (1997). In *The teachings of yoga* (Georg Feuerstein, Trans. & Ed.) Boston, MA: Shambhala.

Read, Tim. (2014). *Walking shadows: Archetype and psyche in crisis and growth.* London, UK: Muswell Hill Press.

Rees, William E., Wackernagel, Mathis, & Testemale, Phil. (1996.) *Our ecological footprint: Reducing human impact on the earth.* Gabriola Island, Canada: New Society Publishers.

Rees, William. (2010). The Human Nature of Unsustainability. In Heinberg, Richard & Leich,Daniel. *The post carbon reader: Managing the 21st century sustainability crisis.* Santa Rosa, CA: Post Carbon Institute.

Romanyshyn, Robert. (2002). *Ways of the heart: Essays toward an imaginal psychology.* Pittsburgh, PA: Trivium Publications.

Rothschild, Babette. (2000). The body remembers: The psychophysiology of trauma and trauma treatment. New York, NY: W. W. Norton & Company.

Ruffing, Janet. (1997). "To have been one with the earth...": Nature in contemporary Christian mystical experience. *Presence: The Journal of Spiritual Directors International, 3*(1), 40-54.

Rumi, Jalal al-Din. (trans. 1995/2004). *The essential Rumi.* (Coleman Barks,Trans.). New York, NY: Harper Collins.

Ruumet, Hillevi. (2006). *Pathways of the soul: Exploring the human journey.* Victoria, Canada: Trafford Publishing.

Sabina, Meredith (Ed.) (2002). *The Earth has a soul: C.G. Jung on nature, technology & modern life.* Berkeley, CA: North Atlantic Books.

Sadoff, Robert L. (1966). On the nature of crying and weeping. *Psychiatric Quarterly, 40*(3), 490-503.

Scally, Aylwyn &Durbin, Richard. (2012). *Nature Reviews Genetics, 13,* 745-753.

Schlain, Leonard. (1998). *The alphabet versus the goddess.* New York, NY: Penguin Group

Sessions, George. (1995). Preface In George Sessions (Ed.), *Deep ecology for the 21st century: Readings on the philosophy and practice of the new environmentalism.* Boston: Shambhala.

Shepard, Florence R. (1997). Preface. In Paul Shepard, *Coming home to the pleistocene.* Washington, D.C.: Island Press/Shearwater Books.

Shepard, Paul. (1996). *The Others: How animals made us human.* Washington, D.C.: Island Press/Shearwater Books.

Shepard, Paul. (1996). Preface. In Paul Shepard (Ed.), *A Paul Shepard reader: The only world we've got.* San Francisco, CA: Sierra Club Books.

Shepard, Paul. (1978/1998). *Thinking animals: Animals and the development of human intelligence.* Athens, GA: The University of Georgia Press.

Smirnova, Marina. (2013). *Atonement with the dreadful manifestations of the sacred in Holotropic Breathwork: Interpretive phenomenological analysis of the breather's embodied experience and the meaning arising within and out of it.* Unpublished doctoral dissertation, Sofia University, formerly Institute of Transpersonal Psychology, Palo Alto, CA.

Sparks, Tav. (2009). *Movie yoga: How every film can change your life.* Santa Cruz, CA: Hanford Mead.

Snyder, Joan. (1989). *The experience of really feeling connected to nature.* Unpublished doctoral dissertation, Union Institute Graduate School, Cincinatti, OH.

Squires, Emily & Belzer, Len. (2000). *Spiritual places in and around New York City.* New York, NY: Paraview Press.

Steindl-Rast, David. (1984). *Gratefulness, the heart of prayer: An approach to life in fullness.* Ramsey, NJ: The Paulist Press.

Stevens, Anthony. (1990). *On Jung.* New York, NY: Penguin.

Strong, David. (1995). *Crazy Mountains: Learning from wilderness to weigh technology.* Albany, NY: SUNY.

Storm, Lance & Thalbourne, Michael A. (2006). *The survival of human consciousness: Essays on the possibility of life after death.* Jefferson, NC: McFarland & Company.

Sullivan, Robert. (2006). *Rats: Observations on the history and habitat of the city's most unwanted habitants.* New York, NY: Bloomsbury.

Swan, James A. (1990). *Sacred places: How the living earth seeks our friendship*. Santa Fe, NM: Bear & Company.

Swan, James. (1992). *The power of place.* Wheaton, IL: Quest Books.

Swimme, Brian & Berry, Thomas. (1994). *The universe story: From the primordial flaring forth to the ecozoic era—a celebration of the unfolding of the cosmos.* New York, NY: HarperOne.

Tarnas, Richard. (1991). *The passion of the western mind: Understanding the ideas that have shaped our world view.* New York, NY: Ballantine Books.

Tart, Charles. (1987). *Waking up: Overcoming the obstacles to human potential.* Boston, MA: Shambhala.

Tatelbaum, Judy (1980). *The courage to grieve: Creative living, recovery and growth through grief.* New York, NY: Harper & Row.

Taylor, Jeremy. (1983). *Dream work: Techniques for discovering the creative power in dreams.* Mahwah, NJ: Paulist Press.

Taylor, Jeremy. (2009). *The wisdom of your dreams: Using dreams to tap into your unconscious and transform your life.* New York, NY: Tarcher.

Ulrich, R. S. (1984) View through a window may influence recovery from surgery. *Science, 224,* 420–421.

Van Heukelem, Judith F. (1979). "Weep with those who weep": Understanding and helping the crying person. *Journal of Psychology and Theology, 7*(2), 83-91.

Vinge, Vernor. (1993). The coming technological singularity: How to survive in the post-human era. In Landis, G.A. (Ed.) *Vision-21: Interdisciplinary science and engineering in the era of cyberspace*, pp. 11–22.

Vingerhoets, Ad (2013). *Why only humans weep: Unraveling the mysteries of tears.* Oxford, UK: Oxford University Press.

Ward, Peter. (2001). *Future evolution.* New York, NY: Times Books.

Wasowski, Andy & Wasowski, Sally. (2006). *Building within nature: A guide for home owners, contractors, and architects.* Minneapolis, MN: University of Minnesota Press.

Weisman, Alan. (2007). *The world without us.* New York, NY: St. Martin's Press. .

Weiss, Joseph. (1952). Crying at the happy ending. *Psychoanalytic Review, 39*(4), 338.

Wells, Nancy M. & Evans, Gary W. (2003). Nearby nature: A buffer of life stress among rural children. *Environment and Behavior, 35*(3), 311-330.

Wilber, Ken. (1981). *Up from Eden: A transpersonal view of human evolution.* New York, NY: Quest.

Wilber, Ken. (1983). *A sociable God: Toward a new understanding of religion.* Boston, MA: Shambhala.

Wilber, Ken. (1993). *The spectrum of consciousness.* Wheaton, IL: Quest Books.

Wilber, Ken. (1996). The *Atman project: A transpersonal view of human development.* Wheaton, IL: Quest Books.

Wilber, Ken. (2007). *The integral vision: A very short introduction to the revolutionary integral approach to life, god, the universe and everything.* Boston, MA: Shambhala.

Wilson, Edward O. (1984). *Biophilia.* Cambridge, MA: Harvard University Press

Wolfe, Thomas. (1934/1990). *You can't go home again.* New York, NY: Scribner.

Wrangham, Richard & Peterson, Dale (1996). *Demonic males: Apes and the origins of human violence.* Boston, MA: Houghton Mifflin.

Zelenski, John M. & Nisbet, Elizabeth K. (2014). Happiness and feeling connected: The distinct role of nature relatedness. *Environment and Behavior , 46*(1), 3-23.

Motion Pictures, Television Series, and Songs

Coppola, Francis Ford & Aubry, Kim. (Producers). & Coppola, Francis Ford. (Director). (1979). *Apocalypse now.* USA: Zoetrope Studios.

Cubitt, Allan, Thomson-Glover, Justin, Irwin, Patrick, & Anderson, Gillian. (Producers). (2013-present). *The fall.* UK: Endemol Shine International.

Ellison, Megan, Landay, Vincent & Jonze, Spike. (Producers). & Jonze, Spike. (Director). (2013). *Her.* USA: Annapurna Pictures.

Fellows, Julian. (Creator). (2010-present). *Downton Abbey.* UK: Carnival Films and Masterpiece.

Heyman, David & Cuarón, Alfonso. (Producers). & Cuarón, Alfonso. (Director). (2013). *Gravity.* USA: Warner Bros. Pictures.

Hunte, Angela, Keys, Alicia Keys, Shuckburgh, Alexander, Keyes, Burt, Sewell-Ulepic, Jane't "Jnay" Sewell-Ulepic, Carter, Shawn, & Robinson, Sylvia. (2009). Empire state of mind. Recorded by Jay Z & Alicia Keyes. On *The Blueprint 3.* New York, NY: Oven Studios.

John, Elton & Taupin, Bernie. (1972). Rocket man. Recorded by Elton John. On *Honkey Château.* Hérouville, France: Uni (US), DJM (UK).

Kubrick, Stanley. (Producer & Director). (1968). *2001: A space odyssey.* USA: Metro-Goldwyn-Mayer (MGM).

Morissette, Alanis & Ballard, Glen. (1996). Ironic. Performed by Alanis Morissette. On *Jagged Little Pill.* USA: Warner Bros. Records.

Nelson, Erik. (Producer). & Herzog, Werner. (Director). (2005). *Grizzly man.* USA: Real Big Productions.

Pollack, Sydney. (Producer & Director). (1985) *Out of Africa.* USA: Universal Studios.

Weiner, Matthew. (Creator). (2007-present). *Mad men.* USA: Lionsgate Television.

Index

Proof

43613727R00204

Made in the USA
Charleston, SC
30 June 2015